Data-Driven Approaches for Effective Managerial Decision Making

Anubha
Jaipuria Institute of Management, Ghaziabad, India

Himanshu Sharma
IILM Institute for Higher Education, New Delhi, India

A volume in the Advances in Business Information Systems and Analytics (ABISA) Book Series

IGI Global
PUBLISHER of TIMELY KNOWLEDGE

Published in the United States of America by
IGI Global
Business Science Reference (an imprint of IGI Global)
701 E. Chocolate Avenue
Hershey PA, USA 17033
Tel: 717-533-8845
Fax: 717-533-8661
E-mail: cust@igi-global.com
Web site: http://www.igi-global.com

Library of Congress Cataloging-in-Publication Data

Names: Anubha, 1977- editor. | Sharma, Himanshu, 1991- editor.
Title: Data-driven approaches for effective managerial decision making / edited by Anubha, and Himanshu Sharma.
Description: Hershey, PA : Business Science Reference, [2023] | Includes bibliographical references and index. | Summary: "Data-Driven Approaches for Effective Managerial Decision Making investigates management concepts and applications using data analytics and outlines future research directions. The book also addresses contemporary advancements and innovations in the field of management. Covering key topics such as big data, business intelligence, and artificial intelligence, this reference work is ideal for managers, business owners, industry professionals, researchers, scholars, academicians, practitioners, instructors, and students"-- Provided by publisher.
Identifiers: LCCN 2022049520 (print) | LCCN 2022049521 (ebook) | ISBN 9781668475683 (hardcover) | ISBN 9781668475690 (paperback) | ISBN 9781668475706 (ebook)
Subjects: LCSH: Decision making. | Production management. | Big data.
Classification: LCC HD30.23 .D37158 2023 (print) | LCC HD30.23 (ebook) | DDC 658.4/03--dc23/eng/20221024
LC record available at https://lccn.loc.gov/2022049520
LC ebook record available at https://lccn.loc.gov/2022049521

This book is published in the IGI Global book series Advances in Business Information Systems and Analytics (ABISA) (ISSN: 2327-3275; eISSN: 2327-3283)

British Cataloguing in Publication Data
A Cataloguing in Publication record for this book is available from the British Library.

All work contributed to this book is new, previously-unpublished material.
The views expressed in this book are those of the authors, but not necessarily of the publisher.

For electronic access to this publication, please contact: eresources@igi-global.com.

Advances in Business Information Systems and Analytics (ABISA) Book Series

Madjid Tavana
La Salle University, USA

ISSN:2327-3275
EISSN:2327-3283

MISSION

The successful development and management of information systems and business analytics is crucial to the success of an organization. New technological developments and methods for data analysis have allowed organizations to not only improve their processes and allow for greater productivity, but have also provided businesses with a venue through which to cut costs, plan for the future, and maintain competitive advantage in the information age.

The **Advances in Business Information Systems and Analytics (ABISA) Book Series** aims to present diverse and timely research in the development, deployment, and management of business information systems and business analytics for continued organizational development and improved business value.

COVERAGE

- Strategic Information Systems
- Information Logistics
- Forecasting
- Decision Support Systems
- Business Intelligence
- Business Process Management
- Business Information Security
- Data Strategy
- Algorithms
- Business Systems Engineering

IGI Global is currently accepting manuscripts for publication within this series. To submit a proposal for a volume in this series, please contact our Acquisition Editors at Acquisitions@igi-global.com or visit: http://www.igi-global.com/publish/.

The Advances in Business Information Systems and Analytics (ABISA) Book Series (ISSN 2327-3275) is published by IGI Global, 701 E. Chocolate Avenue, Hershey, PA 17033-1240, USA, www.igi-global.com. This series is composed of titles available for purchase individually; each title is edited to be contextually exclusive from any other title within the series. For pricing and ordering information please visit http://www.igi-global.com/book-series/advances-business-information-systems-analytics/37155. Postmaster: Send all address changes to above address.

Titles in this Series

For a list of additional titles in this series, please visit: http://www.igi-global.com/book-series/

Building Secure Business Models Through Blockchain Technology Tactics, Methods, Limitations, and Performance
Shweta Dewangan (ICFAI University, Raipur, India) Sapna Singh Kshatri (Shri Shankaracharya Institute of Professional Management and Technology, India) Astha Bhanot (Princess Nourah Bint Abdulrahman University, Saudi Arabia) and Mushtaq Ahmed Shah (Lovely Professional University, India)
Business Science Reference • © 2023 • 283pp • H/C (ISBN: 9781668478080) • US $250.00

Enhancing Business Communications and Collaboration Through Data Science Applications
Nuno Geada (ISCTE - University Institute of Lisbon, Portugal) and George Leal Jamil (Informações em Rede Consultoria e Treinamento, Brazil)
Business Science Reference • © 2023 • 262pp • H/C (ISBN: 9781668467862) • US $270.00

Revolutionizing Business Practices Through Artificial Intelligence and Data-Rich Environments
Manisha Gupta (Sharda University, India) Deergha Sharma (The NorthCap University, India) and Himani Gupta (Jagannath International Management School, India)
Business Science Reference • © 2022 • 300pp • H/C (ISBN: 9781668449509) • US $250.00

AI-Driven Intelligent Models for Business Excellence
Samala Nagaraj (Woxsen University, India) and Korupalli V. Rajesh Kumar (Woxsen University, India)
Business Science Reference • © 2023 • 267pp • H/C (ISBN: 9781668442463) • US $250.00

Handbook of Research on Foundations and Applications of Intelligent Business Analytics
Zhaohao Sun (Papua New Guinea University of Technology, Papua New Guinea) and Zhiyou Wu (Chongqing Normal University, China)
Business Science Reference • © 2022 • 425pp • H/C (ISBN: 9781799890164) • US $325.00

IGI Global
PUBLISHER of TIMELY KNOWLEDGE

701 East Chocolate Avenue, Hershey, PA 17033, USA
Tel: 717-533-8845 x100 • Fax: 717-533-8661
E-Mail: cust@igi-global.com • www.igi-global.com

Table of Contents

Detailed Table of Contents

The healthcare industry produces an outsized amount of knowledge, including medical records, compliance with regulatory requirements, and patient information. Most of these records were stored in a hard copy file system, but the current trend targets digital data. Driven by the need for resources and the ability to enhance the quality of healthcare that currently reduces costs, these big data sets hold the promise to support a large range of health and medical services. Thus, big data in healthcare focuses on digital data sets that are so large and sophisticated that it's almost impossible to manage with conventional software or hardware, nor will they easily be operated by conventional information management methods and tools. This chapter discusses big data analytics in healthcare, how it could be a game changer in reducing the cost of treatments for hospitals and patients, help in treating chronic diseases by suggesting methods as simple as lifestyle changes, and how it could change the whole healthcare industry.

Fluctuations in voltages and power mismatches are common in modern power grids due to the dynamic changes in the load and generation levels. Ancillary services are provided by specialized engineering firms to assist the market operators in operating the power networks and to manage the power mismatches. Ancillary services require a lot of data including the load data, system data, and control device data to take appropriate decisions based on standardized computational processes. This chapter introduces the overall process of determining the required reactive power flows based on load data aggregation in low voltage (LV) networks. The proposed method utilizes the adjustment of DER inverter reactive power using the IEEE 1547 standard reactive power control mode, constant-reactive mode (Cons-VAr), and voltage-reactive power mode (Volt-VAr). The suggested process is applied to a modified IEEE 5-bus network. ETAP software is used simulations for 12-month period.

To assist the management and support the strategic decisions, statistical and computational methodologies are being progressively incorporated into decision support systems. To accurately anticipate the financial data, researchers must properly comprehend its utilization. Therefore, a method-based literature evaluation with an emphasis on the predictive analytics field is proposed in this chapter. Regression, clustering, association, and time series models are thoroughly covered in this research. It extends current statistical explanatory modelling into the field of computational modelling. These model results help financial managers and risk management experts get better results. The numerous financial predictive analytic techniques are brought together in this review under one area. This is regarded as a solid foundation since it shows that when more than 40 papers have been identified as eligible, systematic reviews can be employed at the domain level. This search was conducted by the SPAR-4-SLR (scientific procedures and rationales for systematic literature reviews) protocol.

The objective of this chapter is to find the impact of crude oil price fluctuations on the stock market return of China. Further, the study extended to find the magnitude and the level of exposure to stock market return from the exchange rate. The study used quarterly time series data from 2008 to 2022 to measure the exposure magnitude to the stock market return from variability in crude oil price, exchange rate, interest rate, and GDP. The study used the ARDL bound test and VDC analysis as methodology and checked for multiple breakpoints. The study findings suggested a long running cointegration among crude oil price, exchange rate, interest rate and stock market return. Results indicated that disequilibrium in the short run to stock market return would converge back itself. The investigation concluded that oil and exchange rates transmit shocks to the stock market return. But the oil exposure to the stock market return is the highest, whereas the GDP causes the least volatility.

The target efficiency of the Hessian shuttle loom was much lower than the Sacking loom due to the lighter construction of the Hessian fabric and lower yarn count. It was found that variation of actual CV% of efficiency percentage of Hessian Shuttle loom was comparatively higher than Sacking loom. It is due to the high variation of the number of loom running /day and the lighter construction of the Hessian fabric. In the case of Victor loom, there is a positive co-relationship between Kgs/loom/shift and machine efficiency. Here the value of R is positive. In the case of the S 4 loom, there is a strong positive co-relationship between machine efficiency and kgs/loom/shift. Here the value of R is 0.98 which indicates a strong positive relationship between the two variables. The relationship is statistically significant at a 95% confidence level. In the case of sacking quality narrow shuttle loom, it is found that kgs/loom/shift is positively correlated with loom efficiency %.

Preface

In today's rapidly evolving business landscape, managers face the daunting challenge of navigating the vast amount of data generated by various sources. Failure to make sense of this data can lead to missed opportunities, poor decision-making, and ultimately, the inability to compete in the marketplace. To address this pressing issue, we, the editors, Dr. Anubha from Jaipuria Institute of Management, Ghaziabad, India and Dr. Himanshu Sharma from IILM Institute for Higher Education, New Delhi, India, are pleased to present "Data-Driven Approaches for Effective Managerial Decision Making," a comprehensive guide that demonstrates the power of data science in driving informed and strategic decision making across a multitude of industries.

This book combines our extensive experience and knowledge in data science and management. It is designed to benefit researchers, academicians, students, and practitioners alike, equipping them with the necessary tools to harness the full potential of data science.

Our primary objective is to provide a practical guide that empowers managers to leverage data science for making informed decisions. By covering various domains such as marketing, finance, human resource management, operations, and services (healthcare, hospitality, etc.), this book offers readers a comprehensive perspective on how data science can be applied across different industries.

Moreover, the book outlines future research directions in the field of data science and management, offering readers a roadmap to further explore and innovate in their respective domains. Whether you are new to data science, machine learning, and analytics or an experienced professional looking to stay updated with the latest developments in the field, this book serves as a valuable resource.

We sincerely thank all the contributors who have dedicated their time and effort to share their insights and knowledge with the readers. It is our hope that this book will inspire and motivate researchers, scholars, students, and professionals to explore new avenues in the field of data science and management.

As the book's editors, we are excited to present a collection of insightful and thought-provoking chapters that provide a comprehensive understanding of the latest developments in data analytics across various industries. These chapters not only offer valuable insights for academics and researchers but also serve as an essential resource for practitioners, business leaders, and policymakers interested in staying current with the latest trends and best practices in these fields.

We encourage you, as a reader, to delve into these chapters and allow them to enlighten you on the vital role data analytics play in today's rapidly changing business landscape. We trust that this book will contribute to the ongoing conversation about the importance of data-driven decision-making, fostering further research and collaboration in this area.

Chapter 1. Data Analytics Applications in Healthcare, Hospitality, Marketing, and Security

This chapter delves into the potential of data analytics in various industries, including healthcare, hospitality, marketing, and security, demonstrating how it can enhance decision making, optimize operations, and provide a competitive advantage.

Chapter 2. Data-Driven Framework for Quantification of Reactive Power Using Aggregated Load Data

The authors present a method-based approach to determine reactive power flows in low voltage networks using load data aggregation, with potential applications in improving power system reliability and stability.

Chapter 3. A Systematic Review of the Literature on Financial Applications of Predictive Analytics

This chapter offers an extensive review of financial predictive analytics techniques, emphasizing their potential applications in portfolio optimization, credit risk management, fraud detection, and customer segmentation.

Chapter 4. Factors Influencing Potential User Behavior Towards Usage of Cloud Computing

The authors explore factors such as perceived ease of use and security that significantly influence users' intentions to adopt cloud computing, providing valuable insights for cloud service providers and policymakers.

Chapter 5. Sustainability of Mobile Wallets in the Era of Low Cost DaLow-Cost in India

This chapter investigates factors affecting the sustainability of mobile payment wallets in India, emphasizing the importance of user satisfaction, perception, and security measures for service providers.

Chapter 6. Sustainable Business, Economy, and Environment Practices: An Introduction to Environmental Accounting

The authors discuss the importance of environmental accounting for businesses, illustrating how it can help reduce environmental impact, improve environmental performance, and promote sustainable development.

Chapter 7. Analyzing Artificial Intelligence From Social Science Perspectives: Artificial Intelligence and Human Intelligence

This chapter delves into the ethical implications of artificial intelligence for human rights and values, emphasizing the need for a comprehensive ethical framework to ensure AI benefits society as a whole.

Chapter 8. Data Democratization: Empowering Employees for Data-Driven Innovation

The authors examine the concept of data democratization, providing a conceptual framework and empirical study that suggests embracing data democratization can improve decision-making, employee engagement, and competitiveness.

Chapter 9. Financial Literacy and Perceived Risk Attitudes as Drivers of Investment Intentions in the Digital Era: A Case Study of Delhi-NCR

This chapter investigates the influence of financial literacy and risk attitudes on investment intentions in the digital era, highlighting the importance of promoting financial literacy for widespread investment participation.

Chapter 10. A Study on Oil Price Volatility Exposure to Stock Market Return Evidence From China

The authors analyze the relationship between crude oil price fluctuations and the stock market return in China, emphasizing the importance of considering external factors like oil prices on stock market performance.

Chapter 11. Data Analysis on Weaving Productivity of a Jute Industry in West Bengal, India

This chapter examines the productivity of the jute weaving industry in West Bengal, India, using Data Envelopment Analysis and suggesting the need for investment in technology and training to improve productivity and competitiveness.

Chapter 12. Barriers: Investigating the Factors Impacting Sustainability of Students' Online Learning

The authors investigate the obstacles faced by students in Delhi-NCR while using e-education, finding that technical issues are the primary obstacles and highlighting the need for improved digital infrastructure and training.

Chapter 13. Ethical Business Marketing: The Practices to Compete Successfully in Business

This chapter emphasizes the significance of ethical marketing practices for gaining a competitive advantage in the Indian FMCG sector, identifying practices such as fair pricing, environmental sustainability, and social responsibility.

In conclusion, *Data-Driven Approaches for Effective Managerial Decision Making* stands as a vital resource for anyone seeking to navigate the complex world of data science and its applications in management. Our hope is that this book will not only serve as a comprehensive guide, but also as a catalyst for further exploration, innovation, and collaboration in the realm of data-driven decision-making. By providing a diverse array of perspectives from renowned experts in the field, we aim to spark an ongoing conversation on the importance of data analytics and data-driven techniques across industries. We are confident that this book will prove to be an invaluable asset for researchers, scholars, students, professionals, and anyone interested in harnessing the power of data science to drive better decision-making in today's rapidly evolving landscape.

Anubha
Jaipuria Institute of Management, Ghaziabad, India

Himanshu Sharma
IILM Institute for Higher Education, New Delhi, India

Chapter 1
Data Analytics Applications in Healthcare, Hospitality, Marketing, and Security

Ramani Selvanambi
Vellore Institute of Technology, India

Jatin Kumar Dhankhar
Vellore Institute of Technology, India

Paurush Batish
https://orcid.org/0000-0002-1155-5138
Vellore Institute of Technology, India

Rakshit Soni
Vellore Institute of Technology, India

Marimuthu Karuppiah
https://orcid.org/0000-0001-7379-2641
Presidency University, Bengaluru, India

ABSTRACT

The healthcare industry produces an outsized amount of knowledge, including medical records, compliance with regulatory requirements, and patient information. Most of these records were stored in a hard copy file system, but the current trend targets digital data. Driven by the need for resources and the ability to enhance the quality of healthcare that currently reduces costs, these big data sets hold the promise to support a large range of health and medical services. Thus, big data in healthcare focuses on digital data sets that are so large and sophisticated that it's almost impossible to manage with conventional software or hardware, nor will

DOI: 10.4018/978-1-6684-7568-3.ch001

they easily be operated by conventional information management methods and tools. This chapter discusses big data analytics in healthcare, how it could be a game changer in reducing the cost of treatments for hospitals and patients, help in treating chronic diseases by suggesting methods as simple as lifestyle changes, and how it could change the whole healthcare industry.

INTRODUCTION

The healthcare organization produces an outsized amount of knowledge, including medical records, compliance with regulatory requirements, and patient information. Most of these records were stored in a hard copy file system, but the current trend targets on digital data. (Raghupathi et al., 2014). Driven by the need for resources and the ability to better the quality of medical care that currently reduces costs, these big data (also known 'big data') holds the promise to support a large range of health and medical services, including alternative disease monitoring, treatment support, and human's management of health.

As the world keeps on evolving and changing it has become very significant for the large amounts to data that is generated every day to be digitalized one way or another and this need is especially needed in the healthcare department. During the pandemic or COVID times, the need for advanced development in the sectors of medical facilities is required because the places where these facilities aren't available and most of the things aren't digitalized have suffered the most. Let's take a small survey to see how technology can be a very dominating factor other than top-notch management that gave certain countries an edge over the others during pandemic times. The countries that is discussed here are places such as New Zealand, Singapore and Germany. Even though these countries didn't have the best healthcare system as stated in the World Index of Healthcare Innovation, where Germany, New Zealand, and Singapore are given 17, 19, and 27 ranks respectively, they still managed to survive the corona outbreak. So, the question is, what were the rights decisions and approaches that they all had in common?

All these countries used analytical methods to more effectively allocate the hospital resources that included the beds, hospital staff, medicines etc. to reduce the mortality rates in the areas hardest hit by the virus. They collected various data regarding the virus and the reach of its spread and thus established certain perimeter zones for those areas so that they could be handled with intensive care. (Asante-Korang et al., 2016). Their research workers worked every single day to track the progress of the spread of disease and also its impact on the general population, telling how the patient reacted to a certain type of treatment and check the severity of a particular strain on the patients. They established a proper network among various hospitals across the country and the digitalization of patient records eased their entire process. Other than the patient data and the hospital data, the government was also generating data on the places where new facilities could be constructed such as research centres or new hospitals and allocating people for those tasks by giving priority to places that were affected the most by the coronavirus. Thus, the importance of digitalizing hospital records and the requirement for analytics of data in the healthcare department depending on the present pandemic situation are realised.

This chapter focusses on how Data Analytics has helped other industries such as Artificial intelligence, Military research, and the cryptographic markets. Starting with Artificial Intelligence, one can see the immense development in this sector, mainly by making efficient machine learning algorithms, comprising of basic and advance statistical mathematics, which gives us efficient and real time results to train the machine to react to a set of instructions and scenarios in the most human yet robotic method possible. Now-a-days, there are Google assistant, Siri, Cortana from Microsoft, and Alexa from Amazon etc., as our personal assistants, that have stored tones of data relevant to the people based on their demographic location, such that they can talk to you in your own native language. These assistants can be used for almost any day to day purpose, be it setting a reminder, keeping our birthday events aligned or keeping certain information safe with them. It is been known to have an Intelligence Quotient of 6 which may be very less in comparison to human beings, but still a very decent improvement for Artificial Intelligence. In a certain test done to compare these three competitors, Google Assistant, Siri and Alexa, they were asked a set of 800 questions, where Google won the race by answering all the corrections correctly.

The next section would discuss healthcare analytics and their significance in day-to-day life and would be a summary of everything studied till then. The section 3 of this chapter will focus on the research applications that need to be done in this field and what data that is already available to us can be useful. In the fourth section discusses on how big data could help in clinical operations other than just in the management area, by helping the doctors to narrow down the problem, which could help in diagnostics and further the role of big data in patients test records and scans. This role could revolutionize the healthcare industry and make us achieve milestones. This chapter also elaborates on the implications, limitations, and possibilities for further study.

LITERATURE REVIEW

Some researchers also predicted that in 20 – 25 years, Data analytics would have occupied its seat in all the major parts of the world jobs. This gives an edge to the technology as they now have managed to feed the constant growing data to a machine that can take all of it as input, organise it and restructure it to make useful applications such as Google maps or Google earth etc, that could give us real-time traffic information by tracking the devices speed around the vehicles.

(Martin-Sanchez et al., 2017). Another major area where big data is useful is growing cryptographic market, where most of the world has its focus right now. Elon musk, the Tesla billionaire, made a ton load of money in the year 2019-2021 largely due to his Tesla and SpaceX shares shocked the entire world. His interests in the cryptographic world also gave a huge growth to some of the small crypto currencies such as Dogecoin. This gave the industry researchers a goal to research in this field where they could explain and even predict the next stock market scenarios with machine learning algorithms and statistical analysis of big data.

Analytics of big data in medical care would also help in public health management such as analysing patterns of diseases, detecting disease outbreaks and suggesting step to be taken to control such outbreaks, (Archenaa et al., 2015). It would also help in evidence-based medicine and genomic analytics. Analytics can also help in detecting and analysing large number of requests for claims to reduce fraud, abuse, and waste. It will be really helpful in remote monitoring and patient profile analytics so as to suggest preventive care methods to patients who are at risk of developing certain diseases which can be prevented by lifestyle changes.

Many medium and small businesses can provide analytics service for data chunks that provide competition to big businesses (Sagiroglu et al., 2018). One can learn a lot from messy data if it's big. Most of the modern tools and techniques are capable of performing advanced analysis on raw source data, non-standard data and poor-quality data. This is considered a good thing as discovery and predictive analytics mainly depend on the details.

Health data volume is thought to expand drastically in the coming years (Chen et al., 2005). Also, models of reimbursement of medical services are changing; significant use and pay for achievements are arising as critical latest supporters in the present medical services environment. Despite the fact that profit is not and must not to be a required motivator, it is fundamentally important for healthcare organizations to obtain the tools required, infrastructure, and methods to use big data successfully, or else they can risk losing possibly a great many dollars in income and profit.

Most of the healthcare data is either present in a hardcopy format or even when it is digital, it is in a much unstructured format or a semi-structured format. This poses a huge problem for the health department, as even after having a huge amount of data it is too difficult to extract the right information that can be useful at very critical times with the present tools and technologies. Also, human beings have a very finite ability to process data and when the data grows in size, there is generally a need for analytical tools to make the wide range of data useful. The need to correctly reformat medical data in a very structured way is essential and seen how digitalization can help both the patients and the government even in the most critical times such as in case of a pandemic. Based on these few details, this chapter is structured into five detailed sections. Each section is of its own importance and hence will be highlighting some detailed key points that can be used to understand and analyse whether big data is really a future in the healthcare department and could it revolutionize the healthcare industry.

BIG DATA ANALYTICS

Healthcare data that may incorporate medical images, EMR reports and so forth are comprehensively separated into structured information and unstructured information. The enormous amount of data does help in adding to the worth and enhancing the nature of medical care by advanced analysis as well as patient care refinement. The large volume of data identified with healthcare could be figured through processing that is distributed, with the assistance of big data and cloud centres. This section is divided into what big data is and what it actually means in healthcare along with the various attributes of big data and how its attributes increase in healthcare, so as to define it according to its formations and use in the industry of healthcare.

Introduction to Big Data Analytics

While size does matter in big data's understanding, there are many other defining attributes of big data which refer to data velocity and data variety. Most of the definitions of big data focus on data size; it can be defined more aptly using the three Vs as shown in Figure 1. The three Vs (namely Volume, Variety, and Velocity) not only give a robust definition of big data, but they also bust the myth of big data only being large in volume.

Figure 1. Big data's three Vs

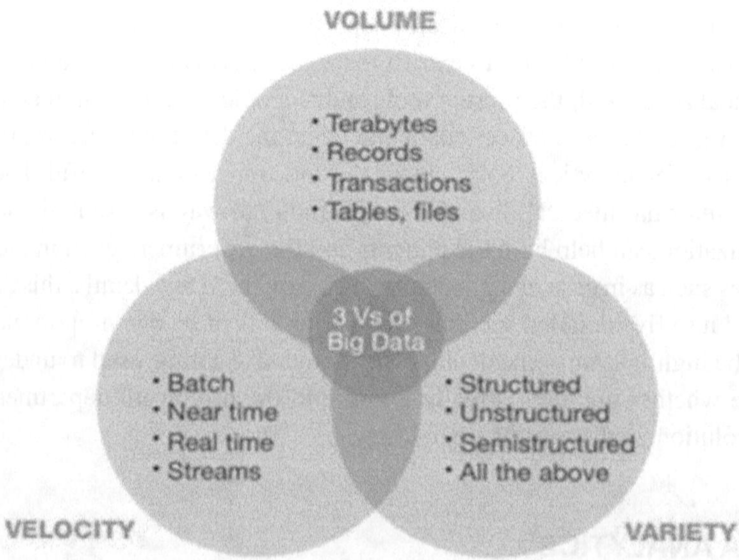

Data Volume

It has been clear from the beginning that volume is big data's main attribute. With this in mind, a lot of humans define big data in terms of memory, namely terabytes and/or petabytes. Though, big data also can be recognized using a number of things such as counting of records, tables, transactions and/or files. While nowadays many industries find it way more appropriate to recognize in term of time the big data.

Data Variety

Big data is extensively contrasting in accordance to types of data, sources and entities that are represented. A very important reason that calls big data as actually large is that it has been coming from various types of sources. Big data variety has three types mainly: unstructured, semi-structured and structured. The structured data does insert a warehouse of data that has already been sorted and tagged, whereas unstructured data is random in nature and really difficult to be analysed. Most of the new sources of big data are hospitals, social media, cloud storages, logs, and web sources.

Data Velocity

Velocity is a need for all other processes and not just for the big data. For processes that are time restricted, big data ought to be utilized by organizations as it does stream so as to maximize their value. Big data could be described by the velocity it has. You can also think of velocity as the data's frequency that has been delivered or frequency of information that had been generated. The real time collecting of big data is no latest approach: many firms have been collecting click stream data already for years from many sites, so as to analyse and recommend purchases ads to users.

Defining Big Data Analytics

As everyone knows, big data analytics is a process where advanced techniques of analytics operate on big data. But to understand its true meaning, it is needed to dive in a little deeper. Analytics is just mining data to get a pattern or information out of it. Big data simply provide a large sample case for analytics so as to improve the results. It is clear that the general rule states, more the number of samples, better the results of analytics. Most of the tools that are designed for data mining or statistical analysis tend to be optimized for large data sets. The tools for analytics and databases now can handle large amounts of data. These are far better tools to handle analytics on big data than ever.

The analytics economics is more embraceable now than ever before. This has many factors behind it mainly the huge downfall in the cost of data storage and the bandwidth for processing. The fact that the storage and analysis of big data is affordable now, big data analytics is not limited to big companies only. The analytics of big data provides much better insights that reveal and leverage business change. The already fast phase of its development has been quickened by the recession. The recovery brings even more and more change. The normal business has in fact beyond all recognitions changed, all because of latest recession in the economics and recovery from it. This change is very noticeable. Wholesale recognition is shared by the businesspeople, which says that this change must be analysed so as to get to know the business. Big data can be considered a unique asset that does merit the leverages. This is the whole point of analytics of big data. The technologies in the present and the great routines are fascinating, and there is a sense of confidence and great feeling about oneself in handling terabytes of data. But it is not to be done for big data. It should be done for merging big data and discovery analytics so as to find new insights they give your business.

Examples of fields where large amount of data available are astronomy, genomics, biological science and exploration, atmospheric science, biogeochemical, life sciences, catastrophic event and resource management, private sector, scientific research, clinical records, government, financial services, sensor network and telecommunications, military reconnaissance, social networks, retail, weblogs, archive, texts, photography, video, sound, search indexing, click streams, call detail records, RIFD, POS data, and cell phones. Any industries organizations that do have big data can profit by carefully examining it to acquire experiences and profundities to take care of genuine real-world issues.

Big Data Analytics in Healthcare

Historically, large amounts of data have been generated by the healthcare industries, be it regulatory requirements and compliance, patient care, and record keeping. Although, most of these data is stored in paperback but the efforts to digitalize it are at the peak. In order to comply with requirements that are mandatory and the possibility of improving the medical care services quality as well as reduction of the costs, this big data does hold the key to support a huge variety of healthcare and medical functions, and also disease surveillance, population health management and clinical decision support.

Big data in medical care industry points to electronic health data which is so huge that it is very tough (nearly impossible) to be managed from software of traditional neither technology; nor they can be managed without a trouble with data management methods and tools which are common. All the data in totality related to a patient's health refers to big data in healthcare organizations. It does include everything from clinical decision and CPOE, data of patient in the form of electronic patient record (ERP), data generated from machines and sensors, social media posts, articles, and feeds of news in healthcare journals. For the big data scientists, there is a great opportunity among this huge amount and arrays of data in healthcare. The analytics of big data holds the promise to very much improve the care, saving the life of people and reduce the costs of treatments, if the associations are discovered and the patterns and the trends within the data are understood. Thus, better informed decisions can be made if the explosion in data is taken advantage of in big data analytics in healthcare organizations.

The promise for big data examination in medical services to prompt improved results does exist across various situations, for example: by analysing the characteristics of the patients and the expense and findings of care to find the most financially appropriate and clinically appropriate therapies and offer investigation and tools, in this way influencing the behaviour of supplier; advanced analytics applied to patient profiles (e.g., division and predictive modelling) to proactively distinguish lifestyle changes and/or preventative care initiative benefitting individuals; small-scale profiling of diseases to distinguish events that could be predicted and so supporting the predictive initiatives; medical procedures data to be gathered and published, so as to assist patients in determining the best value care protocols or regimes; recognizing, anticipating and limiting misrepresentation by the implementation of advanced analytics frameworks for detection of fraud and confirming the consistency and precision of claims; and, carrying out more closer to real-time, claim authorizations; making latest income streams by combining and accumulating records of clinics of patients and datasets of claims to give information and help to third-parties, for instance, authorization of data for the help of pharmacists drug organizations in distinguishing in clinical trials patients for incorporation (Sandryhaila et al., 2014).

Advantages to Healthcare

The costs of the healthcare have been exponentially rising, whereas there has been difficulty for the members to cope up with the rising costs. So as to bring satisfied customer experience and treatment, the bringing down of the costs have been one of the top priorities for the health industries. On the contrary, there has been an outstanding growth in chronic diseases, such as diabetes. Because of this reason, there have been a huge utilization of resources of healthcare thereby increasing the costs.

By the digitization, combination and significant use of big-data, the healthcare industries that range from single-physicians' chambers and groups of multi-providers to huge networks of hospitals and significant care organizations do stand to realization of huge profits and benefits. Some of the potential benefits can include early-stage detection of diseases where they can be treated with more ease and effectiveness, management of health of specific individuals and population health and quicker and efficient detection of healthcare frauds. The key areas where big data analytics would help in reducing wastage and increasing efficiency are clinical operations and research and development.

The Big Data Analytics 4Vs in Healthcare

Even in medical care, the analysis of big is defined by the three main big data attributes known as: volume, velocity and variety. In time, the data related to health will be created and gathered continuously, which will result in huge amount of data. Data is gathered continuously and at a pace that is fast or say velocity. The consistent progression of new information aggregating at exceptional routine presents new problems. Similarly, as the variety and volume of data that is gathered and put away has advanced, so has the velocity at which data is created and that is fundamental for getting back, analysing, contrasting and decisions being made dependent on the choices.

As according to the idea of health information has advanced, so has the analysis strategies scoped up to the complicated and modern analysis important so as to adjust the velocity, variety, and volume. Gone are the times of information gathered solely in electronic health records and different configurations which are structured. Progressively, the data is in unstructured and multimedia design. The gigantic variety of information—unstructured, semi-structured and structured—is a measurement that does make healthcare information both fascinating, challenging, and difficult (Raju et al., 2020). Already, structured and unstructured latest streams of data, are being cascaded into the medical world from devices used for fitness, genomics and genetics, research of social platforms and other sources.

Some of the researcher and practitioners have already introduced a new attribute of big data, the fourth, known as 'data assurance', or veracity. Which is, analytics, the big data and outcomes would be free of errors and trustworthy? Veracity, of course, is still a target and not the reality. The issues of quality of data is still a major worry in healthcare for two reasons mainly: depending on the accurate data are life or death situations, and the healthcare data quality is, the unstructured information especially, is hugely variable in nature and more often wrong. There is an assumption in veracity about the side-by-side scoping up in architectures and granularity and methodologies, platforms, tools, and algorithms performance to cope up with the big data demands.

The '4Vs' are a proper beginning stage for a debate about analytics of big data healthcare as shown in Figure 2. Yet, there are different problems to be considered, like the number of platforms and architectures, and the predominance of the sources which are open are worldview in the accessibility and possibility of tools being available. Consider, as well, the need for user-friendly interfaces and the challenge of developing methodologies. While the general expense of software and hardware is falling, these problems must be routed to maximize and extract the capability of big data analytics in healthcare services.

Analytics of Big data can change possibly the manner in which providers of healthcare make use of new technologies to acquire knowledge from their clinical and other information stores and make detailed decisions based on them. In the coming years, the fast, widespread utilization and implementation of analytics of big data across the healthcare organization can be seen. Keeping that in mind, the few hurdles discussed above will be explored in the next section.

Figure 2. Big data's four Vs in healthcare

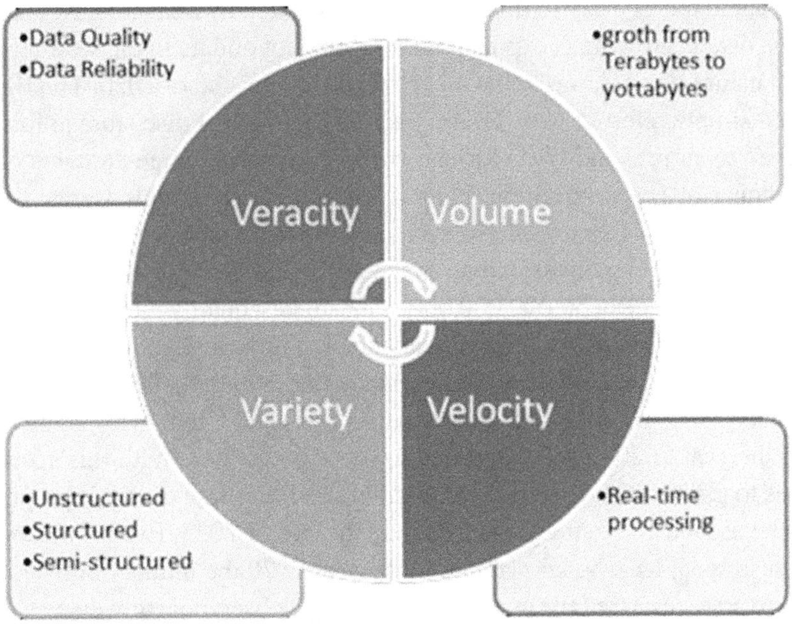

HEALTHCARE ANALYTICS AND ITS APPLICATION

Now that having discussed big data and its role in the development of some of the major industries and their pros and cons, let us move forward to the next section in this chapter, which will deal with data analytics in healthcare operations. From this section onwards the process to integrate big data with healthcare applications are defined and suggested some fields where big data analysis could be useful in a hospital and hence come forward with a solution that works along with some future research. Let us first know about the medical record system in hospitals.

Medical records act as building blocks of data in healthcare, particularly for sourcing patient data, and are typically stored in either a temporary location, until the patient has contact with the hospital when they are either undergoing treatment or are either enrolled in a program, or these records are stored in a hardcopy format as files printed pages and after some duration of time they are shredded if they are of no use to the hospital (Alexandru et al., 2016). In both scenarios, most of the time records aren't kept by the hospital over a longer period and hence cannot be useful for future studies. This is a huge drawback for the medical community because they can't capitalize on the information that could be useful to them in the long run. The question that comes to the minds is why is it the hospitals don't store all this data and how much is this data.

Let us just take healthcare out of the equation and check the amount of data that is generated every day in this global age. As stated by Seagate UK, the rate at which the data is growing is exponential. The amount of data in the world that was digital in nature was assessed to be 44 zettabytes by the end of 2020. The Blue-ray disc often simply referred to as Blu-ray is a digital optical disc storage format. It is designed to surpass the DVD format, capable of storing huge amounts of data, such as hours of High-definition Videos, Movies etc. In simple terms, they are mostly used to store HD movies. Now a movie can be of any size ranging from 1-2 Gigabytes to 19-20 Gigabytes, based on the audio and video quality of the movie. By this means, storage of 50,000,000,000 of the highest quality movies are possible. Let us take another example, a more realistic one, if each Gigabyte in a zettabyte were a brick, 258 Great Walls of China (made of 3,873,000,000 bricks) could be built. In the year 2016, the global internet traffic reached 1 zettabyte and now at the dawn of the year 2020, it was supposed to be 44 zettabytes. With this speed, if it continues to grow at the same rate or possibly at a faster rate than it is proposed to grow to be around 175 zettabytes of data by the end of 2025. Even if this number doesn't scare you, let it be known that in the year 2020 the number of bytes in the digital universe surpassed the number of stars in the observable universe by at least 40 times! Even if some of the data isn't stored on a long-term basis, still there would be a 581% increase in the global data.

The hospital data is supposed to be growing at almost the same rate as everything. It is presumed that each patient generates at least 80 MB of digital data. These patient records are largely stored on a short-term basis in softcopy format and when the patient is discharged, the data is given to the patient as a hardcopy in a report format and hence only a short summary is kept for some time. Since most of this data is deleted, at the present situation the patient information can't be used for any future diagnosis. Electronic healthcare records also play a key role in a patient's recovery. Most of the time when patients are either old or have a memory condition, they forget to take their medicine or usually end up getting confused about the dosage of medicine, if prescribed more than one medicine. In these cases, these records trigger a warning and reminders about when patients should get a new track prescriptions or lab test to check if a patient has been following orders of the doctor. But most of these facilities are only limited to certain sections of society as these facilities require money (Kim et al., 2017).

Things could be made a lot cheaper, if a broad database system is made to operate within a state or city or a small town, that could manage most of these hospital records on a short-term basis so that if the patient decides to move to another hospital or if get a second opinion, things would be much simpler for a large section of the population. The conditions with the government hospitals in rural India or any other developing country, is that sometimes the illiterate patients forget the dose they were prescribed, and just remember the colour of the tablet. As vague as it sounds, it a fact, that gives headaches to the doctors diagnosing them. Other than these patients, there can be cases where the patient test results are lost by the patients or misplaced. For this service it should be mandatory to store and fetch the patient records by giving them unique credentials though with, if the hospital is provided permission, they can access the disease with much more ease and less confusion. However, this comes with certain limitations which would be discussed in the next section. Let's now dive into the psychology of a patient.

Patient Engagement

With the rise in popularity of the Fitbit watches, healthcare logs of some popular doctors and fitness mobile applications, it is evident that most of the people are obsessed about smart devices tracing their calorie burn rate, heart rate diet intakes, sleeping habits etc. So why not make use of the data that can be tracked frequently, and the patient is okay with it. This data could be further coupled with some pre-existing textbook symptoms to diagnose some potential health risks that the patients would be unaware of. For example, an elevated heart rate and chronic insomnia can signal a risk of heart disease for future. This idea may sound rare but can be very useful. In cases where a person is suffering from a drug overdose or an epilepsy disorder or maybe and heart attack, a pulse rate alert could be generated by these watches which could alert the family doctor or an associated hospital. This data could also be compressed and stored in a cloud platform where doctors can monitor their patients when they are not admitted more advanced devices could be made where patients could themselves track their blood pressure and in case of emergency instead of worrying about their situation they could just know if something is wrong with it. It could largely help the patients as well as the doctors as sometimes the conditions come and go in certain medical cases, where due to lack of information the patients aren't able to explain what was wrong with their health conditions at that time, but on the other hand a medical record would be of large help.

Statistical Treatments

Big data in medical fields can also be used to store and analyse large amount of medical data such as treatment plans and recovery rates of patients for a specific treatment plan (Kaul et al., 2015). The duration of the treatment, patient pre-existing conditions, age, gender, and other relevant information can be analysed using supercomputers to propose the grey area where disease can be very harmful to a patient and the best time to detect such a disease. Such kinds of research may be thought as a very tedious and a useless way to generate a solution, mainly because human body is the Baltimore of genetic diseases. There are over 4000-6000 genetic disorders, many of these diseases are fatal and some of these diseases don't even have a proper cause due to a huge variation among human races. For example - Schizophrenia is a serious mental disorder that is usually accompanied by psychosis, where people can't differentiate between the reality and their thoughts. Disease like Schizophrenia happens without a proper reason and there is just no solution for some of these diseases. But researchers believe that most of these areas are under-researched and due to lack of material they aren't able to proceed forward with the solutions. But these research based on treatments and common relation between patients' symptoms have proved to be very useful in certain cases which aren't explainable to us right now, but a reason could be given in future.

For example, researchers have found that and antidepressant Desipramine, has the ability to help cure lung cancer's certain types. However, nothing can be done this direction unless the patient database from different demographic locations and intuitions such as hospitals, non-profit research organisations, medical universities etc., are linked up together. The researchers could research on the data, received from the other institutions located in different demographic locations having a wide range of biopsy reports. Genetic sequencing of some of the tissues infected with cancer could be done that the hospitals get from doing clinical trials and making this data available to the rest of the world by making a huge database granting access. But this approach can be very dangerous to the patient's privacy and has a lot of obstacles. The patient has their own right to allow limited people to check their medical reports and the doctors can't talk about them anywhere the patient doesn't want to.

Overdose and Suicide Prevention

As per the reports mentioned on the WHO website (World Health Organisation), it is said that almost 0.5 million people die every year because of drug use, and most of these deaths approximately 70% are caused due to opioid overdose. Another interesting fact about drug use is that only 10% of the people are receiving a proper treatment for it. This is a major problem among the youth all over the world, and thousands of lives are ruined by it. Another big issue is suicide among young people. It is believed that nearly one of every eight children in the US has a suicidal thought every night. One question arises, how big data analysis of healthcare can help to be useful in this situation. It is commonly believed that most of the people who have suicidal thoughts are known to have a mental illness most often depression. Unfortunately, these conditions are often ignored by people and mental illness isn't talked about as much as it should be (Wang et al., 2018). The data scientists at blue cross blue shield have done research and found out about a series of factors that are often seen in potential drug users and some common habits are also known among drug users or suicidal people. These diseases could be further prevented by knowing a trigger sequence, as to when to alert the person about their mental health.

To understand this, let's take an example of how machine learning works. Common applications such as Facebook, Amazon, YouTube etc. are known to collect user data and hence give them more content related to it. For instance, if you search anything on Amazon or Flipkart, you will see the same type of advertisements in your YouTube advertisements or, when you are using your Twitter account and you follow a specific type of page or account, let's say an election is coming around, then you would only see one side of the story, the one that you follow. Let's take a more relevant example, if by any reason, you are awake till 4 am in the morning and are searching for videos, that can help you overcome a certain type of addiction and this is pattern is continued for every 3-4 days, then your Facebook will know that you are seeking medical help. So, then Facebook will show groups and advertisements that are related to mental health and psychology. Sometimes these patterns taken by such services can very likely help save a person's life. This might be taken as a privacy breach by majority of people, but for those people who are willing to give consent to take user data and conduct surveys to analyse behavioural pattern among people, can be very useful for Artificial Intelligence and future research. Parents can make use of such services to keep their kids in a proper check, just like parental control feature but one where they can get alerted if their child is either struggling with something. There was a study from the Mental Health Research Network and KP, where they collected a set of most frequent questions that were relevant to depression, which helped them identify the certain people, who had an advanced risk of suicide. The research was a success because of its tremendous accuracy where they used a predictive algorithm which separate 1% of the patients in the research as critical, and the chance of suicide among these people were more than 200 times .These research data just show us the relevance of statistics in day to day life and how so many people, living in different parts of the world aren't so different from each other and could benefit from this research.

Hospital Management

Other than diagnosis and patient engagement, big data can also be extremely useful for hospital management process. The data need not be just the medical data that is patient specific, but it can also be research-based data (Chen et al., 2017). With the increase in Machine learning algorithms and Artificial learning with statistics tools, a large amount of research is currently being done to improve clinical trial design and to reduce trial failures, by matching the treatments available with individual patients, which would in turn speed up the process and new treatments would be available in the market. Most of the times hospitals have to choose the right number of people to put on staff at a given time. More number can lead to higher labour costs and a waste of resources, and at the same time lesser number of staff means more chaos in the work environment which could lead to bad decisions. So, to analyse this situation, most of the big hospitals maintain a statistical record as to when what number of patients are admitted. These hospitals are able to predict the flu seasons or pregnancy seasons, based on a proper statistical record and hence are able to prepare beforehand. This is largely helpful for the hospital records because they can arrange beds and medicines based on a short-term basis that can come in handy to them, in case of emergency and save a good deal of money and other hospital resources. This simple research can be done based on the demographic location of the hospital and the current season, where only a limited amount of data can be used to predict future scenarios over time.

Image Analysis

Digital imaging in medical fields plays a crucial role, starting right from CT Scans (Computerized Tomography Scans), X-ray scans, MRI scans (Magnetic resonance imaging Scans), PET Scans (Positron emission tomography), Ultrasounds etc. All these scans are very crucial in their own respective ways. A CT scan is mainly used by the doctors to diagnose any kinds of muscle and bone disorders in human body. They are a very good tool that helps the doctors to pinpoint the exact location of any kinds of tumours, clots or any infection in the body which may hard the patient. If the patient has a neurological problem, then he is then subjected to MRI Scans or PET Scans. The key feature about PET scans that make them stand out from both MRI and CT scans are that these are used to detect any changes that are happening in an organ in real-time, whereas MRI and CT can only detect the changes after they have happened, mainly to diagnose the extent of damage received to the organ. All these scans are thus lifesavers, if only the physician doesn't miss any emerging change or a very small change on the scan, which could thus cause an irreversible damage to the patient's condition. On many occasions it is seen that when these conditions are still in the emerging phase, a professional may only be focused on the symptoms of the problems and may miss to observe it. So, there is need for some analytical tools that can help to extract the biological information from these images and pinpoint some minor changes, if observed, that may not be seen by the doctor, so that the physician can therefore diagnose with much more ease and accuracy. The machine is required to do a pattern recognition based on the dataset provided by the tons of images and the training algorithms designed by experts, which in-turn could teach the machine to create a diagnosis and give a proper treatment to the patient. Over time this could increase the decision-making ability of the machine to a good extent which would give a much more accurate and precise diagnosis.

OPTIMIZING CLINICAL OPERATIONS

The huge amount of big data collected across the trial method offers Drug Company and biotech the chance to harness the knowledge in these huge data sets for improved clinical trial style, patient enlisting, website choice, observance insights and overall deciding. Harnessing and unlocking the potential in existing information sources, together with biomarker, genomic, EHRs, claims information, universe information and trial information, will ultimately cause improved drug development.

In pharmaceutical business, information is largely accessible, like historical clinical trials, drug databases, electronic medical records, sensors information, human ordering, real world expertise, scientific publications and social media information. Institutions have been building an enormous information analytics platform and have outlined a group of common analytics models that may be applied to several sorts of clinical trials. With massive information and advanced analytics, they will facilitate clinical scientists create data-driven choices and reach conclusions quicker and a lot of accuracy. Massive information analytics cannot solely accelerate clinical trials, however conjointly facilitate, and cut back the risks and prices related to clinical trials. Massive information analytics plays vital role in future clinical trials.

BMS (Bristol Myers Squibb) chose to coordinate all corporate examination capacities under one association to drive endeavour level dynamic through information. The ideal outcome is coordinated, prescient examination that helps drive R&D procedure and execution, with clear connections to long haul monetary effects. This introduction features the idea and the early outcomes including the difficulties and talks about the social parts of the change, which are substantially more mind-boggling obstacles than getting experiences from an abundance of information.

Patient enrolment and maintenance are seemingly the best difficulties to the convenient execution of clinical preliminaries. This is especially obvious on account of preliminaries including biosimilars and those zeroed in on uncommon illnesses. For biosimilars, enlistment achievement normally relies on trouble of admittance to repayment for the originator item and might be prevented by rivalry from concentrates with other biosimilars and those with new compound substances. For uncommon sicknesses, enrolment achievement depends on discovering enough patients as well as on holding them for the term of the preliminary. Verifiable accomplishment with patient enlistment—notwithstanding site capabilities—should be considered in corresponding with current market rivalry and results in an always changing patient enrolment climate. Numerous organizations supporting the biopharmaceutical business, like Contract Research Organizations, have started to use complex information demonstrating devices and methods to discover extra patients for biosimilar and uncommon illness preliminaries and additionally to discover patients all the more rapidly. What's more, these organizations look to all the more likely comprehend the number of inhabitants in intrigue and refine their measurable suppositions when leading clinical preliminaries or genuine investigations. The biggest and most grounded organizations that help the biopharmaceutical business presently have unrivalled admittance to enormous information from clinical preliminaries, electronic wellbeing records, clinical cases, research facility tests, and solutions (Harris et al., 2016).

The clinical advancement data storm is arriving at minimum amount for drugs. Utilization of changed information for focused results stays troublesome, regardless of studies that create proof of the danger advantage profile of investigational items. New advances are unifying the capacity to use scientific prepared information for developments in clinical activities and clinical science. With the utilization of clinical information as-a-administration and meta-information centre, concentrated clinical information lakes have the ability to improve information quality, proof age, and time-to-experiences. The Alzheimer's disease Neuroimaging Initiative (ADNI) is an enormous, normal history study crossing the range of Alzheimer's sickness that gives an available information storehouse proposed to additional comprehension of the illness through the incitement of new examination. The current examination utilized clinical and biomarker information from ADNI to help plan a huge Phase 2b investigation in Early AD with a monoclonal neutralizer focused against dissolvable beta amyloid totals. Additionally, longitudinal ADNI information was utilized in a progression of investigations to build up a complete clinical information checking approach in the continuous Phase 2 examination with techniques that can be applied extensively across an assortment of datasets and remedial zones.

Ways to Optimize Clinical Trials

Huge pharma and little biotech the same are searching for imaginative approaches to improve preliminary results and, thus, lower preliminary expenses—this implies expanding the proficiency where they select patients, checking all the more intently how medications are provided and being more adaptable about preliminary plan. Here's a gander at how large information investigation can advance clinical preliminaries:

Patient Centricity

Patient centricity has certainly been one of the significant trendy expressions inside the business in the course of the most recent couple of years. This is currently essential for clinical preliminaries as well. Patients are utilizing their web expertise and drawing on the expanding impact of backing gatherings to get more associated with all parts of their clinical preliminaries. In equal, patients are likewise shaping more care groups to examine their infection and accessible medicines and these care groups regularly proceed past the preliminary. Experiences from these patients and gatherings can profit pharma, permitting them to change patient conventions to all the more likely suit true conditions and improve patient personal satisfaction.

Tapping into Technology

Cell phones are not only for Instagram and text informing any longer. As customers become progressively alright with utilizing their cell phones for everything from web banking to shopping on the web, they are additionally getting progressively OK with sharing wellbeing data over their cell phones. Pharma and biotech are utilizing versatile informing to expand patient enrolment in front of preliminaries and afterward keep patients on target during clinical preliminaries. Organizations like mProve Health have shown that utilizing portable stages expands patient enlistment by 30% and can decrease the expense of preliminaries. Portable applications can likewise remind patients about arrangements, when to consume medications and even give directions.

Data You Can Wear

Developing utilizing innovation in clinical preliminaries, there is a development to have patients brings their own gadgets. While patients might be more alright with their own gadgets, there are still worries about how secure the information might be and what occurs if a patient loses their device. Clinicians and pharma are additionally taking advantage of the utilization of wearables to improve patient information since the gadget can be with patients consistently.

Automated Site Supplies

Some pharma and biotech organizations have started to utilize PC controlled stockpile frameworks to mechanize drug apportioning and oversee site inventories. The training is turning out to be more normal since it considers less waste inside the inventory network and gives organizations a tighter handle on the measure of medication utilized.

Advantages of Clinical Trial Analytics

By solidifying operational information on a clinical preliminary examination stage with prescient investigation capacities, Biopharma organizations can improve their capacity to observe whether an information inconsistency is a genuine danger—helping stage more profitable and proficient visits. Settle on key business measurements.

To start with, assess your business and choose where you need to centre your endeavours. What data improve operational choices? Gain concurrence on what ought to be estimated, how it will be estimated, and how that data will be joined into choices across the clinical preliminary worth chain.

Fit information to empower more educated choices. Normalizing information accumulated from many inward and outside sources might be your greatest impediment. Interpreting different names and codes is a monotonous interaction that needs top to bottom clinical information and a comprehensive perspective on the clinical preliminary cycle. When information norms are set up and incorporated into the interaction, continuous support is more straightforward. Gain a start to finish perspective on your information. A combined perspective on the information gathered and took care of isn't sufficient. In the event that you utilize a few clinical merchants to address explicit issues and diminish hazard, merging all your information—whatever the source—on one shared insightful stage can cultivate intelligence and coordinated effort. It ought to give job-based bits of knowledge across crucial measurements, going from enrolment rate and screen disappointment rate to hazard extent and convention deviations (Iyamu & Mgudlwa, 2018).

Install knowledge across the cycle. A compelling coordinated stage consolidates progressed examination, including prescient investigation, at each phase of the interaction to uncover significant bits of knowledge that were troublesome or maybe outlandish to accomplish previously. It likewise joins a self-learning framework intended to improve expectations and remedies over the long run. Information representation devices can proactively convey dependable logical bits of knowledge to clients.

Change experiences right into it. A community stage that consolidates prescient and prescriptive investigation can educate proactive choices to dodge issues before they occur. Progressed clinical endeavours may likewise receive altered and versatile bumps that can help defeat intellectual inclinations, prompting more target choices. Execute to drive enduring change. Furnishing your kin with simple admittance to the information they need, when they need it, can help make their positions simpler, more gainful, and really captivating. Yet, it's not difficult to slip once more into old propensities, which is the reason powerful preparing and change the board ought to be incorporated into your execution plans with an end goal to acquire supported long-haul benefits.

CHALLENGES AND LIMITATIONS

In most firms circumstances the data is too vast or too fluctuating or it surpasses current processing capacity. Big Data possess the ability to ameliorate and make it efficient and more smart choices. Big Data is normally comprehensive of data sets that range past the capacity of routinely utilized programming tools to catch, minister, and handle data inside a significant amount of time. Big Data is a bunch of methods and designing that request another type of incorporation to disentangle tremendous mysterious worth from huge data sheets that are assorted, compound, and gigantic scale. Walmart deals over a million customer transactions every hour or so. Facebook operates with more than 40 billion photos which are from the user base it has. Big Data is need of a technology to effectively manage huge amount of data (Zhang et al., 2008).

Big Data Analytics

Of late Big Data has had been a part of a lot of work places like the health-care, retail, biochemistry, administration department of public and other researches in science which are interdisciplinary. Applications which are web-based deal with Big Data often, such as computing in social field, documents and texts on the internet and indexing based on internet search. Social computing involves online communities, analysis of networks of social fields, recommender systems, markets based on prediction, etc. Keeping in Big Data's perspective, it generates modern prospects for knowledge development tasks for the researchers which are new. However, certain obstacles are brought with the opportunities.

In order to handle the challenges, access to the knowledge of different computational complications, computational methods and information security for big data analysis is vital. For instance, great number of statistical ways that works out for data size which are small do not measure to enormous data. Likewise, many techniques for computation, which fulfil data smaller in size, their demands pose hindrance in analysis of Big Data. Multiple oppositions health sector comes across were getting worked over by researcher on a large scale (Smith & Koppel, 2014). Here, Big Data analysis challenges are categorized in four main divisions which are analysis and storage of data; computational complexities and discovery of knowledge; visualization of data and its scalability and information security.

Data Storage and Analysis

In coming modern time, the magnitude of information has increased immensely by a lot of various mediums such as aerial sensory technologies, telephone devices, radio frequency identification readers, remote sensing, etc. Such data is now accumulated on grant cost and eventually result in omitting gradually, due to lack spatial storage. Hence, the primary obstacle for analysis of Big Data is record space and high speed of output/input. With reference to this context, data approachability must be then primary essence for the representation and discovery of knowledge. The ground cause being that, it must be availed conveniently and readily for later usage. Using history as a reference, analyst used hard disk drives (HDD) to record information but it exhibited much slow arbitrary performance of output/input than input/output which is sequential. In order for this challenge to be resolved, the conception of phrase change memory (PCM) and solid-state drive (SSD) was brought forth. Unfortunately, the current technologies for storage purposes cannot demonstrate the required performance for managing Big Data (Tse & You, 2011).

In addition to that, another setback that Big Data analysis subjected to is data diversity. With huge-expanding sets of data, data mining task has notably raised. Also, reduction of data, feature selection and selection of data is an indispensable activity when handling huge sets of data. This presents for researchers a very unusual challenge. It is so, because algorithms in present-day might not be able to react in expected duration while being dealt with this dimensional information. This procedures automation and modifying algorithms of machine learning to maintain coherence is foremost limitation. In continuance of the scenario, clustering of huge sets of data that would help in Big Data analysis is of major concern. Modern technologies which could be MapReduce and Hadoop enable huge unstructured and semi-structured amounts of data in a considerable time range. The main engineering drawback is the extent to which data is efficiently extracted to attain better knowledge. A classic approach towards this end would be to transmute the unstructured or semi-structured information into information which is structured and then implementation of data mining algorithms to knowledge obstinance. The central hinder in this situation would be to focus better on constructing systems for storage and to upgrade the tools for analysis of data that ensures for the output when information is derived from sources of various kinds. Furthermore, the designing of algorithms for machine learning for data analysis is important for upliftment of scalability and efficiency (Munn et al., 2018).

Knowledge Discovery and Computational Complexities

Discovery of knowledge and presentation remains the crucial issue in Big Data. It consists of numerous sub fields such as archiving, authenticating, information retrieval, preservation, management of and representing it. Various tools are put to operation such as rough set, fuzzy set, near set, soft set, principal component analysis, formal component analysis, etc. to name some. In addition to this many hybridized techniques are also formulated to process real life problems. Such techniques are problem subjective. Further some techniques might not be appropriate for large datasets in a sequential computer. Simultaneously, some of the techniques have good features of scalability over parallel computer. Since the size of Big Data is consistently increasing, present tools may not be useful to attain significant information. The trendiest approach for large dataset handling is then data marts and warehouses. Data warehouses are primarily accountable for the storage of information that will be received via systems that are operational whereas small knowledge store is positioned on an information warehouse and analysis is assisted (Kankanhalli et al., 2016).

Analysis of huge sets of data demands extra complexities in computation. The main problem will be the management of deviation and ambiguity in the sets of data. Overall, a modelling which is systematic in nature in the complexities in computations is used. It might be a challenge to set a mathematical system comprehensive in nature that would be applicable to the Big Data broadly. But a field specified analytics of data can be resolved with ease by detangling complexities certain in nature. A periodical advancement can stimulate analysis of Big Data for multiple regions. Many studies and research have taken place by the use of techniques of machine learning in this direction along with minimum memory requirements. The prime goal in such research would be to lessen the processing of cost of computations and complications (Wills, 2014).

Thus, present the tools for analysis of Big Data has performance which is poor in managing complications of computations, inconsistencies, and uncertainty. It would result in a major limitation development of technologies and techniques that could handle computational complexities, inconsistencies and uncertainties in a manner that is effective.

Scalability and Visualization of Data

The very essential hurdle for analysis techniques of Big Data would be its security and scalability. In past years', heed have been paid by the researchers to hike-up analysis of data and processors of it speed up, accompanied by the law proposed by Moore. For the previous one, multi-resolution and techniques of analysis which are on-line to develop sampling. Techniques to Increment have well property of scalability with respect to analysis of Big Data. With the fast increase in size of the data, then speed of CPUs, there is a sharp shift in technology of the processor being integrated with expanding number of millions. Real time uses for example networks in social fields, navigation, searches on the internet, finance, timeliness, etc. which requires computing in parallel.

The aim of data visualization is to show those more appropriately by employing graph theory's some techniques. Visualization by graphics holds the thread between information with interpretation that is proper. However, platforms which are online like Amazon, Flipkart, and eBay has millions of users and billions of products to sell each month. A lot of data is generated by this. For this case a tool called Tableau is used for visualization of Big Data. It holds the potential to convert huge and complicated data into pictures which are intuitive. These assists employees of the company to monitor most recent feedback of the customers visualize search relevance and analysis of their sentiment. However, present tools for visualization of big data tools generally have bad performances in scalability, functionalities and time for the response (Saranya & Asha, 2019).

It could hence be concluded that many challenges have been generated by big data for the development of software and hardware which thus leads to computing which is parallel, distributed computing, cloud computing, process visualization and scalability. For this limitation to be resolved, researchers are trying to postulate more models of mathematics for computational science.

Information Security

In the analysis of Big Data, huge amount of information is analysed, correlated and mined for patterns which are meaningful. All organizational structures have non-similar policies to protect information sensitive to them. Maintaining sensitive data is an essential issue in analysis of Big Data. There appears to be an enormous risk attached to Big Data. Therefore, security of information remains a problem of Big Data analytics. Safe guarding against Big Data can be advanced by engaging in authentication, encryption and authorization. Multiple security measures that Big Data application comes across are real time security monitoring, variety of different devices, scale of network and intrusion system lacking. The hindrance posed by Big Data has called the focus of security of information. Thus, it becomes crucial that one focuses on the development of a security policy model that has multi-level and system for prevention (Tresp et al., 2016).

Big Data Analytics in Healthcare

With massive benefits that are potential, the medical care sector is in its emergent for Big Data analytics adoption. Even with large quantity of information accessible, there has been an absence of skills regarding what information to be used and for which reasons specific. In addition to that another major challenge is absence of suitable infrastructure of IT department and transitioning from employing records based on paper to the use of processing of data which is distributed. The impedance for re-modifying process and validating tools and technology that determines the system for medical care and requirement for large beginning investment, does make it more problematic to implement technologies of Big Data. Studies assert that due to lack of knowledge about the algorithm and tools which are appropriate for analysis and absence of scientists which are clinically trained and managers of Big Data rendering outcomes of Big Data, healthcare gets marginalized from even exercising its potent Big Data analytics. To return to the challenging aspect of it, remains that it operates without any human supervision this might result in pernicious conclusions. Hence, there is a demand for convenient, easy and see-through analytics system of Big Data which could be used for cases that are real-time (Krishnan, 2016).

From perspective of technicality, limitations include assimilation of semi-structured, structured and unstructured information from a variety of places. Academics asserts that technological issue in Big Data analysis consists of soiled/fragmented data, validation, data structure, limitations of observational data issues, data inaccuracy and inconsistency (veracity), data standardization issues, network bandwidth, semantic interoperability, cost and scalability. Limitations like false positive associations and missing data also increase it. Issues of security can pose serious problems to healthcare.

The privacy and confidentiality of patients are prioritized the most in health care. However, data sharing for insights among stakeholders can compromise the security and privacy. Informed permission security, and privacy would be the central focus areas. Negligence in data rules and standards are few of the operational issues faced by analytics of Big Data in health care. Another important limitation that it faces is that it falls back with reference to other industries, which becomes the principal reason that cases are difficult to locate. With ever expanding amount of unstructured information, there is an imperative requirement for progressive techniques in analytics, like algorithms of deep ML that enables computer to sight relatable items in huge unstructured data quantities and to conclude relationships without certain framework or instructions for programming. However, deep learning has drawbacks of its own (Shahbaz et al., 2020).

An essential problem would be to know whether to implement the whole input capital of Big Data available while analysing information with algorithms of deep learning. The broad focus would be to put algorithms of Deep Learning to work to manage high-level information representation approach that would be based on a input corpus portion and then apply with the learned, the residual input corpus designs for deriving the data representations and abstractions. With reference to this context, a dilemma to investigate what amount of input information is conventionally obligatory for the training of useful (good) information representations by algorithms of Data learning which can be concluded general for new information in the specific Big Data domain of application. On further expanding the mentioned issue, recall the analytics of Big Data, which centres on the input data types variation and domains in Big Data. Hence, by considering the alteration between the data source which is input (for representations training), the issue thus becomes a part of domain adaptation for Big Data Analytics with deep learning (Shah et al., 2019).

HEALTHCARE DATA ANALYTICS TOOLS

Flatiron Healthcare Data Analytics Tool: Healthcare institutions are already using the healthcare data analytics tools provided by this organisation to manage the data of more than two million patients.

Digital Reasoning Systems for Healthcare Analytics: Healthcare system that uses artificial intelligence (AI) and natural language processing (NLP) to give medical facilities effective tools for quickly and conveniently analysing and processing complex patient information.

Ayasdi – AI for Healthcare Analytics: Ayasdi provides ready-to-use healthcare data analytics tools to improve hospitals' and clinics' operational effectiveness in a number of areas, including population health forecasting, clinical variation management, and rejections management.

Health Fidelity – NLP Enabled Solution for Healthcare Analytics: Using strong analytical techniques, a natural language processing engine is designed to help healthcare professionals identify areas of risk in their practise.

In order to meet the expectations and needs of its customers, hospitals and other similar institutions have been forced to implement Big Data analytics. In order to improve decision-making and the overall quality of services, more healthcare workers are using quality measurement tools. Understaffing can be discovered and given priority using BI technologies. Such systems can examine EHRs, genetic studies, and other data to offer effective medicines that are tailored to each patient's particular needs and current state.

Some of the other tools most popularly used in 2023 are PowerBI, SiSense, Tableau, Qlik Sense, and Driver Platform.

RESEARCH APPLICATIONS

This section focuses on the research applications in the Healthcare Data Analytics. This section, will focus on how data analytics has made huge changes in healthcare industry and how applications of big data can be helpful in various fields like detecting spreads of a virus, finding new mechanisms to fight a certain disease, improve the quality of the medical facility and provide high quality treatment techniques.

Analytics of Big Data has a great probability to change the health industry in a sharp and efficient way. The huge amount of data being produced daily in the healthcare remains unidentified. Big data can provide integration to this un-identified data by recognizing certain patterns and maintain the huge data simply. One of the major applications of the big data is its use in daily practice, how the analysis could be done for early detection of any particular disease, or detecting a spread of a virus and prediction of the disease trajectory. By getting this information, it helps the medical clinics and hospitals in targeted and cost-effective treatment of patients, and reduces in the resource's wastage. Moreover, it identifies patterns and routines of the patient, thus providing recommendations to certain people it tells how to maintain one-self in good health condition. Analytics of big data also presents a great chance in clinical data efficient use and its integration in a wide range of applications, like monitoring of diseases. Integrating analytics of Big Data into healthcare can provide huge success for the medical industry. It can help them to identify the various aspects of healthcare and their cost, how these prices can rise in the future. Big Data can help them to detect any fraudulent claims, how policy changes can impact the healthcare quality, how the cost of a certain treatment varies from one place to another and which treatment proves to be most efficient for a certain disease. Big Data can also help in detecting early signs of a huge epidemic, like the Corona, in advance and can be of a huge help to the healthcare industry to prepare in advance and minimize the damage. Now, let's explore certain research applications and see how an approach of analytics can better the quality of patient care and improve the medical facility (Rehman et al., 2021).

Patient Prediction

First application is the prediction of number of patients. By predicting the number of patients, a hospital can plan the amount of staff that is needed so that there are neither too many workers, resulting in neither unnecessary labour, nor the hospital is under staffed and is unable to provide services to all the patients. Big data helps to solve this problem by using a variety of sources and make predictions of how many patients can come up daily or even hourly to the hospital. These analyses and records allowed them to see a pattern in the admission rates of the patients. By these reports, they can easily predict the patient load and helps in planning adequate resources and staff to take care of the patients.

Real-Time Analysis

Real time analysis means the ability to analyse the medical data on the spot, providing doctors with a proper report of the patient's health and make decisions accordingly. Real time detection mainly focuses on the fact that doctors can access the data of the patient from their homes. Certain wearable devices like a wrist band can collect the patients' health data and the doctors can access this data through the cloud. If a patient has a blood pressure problem, and the blood pressure increases severely, the wearable devices will instantly update the doctor in real-time who can then take necessary actions to reach the patient and adapt necessary treatment to lower the blood pressure. Thus, Institutions and healthcare clinics can use these sophisticated tools to collect the data received from the devices and monitor it so that they can take actions when required (Smys & Raj, 2019).

Cure Cancer

More important application of the big data can be in the treatment of cancer. Medical researchers have been working on the big data and have inferred a plan where they can examine the tumour samples that are connected with the patient's data. Use of this information, they can work on treatment plans and how these will react to different treatments and what are the recovery rates. This data can be of huge benefit. For example, Desipramine has the lung cancer curing abilities. However, there are a few issues and hurdles in the way like problems with data systems, patients not willing to share their information with the hospitals and also would require a lot of time, money and efforts to come up with the progress of curing cancer with help of big data analytics.

Electronic Health Records (EHRs)

Over the past few years, Electronic Health Records (EHRs) are being widely used in the medical industry around the globe. EHRs help to gather important and useful knowledge of the disease and provide great insights to the pattern of the patients' disease. It is basically an electronic report of the patients' medical background that includes all the data relevant to the patients' medical history which includes past diseases, immunizations and vaccines, test reports and allergies.

A key feature of and electronic health record is that the document ca be managed in a digital format and can be shared with different hospitals or clinics when needed. For example, a patient has a well maintained EHR at a certain clinic nearby their home. The doctors in that clinic know about the medical history of that patient and have a proper record maintained. Now, if the same patient meets with a medical emergency in some other part of the country, the health clinic or the hospital there can have access to the EHR of the patient, and have a proper understanding of the patients' background and hence plan a more efficient diagnosis of the patient. Thus, with an electronic record, the information is available at any certain place and time whenever it is needed (Bora, 2019).

Improved Supply Chain Management

A medical institution depends largely on the supply management. It is very important to maintain proper supply from the products needed for patient care to all the medical equipment of the institution. Supply chain management focuses on everything related to supply and the finances involved with it. Big Data Analytics can help keep an efficient supply chain by analysing the performance metrics, and make accurate and cost-efficient decisions as to what needs to be purchased and what not. This not only helps to keep the adequate supply in the institution, but also ensures proper usage of the institutions' funding. By using Big Data supply chain management; a hospital can deliver crucial treatment to patients without any delay or lack of equipment.

Medical Imaging

Medical Imaging is the process of analysing the human body through virtual images like X-Rays, which can be used for diagnosis and treatment of diseases. Ideally, medical imaging can be done using various techniques like the X-Rays, MRI, and Ultrasound and so on. This provides us with a manual image of the human body which is examined by the doctors and experts. But, using Big Data, medical imaging can be taken to the next level. Big data can change the way medical imaging works. Rather than just having a manual image of the body part, big data analytics can develop algorithms which can analyse the image and compare it with hundreds of such images in the database. Big data can develop algorithms where the image the comparison of the image could identify the pattern and give an outcome as to what the disease/problem is. This means that the doctors wouldn't have to examine the images, but rather have a look at the final outcome which would be much more efficient. Thus, big data analytics can provide a huge value in the process of medical imaging.

Security

Nowadays, whether it is a multi-national company or an institution or a healthcare organization, data breach has become so common. A healthcare organization has an immense amount of personal data of thousands of people, and any data breach can cause a lot of trouble. By using big data, these data breach can be prevented to a large extinct. Advanced security techniques like firewalls, anti-virus software, etc., can help prevent fraud and keep the data safe from any breach. Thus, the advancement in the security environments using big data is a huge application of analytics of big data in the healthcare industry (Rao, 2015).

Telemedicine

Telemedicine has been available in the industry for a long time but with the appearance of videos online tools, telephones, gadget that can be used remotely, and wearable's, has it had the option to come forward into full sprout. The "alludes" terms to the conveyance of far off administrations of the clinics utilizing advancements. Telemedicine is basically used for essential counsels and diagnosis of patients, distant monitoring of patients, and clinical training for experts of health. Some more important telesurgery uses are – specialists can be performing activities with the help of real time data and robots without truly being in a similar area with a patient.

Telemedicine is used by clinicians to give customized treatment designs and preventing re-affirmation or hospitalization. Such utilization of analytics investigation of medical care can be connected to the utilization of big data predictive analysis as seen before. It permits clinicians to anticipate intense clinical occasions ahead of time and prevent any further worsening of condition of patients. By getting patients away from clinics and hospitals, telemedicine assists with decreasing expenses and improve the nature of administration. Patients can try not to stand by in lines and specialists don't need to waste their energy on consultations and administrative work. Telemedicine additionally improves the accessibility of care as patients' state can be checked and counselled anyplace and whenever needed.

Suicide Prevention

It is no secret how many people commit suicide every single day. According to a research, almost a million people die from suicide globally. These figures are highly alarming. While this is a very sensitive issue, big data analytics can be of a great help in making a difference which can help prevent suicides. Analysis can be done by healthcare organizations to everyone who comes to the hospitals and identify the patients who are at a risk of suicide attempt or can harm themselves.

A study conducted by a certain Research Network showed results of great accuracy. Electronic Health Records (EHRs) and some basic questions regarding depression were asked, and people were identified who can attempt a suicide or harm themselves. Using this big data predictive algorithm, it was found that top 1% of patients were more likely to attempt suicide linking to certain datasets. By proper counselling and care of these individuals, suicides can be prevented and many lives can be saved. This application of Big Data Analytics shows that how analysis of healthcare data can help save lives. Using predictive algorithms to treat people in depression or suicide attempts is a huge aspect and if proper treatment is provided, a person's life is saved.

Big Data Analytics is an emerging technology in the advancement of healthcare. Costs are a lot higher than they ought to be, and it have been on the rise for as long as 20 years. Obviously, we need some elegant, data driven intuition around there. Also, current motivations are changing too; numerous insurance agencies are changing from charge for-administration plans to plans that focus on patients' treatments. With the growing digital and information technology, big data could play a major role in shaping the healthcare facilities and taking it to the next level. Improved healthcare quality, cost-efficient care, predictive analysis of a certain disease, diagnosis management is some of the major areas where the efficiency of the medical facility has improved exponentially. Thus, Big Data analytics has a huge scope, and once people understand its characteristics and tackle the challenges associated with it, the healthcare value of the medical facility would be maximized (Alotaibi et al., 2020).

CONCLUSION

Information is at the top of the hierarchy in every field. Information with meaning is referred to as data and if in very large amount is called big data. Enormous amount of data is required in various fields. Some examples would be keeping of records and data related to patient in healthcare organizations, etc. The true aim of all organizations and industries is digitizing this data in today's digital world effectively with least expenses. In healthcare industries, the cost-effective methods cannot be directly chosen. They have to carefully inspect as healthcare is a field which deals directly with human life. It is an observational fact that a large amount of data is being generated by healthcare sector as well. So, there is need of a technology which is robust in nature, so as to utilize these huge datasets in real time and effectiveness so as to help the patients get improved results. The big data dies help in giving significant steps by the relationship among different datasets and data patterns with the assistance of algorithms of machine learning. Big data is only the assortment of data in unstructured and structured format. Machine learning is the key to big data analytics in healthcare. Machine learning concepts and tools are being used on big data by researchers to get best results. A productive and efficient tool could be developed so as to overcome issues in bid data analysis. It would have the ability to manage imbalanced and noisy files. It could also take care of inconsistency and uncertainty that would ultimately resolve the troubles of analytics of big data in healthcare.

REFERENCES

Alexandru, A., Alexandru, C. A., Coardos, D., & Tudora, E. (2016). Big data: concepts, technologies, and applications in the public sector. *International Journal of Computer Electrical Automation Control and Information Engineering*, *10*, 1629-35.

Alotaibi, S., Mehmood, R., & Katib, I. (2020). The role of big data and twitter data analytics in healthcare supply chain management. Smart Infrastructure and Applications, 267-279. doi:10.1007/978-3-030-13705-2_11

Archenaa, J., & Anita, E. M. (2015). A survey of big data analytics in healthcare and government. *Procedia Computer Science*, *50*, 408–413. doi:10.1016/j.procs.2015.04.021

Asante-Korang, A., & Jacobs, J. P. (2016). Big data and pediatric cardiovascular disease in the era of transparency in healthcare. *Cardiology in the Young*, *26*(8), 1597–1602. doi:10.1017/S1047951116001736 PMID:28148322

Bora, D. J. (2019). Big data analytics in healthcare: A critical analysis. Big Data Analytics for Intelligent Healthcare Management, 43-57 doi:10.1016/B978-0-12-818146-1.00003-9

Chen, J., Dougherty, E., Demir, S. S., Friedman, C., Li, C. S., & Wong, S. (2005). Grand challenges for multimodal bio-medical systems. *IEEE Circuits and Systems Magazine*, *5*(2), 46–52. doi:10.1109/MCAS.2005.1438739

Chen, M., Hao, Y., Hwang, K., Wang, L., & Wang, L. (2017). Disease prediction by machine learning over big data from healthcare communities. *IEEE Access : Practical Innovations, Open Solutions*, *5*, 8869–8879. doi:10.1109/ACCESS.2017.2694446

Harris, S. L., May, J. H., & Vargas, L. G. (2016). Predictive analytics model for healthcare planning and scheduling. *European Journal of Operational Research*, *253*(1), 121–131. doi:10.1016/j.ejor.2016.02.017

Iyamu, T., & Mgudlwa, S. (2018). Transformation of healthcare big data through the lens of actor network theory. *International Journal of Healthcare Management*, *11*(3), 182–192. doi:10.1080/20479700.2017.1397340

Kankanhalli, A., Hahn, J., Tan, S., & Gao, G. (2016). Big data and analytics in healthcare: Introduction to the special section. *Information Systems Frontiers*, *18*(2), 233–235. doi:10.100710796-016-9641-2

Kaul, C., Kaul, A., & Verma, S. (2015). Comparative study on healthcare prediction systems using big data. *2015 International Conference on Innovations in Information, Embedded and Communication Systems (ICIIECS)*, 1-7.

Kim, M. K., & Park, J. H. (2017). Identifying and prioritizing critical factors for promoting the implementation and usage of big data in healthcare. *Information Development, 33*(3), 257–269. doi:10.1177/0266666916652671

Krishnan, S. M. (2016). Application of analytics to big data in healthcare. *2016 32nd Southern Biomedical Engineering Conference (SBEC)*, 156-157. 10.1109/SBEC.2016.88

Martin-Sanchez, F. J., Aguiar-Pulido, V., Lopez-Campos, G. H., Peek, N., & Sacchi, L. (2017). Secondary use and analysis of big data collected for patient care. *Yearbook of Medical Informatics, 26*(01), 28–37. doi:10.15265/IY-2017-008 PMID:28480474

Munn, Z., & Qaseem, A. (2018). Disappearance of the National Guideline Clearinghouse: A huge loss for evidence-based health care. *Annals of Internal Medicine, 169*(9), 648–649. doi:10.7326/M18-2216 PMID:30167676

Raghupathi, W., & Raghupathi, V. (2014). Big data analytics in healthcare: Promise and potential. *Health Information Science and Systems, 2*(1), 1–10. doi:10.1186/2047-2501-2-3 PMID:25825667

Raju, B., Jumah, F., Ashraf, O., Narayan, V., Gupta, G., Sun, H., & Nanda, A. (2020). Big data, machine learning, and artificial intelligence: A field guide for neurosurgeons. *Journal of Neurosurgery, 1*, 1–11. doi:10.3171/2020.5.JNS201288 PMID:33007750

Rao, S., Suma, S. N., & Sunitha, M. (2015). Security solutions for big data analytics in healthcare. *2015 Second International Conference on Advances in Computing and Communication Engineering,* 510-514. 10.1109/ICACCE.2015.83

Rehman, A., Naz, S., & Razzak, I. (2021). Leveraging big data analytics in healthcare enhancement: Trends, challenges and opportunities. *Multimedia Systems, 1*, 33.

Sagiroglu, S., & Sinanc, D. (2013). *Big data: A review. In 2013 international conference on collaboration technologies and systems*. CTS.

Sandryhaila, A., & Moura, J. M. (2014). Big data analysis with signal processing on graphs: Representation and processing of massive data sets with irregular structure. *IEEE Signal Processing Magazine, 31*(5), 80–90. doi:10.1109/MSP.2014.2329213

Saranya, P., & Asha, P. (2019). Survey on Big Data Analytics in health care. *2019 International Conference on Smart Systems and Inventive Technology (ICSSIT),* 46-51. 10.1109/ICSSIT46314.2019.8987882

Shah, G., Shah, A., & Shah, M. (2019). Panacea of challenges in real-world application of big data analytics in healthcare sector. *Journal of Data. Information & Management*, *1*(3), 107–116.

Shahbaz, M., Gao, C., Zhai, L., Shahzad, F., & Hu, Y. (2019). Investigating the adoption of big data analytics in healthcare: The moderating role of resistance to change. *Journal of Big Data*, *6*(1), 1–20. doi:10.118640537-019-0170-y

Smith, S. W., & Koppel, R. (2014). Healthcare information technology's relativity problems: A typology of how patients' physical reality, clinicians' mental models, and healthcare information technology differ. *Journal of the American Medical Informatics Association : JAMIA*, *21*(1), 117–131. doi:10.1136/amiajnl-2012-001419 PMID:23800960

Smys, S., & Raj, J. S. (2019). Internet of things and big data analytics for health care with cloud computing. *Journal of Information Technology*, *1*(01), 9–18.

Tresp, V., Overhage, J. M., Bundschus, M., Rabizadeh, S., Fasching, P. A., & Yu, S. (2016). Going digital: A survey on digitalization and large-scale data analytics in healthcare. *Proceedings of the IEEE*, *104*(11), 2180–2206. doi:10.1109/JPROC.2016.2615052

Tse, J., & You, W. (2011). How accurate is the electronic health record?–a pilot study evaluating information accuracy in a primary care setting. In *Health Informatics* (pp. 158–164). The Transformative Power of Innovation.

Wang, Y., Kung, L., & Byrd, T. A. (2018). Big data analytics: Understanding its capabilities and potential benefits for healthcare organizations. *Technological Forecasting and Social Change*, *126*, 3–13. doi:10.1016/j.techfore.2015.12.019

Wills, M. J. (2014). Decisions through data: Analytics in healthcare. *Journal of Healthcare Management*, *59*(4), 254–262. doi:10.1097/00115514-201407000-00005 PMID:25154123

Zhang, H., Morrison, M. A., DeWan, A., Adams, S., Andreoli, M., Huynh, N., & DeAngelis, M. M. (2008). The NEI/NCBI dbGAP database: Genotypes and haplotypes that may specifically predispose to risk of neovascular age-related macular degeneration. *BMC Medical Genetics*, *9*(1), 1–10. doi:10.1186/1471-2350-9-51 PMID:18541031

Chapter 2
Data-Driven Framework for Quantification of Reactive Power Using Aggregated Load Data

Nghipundaka Jeremia
https://orcid.org/0000-0001-9635-5428
Namibia University of Science and Technology, Namibia

K. S. Sastry Musti
https://orcid.org/0000-0003-4384-7933
Namibia University of Science and Technology, Namibia

ABSTRACT

Fluctuations in voltages and power mismatches are common in modern power grids due to the dynamic changes in the load and generation levels. Ancillary services are provided by specialized engineering firms to assist the market operators in operating the power networks and to manage the power mismatches. Ancillary services require a lot of data including the load data, system data, and control device data to take appropriate decisions based on standardized computational processes. This chapter introduces the overall process of determining the required reactive power flows based on load data aggregation in low voltage (LV) networks. The proposed method utilizes the adjustment of DER inverter reactive power using the IEEE 1547 standard reactive power control mode, constant-reactive mode (Cons-VAr), and voltage-reactive power mode (Volt-VAr). The suggested process is applied to a modified IEEE 5-bus network. ETAP software is used simulations for 12-month period.

DOI: 10.4018/978-1-6684-7568-3.ch002

INTRODUCTION

The development of the upcoming decentralized power grid, which will include small-scale power systems made up of distributed generation, flexible loads, and storage systems, has been supported by the surge in grid-connected renewable energy sources. However, dynamic changes in the load and random nature of renewable energy sources result either in excess energy production or energy deficit. Either way, the utility loses revenue besides facing other risks. Further, active and reactive powers need to be managed separately to maintain the voltage and frequency stabilities of the grid. In other words, real-time management of modern smart grids is a complex task. To raise energy production levels, system operators need an accurate estimation of the load, which is generally obtained from the meters from various parts of the power grid. For managing the energy pool over the next day or over the next week, load needs to be predicted or forecasted. The tasks of load estimation (for real-time) and forecasting (for immediate future) is typically done on aggregated load data. Modern grids do employ well-trained professionals to attend the task of aggregation. The presence of an aggregator serving as a middleman between the prosumers, distribution and transmission network operators is the key to manage the supply-demand mismatch. In the case of larger networks, an independent market operator is employed who controls the aggregated resources to achieve a specific load demand modification, defines ongoing demand response programs (Musti, 2020a; Öztürk et al., 2022). Thus, managing the supply-demand mismatch requires aggregation of both loads and generation sources (typically in the intervals of 15 minutes) that are connected to the grid in different geographical locations. It is clear that a lot of data is being collected and monitored for aggregation purposes. In other words, management of smart grids is data intense activity as several decisions need to be taken based on the dynamically varying data (Musti, 2020b). Though there are several components, stakeholders and influencing factors associated; four major aspects – energy markets, load data obtained from different locations, computational processes and the key decisions required be to made – are the important ingredients in managing the supply-demand mismatch. This chapter deals with these major aspects in order to explain the importance of data, computations and the process of making the decisions in operating the modern smart grids.

Reactive power is a vital component in managing the inductive and capacitive loads. Without adequate reactive power, transformers (responsible for energy transformation) cannot function. Voltage levels are essentially managed either by increasing or decreasing the reactive power supply (Georgios et. al, 2022). In most cases, reactive power needs to be supplied as a resource to keep the voltage stability within the limits. The task of controlling the reactive power supply needs aggregated data from various load points. Since this is a complex task, reactive power can be provided as an ancillary service in power markets. Ancillary services are additional services beyond the supply of energy that are required to maintain the reliability and security of the power system. Reactive power as an ancillary service can be provided by generators, synchronous condensers, or static VAR compensators. These resources can be dispatched by the system operator to provide reactive power support as needed to maintain system stability. Reactive power control needs to be done in real-time and thus the process assumes high significance. Control extents are determined through complex computations that require a lot of data. If the reactive power is not managed well in real-time, the system voltage fluctuates and this in-turn can result in equipment damage (Falabretti et al., 2022).

Since these energy resources are typically owned by different stakeholders in a modern, decentralized energy markets, the reactive power is typically traded based on the needs such as for next day, over next week or fortnight, or over next month etc. The day-ahead energy market is a part of the electricity market where electricity is traded for delivery on the next day. It is a short-term market that operates on a daily basis and allows electricity producers and consumers to buy and sell electricity to meet their respective needs. In this market, electricity generators submit offers to sell their electricity at various prices for each hour of the next day, while electricity consumers submit bids to buy electricity at different prices for each hour of the day ahead. The market operator then matches the offers and bids to determine the market clearing price for each hour of the day ahead. Since energy production is heavily dependent on seasons of the year and other environmental factors, prices do fluctuate. Thus, the day-ahead energy trade assumes a very important role, as it provides a way for producers and consumers to manage their exposure to volatile energy prices and ensure that there is enough supply to meet demand. Since, it is regulated through a well-defined framework, it is possible to control the overall price range efficiently and fairly, reflecting the real-time conditions of the market.

From the above, it can be seen that reactive power requirements need to be estimated and appropriate control measures need to be taken in real-time in order to manage the bus voltages and power mismatches. At the same time, energy trade and operation of smart grids are essentially managed through technical decisions that require a lot of data (Musti, 2020b). Thus, this chapter has the objective of demonstrating the role of data and computations that help various stakeholders to determine the reactive power requirements for the smart grids. To accomplish this objective, the chapter first presents an in-depth literature review, deduces the rationale for the topic and then formulates the required investigative framework.

LITERATURE REVIEW

In order to effectively and efficiently meet their needs, various ancillary services are required such as reactive power management, frequency regulation, and capacity planning. In most cases a few small-scale industries are set up to (Musti and Kapali, 2021) provide various ancillary services. Such technical activities require intense technical analysis leading to the determination of specific KPIs. Load data is essential for most of such activities to determine various KPIs, which can be used either in planning studies, technical studies, and even in real-time operation and control of the grid itself. Real-time control generally involves sending appropriate control signals from utility to different loads. For such tasks, the load data from different feeders, measuring points, and substations need to be aggregated. There are several aggregation methods used in power systems, which includes bottom-up, coordinated, and bus-split (Gao et al., 2021).

- Bottom-up (BU) method
  Commercial and residential loads are combined using this technique. Loads must be classified as static or dynamic; a static load's feeder voltage is unaffected by the connecting and disconnecting of the load. The lower transformers supply energy to associated changing loads.
- Coordinated method
  In this method, the loads are ranked and priority is only given to certain loads based on characteristics such as power demand, capacity, and frequency. The load is ranked to avoid statistical methods of determining the load power demand. It has the advantage of having less dependency on the load model and load type.
- Bus-split (BS) method
  In this method, the aggregation is done on three-phase loads such as an induction motor.

The microgrid offers islanded and grid-connected operation and can be connected to the main grid as a regulated load or generator (Ahmad Khan et al., 2016). As dispersed energy resources are used more frequently, and have high uncertainties, the coordination of large numbers of distributed generators in a single microgrid becomes complex and infeasible. A technique to solve this issue is a cluster of microgrids (peer-to-peer microgrids), which is a self-healing configuration where the distribution network is divided into several interconnected microgrids which are geographically close. These clusters offer economic benefits to both the utility and the individual microgrids (Ganjian-Aboukheili et al., 2020). This means, it is possible that data extraction can be simplified as a part of the network is better organized and that the burden on the system aggregator is reduced; and thus, managing is more efficient and economical (Mahmoudi et al., 2018). Clusters and/or microgrids have the advantage of reducing dependency on the utility grid by supplying on-site customers. They are also capable of supplying extra generated power and services of the grid such as (but not limited to); frequency control and regulation, voltage support, spinning reserves, blackout recovery support, and load reduction during peak hours. Microgrids are evolving to be the building block of smart grids and they can be designed in various methods such as AC-coupled micro-grids which mostly dominate the present electric systems, DC-coupled micro-grids, and hybrid AC/DC coupled micro-grids (Ganjian-Aboukheili et al., 2020).

To ensure the cluster's safe and dependable operation in the grid-connected and standalone operation modes, linking many micro-grids into a cluster necessitates controlling and managing energy architecture One can create a smooth changeover between the operating modes by strategically controlling the switchgear at the point of common coupling. In the event of a grid breakdown, the microgrid can be used either in online mode or in stand-alone mode (Merai et. al, 2018; Martínez-Ramos et.al, 2018; Sastry, 2007). Since the distributed energy resources (DERs) generates DC output power, they are linked to the AC busbar by a DC/AC convertor. When operating in Islanded mode the DERs share the power generated in order to fulfill the load demand. Aggregated systems of DERs can effectively perform grid services as compared to individual operations. There are several methods of adjusting the reactive power from DERs, such as the wireless method and the communication-based method. In the wireless method, the reactive power compensation is only done locally depending on load demand, while in the communication-based approach, the reactive power of the DERs is adjusted in terms of optimal power flow (Nie et al., 2022).

Load estimation is an essential activity in the energy supply industry(ESI), as several planning studies depend on the estimated load. One of the recent approaches is load aggregation. Electric load aggregation is a strategy employed by independent energy consumers to band together and secure more affordable rates than they could if they shopped around separately (Zoričić et al., 2022). Aggregation can be accomplished through a simple pooling arrangement or by forming clusters, in which case separate contracts are made between the supplier and each aggregate group member. In 2022, Zoricic et. al. outlined the benefits of load aggregation and they concluded that it helps to enhance the load factor, making the resource price more stable, allowing the price to be more competitive and increase the buying power of the customers (Zoričić et al., 2022). Aggregated demand response from DERs is emerging as a leading solution in the energy markets as the amount of renewable electricity in the energy mix increases. In order to evaluate the present and future flexibility capability of a cluster of DERs, a flexible aggregation platform was created, enabling aggregators to build a robust virtual power plant (Ran et al., 2019). A DER aggregation model was proposed by Gao et al.(2021) created in the style of a Stackelberg game. When the price is equivalent to the wholesale market price and prosumers decide to sell the same quantity of energy as if they were directly participating in the wholesale market, then, this model permits an efficient equilibrium. In 2020, Alshehri et. al reviewed the integration of microgrids and the role of distribution system operators. Their work contended that the electrical market should allocate resources at the lowest possible cost to maximize market efficiency. According to Öztürk et al (2022), as the penetration of DERs increases, as well as the rising quantity of electrical loads, it makes it difficult to balance supply and demand. Therefore it results in power grid operational difficulties. A good number of authors have explored the involvement of aggregators in Demand Response activities (Abrishambaf et al., 2020; Musti, 2020a). Thomas et al.(2022) proposed a method of performance quantification of flexibility aggregation in flexibility coordination schemes(FCS). In comparison to microgrids with single active grid connectivity, those that import and export power through several active grid interconnections will be more dependable (Rizvi & Abu-Siada, 2022).

In the context of energy markets, the ancillary services are defined as the services necessary to maintain the security, dependability, and quality of the grid's power supply and that is necessary to keep it operating properly (Falabretti et. al, 2022; Cardoso et. al, 2022). Ancillary services can be placed into two general groups, which are frequency controlled and network controlled services. Supply and the pricing of reactive power is a well-known ancillary service that is generally designed for assisting the aggregators and also system operators. Despite its critical function in keeping system characteristics within allowable limits, real-time market-based procurement of reactive power is not being implemented (Cardoso et. al, 2021). To reduce the voltage imbalance at the points of connection and point of common coupling, DER inverter control solutions have been devised (Ehtesham & Junaid, 2022). Abbasi (2022) presented a method of a boost inverter-based single-stage electrical vehicle charger with a DC-side capacitor can provide vehicle to grid reactive power correction without negatively impacting the electric vehicle battery. Almeida et. al.(2021) have provided a thorough analysis of topological developments in PV-Grid Tied Inverters, outlining their benefits, drawbacks, and key characteristics.

Gastalver-Rubio et. al (2019) presented distributed voltage control scheme was proposed for optimally coordinating distributed generation units and the on-load tap changer transformers to regulate the voltages within the acceptable range. A few authors presented solutions for Volt-VAr optimization to control the legacy voltage regulators and synchronizing their functioning with intelligent inverter control. Table 1 shows the literature summary in terms of measured outcomes and tools/ software solutions that were used.

Table 1. Literature summary

Authors	Content Treated	Outcomes Measured	Tools/Software
Wolgast et al. (2022)	The energy system's emancipation opens the door to market-based solutions for the provision of reactive power	Reactive energy for market procurement; Voltage control problems in future distribution and transmission grids	Not stated
Merai et al. (2018)	The use of the self-balancing differential evolution algorithm minimize power loss	Energy losses, Reactive energy; Control and energy prices	Not stated
Charalambous et al. (2019)	a technique for adjusting the power factor and load asymmetries of microgrids using improved capabilities made possible by grid-tied inverters for solar power and energy storage systems	Power losses using the energy capacity	SCADA
Alshehri et al. (2019)	The aggregator's focus on generating profits could counteract the advantages of large-scale DER involvement in wholesale power markets.	Market efficiency brought large-scale deployment of DERsLosses due to aggregator monetary gain	Not stated
Cardoso et al. (2017)	Participation in ancillary service markets.	sizing of resource; Dispatching operation	Not stated
Xie & Wu (2022)	An improved generic algorithm for reactive power optimization in windfarms	Minimum compensation capacity; The minimum voltage deviation of the load nodes	Matlab
Baviskar et al. (2021)	the use of wind power facilities to manage reactive electricity in order to minimize distribution network losses	Real power loss; Profile for voltage; Reactive energy	SCADA

Three smart inverter functionalities Volt-Var, Volt-Watt, and the concurrent Volt-Var and Volt-Watt controls have been evaluated for effectiveness using a variety of performance metrics (Abbasi, 2021; Beyer et. al., 2021; Gastalver-Rubio et. al., 2019). A centralized, coordinated, and differentiated evolution based on Volt/VAR control was suggested by (Nirmala & Venkatesan (2022) to get rid of the voltage variations brought on by excessive photovoltaic integration in distribution networks. (Nie et al., 2022), have done a review on the different types of reactive power compensation methods in microgrids in terms of devices, control methods, and algorithms. Renewable resources such as solar PV have many benefits such as low cost after installation, and flexibility as it can be mounted on rooftops, ground, and on buildings. With all these benefits, a large increase in the integration of solar PV penetration causes serious power issues (Gastalver-Rubio et al., 2019). Hauwanga & Musti, (2022) have investigated the power losses and costs according to the location of the point of common coupling in smart grids. In 2021, Pitra & Musti investigated that in order to ascertain the effects of the duck curve, a two-step methodology was devised. A significant portion of the load that cannot be met during off-peak hours when a huge amount of solar energy is incorporated into the grid, which results in extra energy not being used during peak hours (Pitra & Musti, 2021). Several authors suggested possible control strategies for reactive power control in microgrids. It was suggested to use a hybrid Volt/Var control strategy based on machine learning (Abbasi, 2022). This method has benefits of being applicable in both centralized and decentralized power systems but its limitation is that it cannot be used in online mode. Gastalver-Rubio et al. (2019) have proposed a control strategy of Volt/VAR control by considering the predefined voltage range at the point of common coupling. This method is limited to smaller systems as in large systems, the voltage difference at the point of common coupling and far-end nodes is very large.

SIGNIFICANCE OF THE STUDY

Very few works in the literature have focused on distributed energy resource aggregation in the absence of an aggregator. From the literature, many authors have done studies on providing reactive power as an ancillary in MV and LV networks. A majority of the reactive power compensation studies are based on the data collected from power electronic controlled device solar PV systems, Electric vehicles, Energy storage devices, as well as distributed generation. However, there is gap in the research on how the researchers generated the load and generation data. There is limited research for creating day to day and each hour demand profiles for loads as well updating of demand profiles of loads. There is no clear contribution that explains determination of reactive power flows utilizing the data aggregation.

The importance of this study is to demonstrate how data aggregation of DERs in medium voltage (MV) distribution networks can employ the IEEE 1547 reactive power regulation modes. In order to control reactive power at the point of connection, this work uses solar PV and battery energy storage inverters, which is an emerging solution to reactive and active power control because the inverters have the ability to inject and absorb reactive power while simultaneously generating active power. Almeida et al. (2021) pointed to the possible use of using the data from various devices for determining the reactive power flows. When an inverter runs at leading power factor, it injects reactive power, and when it operates at trailing power factor, it absorbs reactive power. Keeping in view of above aspects, this work has the following objectives.

1. Generation of information for both loads and DERs through appropriate data models
2. Examining the prospects for offering auxiliary services, such as load aggregation, and reactive power compensation through systematic computational models
3. Investigate how reactive power compensation is affected when the DERs are not aggregated. (in other words, to investigate the accuracy of reactive power estimation without data processing)

To accomplish the above objectives, this chapter first designs and simulation of a low voltage microgrid based on a typical five bus network that is custom developed for this work. This 5-bus network is derived by modifying the standard IEEE-5bus system, while preserving all the original, standard features of the network and then solar power injection and inverters are added. Thus, these modifications are done in such a way that the network has all the native features and also the required components for the load aggregation and Volt-Var estimation studies. Thus, the modified network has two solar PV plants at buses 3 and 5; battery energy storage systems (BESS) at buses 2 and 4. However, both BESS and solar energy plants need inverters; and thus they are located at the respective buses. Figure 1 shows the network that is developed for the current study.

Figure 1. Proposed 5-bus low voltage microgrid

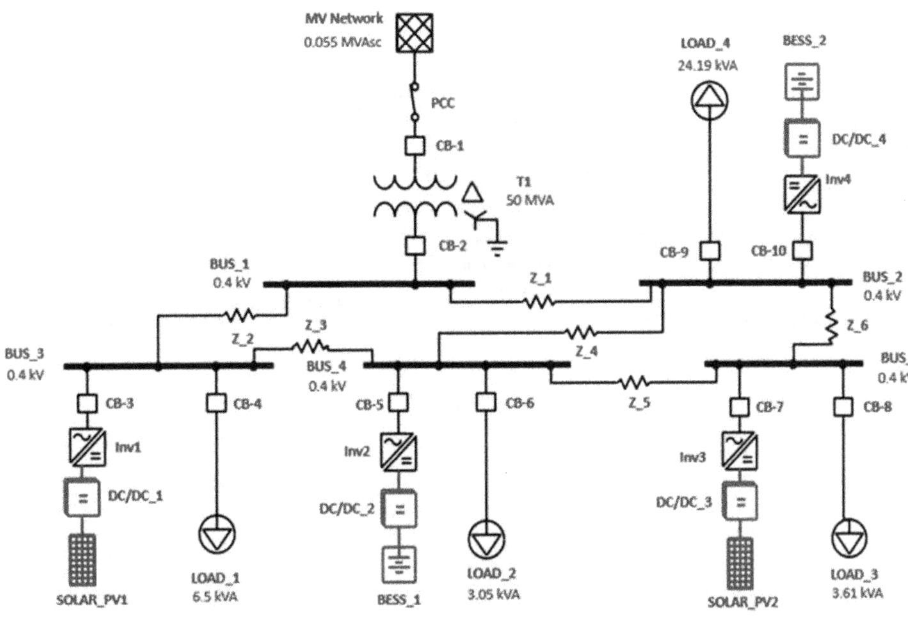

METHODOLOGY AND OVERALL FRAMEWORK

The low voltage(LV) network based on a modified IEEE 5-bus system was designed in ETAP software, it consists of two solar PV systems, two battery energy storage(BESS) systems, and four lumped loads. Each load in this system represents various static loads and motor loads that can consume reactive power in the system. The 5-bus system's five connected buses must have a load on them in order to replicate the hourly load fluctuations on those buses. Apart from the above data, I-V and P-V characteristics of solar PV panels are also required in simulating the generation case data and then in undertaking the load flow studies. Also, system data for a load such as the line data and bus data are required for conducting the load flow studies. Naturally, the simulations and the computational processes require a well-structured framework. Figure 2 shows the framework that is developed in this work, for computing the volt-var requirements.

Figure 2. Framework for computing the volt-var requirements

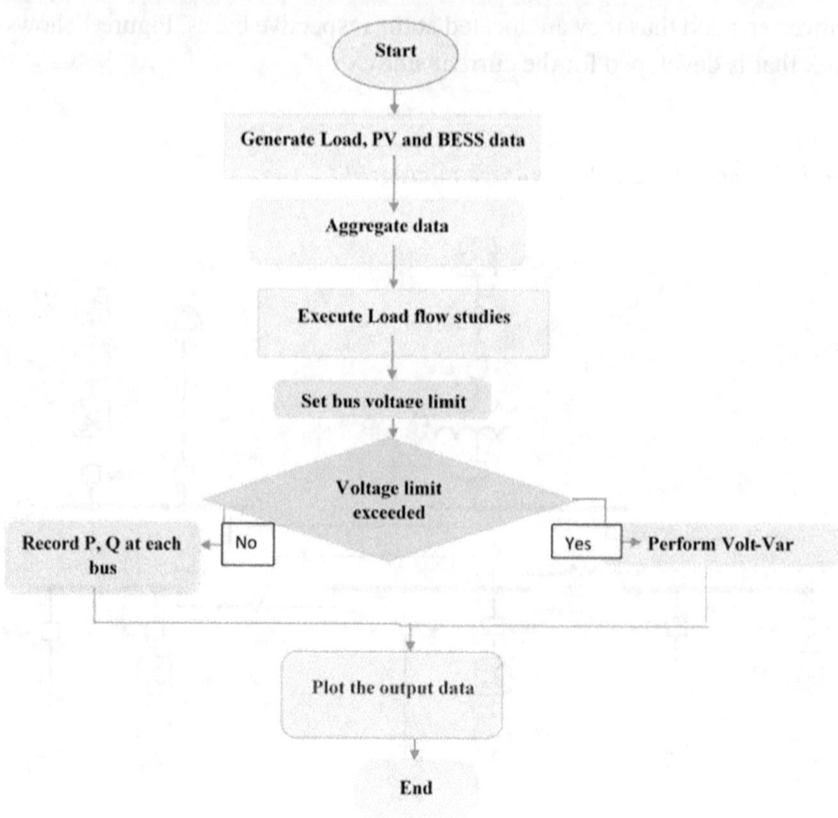

For the load data part., a tool has been designed in Microsoft excel using Visual Basic programming (VBA) to generate the aggregated that of the duration selected by the user. This tool provides flexibility as the user is free to select the number of days and the exact date they would like to generate the data. Extensive discussion on this Excel tool is avoided as the same is out of scope of this work. At the same time, it should be noted that the data and information required for the load aggregation are obtained out of simulations based on normal operating conditions. The load profile at each bus is generated and the aggregated load and generation active and reactive powers are plotted for a 24-hour basis with a 30min interval, which is the standard for load profile generation. The solar PV and Battery energy storage is connected to boost converter that converts the output voltage to higher voltages required at the buses. The inverter then changes the direct current power to alternating power, which is the total apparent power of the system. Aggregated active power for the base case, as generated the by MS-Excel tool is shown in Figure 3; and the reactive power is shown in Figure 4. From Figure 3, it is clear that the different energy resources such solar-PV and BESS do exist in smart grids and the overall energy profile can be dynamically varying due to inherent intermittency issues and also capacity limits on storage systems.

Figure 3. Base case aggregate active power of load, PV, and BESS

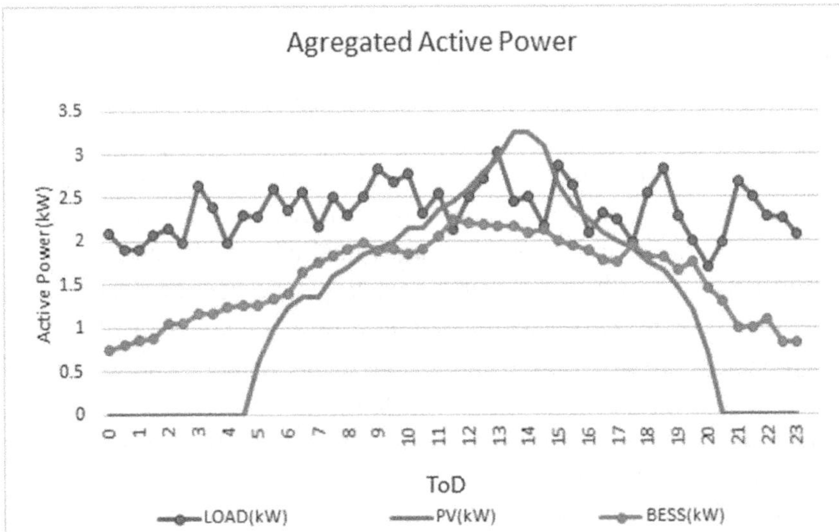

Figure 4. Base case aggregate reactive power of load, PV, and BESS

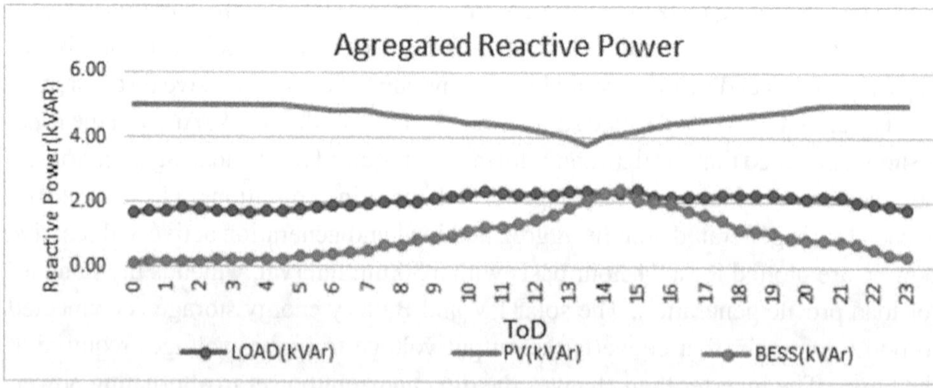

From the Figures 3 and 4 it can be seen that aggregated load information on both active and reactive powers needs to be gathered for every 30 minutes. Importantly, this aggregated load information changes from weekdays to weekends. Also this information changes over different seasons of the year. This is the reason behind considering day-ahead, month-ahead and/or quarter ahead schedules in energy trade. Naturally, load aggregation can result in various benefits (Falabretti et. al, 2022; Gao et. al, 2021) especially in taking appropriate and timely decisions. Some of the key benefits of load aggregation are illustrated below:

- **Load Factor Improvement:** The load factor is defined as the proportion of overall power consumption to peak power consumption. Through load aggregation, clusters of consumers can increase their purchasing power by utilizing load diversity to raise the aggregate load factor of the cluster. When loads of multiple customers are combined, the non-coincident peaks and valleys in the load profiles of individual consumers tend to cancel out one another. This effect causes the overall load profile to be flatter, the load factor to increase, and the total cost of energy per unit of energy for the entire aggregate group to decrease. Load factor improvement is very important as it is computed typically for each billing cycle and consumers generally get financially benefited as several known tariff structures apply penalties for peak power consumptions.
- **Price Stability:** It is possible to negotiate a range-bound price for energy from an energy market operator once the aggregated load information is known. However, such pricing contracts are generally valid for a predetermined amount of time, like a month or a season.

- **Competitive Pricing:** When aggregated load information is combined with effective demand response programs, the aggregator generally reduces the energy tariff to stay competitive in the market. Just as above, it should be noted that basic energy service prices change all the time, long-term savings cannot be guaranteed.
- **Increased Buying Power:** Industrial consumers with large energy requirements often have more negotiating powers with their energy suppliers and typically enjoy good financial standing. This results in increased purchasing power. The aggregator generally tends to offer financial incentives to ensure bulk energy sales well in advance that can help in safer cash flows.

From the above, several benefits can be seen from load aggregation. However, to enjoy such benefits, gathering data is critical first step (Martínez-Ramos et.al, 2018). From the data, various parameters need to be computed so that informed decisions can be taken. For the sake of clarity and completeness, the mathematical models and various assumptions are provided below.

COMPUTATIONAL MODEL

The power injected at bus i in a distribution system with N nodes is given by;

$$S(inverter)at\ bus_i = S(inverter_i) - S(load,i) \tag{1}$$

Where; S represents the apparent power.

$$S = (Pi + jQi) \tag{2}$$

P and Q represent the real and reactive power, while represents the bus under study. The flow of power of the system is defined by N simultaneous equations generated by equation (1). N represents the number of nodes/buses in the system. The voltage variation at each bus can be represented as:

$$\Delta V = V1 - V2 = I(R+jX) \tag{3}$$

Where I is the current at the respective buses;

$$\mathrm{I1} = \left(\frac{(PL1 - Ppv1) + j\left(QL1 - Q_{pv1}\right)}{Vbus3} \right) \tag{4}$$

$$\mathrm{I2} = \left(\frac{(PL2 - Pbess\_1) + j(Ql2 - Qbess\_1)}{Vbus4} \right) \tag{5}$$

$$\mathrm{I3} = \left(\frac{(PL3 - Ppv2) + j\left(QL3 - Q_{pv2}\right)}{Vbus5} \right) \tag{6}$$

$$I4 = \left(\frac{(PL4 - Pbess_2) + j\left(QL4 - Q_{bess_2}\right)}{Vbus2} \right) \tag{7}$$

Substituting equation (3) to equation (6) into equation (1) to

$$\Delta Vbus3 = \left(\frac{(PL1 - Ppv1) + j\left(QL1 - Q_{pv1}\right)}{Vbus3} \right) * (R + jX) \tag{8}$$

$$\Delta Vbus4 = \left(\frac{(PL2 - Pbess_1) + j(Ql2 - Qbess_1)}{Vbus4} \right) * (R + jX) \tag{9}$$

$$\Delta Vbus5 = \left(\frac{(PL3 - Ppv2) + j\left(QL3 - Q_{pv2}\right)}{Vbus5} \right) * (\mathrm{R} + \mathrm{j}\,\mathrm{X}) \tag{10}$$

$$\Delta Vbus2 = \left(\frac{(PL4 - Pbess_2) + j\left(QL4 - Q_{bess_2}\right)}{Vbus2} \right) * (R + jX) \tag{11}$$

Where R+Jx represents the resistance and reactance of the respective transmission line section. Now, considering real and imaginary parts of the voltage, the change at the point of connection can be modelled as;

$$\Delta Vbus2 = \left(\frac{(PL4 - Pbess_2)R + (QL4 - Q_{bess_2})X}{Vbus2} \right) \tag{12}$$

$$\Delta Vbus3 = \left(\frac{(PL1 - Ppv1)R + j(QL1 - Q_{pv1})X}{Vbus3} \right) \tag{13}$$

$$\Delta Vbus4 = \left(\frac{(PL2 - Pbess_1)R + (Ql2 - Qbess_1)X}{Vbus4} \right) \tag{14}$$

$$\Delta Vbus5 = \left(\frac{(PL3 - Ppv2)R + (QL3 - Q_{pv2})X}{Vbus5} \right) \tag{15}$$

Where; *PL*1, *PL*2, *PL*3, & *PL*4 is the real power for the load1, load2, load3 and load4 respectively. QL1, QL2, QL3 & QL4 is the reactive power of the loads. PV1, PV2 is the real power from the solar panels. $Pbess_1$, $Pbess_2$ is the real power and $Qbess_1$, $Qbess_2$ is the reactive power from the battery storage. Vbus1, Vbus2, Vbus3, Vbus4 & Vbus5 is the voltage at the respective bus. Mathematical expressions for the reactive power that the Volt-Var control injects or absorbs include:

$$Q(T) = \begin{cases} Q1(t); \ if \ V(t) \le V1 \\ \dfrac{V2 - V(t)}{V2 - V1} * Q1(t); \ if \ V1 < V(t) \le V2 \\ 0; \ if \ V2 < V(t) \le V4 \\ \dfrac{V3 - V(t)}{V3 - V4} *; \ if \ V3 < V(t) \le V4 \\ Q4(t); \ if \ V(t) > V4 \end{cases} \tag{16}$$

Some of the assumptions made during the design and data development are listed below.

- Loads 1, 2, 3, and 4 are assumed to be lumped.
- Constant power model is used for representing all the loads.
- Data development is based on Day-Ahead and on a short and Medium term forecast since a range of data needs to be considered.
- It is assumed that the reactive power compensation is done locally, in other words the reactive power consumed by a load is compensated by the inverter connected at that same bus.

LOAD AGGREGATION

The first iteration of load aggregation was developed for use in the design, expansion, and planning of power systems. Later, load aggregation was utilized to build grounding systems, voltage compensators, and reactive power compensators. As the generation, transmission, and distribution levels of power systems rose, load aggregation made additional strides for applications in stability, control, and protection of power systems. In transmission systems, loads have been applied to power flow and voltage restoration devices as well as to control loads in MV&LV distribution systems. Aggregation of loads is the process of combining a load's active and reactive power requirements (Thomas et al., 2022). It should be noted that two important data points – Load model itself and the load profiles (typically forecasted load) are essential for determining the aggregated load.

STANDARD IEEE 1547 GRID SERVICES

There are six grid services that follow the IEEE 1547 standard (Nie et al., 2022b). Based on the scope of this chapter, two important services will be discussed in this chapter.

1. **Constant-VAR Mode:**
   The system seeks to maintain a steady injection or absorption of reactive power while operating in this mode.
2. **Volt-VAR Mode:**
   In this mode of operation, the system aims to adjust the reactive power to compensate for voltage variation based on a piece-wise Volt-Var power response curve

REACTIVE POWER PRICING

There is a growing need for reactive power compensation due to increase voltage collapse in LV systems, loads operating at low power factor. Customers are often required to maintain a power factor of 0.95 lag and if the power factor falls below 95%, penalty charges depending on the tariff are enforced.

Reactive power ancillary service can be priced in two different ways (Falabrettiet al., 2022).

- By establishing distinct reactive power pricing in addition to the kWh tariff
- By establishing a kVAh price that accounts for both reactive and active electricity

Generally, most industrial and commercial consumers are expected to maintain the power factor (and thus manage their own reactive power consumption so that it stays within the set limits) in order avoid penalties. Thus, consumers mostly draw a very less amount of reactive power from the grid as the static VAR capacitors installed by them constantly supply a large portion of internal reactive power needs. This practice yields a power factor that is almost unity. Reactive power pricing has advantages including increased system voltage, increased transmission capacity, and increased margin against voltage collapse. For the simple reason that it is required for the effective transmission of active power, reactive power is frequently seen as an essential ancillary service.

The following data was used for the base case design in the ETAP software simulation

Table 2. Inverter data

Bus Number	Bus 3	Bus_4	Bus 5	Bus 2
Inverter number	Invert 1	Invert 2	Invert 3	Invert 4
DC Power(Kw) Design	3.34	3	3.25	1.62
AC Power(Kw) Rating Design	3.24	2.7	3.15	1.571
Rating (kVA)	3.24	2.7	3.15	1.62
AC Volts(kV)	0.360	0.375	0.225	0.380
Efficiency	97%	90%	97%	97%
Nominal Op. Voltage Range	90-110%	90-110%	90-110%	90-110%
Dc Power(Kw) Nominal	2.836	2.4	2.757	1.375
AC Power(KW) Rating Nominal	2.592	2.16	2.52	1.257

Reactive power dissipates faster than active power because the reactive power absorbed in the transformer or transmission line is proportional to the square of the current. Hence it is a common practice to install reactive power compensation devices at the load side, since reactive power does not travel well over long distances due to losses, charging admittances and injections (Xie & Wu, 2022). However, loads keep on changing and also the transformer taps. Thus, the reactive power requirements need to be computed dynamically and inverters need to be controlled based on the computations. ETAP software is used in this work to investigate the reactive power requirements for various case scenarios. Table 2 shows the inverter data that needs to be utilized in the simulation process.

Similarly, data points related to the solar PV system and the BESS are required. These are provided in Tables 3 and 4.

The following data was extracted from the ETAP software during the simulation.

Table 3. Solar PV data

Bus Number	Bus 3	Bus 5
Solar PV generation num	SOLAR_PV1	SOLAR_PV2
Total Panels	12	60
Voltage DC(V)	231	177.2
Active Power(kW)	2.15	3.76
Current(A) DC	14.92	21.21
Total Cells	72	36
Number of Series connection	6	10
Number of Parallel connection	2	6
Watt/panel	179	62.7

Table 4. Battery storage data

Bus Number	Bus 4	Bus 2
Battery Storage num	BESS_1	BESS_2
Number of cells	4	6
Rated Voc(V)	8.252	12.36
Total capacity(AH)	1000	200
Capacity(Kw)	2.50	2.0
Discharge Time(hours)	8	8

RESULTS

All the above data is carefully processed into the ETAP software and then load flow studies were conducted. Load flow studies need to be conducted for all 24 data sets since each data set is spaced by 30 min from the other. Output was collected from the ETAP and further utilized in the process of volt-var computations. Since the load variation is different over the seasons, the load data needs to be processed for different seasons. Load will be different during weekdays and the weekends.

Figure 5. Aggregated reactive power profile over different seasons

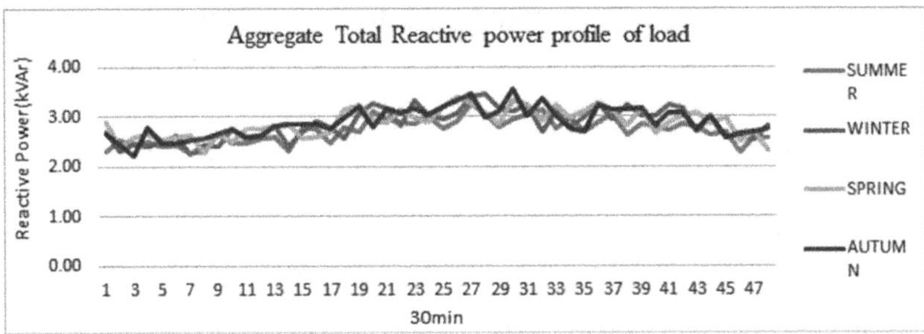

Thus, computations have to be carried out continuously on various data sets. This inherent requirement in this problem itself points to the need of developing an automated process and/or framework for data processing, computing, and decision making process, which is the essence of this chapter. Figure 5 shows the aggregated reactive power profile of the load over the seasons in a year. As stated above, loads need to be represented and categorized for weekdays and weekends separately. Figure 6 shows the aggregated average load values during the weekdays and the weekends in a year.

Figure 6. Annual average load profile with weekdays and weekends

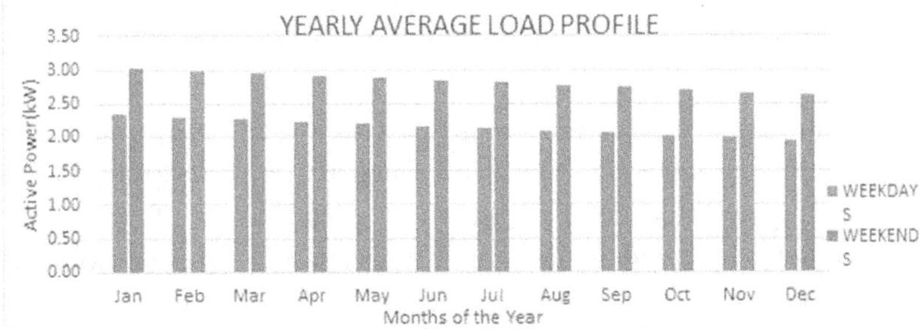

DISCUSSION

From the above, several aspects can be observed. Aggregation can be done through a straightforward pooling arrangement or by creating clusters, whereby individual contracts are arranged between the suppliers and each aggregate group member. Reactive power management is a complex and real-time process. Required volt-vars can be determined through complex mathematical models and yet market design models can influence these computational models. In a nutshell, the entire process requires data aggregation followed by appropriate decisions (control signals) for controlling the inverters. The volt-var computational process is highly data-driven and indeed is a typical example that readily can qualify for track of decision-making based on data/ information. Such automated decision-making systems naturally result in transparency, computational consistency, and stable operation. However, it should be noted that at present there is no single tool that handles the process from end to end. For instance, data needs to be generated (or obtained through meters) in 30-minute intervals. Then load flows need to be done for all 24 data sets in a single day and this requires manual processing for all the intervals as at present there is no dedicated software to loop the studies. This work used ETAP software and all the load flows are executed manually.

Further, there are a good number of assumptions in the approach adopted and also several anomalies in the works contributed by various authors in this area over the years. For instance, this work does not consider the pricing of reactive power; and determines the volt-var requirements. In reality, complex pricing of reactive power does exist. There are two possible views exist. Firstly, the reactive power, though priced, is consumed in smaller amounts by bulk consumers as they will have static capacitors that typically and generally achieve 95% power factor. If such consumers tend to draw reactive power beyond the set limits, then penalties will be applied based on prevailing reactive power tariffs. Secondly, reactive power is required for the active power flows and especially for the operation of transformers that operate between transmission and distribution companies. This is where the computations that determine the volt-var requirements assume more significant importance; though they certainly help in LV networks as well. Further, this chapter considered only inverters to produce reactive power, but there are a range of power apparatus that can do the job of producing the reactive power. A range of factors such as the length and operating voltage of the transmission lines influence volt-var requirements and these are not considered in this work as well. Energy market models, particularly energy trading conditions also influence overall costs of procuring the required reactive power. Essentially, there are a good number of aspects; such as – data collection for load aggregation, market design, trading conditions, reactive power tariff structures, network characteristics, computational processes etc,; in managing load aggregation for reactive power management. Then, decisions for volt-var controls need to be made either based on a day-ahead model or week-ahead, or even month-ahead depending on the requirement. Future studies may consider developing a single tool. Since the problem of load aggregation and reactive power management involves a lot of data; several opportunities exist in applying big data tools and machine learning algorithms.

CONCLUSION

This chapter presented the problem of load aggregation for volt-var estimation in a 5-bus smart grid. Complexity of reactive power management problem is explained in terms of data development and computational processes. Suitable assumptions have been made to reduce the complexity. A well-structured framework is proposed for determining the required volt-vars. Standard IEEE 5 bus system is modified by adding storage systems and inverters. The proposed framework is applied on the custom developed 5 bus system for varying loads over a calendar year. Scope for further work is presented and the need to develop automated tools and possible prospects of applying machine learning algorithms is highlighted.

REFERENCES

Abbasi, A. G. (2022). *Coordinated Volt-Var control in multiple smart inverters in Smart Distribution Networks for Voltage Regulation* [Master's thesis]. Arctic University of Norway. https://munin.uit.no/bitstream/handle/10037/25764/thesis.pdf

Abrishambaf, O., Faria, P., & Vale, Z. (2020). Aggregation of Consumers Participation in the Ramping of a Demand Response Event. *International Conference on the European Energy Market, EEM*. 10.1109/EEM49802.2020.9221914

Ahmad Khan, A., Naeem, M., Iqbal, M., Qaisar, S., & Anpalagan, A. (2016). A compendium of optimization objectives, constraints, tools and algorithms for energy management in microgrids. In *Renewable and Sustainable Energy Reviews* (Vol. 58, pp. 1664–1683). Elsevier. doi:10.1016/j.rser.2015.12.259

Almeida, D., Pasupuleti, J., & Ekanayake, J. (2021). Comparison of reactive power control techniques for solar pv inverters to mitigate voltage rise in low-voltage grids. *Electronics (Basel)*, *10*(13), 1569. Advance online publication. doi:10.3390/electronics10131569

Alshehri, K., Ndrio, M., Bose, S., & Başar, T. (2020). Quantifying Market Efficiency Impacts of Aggregated Distributed Energy Resources. *IEEE Transactions on Power Systems*, *35*(5), 4067–4077. doi:10.1109/TPWRS.2020.2979997

Baseem & Hagos. (2022). Demand response aggregation. *Active Electrical Distribution Network,* 345-358. doi:10.1016/B978-0-323-85169-5.00008-3

Baviskar, A., Das, K., Hansen, A. D., & Menegatos, P. (2021): Loss Minimization in Distribution Network using Wind Power Plant Reactive Power Support. doi:10.36227/techrxiv.14554845.v1

Beyer, K., Beckmann, R., Geißendörfer, S., von Maydell, K., & Agert, C. (2021). Adaptive online-learning volt-var control for smart inverters using deep reinforcement learning. *Energies*, *14*(7), 1991. Advance online publication. doi:10.3390/en14071991

Cardoso, F., Stadler, G., & Mashayekh, M. (2021). *The impact of Ancillary Services in optimal DER investment decisions.* Lawrence Berkeley National Laboratory Recent Work Title. https://escholarship.org/uc/item/112337hb

Charalambous, A., Hadjidemetriou, L., Zacharia, L., Bintoudi, A. D., Tsolakis, A. C., Tzovaras, D., & Kyriakides, E. (2019). Phase balancing and reactive power support services for microgrids. *Applied Sciences (Basel, Switzerland)*, *9*(23), 5067. Advance online publication. doi:10.3390/app9235067

Ehtesham, M., & Junaid, M. (2022). Reactive power control strategy for integrated photovoltaic inverter. *International Journal of Power Electronics and Drive Systems*, *13*(3), 1713–1720. doi:10.11591/ijpeds.v13.i3.pp1713-1720

Falabretti, D., Gulotta, F., & Spinelli, L. (2022). Participation of Aggregated DERs to the Ancillary Services Market: A Monte Carlo Simulation-Based Heuristic Greedy-Indexing Model. *Energies*, *15*(3), 1037. Advance online publication. doi:10.3390/en15031037

Ganjian-Aboukheili, M., Shahabi, M., Shafiee, Q., & Guerrero, J. M. (2020). Seamless Transition of Microgrids Operation from Grid-Connected to Islanded Mode. *IEEE Transactions on Smart Grid*, *11*(3), 2106–2114. doi:10.1109/TSG.2019.2947651

Gao, Z., Alshehri, K., & Birge, J. R. (2021). On Efficient Aggregation of Distributed Energy Resources. *2021 60th IEEE Conference on Decision and Control (CDC),* 7064-7069. 10.1109/CDC45484.2021.9683117

Gastalver-Rubio, A., Romero-Ramos, E., & Maza-Ortega, J. M. (2019). Improving the Performance of Low Voltage Networks by an Optimized Unbalance Operation of Three-Phase Distributed Generators. *IEEE Access : Practical Innovations, Open Solutions*, *7*(7), 177504–177516. Advance online publication. doi:10.1109/ACCESS.2019.2958206

Georgios, C. (2022). Distributed methodology for reactive power support of transmission system, Sustainable Energy. *Grids and Networks*, *31*, 100753. Advance online publication. doi:10.1016/j.segan.2022.100753

Hauwanga, A. S., & Musti, K. S. S. (2022). Evaluation of Energy Losses and Costs Based on the Location of PCC in Smart Grids. *IEEE 11th Int. Conference on Communication Systems and Network Technologies (CSNT),* 76-82. 10.1109/CSNT54456.2022.9787642

Mahmoudi, M., Fatehi, A., Jafari, H., & Karimi, E. (2018). Multi-objective micro-grid design by NSGA-II considering both islanded and grid-connected modes. *IEEE Texas Power and Energy Conference,* 1–6. 10.1109/TPEC.2018.8312105

Martínez-Ramos, J. L. (2018). Provision of Ancillary Services by a Smart Microgrid: An OPF Approach. *Int. Conf. on Smart Energy Systems and Technologies (SEST),* 1-6. 10.1109/SEST.2018.8495883

Merai, M., Naouar, M. W., Slama-Belkhodja, I., & Monmasson, E. (2018). Grid connected converters as reactive power ancillary service providers: Technical analysis for minimum required DC-link voltage. *Mathematics and Computers in Simulation*, *158*, 344–354. doi:10.1016/j.matcom.2018.09.016

Musti, K. S. (2020b). *Circular Economy in Energizing Smart Cities. In Handbook of Research on Entrepreneurship Development and Opportunities in Circular Economy.* IGI Global., doi:10.4018/978-1-7998-5116-5.ch013

Musti, K. S., & Kapali, D. (2021). Digital Transformation of SMEs in the Energy Sector to Survive in a Post-COVID-19 Era. In N. Baporikar (Ed.), *Handbook of Research on Strategies and Interventions to Mitigate COVID-19 Impact on SMEs* (pp. 186–207). IGI Global. doi:10.4018/978-1-7998-7436-2.ch009

Musti, K. S. S. (2020a). Quantification of Demand Response in Smart Grids. *IEEE India Council Int. Conf. (INDISCON)*, 278-282. 10.1109/INDISCON50162.2020.00063

Musti, K. S. S., Iileka, H., & Shidhika, F. (2020). *Industry 4.0 Based Enterprise Information System for Demand-Side Management and Energy Efficiency. In Novel Approaches to Information Systems Design*. IGI-Global. doi:10.4018/978-1-7998-2975-1.ch007

Nie, J., Liu, Y., Zhou, L., Jiang, X., & Preindl, M. (2022). Deep Reinforcement Learning Based Approach for Optimal Power Flow of Microgrid with Grid Services Implementation. *IEEE Transportation Electrification Conf. & Expo*, 1148–1153. 10.1109/ITEC53557.2022.9813862

Nirmala, R., & Venkatesan, S. (2022). Inverter current control for reactive power compensation in solar grid system using Self-Tuned Fuzzy Logic Controller. *Automatika (Zagreb)*, *63*(1), 102–121. doi:10.1080/00051144.2021.2009653

Offergeld, T., Mattus, N., Schmidtke, F., & Ulbig, A. (2022). On Aggregation Performance in Privacy Conscious Hierarchical Flexibility Coordination Schemes. *Proceedings of the 11th Bulk Power Systems Dynamics and Control Symposium (IREP)*. 10.48550/arXiv.2207.03439

Öztürk, E., Rheinberger, K., Faulwasser, T., Worthmann, K., & Preibinger, M. (2022). Aggregation of Demand-Side Flexibilities: A Comparative Study of Approximation Algorithms. *Energies*, *15*(7), 2501. Advance online publication. doi:10.3390/en15072501

Pitra, G. M., & Musti, K. S. S. (2021). Duck Curve with Renewable Energies and Storage Technologies. *13th International Conference on Computational Intelligence and Communication Networks (CICN)*, 66-71. 10.1109/CICN51697.2021.9574671

Ran, B., Nutma, J., & Klever, M. (2019). Maximizing the utilization of DERs with the Interflex Aggregation Platform for Flexibility. CIRED-2019 Conference, Madrid, Spain, doi:10.34890/781

Rizvi, S., & Abu-Saida, A. (2022). Active Power Sharing in a Micro-Grid with Multiple Grid Connections. *Designs*, *6*(2), 24. Advance online publication. doi:10.3390/designs6020024

Sastry, M. K. S. (2007). Integrated Outage Management System: An effective solution for power utilities to address customer grievances. *International Journal of Electronic Customer Relationship Management*, *1*(1), 30–40. doi:10.1504/IJECRM.2007.014424

Wolgast, T., Ferenz, S., & Nieße, A. (2022). Reactive Power Markets: A Review. IEEE Access, 10, 28397–28410 . doi:10.1109/ACCESS.2022.3141235

Xie, Y., & Wu, Y. (2022). Investment Strategy of Reactive Power Compensation Scheme in Wind Turbine Distribution Network Based on Optimal Allocation. *Journal of Sensors*, *2022*, 1–8. Advance online publication. doi:10.1155/2022/7037451

Zoričić, D., Knežević, G., Miletić, M., Dolinar, D., & Sprčić, D. M. (2022). Integrated Risk Analysis of Aggregators: Policy Implications for the Development of the Competitive Aggregator Industry. *Energies*, *15*(14), 5076. Advance online publication. doi:10.3390/en15145076

KEY TERMS AND DEFINITIONS

Aggregator: Aggregator in a typical energy supply industry, gathers data of demand and supply from various parts of the power network; and then pools them and then sells the energy (or capacity) to the Distribution System Operators (DSOs). The role of aggregator is critical in ensuring the transparency and competitiveness in energy markets.

Ancillary Service (in Energy Supply Industry): Engineering services that are required to support the power grid operation in order to preserve grid security, dependability, and quality of power are typically termed as ancillary services. In modern era, ancillary services are typically provided by small scale engineering firms which specialized in the power grid operation and related activities. Some of the common ancillary services include - generation scheduling, load dispatch, frequency regulation, voltage management etc.

Electricity Supply Industry (ESI): ESI is a complex industry that consists of different segments in which different organizations and businesses exist and operate. The major segments include the generation, transmission and distribution systems. ESI also will have other stakeholders such as an independent system operator, a state appointed regulator, an aggregator, consumers and prosumers etc. Energy is traded as the main commodity in the ESI. Modern ESIs are typically decentralized and regulated as per the prevailing energy laws and standards.

Inverter: It is a power-electronic device that converts DC power into AC power using specialized electronic components that can be controlled locally and/or remotely. The voltage level and the frequency of the output power depend on design and operation of a specific inverter.

Load Aggregation: Electric load aggregation is a technique used by various stakeholders to form an alliance to find or negotiate cheaper energy pricing than the prevailing market prices. Aggregation can be done through a straightforward pooling arrangement or by creating clusters, whereby individual contracts are arranged between the suppliers and consumers. Naturally, load aggregation requires a lot of data for understanding the requirements and also for successful grid operation.

Chapter 3
A Systematic Review of the Literature on Financial Applications of Predictive Analytics

Sudhansu Sekhar Nanda
https://orcid.org/0000-0003-0974-181X
Kirloskar Institute of Management, India

ABSTRACT

To assist the management and support the strategic decisions, statistical and computational methodologies are being progressively incorporated into decision support systems. To accurately anticipate the financial data, researchers must properly comprehend its utilization. Therefore, a method-based literature evaluation with an emphasis on the predictive analytics field is proposed in this chapter. Regression, clustering, association, and time series models are thoroughly covered in this research. It extends current statistical explanatory modelling into the field of computational modelling. These model results help financial managers and risk management experts get better results. The numerous financial predictive analytic techniques are brought together in this review under one area. This is regarded as a solid foundation since it shows that when more than 40 papers have been identified as eligible, systematic reviews can be employed at the domain level. This search was conducted by the SPAR-4-SLR (scientific procedures and rationales for systematic literature reviews) protocol.

DOI: 10.4018/978-1-6684-7568-3.ch003

INTRODUCTION

This chapter analyses and investigates how forecasts are made by academics in the fields of finance and computational studies using predictive analytic techniques. Systematic identification of methods and used cases are provided, using the information from financial information systems, which can be obtained internally or externally (IS). This chapter serves as a review; it does not go into detail on the modelling procedure. Many textbooks appropriately address this (Kuhn and Johnson, 2013). Instead, it is a collection of computational and statistical explanations for the financial services sector. It is pertinent to the IS field since Decision Support Systems are increasingly using predictive methodologies (DSS).

The term "finance" refers to a broad range of capital market activities, including portfolio and intertemporal decisions (Summers, 1985). Time series produced by these processes are widely used to forecast the future (Gooijer and Hyndman, 2006).

Predictive analytics are utilized in the world of finance to analyze historical IS data sets. The phrase refers to both predictive computational techniques and explanatory statistics. Predictive computational algorithms are categorized as forward-looking (Tsay, 2005). The researchers who employ such techniques must be at ease that the study begins with the help of data rather than a theory (Muller et al., 2016; Prado, 2020).

Descriptive data from a data warehouse is required for DSS to perform predictive analytics. This becomes more of a challenge when dealing with the heterogeneous, autonomous, complex, and changing "Big Data" frequently seen in finance due to the vast, diverse, and complex data (Wu et al. 2013).

This brings up a crucial issue for IS. It's important to distinguish between information and data that is generated inside and externally. The datasets that must be imported into an IS are therefore covered in Section 2 of this paper, whereas datasets created by an IS are covered in Section 3. It is necessary to use an interactive software-based system to address ways to internally collected raw data. A mechanism for collecting distributed data or appropriate imported data sets is needed to address approaches to external data.

The learning process in predictive computational algorithms can be either supervised or unsupervised (Dixon, 2020). IS data sets and predictive analytics can be combined to categorize event outcomes. It is possible to use it to predict numerical values, such as a fraudulent credit card transaction, or a fabricated insurance claim. Finally, it can be used to forecast time series, as was already described. As already noted, the information in the IS might come from both internal and external sources.

For effective predictive analytics, the data's outliers must be identified. The cross-sectional distributional features of financial ratios are significantly impacted by outliers (Frecka and Hopwood, 1983). These are very helpful for spotting questionable financial transactions that identify outliers in financial data, as an illustration (Adams et al. 2019).

The predictive model can be incorporated once the data has been prepared which can be categorized as either parametric or nonparametric (Zhao 2008).

METHODOLOGY

The most significant applications of predictive analytics in finance were determined by doing a thorough literature analysis utilizing many search engines. This search was conducted by the SPAR-4-SLR (Scientific Procedures and Rationales for Systematic Literature Reviews) protocol (Paul et al. 2021).

This approach is employed to refine knowledge in a certain field. It makes sure no duplicate research is included and puts emphasis on claims of innovation. The various used cases and approaches were compiled, organized, and evaluated. Over 187 significant contributions were found in the domain search, indicating enough maturity to warrant the study. This is regarded as a solid foundation since it shows that when more than 40 papers have been identified as eligible, systematic reviews can be employed at the domain level (Paul and Criado, 2020).

There were two major categories found. Firstly, inference-drawing statistical techniques, and then computational techniques that identify broad predictive patterns apply to DSS and can be used to perform predictive analytics on several financial factors. Two research questions (RQ) were posed to serve as the foundation for the construction of the predictive analytic domain.

Q1: Top financial contributors used predictive analytics in their research.
Q2: Enquired about the research context and methodological decisions made when using predictive analytics.

In sections 3 and 4, the existing literature that relates to the search criteria is thoroughly reviewed. The primary statistical, classification, regression, clustering, association, and time series models were used in these studies. To make sure all study methodologies were covered, these search phrases were added to the important research fields. The conclusions from this methodical approach are then covered.

CLASSIFICATION METHODS

Many aspects of finance are impacted by predictions made using classification matrices, including portfolio design, risk management, option pricing, and strategic hedging. Financial DSS generates forecasting reports using classification methods. For instance, you could use the classification approach and a Support Vector Machine (SVM) to forecast the direction of the stock market, which is either up or down (Huang et al. 2005).

To identify anomalies related to the time of day, week, or month, volatility clustering, heavy tails, and high-frequency and ultra-high-frequency trade data are analyzed using predictive tables. Take the 1.28 million buy transactions and 1.30 million sale transactions, for instance, and analyze the transaction batch frequency (Broby et al. 2007). The pace of transactions with this type of analysis makes mistakes more likely (Thought, 2019). Furthermore, at times when there is no trade, that data must be synthesized using linear interpolation.

There are several quadratic financial problems. In the first case, points on a quadratic function can be predicted using graphs. In the latter, conditional variances, covariances, and correlations of financial returns can be analyzed using covariance matrices.

Similarity functions are crucial to the process of financial forecasting. especially when employing specific linear and nonlinear classifiers, neural networks, and parametric and nonparametric regressions. In finance, using similarity functions is typically necessary for making case-based choices. For instance, by recognizing analogous prior instances of financial difficulties, bankruptcy can be predicted (Fabozzi et al. 2011). The matching and retrieval of the preceding cases is this approach's key characteristic. This weighs the characteristics of a previous bankruptcy. The retrieval step of the matching process then compares the features of these earlier bankruptcies to those of the company or companies under investigation.

When dealing with non-linear issues, computational methods in DSS are more beneficial. These non-linear financial prediction issues are particularly well-suited for computation by ANN and Support Vector classifiers to determine the value of an output (Park and Han, 2002). ANNs combine a collection of inputs and then compute bias corrections and apply weights thanks to this. The ANN discovers the ideal result by adjusting these weights. A few of these articles in science publications employ technical indicators, which are discouraged by academics studying finance (Coakley and Brown, 2000).

REGRESSION METHODS

Predictive finance, the most popular type of forecast model in DSS, heavily uses regression techniques, which are also utilized in explanatory modelling.

The capital asset pricing model is the most used one in finance (CAPM). In essence, this is a model of linear regression with one factor:

E(Ri) = Rf B + (E(Rm) Rf)

It is premised on a linear relationship between the market return explanatory variable E(Rm) and the expected return dependent variable E(Ri). Thus, this can be used to illustrate the relationship between systematic risk, the percentage of returns that cannot be eliminated through diversification, and the projected return on assets. The CAPM is frequently used in papers to make predictions.

A measure of the researcher's level of confidence in the output prediction must be added to the numerical output when using regression analysis to generate predictions. These might be expressed as tolerance intervals or confidence predictions. Financial studies using panel regressions frequently manipulate data to reach desired p-values to test for these risk factors (Menkhoff and Taylor, 2007).

Using quantile regression is another technique to include a level of confidence (Fama and French, 2004). Instead of calculating the mean, it computes the conditional median. It has the benefit of allowing for sample ordering and sorting. For instance, there is skew and dispersion between a company's highest-paid employees and lowest-paid ones. This method is used to determine if employees who are conditionally (predicted) paid higher wages than those who are conditionally paid lower wages (Harvey and Liu, 2021).

CLUSTERING AND ASSOCIATION RULE METHODS

These are crucial methods in finance for comprehending time series that make it easier to visualize the connections between the data (Koenker and Hallock, 2001).

Machine learning (ML) models are used by Association Rules (AR) to search databases for patterns or associated events. It is offered as a method of identifying bank fraud (Hallock and Madalozzo, 2010). Data mining can be used to identify the occurrences that are typically connected with fraud.

Both association rules and clustering algorithms can be applied in computational finance in addition to other techniques. For instance, by utilizing clustering in conjunction with a neural network-based model, financial insolvency can be forecasted (Aghabozorgi et al. 2015).

TIME SERIES MODELS

A time series' internal organization may also display autocorrelation, like when a stock's price responds to new information gradually rather than immediately. Therefore, moving average (MA), autoregressive moving average (ARMA), and autoregressive integrated moving average (ARIMA) models as well as autoregressive (AR), can all be used in predictive analytics (Tackett, 2013).

Many applications of conditional asset pricing use the GARCH and ARCH models. Securities' conditional covariances change over time and play a significant role in determining how risk premia change over time (Shah and Murtaza, 2000). To forecast trends and cycles, time series models and Bayesian models are frequently integrated into the field of economics (Franses and Van, 2000).

PREDICTIVE ANALYTICS USING EXTERNAL DATA

When we talk about "external data," we're talking about "syndicate data," which is information obtained from companies like Bloomberg, Reuters, Datastream, and NielsenIQ. Machine learning is particularly well adapted to the external data sets.

The integration of external data into bank's IS or data warehouses have not received much attention in the literature. Indeed, because of problems with cost and complexity, not all institutions have an integrated data warehouse (Bollerslev et al. 1998).

ECONOMIC PREDICTION

Several peer-reviewed economics studies employ predictive techniques. Regressions in this sense can be linear or logistic. Numerous previously discussed techniques, including classification models, random forests, and penalized regression techniques like least-angle (LARS) and least-absolute-shrinkage and selection operator (LASSO) regressions, are nonlinear.

Using a stochastic vector difference equation for the policy action is the most typical prediction strategy. After that, the analyst used a model based on the theories concerning the exogenous variables such as the Wharton model (MARK III) and different ARIMA models (Lekha and Prakasam, 2017).

Coupled Market State Analysis uses a series of dynamic states to describe a crisis brought on by dynamic market interactions (CMSA) (Pole et al. 2018). The result that was predicted outperformed a variety of different strategies, such as ANN and logistic regressions (Hwang et al. 2004).

But the economy is intrinsically unstable. As a result, there hasn't been much success in forecasting economic variables like the growth in Inflation and GDP (Cao and Cao, 2015). To assist econometricians in selecting between models given a predetermined level of confidence, a Model Confidence Set (MCS) is proposed (Huang et al. 2007).

EARNINGS PREDICTION

Computational techniques are particularly suited to DSS because they handle the dual problems of objectivity and independence in human analysts. But valuation-a typical goal of predictive models in finance-raises a critical question about accuracy that is particularly relevant to this field. SVM may consequently be superior when applied in a systems environment. It has been discovered that the results of the vector regression prediction on quarterly earnings are superior to an ARIMA model (Hansen et al. 2007). The SVM models are suitable for predicting earnings (Fischer et al. 2020). Similar to this, there are a few advantages that genetic algorithms have over other prediction methods (Amani and Fadlalla, 2017).

STOCK PRICE, RETURNS, AND VOLATILITY PREDICTION

The stock market has proven to be particularly difficult to predict because it is thought to be crucial to the process of financial intermediation. Even so, there is a substantial body of work on stock price prediction. The Efficient Market Hypothesis's strong version contends that the prices stated there reflect all available information (Dhar and Chou, 2001). Therefore, the stock market is deemed efficient if prices would not change if all accessible information were made public (Degutis and Novickyte, 2014).

There are several matrices-based estimating models in the literature, but the Dynamic Equicor-relation and the Scalar Dynamic Conditional Correlation (Malkiel, 1989) are the two most widely used academic methods (DECO) (Engle, 2002). Such models depend on the Generalized Auto Regressive Conditional Heteroskedasticity (GARCH) estimations from earlier stages to make their predictions. Large datasets have shown GARCH models to be unfeasible. The research on estimating error in portfolio optimization is likewise fairly extensive and expanding (Trucios, 2019).

The investors and the service providers generate fundamental projections and use them as the foundation for their investing strategy (Britten, 1999). Fewer people make technical predictions based on past price trends. Many of the prediction models are based on the latter, even though it is thought to be ineffective (Ou and Penman, 1989; Fama and Blume, 1966; Horne and Parker, 1967).

A predictive strategy may be founded on several forecasting models, search technologies, real-time pricing feeds, risk premium models, and an estimation of transaction costs (Jensen and Benington, 1970). On the predictability of stock returns based on the time horizon, there is also a lot of research (Timmermann and Granger, 2004).

OPTIMAL PORTFOLIO PREDICTION

When dealing with quadratic problems, predictive models are also utilized to predict the best results. According to modern portfolio theory, it is possible to create a mean-variance "efficient frontier" made up of an ideal portfolio of securities that offers the highest possible expected return for the assumed risk. Market analysis, financial research, and profit estimates make up the three main functions of predictive analytics (Fama and French, 1988). An increasing body of research has been done using this strategy and ML approaches (Ayodele, 2010). The majority of academics categorize the optimization problem as a supervised learning problem (Henrique et al. 2014). Lower estimate error is achieved by the Performance Based Regularization (PBR) ML method's constraint on sample variances (Ban et al. 2018).

To create optimal portfolios, machine learning can also be combined with regression techniques. The quantile regression approach is used, with the justification that it incorporates the features and stochastic relationship of the variables used to estimate the expected returns (Ma and Pohlman, 2008).

AUDIT AND COMPLIANCE PREDICTION

The adoption of computational approaches by the audit and compliance functions has been sluggish, but the third wave of technologies will make these techniques increasingly crucial (Van et al. 2010). Predictive analytics in this field may lack explanatory insights and have more complicated models (Butler, 2019). Enforcement can also benefit from predictive analytics. For instance, money laundering predictions using statistics (Hancock et al. 2016).

CREDIT SCORE PREDICTION

A lender can assess the risk of giving credit based on a borrower's credit history. To predict credit scores, a review of the literature on statistical methods and assessment standards is used (Hashimzade et al. 2016). Testing nonlinear classifiers such as neural networks, support vector machines, generalized boosting, and random forests yield a similar result (Abdou and Pointon, 2011). Early credit scoring relied on a variety of factors, including occupation, employment history, marital status, income, and rent/mortgage payments, which were all collected by a bank's internal IS. The next step involves applying multivariate regression and/or discriminant analysis (Jones et al. 2015).

Accuracy improvement is crucial for credit scoring since it prevents the granting of poor loans. The effectiveness of these can be evaluated using ROC curves and Gini coefficients. Kolmogorov-Smirnov curves can be used to assess things' resilience. Additionally, when using short data sets or poorly defined attributes, ANN has poor performance in small samples (Chatterjee and Barcun, 1970).

PREDICTIVE ANALYTICS USING INTERNAL DATA

Predictive analytics inside a financial organization is primarily based on internally generated data. The IS must be constructed with a good decomposition model as the representational will become more pertinent (Feraud and Clerot, 2002).

Relational database management systems' initial, pioneering databases containing structured data (RDBMS). The second is data obtained through the Internet from an outside source. The third wave is a more recent one that is driven by the internet of things. The primary techniques for using such internal data are then outlined (Wand and Weber, 1995).

CUSTOMER ACQUISITION AND ATTRITION PREDICTION

The approaches for predicting customer acquisition include Monte Carlo simulation, logistic regression, and neural networks. Investigations have also been done to prevent losing clients. When the accuracy of several techniques is examined, discriminant analysis is discovered to be the least accurate, followed by logistic regression, decision trees, and discriminant analysis (Jeble et al. 2016). When using the bank database to forecast ideal levels of client turnover, the SVM is recommended as the best method (Neslin, 2006). A binary Probit Tobit model is examined to see how client acquisition and retention are related (Lazarov and Capota, 2007).

It is suggested to evaluate numerous interaction classifiers and includes emotions into emails to improve customer attrition prediction. The same can be performed in conjunction with logistic regression, SVM, and random forests (Thomas, 2007).

A private client asset manager, for instance, can spot familial ties among high-net-worth individuals. The Knowledge Discovery in Databases (KDD) method is described as a way to perform this at scale (Coussement and Poel, 2009).

CUSTOMER SEGMENTATION AND SALES PREDICTION

The forecasting of sales is another essential component of DSS for management. Both evaluation and prediction-focused research has been done on sales prediction systems. Typically, qualities are divided into "benefit" and "cost" categories. Response time to a client inquiry is an illustration of a benefit attribute in finance. The charge level in comparison to competitors would be a cost attribute (Fayyad et al. 1996).

Using visualization techniques is the greatest way to categorize customers. Link analysis, deviation detection, and dependency modelling summarizing are examples of statistical approaches. Logistic regression, random forests, and regression forests. Customer segmentation makes it possible to target marketing efforts more precisely and even helps with sales forecasting (Cohen et al. 1999).

Insights gathered from internal IS data can be expanded using data from the internet (Zakrzewska and Murlewski, 2005). An ANOVA approach on the observed response is used to examine customer satisfaction based on their dis-confirmation between two products (Churchill and Surprenant, 1982).

Additionally, some research focuses on cross-selling forecasting and customer lifetime value. Keyword similarity was used in a single value decomposition to measure customer online reviews (Herzig et al. 2016) and a kernel-based learning technique is employed to forecast a range of client behaviors (Zhou, 2018).

CREDIT DEFAULT PREDICTION

Credit default prediction uses information from internal IS, as opposed to credit score prediction, which mostly uses external data sets. Decision Tree Regression, Altman Z, ANN, RS, and SVM are examples of predictive techniques (Kitchens et al. 2018).

A default can result from a wide range of additional conditions, making it difficult to predict. On both these and credit-sensitive instruments, there is a sizable body of literature. The default of corporate bonds is the main topic of the literature. This includes studies on reduced-form models that exogenously predict default probabilities, option pricing predictions, and empirical structural models based on the pricing of corporate obligations (Yeh and Lien, 2009; Black and Scholes, 2019). Non-parametric models apply to structures. For different economic situations, bankruptcy prediction models are created using a data mining approach (Jarrow and Turnbull, 1995). Also studied were various bankruptcy models, and it was discovered that a human forecaster performed better than the IS forecasting methods (Sung et al. 1999).

The 1930s are the earliest that bankruptcy prediction literature has been found (Kim and McLeod, 1999). Early models were built using financial ratios or univariate single variables. The majority of research is now multivariate, reflecting the various causes of financial distress. One of the most popular models for predicting financial trouble and bankruptcy is the Z-Score model (Bellovary, 2007). A probit and a logit technique have been suggested, which have helped to improve this multivariate model over time (Altman, 1983; Zmijewski,1984).

FINANCIAL AND CREDIT FRAUD PREDICTION

DSS is used to spot fraudsters early since the financial markets attract them. False financial reports, fraudulent financial schemes, and financial mis-selling are the three main types of financial fraud (Ohlson, 1980). Due to the rarity of fraud, the abundance of explanatory variables, and the variety of fraud, the prediction is made challenging (Reurink, 2018; Perols et al. 2017).

On a huge amount of data, predictive analytics can be used in conjunction with machine learning algorithms, data mining techniques like support vectors and random forest, as well as more conventional logistic regressions (Abbasi, 2015). Peer group analysis has suggested that there is widespread credit card application fraud as well (Ngai et al. 2011).

CYBER-CRIME PREDICTION

DSS predicts cybercrime using both statistical and computational methodologies, just as other predictive techniques. The most popular ones are time series and other kinds of regression. AGI, ANN, ML, genetic algorithms, fuzzy logic, NLP, and robotics are the methods frequently applied on top of one another (Bolton et al. 2001).

IS in Computational approaches must overcome several obstacles, including a lack of accurate threat intelligence, an abundance of real-time network data, and the dynamic nature of the threat (Lekha and Prakasam, 2017). The literature on cybercrime is mostly concerned with a limited range of topics, such as denial of service attacks, business extortion, cyberbullying, stalking, fraud, and robberies (Gandotra et al. 2015).

The majority of the research on prediction focuses on estimating an event's size after it has already begun (Prabakaran and Mitra, 2018). The spontaneous deception by analyzing the language used in interactive online games was an intriguing idea (Fachkha et al. 2013). Maintaining a Reputation Black-List is a genre tree kernel technique that employs fraud cues to anticipate phishing and so improves anti-phishing capabilities to avoid it (RBL) (Hancock, 2016).

DISCUSSION

DSS is progressively incorporating the offered predictive analytics. These systems use external and internal databases as their data sources. Figure 1 illustrates how this process functions to give managers in the financial services industry relevant information. Each DSS is distinct, therefore different approaches will need to be chosen for various jobs. As a result, no one approach or group of methods can be prescribed.

According to the literature, some computational methods have performed better in non-linear issues than explanatory methods that rely on causal linkages. This is supposed to support the argument that financial DSS ought to include both methods to give a wider range of explanatory resources. This makes it possible for non-computer-savvy financial professionals to engage with data stored in an IS and automatically retrieve it to make predictions. These projections set such DSS apart from Management Information Systems (MIS).

It must be emphasized that the approaches discussed in the literature have significant drawbacks. This is because the numerous unsuccessful attempts to apply such strategies are covered less in the literature. This category includes a wide variety of investment methods in finance. Various techniques result in erroneous positive results. This happens in the financial industry because supposedly "successful" techniques are occasionally supported by over-fitting backtests.

Figure 1. The diagram shows a decision support system with incorporated predictive analytics that is part of a banking information system (IS). Both computational approaches and explanatory statistics are capabilities of the DSS. Using internal and external databases, management may make better decisions thanks to the IS. Similar problems can be observed in "successful" techniques that are "based on strong academic research," but which perform poorly when risk is considered.

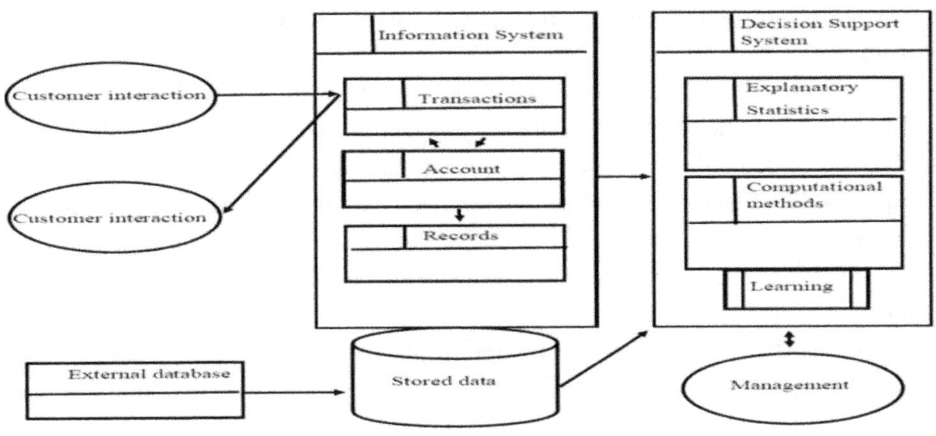

Unstructured data is another topic that the literature does not adequately address. Despite the rise of social media forecasting tools, there has been little discussion of techniques that employ such data. Future research in this field is anticipated to gain momentum. The utilization of language text and context is giving rise to a completely new genre of methodologies (Abbasi et al. 2015). Natural Language Processing (NLP), Information Retrieval (IR), and structured and unstructured Data Mining (DM) approaches will be employed more frequently as social media's position in society changes (Das et al. 2014).

CONCLUSION

In this paper, a wide range of methodologies was provided. A search using a keyword index was conducted that included both computational models and explanatory statistical methods. This was accomplished by reviewing the best authors who have contributed to the fields of information systems, finance, computing, and management science. Their methodological and analytical decisions were noted in the framework of their study. It was demonstrated that academics employed these techniques to provide descriptive outputs, decision forecasts, and outcomes that were optimal. All of these are said to be able to be integrated into DSS to support management decision-making. By combining IS data with computational power, management can improve its capacity for lending, investing, and making financial decisions.

It was demonstrated that academics have employed statistical and computational methods obtained from IS, either outside or internally, to address a variety of financial issues. These include forecasting the economy and company earnings using external data. Predictive models were demonstrated in this regard to have been utilized in conjunction with external data to examine historical time series and aid in return predictions. Descriptive models have also been found to be utilized in finance to quantify correlations and aid in risk prediction. These include modelling credit and risk as well as using data that is generated internally to predict and understand the consumer.

In particular, the chapter discusses the practical application of predictive analytics and model-driven decision assistance. It was discovered that the term "predictive analytics" is equivalent to the detection of anomalies and forecasting using computational models that use data that has been gathered, stored, and processed in the financial industry. Such methods are becoming more and more integrated into IS, improving management's capacity for forecasting. Additionally, it was discovered that different approaches might be taken to deal with different issues. As a result, decisions must be taken from the standpoint of systems design. This supports the idea that IS professionals should be familiar with the literature. Design engineers of

IS and DSS systems might consequently find the list of academic approaches in this paper to be helpful. The conclusion is that as DSS develops, more computational methods will be embedded. These will be useful in the investigation of nonlinearity and difficult financial problems. It is anticipated that more domestically generated IS data would be used in academia to produce academic insights. It is also anticipated that the industry will adopt academic techniques more frequently.

REFERENCES

Abbasi, A., Zahedi, F., Zeng, D., Chen, Y., Chen, H., & Nunamaker, J. F. Jr. (2015). Enhancing predictive analytics for anti-phishing by exploiting website genre information. *Journal of Management Information Systems, 31*(4), 109–157. doi:10.1080/07421222.2014.1001260

Abdou, H. A., & Pointon, J. (2011). Credit scoring, statistical techniques and evaluation criteria: A review of the literature. *Intelligent Systems in Accounting, Finance & Management, 18*(2-3), 59–88. doi:10.1002/isaf.325

Adams, J., Hayunga, D., Mansi, S., Reeb, D., & Verardi, V. (2019). Identifying and treating outliers in finance. *Financial Management, 48*(2), 345–384. doi:10.1111/fima.12269

Aghabozorgi, S., Shirkhorshidi, A. S., & Wah, T. Y. (2015). Timeseries clustering–a decade review. *Information Systems, 53*, 16–38. doi:10.1016/j.is.2015.04.007

Altman, E. I. (1983). *A Complete Guide to Predicting, Avoiding, and Dealing with Bankruptcy*. Corporate Financial Distress.

Amani, F. A., & Fadlalla, A. M. (2017). Data mining applications in accounting: A review of the literature and organizing framework. *International Journal of Accounting Information Systems, 24*, 32–58. doi:10.1016/j.accinf.2016.12.004

Ayodele, T.O. (2010). Types of machine learning algorithms. *New Advances in Machine Learning, 3*, 19–48.

Ban, G. Y., El Karoui, N., & Lim, A. E. (2018). Machine learning and portfolio optimization. *Management Science, 64*(3), 1136–1154. doi:10.1287/mnsc.2016.2644

Bellovary, J. L., Giacomino, D. E., & Akers, M. D. (2007). *A review of bankruptcy prediction studies: 1930 to present*. J Financ Education.

Black, F., & Scholes, M. (2019). The pricing of options and corporate liabilities. In World Scientific Reference on Contingent Claims Analysis in Corporate Finance: Volume 1: Foundations of CCA and Equity Valuation. World Scientific. doi:10.1142/9789814759588_0001

Boero, G., Smith, J., & Wallis, K. F. (2008). Uncertainty and disagreement in economic prediction: The bank of England survey of external forecasters. *Economic Journal (London)*, *118*(530), 1107–1127. doi:10.1111/j.1468-0297.2008.02162.x

Bollerslev, T., Engle, R. F., & Wooldridge, J. M. (1988). A capital asset pricing model with time-varying covariances. *Journal of Political Economy*, *96*(1), 116–131. doi:10.1086/261527

Bolton, R.J., & Hand, D.J. (2001). Unsupervised Profiling Methods for Fraud Detection. *Credit Scoring and Credit Control, 7*, 235–255.

Britten-Jones, M. (1999). The sampling error in estimates of mean-variance efficient portfolio weights. *The Journal of Finance*, *54*(2), 655–671. doi:10.1111/0022-1082.00120

Broby, D., Basu, D., & Arulselvan, A. (2019). The role of precision timing in stock market price discovery when trading through distributed ledgers. *J Business Thought.*, *10*, 1–8. doi:10.18311/jbt/2019/23355

Butler, T., & O'Brien, L. (2019). Understanding regtech for digital regulatory compliance. In *Disrupting Finance* (pp. 85–102). Palgrave Pivot. doi:10.1007/978-3-030-02330-0_6

Cao, W., & Cao, L. (2015). Financial crisis forecasting via coupled market state analysis. *IEEE Intelligent Systems*, *30*(2), 18–25. doi:10.1109/MIS.2015.4

Chatterjee, S., & Barcun, S. (1970). A nonparametric approach to credit screening. *Journal of the American Statistical Association*, *65*(329), 150–154. doi:10.1080/01621459.1970.10481068

Choudhry, T., & Wu, H. (2009). Forecasting the weekly time-varying beta of UK firms: Garch models vs. kalman filter method. *European Journal of Finance*, *15*(4), 437–444. doi:10.1080/13518470802604499

Churchill, G. A. Jr, & Surprenant, C. (1982). An investigation into the determinants of customer satisfaction. *JMR, Journal of Marketing Research*, *19*(4), 491–504. doi:10.1177/002224378201900410

Coakley, J. R., & Brown, C. E. (2000). Artificial neural networks in accounting and finance: Modelling issues. *Intelligent Systems in Accounting, Finance & Management*, *9*(2), 119–144. doi:10.1002/1099-1174(200006)9:2<119::AID-ISAF182>3.0.CO;2-Y

Cohen, W. W., Schapire, R. E., & Singer, Y. (1999). Learning to order things. *Journal of Artificial Intelligence Research*, *10*, 243–270. doi:10.1613/jair.587

Coussement, K., & Van den Poel, D. (2009). Improving customer attrition prediction by integrating emotions from client/company interaction emails and evaluating multiple classifiers. *Expert Systems with Applications*, *36*(3), 6127–6134. doi:10.1016/j.eswa.2008.07.021

Das, S.R. (2014). Text and context: language analytics in finance. Found Trends® Finance. 2014;8:145–261.

De Gooijer, J. G., & Hyndman, R. J. (2006). 25 years of time series forecasting. *International Journal of Forecasting*, *22*(3), 443–473. doi:10.1016/j.ijforecast.2006.01.001

de Prado, M. M. L. (2020). *Machine Learning for Asset Managers*. Cambridge University Press. doi:10.1017/9781108883658

Degutis, A., & Novickytė, L. (2014). The efficient market hypothesis: A critical review of literature and methodology. *Ekonom.*, *93*(2), 7–23. doi:10.15388/Ekon.2014.2.3549

Dhar, V., & Chou, D. (2001). A comparison of nonlinear methods for predicting earnings surprises and returns. *IEEE Transactions on Neural Networks*, *12*(4), 907–921. doi:10.1109/72.935099 PMID:18249921

Dixon, M. F., Halperin, I., & Bilokon, P. (2020). *Machine Learning in Finance*. Springer. doi:10.1007/978-3-030-41068-1

Elliott, R. K. (1992). The third wave breaks on the shores of accounting. *Accounting Horizons*, *6*, 61.

Engle, R. (2002). Dynamic conditional correlation: A simple class of multivariate generalized autoregressive conditional heteroskedasticity models. *Journal of Business & Economic Statistics*, *20*(3), 339–350. doi:10.1198/073500102288618487

Engle, R., & Kelly, B. (2012). Dynamic equicorrelation. *Journal of Business & Economic Statistics*, *30*(2), 212–228. doi:10.1080/07350015.2011.652048

F'eraud, R., & Cl'erot, F. (2002). A methodology to explain neural network classification. *Neural Networks*, *15*(2), 237–246. doi:10.1016/S0893-6080(01)00127-7 PMID:12022511

Fabozzi, F., Focardi, S. M., & Jonas, C. (2011). High-frequency trading: Methodologies and market impact. *Review of Futures Markets.*, *9*, 7–38.

Fachkha, C., Bou-Harb, E., & Debbabi, M. (2013). Towards a forecasting model for distributed denial of service activities. In *2013 IEEE 12th Inter- national Symposium on Network Computing and Applications*. IEEE. 10.1109/NCA.2013.13

Fama, E. F., & Blume, M. E. (1966). Filter rules and stock market trading. *The Journal of Business*, *39*(S1), 226–241. doi:10.1086/294849

Fama, E. F., & French, K. R. (1988). Permanent and temporary components of stock prices. *Journal of Political Economy*, *96*(2), 246–273. doi:10.1086/261535

Fama, E. F., & French, K. R. (2004). The capital asset pricing model: Theory and evidence. *The Journal of Economic Perspectives*, *18*(3), 25–46. doi:10.1257/0895330042162430

Fayyad, U., Piatetsky-Shapiro, G., & Smyth, P. (1996). The kdd process for extracting useful knowledge from volumes of data. *Communications of the ACM*, *39*(11), 27–34. doi:10.1145/240455.240464

Fischer, J. A., Pohl, P., & Ratz, D. (2020). A machine learning approach to univariate time series forecasting of quarterly earnings. *Review of Quantitative Finance and Accounting*, *55*(4), 1163–1179. doi:10.100711156-020-00871-3

Franses, P. H., & Van Dijk, D. (2000). *Non-linear Time Series Models in Empirical Finance*. Cambridge University Press. doi:10.1017/CBO9780511754067

Frecka, T. J., & Hopwood, W. S. (1983). The effects of outliers on the cross-sectional distributional properties of financial ratios. *The Accounting Review*, 115–128.

Gandotra, E., Bansal, D., & Sofat, S. (2015). Computational techniques for predicting cyber threats. *Intelligent Computing, Communication and Devices*, 247–253.

Hallock, K. F., Madalozzo, R., & Reck, C. G. (2010). Ceo pay-for-performance heterogeneity using quantile regression. *Financial Review*, *45*(1), 1–19. doi:10.1111/j.1540-6288.2009.00235.x

Hansen, P. R., Lunde, A., & Nason, J. M. (2011). The model confidence set. *Econometrica*, *79*(2), 453–497. doi:10.3982/ECTA5771

Harvey, C. R., & Liu, Y. (2021). Lucky factors. *Journal of Financial Economics, 141*(2), 413–435. doi:10.1016/j.jfineco.2021.04.014

Hashimzade, N., Myles, G. D., & Rablen, M. D. (2016). Predictive analytics and the targeting of audits. *Journal of Economic Behavior & Organization, 124*, 130–145. doi:10.1016/j.jebo.2015.11.009

Henrique, B. M., Sobreiro, V. A., & Kimura, H. (2019). Literature review: Machine learning techniques applied to financial market prediction. *Expert Systems with Applications, 124*, 226–251. doi:10.1016/j.eswa.2019.01.012

Herzig, J., Feigenblat, G., Shmueli-Scheuer, M., Konopnicki, D., & Rafaeli, A. (2016). Predicting customer satisfaction in customer support conversations in social media using effective features. *Proceedings of the 2016 Con- Ference on User Modeling Adaptation and Personalization,* 115–119.

Ho, S. M., Hancock, J. T., Booth, C., & Liu, X. (2016). Computer-mediated deception: Strategies revealed by language-action cues in spontaneous com- munication. *Journal of Management Information Systems, 33*(2), 393–420. doi:10.1080/07421222.2016.1205924

Huang, W., Lai, K. K., Nakamori, Y., Wang, S., & Yu, L. (2007). Neural networks in finance and economics forecasting. *International Journal of Information Technology & Decision Making, 6*(01), 113–140. doi:10.1142/S021962200700237X

Huang, W., Nakamori, Y., & Wang, S. Y. (2005). Forecasting stock market movement direction with support vector machine. *Computers & Operations Research, 32*(10), 2513–2522. doi:10.1016/j.cor.2004.03.016

Hwang, H. G., Ku, C. Y., Yen, D. C., & Cheng, C. C. (2004). Critical factors inñuencing the adoption of data warehouse technology: A study of the banking industry in taiwan. *Decision Support Systems, 37*(1), 1–21. doi:10.1016/S0167-9236(02)00191-4

Jarrow, R. A., & Turnbull, S. M. (1995). Pricing derivatives on financial securities subject to credit risk. *The Journal of Finance, 50*(1), 53–85. doi:10.1111/j.1540-6261.1995.tb05167.x

Jeble, S., Kumari, S., & Patil, Y. (2016). Role of big data and predictive analytics. *International Journal of Automation and Logistics., 2*(4), 307–331. doi:10.1504/IJAL.2016.080336

Jensen, M. C., & Benington, G. A. (1970). Random walks and technical theories: Some additional evidence. *The Journal of Finance*, *25*(2), 469–482. doi:10.1111/j.1540-6261.1970.tb00671.x

Jones, S., Johnstone, D., & Wilson, R. (2015). An empirical evaluation of the performance of binary classifiers in the prediction of credit rating changes. *Journal of Banking & Finance*, *56*, 72–85. doi:10.1016/j.jbankfin.2015.02.006

Kim, C. N., & McLeod, R. Jr. (1999). Expert, linear models, and nonlinear models of expert decision making in bankruptcy prediction: A lens model analysis. *Journal of Management Information Systems*, *16*(1), 189–206. doi:10.1080/07421222.1999.11518239

Kitchens, B., Dobolyi, D., Li, J., & Abbasi, A. (2018). Advanced customer analytics: Strategic value through the integration of relationship-oriented big data. *Journal of Management Information Systems*, *35*(2), 540–574. doi:10.1080/07421222.2018.1451957

Koenker, R., & Hallock, K. F. (2001). Quantile regression. *The Journal of Economic Perspectives*, *15*(4), 143–156. doi:10.1257/jep.15.4.143

Kuhn, M., & Johnson, K. (2013). *Applied Predictive Modelling Springer*. doi:10.1007/978-1-4614-6849-3

Kumar, A. S., & Chandrakala, D. (2017). An optimal churn prediction model using support vector machine with adaboost. Int J Scientific Res Computer Sci. *Eng and Information Technology.*, *2*, 225–230.

Lazarov, V., & Capota, M. (2007). Churn prediction. *Bus. Anal. Course. TUM Comput. Sci.*, *33*, 34.

Lekha, K. C., & Prakasam, S. (2017). *Data mining techniques in detecting and predicting cyber crimes in banking sector. In 2017 International Conference on Energy, Communication, Data Analytics and Soft Computing (ICECDS)*. IEEE. doi:10.1109/ICECDS.2017.8389725

Ma, L., & Pohlman, L. (2008). Return forecasts and optimal portfolio construction: A quantile regression approach. *European Journal of Finance*, *14*(5), 409–425. doi:10.1080/13518470802042369

Malkiel, B. G. (1989). Efficient market hypothesis. In *Finance* (pp. 127–134). Springer. doi:10.1007/978-1-349-20213-3_13

Menkhoff, L., & Taylor, M. P. (2007). The obstinate passion of foreign exchange professionals: Technical analysis. *Journal of Economic Literature*, *45*(4), 936–972. doi:10.1257/jel.45.4.936

Muller, O., Junglas, I., Vom Brocke, J., & Debortoli, S. (2016). Utilizing big data analytics for information systems research: Challenges, promises and guidelines. *European Journal of Information Systems*, *25*(4), 289–302. doi:10.1057/ejis.2016.2

Neslin, S. A., Gupta, S., Kamakura, W., Lu, J., & Mason, C. H. (2006). Defection detection: Measuring and understanding the predictive accuracy of customer churn models. *JMR, Journal of Marketing Research*, *43*(2), 204–211. doi:10.1509/jmkr.43.2.204

Ngai, E. W., Hu, Y., Wong, Y. H., Chen, Y., & Sun, X. (2011). The application of data mining techniques in financial fraud detection: A classification framework and an academic review of literature. *Decision Support Systems*, *50*(3), 559–569. doi:10.1016/j.dss.2010.08.006

Ohlson, J. A. (1980). Financial ratios and the probabilistic prediction of bankruptcy. *Journal of Accounting Research*, *18*(1), 109–131. doi:10.2307/2490395

Ou, J. A., & Penman, S. H. (1989). Financial statement analysis and the prediction of stock returns. *Journal of Accounting and Economics*, *11*(4), 295–329. doi:10.1016/0165-4101(89)90017-7

Pachamanova, D. A., & Fabozzi, F. J. (2014). Recent trends in equity portfolio construction analytics. *Journal of Portfolio Management*, *40*(3), 137–151. doi:10.3905/jpm.2014.40.3.137

Park, C. S., & Han, I. (2002). A case-based reasoning with the feature weights derived by analytic hierarchy process for bankruptcy prediction. *Expert Systems with Applications*, *23*(3), 255–264. doi:10.1016/S0957-4174(02)00045-3

Paul, J., & Criado, A. R. (2020). The art of writing a literature review: What do we know and what do we need to know? *International Business Review*, *29*(4), 101717. doi:10.1016/j.ibusrev.2020.101717

Paul, J., Lim, W. M., O'Cass, A., Hao, A. W., & Bresciani, S. (2021). Scientific procedures and rationales for systematic literature reviews (SPAR-4-SLR). *International Journal of Consumer Studies*, *45*(4), 1–16. doi:10.1111/ijcs.12695

Perols, J. L., Bowen, R. M., Zimmermann, C., & Samba, B. (2017). Finding needles in a haystack: Using data analytics to improve fraud prediction. *The Accounting Review*, *92*(2), 221–245. doi:10.2308/accr-51562

Pole, A., West, M., & Harrison, J. (2018). *Applied Bayesian Forecasting and Time Series Analysis*. Chapman and Hall/CRC. doi:10.1201/9781315274775

Prabakaran, S., & Mitra, S. (2018). Survey of analysis of crime detection techniques using data mining and machine learning. In *Journal of Physics:Conference Series* (p. 012046). IOP Publishing. doi:10.1088/1742-6596/1000/1/012046

Reurink, A. (2018). Financial fraud: A literature review. *Journal of Economic Surveys*, *32*(5), 1292–1325. doi:10.1111/joes.12294

Shah, J. R., & Murtaza, M. B. (2000). A neural network-based clustering procedure for bankruptcy prediction. *Am Bus Rev.*, *18*, 80.

Summers, L. H. (1985). On economics and finance. *The Journal of Finance*, *40*(3), 633–635. doi:10.1111/j.1540-6261.1985.tb04985.x

Sung, T. K., Chang, N., & Lee, G. (1999). Dynamics of modelling in data mining: Interpretive approach to bankruptcy prediction. *Journal of Management Information Systems*, *16*(1), 63–85. doi:10.1080/07421222.1999.11518234

Ta, V. D., Liu, C. M., & Addis, D. (2018). Prediction and portfolio optimization in quantitative trading using machine learning techniques. *Proceedings of the Ninth International Symposium on Information and Communication Technology*, 98–105. 10.1145/3287921.3287963

Tackett, J. A. (2013). Association rules for fraud detection. *Journal of Corporate Accounting & Finance*, *24*(4), 15–22. doi:10.1002/jcaf.21856

Thomas, J. S. (2001). A methodology for linking customer acquisition to customer retention. *JMR, Journal of Marketing Research*, *38*(2), 262–268. doi:10.1509/jmkr.38.2.262.18848

Timmermann, A., & Granger, C. W. (2004). Efficient market hypothesis and forecasting. *International Journal of Forecasting*, *20*(1), 15–27. doi:10.1016/S0169-2070(03)00012-8

Trucíos, C., Zevallos, M., Hotta, L. K., & Santos, A. A. (2019). Covariance prediction in large portfolio allocation. *Econometrics.*, *7*(2), 19. doi:10.3390/econometrics7020019

Tsay, R. S. (2005). *Analysis of Financial Time Series* (Vol. 543). John Wiley & Sons. doi:10.1002/0471746193

Van Binsbergen, J. H., & Koijen, R. S. (2010). Predictive regressions: A present-value approach. *The Journal of Finance*, *65*(4), 1439–1471. doi:10.1111/j.1540-6261.2010.01575.x

Van Horne, J. C., & Parker, G. G. (1967). The random walk theory: An empirical test. *Financial Analysts Journal*, *23*(6), 87–92. doi:10.2469/faj.v23.n6.87

Wand, Y., & Weber, R. (1995). On the deep structure of information systems. *Information Systems Journal*, *5*(3), 203–223. doi:10.1111/j.1365-2575.1995.tb00108.x

Wu, X., Zhu, X., Wu, G. Q., & Ding, W. (2013). Data mining with big data. *IEEE Transactions on Knowledge and Data Engineering*, *26*, 97–107.

Yao, J., & Tan, C. L. (2001). A study on training criteria for financial time series forecasting. *Proceedings of International Conference on Neural Information Processing*.

Yeh, I. C., & Lien, Ch. (2009). The comparisons of data mining techniques for the predictive accuracy of probability of default of credit card clients. *Expert Systems with Applications*, *36*(2), 2473–2480. doi:10.1016/j.eswa.2007.12.020

Zakrzewska, D., & Murlewski, J. (2005). Clustering algorithms for bank customer segmentation. In *5th International Conference on Intelligent Systems Design and Applications (ISDA'05)*. IEEE. 10.1109/ISDA.2005.33

Zhao, Z. (2008). Parametric and nonparametric models and methods in financial econometrics. *Statistics Surveys*, *2*(none), 1–42. doi:10.1214/08-SS034

Zhou, S., Qiao, Z., Du, Q., Wang, G. A., Fan, W., & Yan, X. (2018). Measuring customer agility from online reviews using big data text analytics. *Journal of Management Information Systems*, *35*(2), 510–539. doi:10.1080/07421222.2018.1451956

Zmijewski, M. E. (1984). Methodological issues related to the estimation of financial distress prediction models. *Journal of Accounting Research*, *59*, 82.

Chapter 4
Factors Influencing Potential Users' Behavior Towards Usage of Cloud Computing

Shruti Bansal
SRM Institute of Science and Technology, India

Ajay Jain
https://orcid.org/0000-0002-6087-0206
SRM Institute of Science and Technology, India

Karuna Gupta
SRM Institute of Science and Technology, India

ABSTRACT

With the aid of cloud computing, numerous services are accessible via the Internet. Among other things, these technologies include storing, managing and processing data, networking, servers, database and software storage. The study aims to recognize the most crucial factors that instigate the Potential User's Behaviour Toward increased usage of Cloud Computing. Technology experts anticipate that as cloud computing becomes more and more popular, most organizations will switch to it by 2025, ending their need for desktop resources. The study aims to assess the impact of certain factors like Perceived Ease of Use and Availability, Security and Privacy, Reliability and Relative Advantage in influencing the intention of the user's towards the usage of cloud computing. Data were gathered using a questionnaire and a convenient sampling method. The data is analysed using the Smart PLS-SEM technique with a sample size of 191. The research finding indicates that all four factors taken in the study significantly influence the users' intention toward the usage of cloud computing.

DOI: 10.4018/978-1-6684-7568-3.ch004

INTRODUCTION

Cloud computing is a prevalent term nowadays. It simply means on-demand delivery of resources like storage space, servers, software, and others over the internet. Cloud computing is being used daily in one manner or another. It probably allows you to do anything online such as sending emails, editing documents, or watching videos and many more. Some simple yet well-known examples of cloud computing are Amazon Prime and Netflix. They entirely rely on computational cloud servers to manage video streaming and provide near-instant video playback to their customers. It requires no setup Investments, encourages energy savings, reduces redundancies etc. Everywhere there is a problem with stiff hardware disks, cloud comes to the rescue. Though it has its disadvantages. Like downtime in cloud servers affects every single organization using them leading to major losses and creating problems for users using them. Since all the content is provided under one umbrella, the company cannot function in any other way (Azure, 2021). Due to its high savings and investment rate when compared to other Asian nations, India is quickly becoming the next major investment destination (Raj, Verma, et al., 2018). In this era of hyper-automation, technology is seen as an enabler or a means of spreading knowledge (Oye et al., 2014). Following water, electricity, oil or gas, and telephone, cloud computing has been named the fifth essential utility (Arias et al., 2012; Sabi et al., 2016). Technology experts anticipate that as cloud computing becomes more and more popular, most organizations and businesses will switch to it by 2025, ending their need for desktop resources (Anderson & Rainie, 2010). Cloud Computing is used now a days in almost all the sectors. Over numerous decades, the Indian banking industry has seen a significant transition and evolved significantly (Raj, Jain, et al., 2018).

This technique uses a process architecture that pools numerous computer resources from several locations in order to accomplish a single objective. It is further defined as "a model for enabling convenient, on-demand network access to a shared pool of configurable computing resources (e.g., network, servers, storage, applications, and services) that can be rapidly provisioned and released with minimal management effort or service provider interaction" by the National Institute of Standards and Technology (NIST) (Mell & Grance, 2011). Contracting out some or all of the information technology (IT) processes offers a elastic and extremely scalable platform for company operations (Armbrust et al., 2010). Increasing client happiness in the age of globalisation is a difficult undertaking, particularly in the service industry (Raj & Bansal, 2019). Despite the many benefits and possibilities of CCT, it also has several security, privacy, and dependability problems. The primary risks connected with using cloud computing are external attacks on infrastructure, provider spying on clients' VMs, and attacks between users, including side-channel attacks and VM attacks (Islam et al., 2016). Truong (2010) asserts that security is a significant barrier for CCT since preserving sensitive and secret data on a public cloud is challenging. Another significant challenge for CCT is consistent, fast internet connectivity (Lin & Chen, 2012).

The Corona Epidemic has had a negative impact on practically all business kinds (Jain et al., 2022). Due to the insufficient standardization of platform technologies and application program interfaces, switching to a different cloud service provider can be challenging, making it difficult for businesses to embrace CCT (Armbrust et al., 2010). The most important barrier to cloud computing adoption is data privacy, data access to audit standards, and data location necessities at the local, national, and international levels (Marston et al., 2011). Security, governance, and a lack of control over service availability are said to be enterprises' top three worries (Aleem & Ryan Sprott, 2012). Additionally, they stated that account, service, and traffic control were the top threats to CCT, followed by data loss and leakage. Adjei (2015) discovered that the growth of trust depends on the cloud service provider's sincerity toward users' interests and that trust is a crucial component for CCT adoption by financial institutions.

It is clear that as businesses linger their digital transformation journeys, modernizing business processes, and optimizing IT infrastructures, cloud computing services, along with automation, orchestration, and data analytics, will become even more important. Ideal application workloads should be able to move easily between cloud service providers (CSPs), or be shared among CSPs, landing wherever the best possible combination of performance, functionality, cost, security, compliance, availability, resilience, and other factors is to be found, while avoiding the dreaded "vendor lock-in." Managing expenses is a significant issue for businesses using various clouds.

LITERATURE REVIEW

While some of the definitions of cloud computing in the literature may vary from one another, they all generally refer to the same idea.

The Primary objective of this research is to recognize the most crucial factors which instigate the Potential User's Behaviour Toward increased usage of Cloud Computing. To meet this objective, this research reviewed the literature on cloud computing on the following aspects: Relative Advantage, Perceived Ease of Use and Availability, Reliability, Security and Privacy.

Perceived Use of Ease and Availability

Businesses and individuals are drawn to cloud computing because it enables them to employ technology, software, and platforms with a very small number of physical equipment and at very low costs (Sultan, 2010). People's ability to quickly access and share information online has had an impact on greater individual customer adoption of cloud computing (Ratten, 2014). The expanded Technology Acceptance Model-TAM model created by (Davis, 1989) will be used to examine whether or not the services provided by cloud computing as a whole are embraced. Utilization Perception (UP) and Usability Perception (UPU) are two characteristics that the Davis, TAM original model uses to determine whether or not a technology, namely cloud computing, is used (PEOU). The model is expanded to include more elements impacting the adoption of cloud computing as (Taylor & Todd, 1995) provide a fuller explanation. The following elements, which are described below, are part of the study's extended model: Risk perception, awareness of cloud computing, computer self-efficacy, and e-skills.

The new fields are given strong theoretical and empirical support (Evans et al., 2011), which makes cloud computing a very appealing topic for research. However, there is a dearth of data on student uptake, who are the primary drivers of new technology adoption. Since studies are no longer solely concentrated in the classroom, the cloud is a useful tool for improving student performance. Additionally, by enabling students to access learning resources at any time and from any location, it is seen as a promising possibility overall, but particularly for educational institutions (Changchit, 2014).

H_1- Perceived Ease of Use and Availability has a substantial effect on users' Intension to use Cloud Computing.

Security and Privacy

There are many different ways to conceptualise the term security and trust, as evidenced by Gefen et al. reviews of the literature. In order to operationalize the effect of being secured while adoption of technical breakthroughs, there are several trust objects and metrics (Gefen et al., 2003). The capacity of the relevant actors to communicate a sense of trustworthiness is taken into consideration for this scope (Stieninger & Nedbal, 2014). Security is a crucial quality of service (QoS) component that, among others, must be taken into account in service requests in the context of cloud computing, according to (Buyya et al., 2009). This element is essential, particularly in scenarios involving public clouds (Walterbusch & Teuteberg, 2012).

Apart from this, there are several concerns regarding data security and privacy, thus Miranda M. and S. Pearson suggested a client-based manager that uses obfuscation and deobfuscation techniques to lower the chance of sensitive data loss and leaking. They equipped the architecture with a variety of functions, including data access, feedback and obfuscation. The fundamental concept is to keep clients' confidential data in cloud storage in encrypted manner. By addressing end-user service difficulties, these solutions offer the advantage of maintaining data privacy. The restriction on aforementioned activity is that vendors must refrain from adding new services for privacy and must cooperate honestly with service providers (Miranda,2009).

H_2- Security and Privacy has a substantial impact on users' Intension to use Cloud Computing.

Reliability

In the context of cloud computing, reliability refers to a system's capacity to regularly deliver its services without hiccup or failure (Sharma, 2016). It may be described as the level of consistency, or outcomes devoid of measurement mistakes, that an instrument can provide (Churchill, 1979). An information system's availability is referred to as its reliability (Kim et al., 2013). Organizations are becoming more and more reliant on their IT infrastructure thus availability is crucial. In most circumstances, a momentary disruption to an organization's IT infrastructure will result in monetary loss as well as reputational harm.

H_3- Reliability has a significant impact on users' Intension to use Cloud Computing.

Relative Advantage

Relative advantage describes how much an innovation is valued as being better than the idea it replaces. Cloud computing solutions offer a number of beneficial features, including the easing of network infrastructure load, decreased infrastructure operation and hardware maintenance, flexibility, easy administration, possibilities for collaboration, possible cost savings, and increased automation (Stieninger & Nedbal, 2014). Due to all these benefits, large publicly listed corporations' have also looked at the perceived value of cloud computing (Opitz et al., 2012). According to (Moore & Benbasat, 1991), the concepts of relative advantage and perceived usefulness are quite similar. Perceived usefulness is defined as the "degree to which a person believes that using a particular technology will improve his or her job performance." (Davis, 1987). Perceived usefulness was discovered to greatly effect satisfaction and influence opinions about the long-term usefulness of such a system in relation to cloud computing in the education sector as well. (Opitz et al., 2012) discovered that desire to employ cloud computing was strongly influenced by perceived utility.

H_4- Relative Advantage has a significant impact on users' Intension to use Cloud Computing.

RESEARCH METHODOLOGY

DATA COLLECTION- Google Forms was used to carry out the survey. We outlined the study's objectives and emphasised its complete anonymity in the introduction. We performed an internet based survey using Google Forms survey and obtained responses from members of the Facebook, Whatsapp and Gmail as a convenient sampling strategy because the users in India spent a lot of time on social networking sites. We focused our research on general public using cloud computing. At the end of October 2022, the survey was ended after a month of being available. The researcher find out that the selected sample is an expert in cloud computing by asking the people whether they are using cloud-computing techniques or not.

RESEARCH OBJECTIVE- To analyze the impact of certain factors like Perceived Ease of Use and Availability, Security and Privacy, Reliability and Relative Advantage in influencing the intention of user's towards the usage of cloud computing.

SAMPLE SIZE- The sample size in the study is 191 which is sufficient enough to represent the entire population.

STATISTICAL TOOL- The model and Hypothesis have been tested in this study by applying the Smart PLS tool- Smart PLS 4.

FACTORS AND THEIR ITEMS WITH CODES- In the present study, four independent factors are taken which are- Perceived Ease of Use and Availability, Security and Privacy, Reliability and Relative Advantage and one dependent variable is taken which is Intension to use Cloud Computing.

DATA ANALYSIS

Factor Loadings

Factor loading describes the degree to which each correlation matrix item interacts with a particular main component. No research item's factor loading fell below the recommended level. 50 (Hair et al.,2016). As a result, none of the items was removed. The factor loadings are listed in Table 2.

Figure 1. Research model

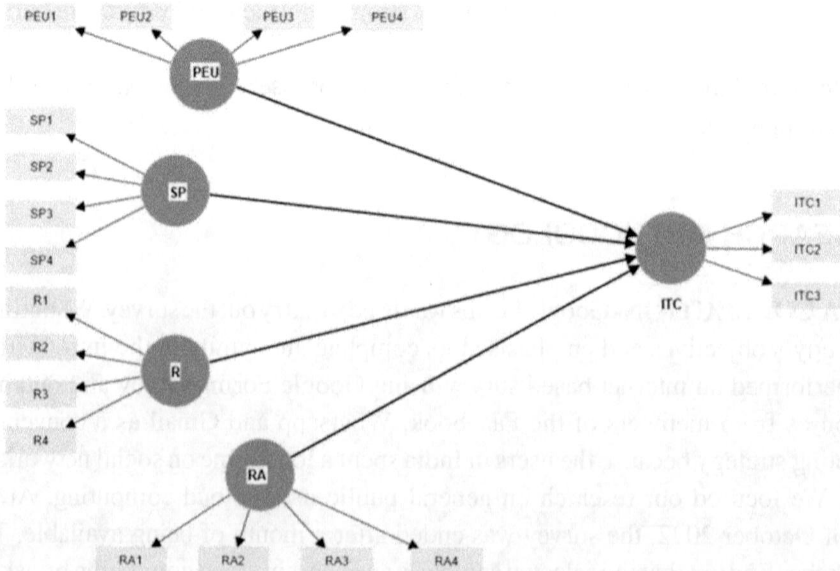

Table 1. Perceived ease of use and availability, security and privacy, reliability, and relative advantage v. intension to use cloud computing

Codes	ItemsAll were in five-point (1=strongly disagree to 5=strongly agree)	Author
IV	INDEPENDENT VARIABLES	
RA	**Relative Advantage- - It is the dimension where there are more benefits and points of interest in a technical environment than there are drawbacks.**	
RA1	The quality of my work would increase if I used cloud computing.	(Mohammed et al., 2016)
RA2	I can effectively manage my work thanks to cloud computing.	(Oliveira et al., 2014)
RA3RA4	I can complete particular jobs faster by using cloud computing.Utilizing cloud computing gives user additional opportunities.	(Oliveira et al., 2014) (Oliveira et al., 2014)
PEU	**Perceived Ease of Use and Availability- The extent to which a person thinks that employing cloud computing would be easy and accessible to user around-the-clock.**	
PEU1PEU2	It is simple to use cloud computing services.It is easy to communicate through cloud computing.	(Tehrani & Shirazi, 2014) (Tehrani & Shirazi, 2014)
PEU3PEU4	Data can be accessed anytime and anywhere through cloud computing. Data can browsed through any device in cloud computing.	(Pańkowska et al., 2020) (Pańkowska et al., 2020)
REL	**Reliability- The likelihood of uninterrupted cloud computing operation in a particular environment for a specific period of time.**	(Alghushami et al., 2020)
REL1	My data has a great "backup" on the cloud against a hard-disk crash.	
REL2REL3	An effective alternative to a USB thumb drive or portable hard drive for my data is cloud computing.I am certain that cloud computing provides excellent uptime and round-the-clock availability of cloud services.	

continues on following page

Table 1. Continued

Codes	ItemsAll were in five-point (1=strongly disagree to 5=strongly agree)	Author
REL4	My data can be safely recovered by the cloud computing service provider even if it is damaged by spam or a malware attack.	
SP	**Security and Privacy- When using cloud computing, customers must feel secure and private.**	
SP1SP2SP3SP4	The cloud computing services have robust security measures in place to safeguard data.I have faith that cloud service providers won't use my data for personal gain or profit.I am confident that any information or data I store in the cloud won't be changed or distorted.The data can be retrieved and backup through cloud computing.	(Mohammed et al., 2016) (Tehrani & Shirazi, 2014) (Pańkowska et al., 2020) (Asadi et al., 2019)
DV	**DEPENDENT VARIABLE**	
ICC	**Intention to use Cloud Computing**	
ICC1	I'm sure I'll use cloud computing services frequently.	(Pańkowska et al., 2020)
ICC2	I'll suggest cloud computing to my family, friends, and connections.	(Tehrani & Shirazi, 2014)
ICC3	I'm willing to employ cloud computing services to their full extent.	(Pańkowska et al., 2020)

Table 2. Factor loadings

	ITC	PEU	R	RA	SP
ITC1	0.854				
ITC2	0.874				
ITC3PEU1	0.903	0.812			
PEU2		0.752			
PEU3		0.828			
PEU4		0.860			
R1			0.720		
R2			0.880		
R3			0.848		
R4			0.871		
RA1				0.858	
RA2				0.868	
RA3				0.834	
RA4				0.831	
SP1					0.910
SP2					0.826
SP3					0.910
SP4					0.821

Indicator Multicollinearity

Hair et al. (2016) found that multicollinearity is not a significant issue if the VIF value is less than 5. The VIF values for the study's indicators are displayed in Table 3, which shows that each indicator's VIF is lower than the advised limit.

Table 3. Collinearity statistics (VIF)-outer VIF values

	VIF		VIF
ITC1	**1.940**	R4	**2.212**
ITC2	**2.073**	RA1	**2.073**
ITC3	**2.329**	RA2	**2.185**
PEU1	**1.768**	RA3	**2.124**
PEU2	**1.528**	RA4	**2.114**
PEU3	**2.037**	SP1	**3.191**
PEU4	**2.208**	SP2	**2.606**
R1	**1.481**	SP3	**3.369**
R2	**2.509**	SP4	**2.270**
R3	**2.211**		

Reliability Analysis

The results for Cronbach's alpha and composite reliability are shown in Table 4. To verify whether test items measuring a concept have scores that are consistent across items, the reliability standards of composite reliability >0.6 and Cronbach's Alpha are utilised (Hair et al., 2016). Cronbach's alpha and the composite dependability are both consistently higher than 0.6, as seen in Table 4. On account of this, reliability is achieved.

Table 4. Construct reliability analysis

	Cronbach's Alpha	Composite Reliability
Perceived Ease of Use and Availability (PEU)	0.830	0.835
Security and Privacy (SP)	0.890	0.913
Reliability (R)	0.851	0.870
Relative Advantage (RA)	0.871	0.882
Intension To Use Cloud Computing (ITC) 0.850		0.856

Convergent Validity

Each of the Table 5 scenarios' computed AVE values is greater than the threshold value of 0.50 on average. It suggests that each study variable and the model's attributes are accurately captured by the questionnaire.

Table 5. Construct validity

	Average Variance Extracted (AVE)
Perceived Ease of Use and Availability (PEU)	0.663
Security and Privacy (SP)	0.753
Reliability (R)	0.693
Relative Advantage (RA)	0.719
Intension To Use Cloud Computing (ITC)	0.770

Discriminant Validity

Fornell and Larcker Criterion

In the correlation matrix, the square roots of the AVE values can be seen diagonally. The squared root of each concept's AVE must be greater than its greatest correlation with any other construct in order to show discriminant validity (Hair et al., 2013). Each indicator should show the highest load it is capable of sensing on the structure. Each construct in Table 6 is larger than its squared relationship with any other construct, as evidenced by the table.

Table 6. Discriminant validity- Fornell-Larcker criterion

	ITC	*PEU*	*R*	*RA*	*SP*
ITC	**0.877**				
PEU	0.639	**0.814**			
R	0.367	0.533	**0.848**		
RA	0.619	0.600	0.536	**0.832**	
SP	0.549	0.562	0.517	0.511	**0.868**

Cross Loadings

In Table 7, the cross-loadings of the aforementioned constructs are high on each other and low on other constructs, demonstrating the achievement of discriminant validity.

Table 7. Discriminant validity- cross loadings

	ITC	PEU	R	RA	SP
ITC1	0.854	0.499	0.566	0.424	0.463
ITC2	0.874	0.548	0.555	0.216	0.398
ITC3	0.903	0.626	0.514	0.332	0.577
PEU1	0.520	0.812	0.356	0.361	0.396
PEU2	0.479	0.752	0.418	0.258	0.353
PEU3	0.500	0.828	0.567	0.481	0.518
PEU4	0.576	0.860	0.602	0.608	0.551
R1	0.421	0.427	0.720	0.603	0.388
R2	0.549	0.567	0.880	0.447	0.473
R3	0.466	0.534	0.848	0.441	0.343
R4	0.599	0.471	0.871	0.348	0.480
RA1	0.343	0.536	0.415	0.858	0.501
RA2	0.345	0.461	0.418	0.868	0.460
RA3	0.276	0.379	0.508	0.834	0.411
RA4	0.264	0.412	0.503	0.831	0.362
SP1	0.572	0.574	0.501	0.480	0.910
SP2	0.363	0.322	0.320	0.242	0.826
SP3	0.472	0.470	0.414	0.476	0.910
SP4	0.461	0.538	0.507	0.553	0.821

Goodness of Fit

The standardised root mean square residuals (SRMR) value calculated in the table above is 0.090, which is below the SRMR cutoff value of 0.1. The NFI's proximity to 1 indicates how well the fit fits. For the current study, the calculated NFI value is 0.734, which is closer to 1. In light of our study requirements, it is also suitable.

Table 8. Model fit

	Saturated model	Estimated model
SRMR	0.090	0.090
d_ULS	1.546	1.546
d_G	0.663	0.663
Chi-square	702.356	702.356
NFI	0.734	0.734

Assessment of Structural Equation Modelling (SEM)

Figure 2. Structural equation modelling (SEM)-initial path model

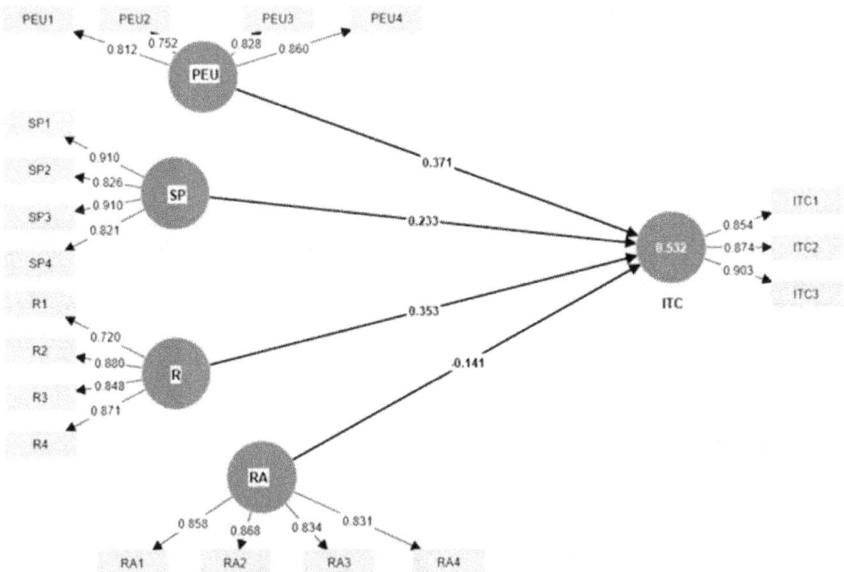

Assessing the Level of R^2

The value of R^2 is 0.532. It depicts that 53.2 per cent of the independent factors selected in the study have an impact on the dependent variable and the rest depend on other factors which are not a part of this stud

Figure 3. Structural equation modelling (SEM)- presenting the final path model

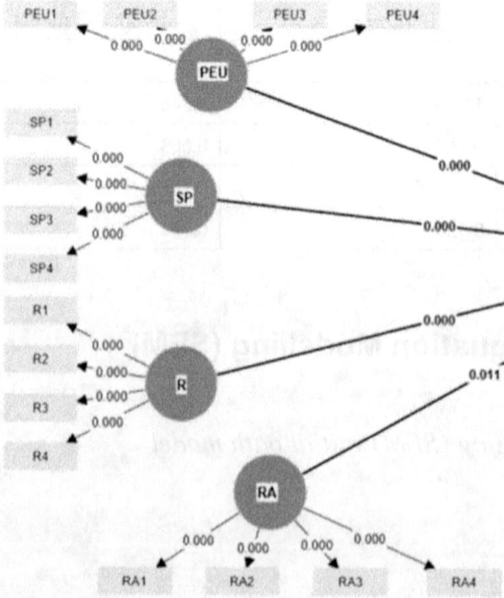

Table 9. Coefficient of determination (R^2)

	R Square	R Square Adjusted
INTENSION TO CLOUD COMPUTING	0.532	0.522

Assessing the Path Co-Efficient

Table 10. Path coefficients values

Original sample (O)	Standard Deviation (STDEV)	T Statistics (|O/ STDEV|)	P Values
Perceived Ease of Use and Availability _ -> Intension to use Cloud Computing.	0.066	5.598	**0.000**
Security and Privacy -> Intension to use Cloud Computing.	0.057	4.077	**0.000**
Reliability -> Intension to use Cloud Computing.	0.085	4.167	**0.000**
Relative Advantage -> Intension to use Cloud Computing.	0.055	2.541	**0.011**

FINDINGS

H_1- Perceived Ease of Use and Availability has a significant impact on users' Intension to use Cloud Computing.

H1 assesses whether users' intentions to use cloud computing are significantly impacted by perceived availability and ease of use. The findings showed that users' intentions to use cloud computing are significantly influenced by perceived availability and ease of use. The calculated p-value for H1 is 0.000, which, at a 95% confidence level, is less than the 0.05 significance threshold. It follows that H1 is approved.

H_2- Security and Privacy has a significant impact on users' Intension to use Cloud Computing.

H2 assesses the effect of security and privacy on users' intentions to use cloud computing. The findings showed that users' intentions to use cloud computing are significantly impacted by security and privacy. The calculated p-value for H2 is 0.000, which, at a 95% confidence level, is less than the 0.05 significance threshold. It follows that H2 is approved.

H_3- Reliability has a significant impact on users' Intension to use Cloud Computing.

H3 analyzes whether a user's intention to use cloud computing is significantly impacted by reliability. The findings showed that users' intentions to use cloud computing are significantly influenced by reliability. The calculated p-value for H3 is 0.000, which, at a 95% confidence level, is less than the 0.05 significance threshold. It follows that H3 is approved.

H_4- Relative Advantage has a significant impact on users' Intension to use Cloud Computing.

H4 assesses the effect of relative advantage on users' intentions to use cloud computing. The findings showed that users' intentions to use cloud computing are significantly impacted by relative advantage. At a 95% confidence level, the calculated p-value for H4 is 0.011, which is less than the 0.05 significance threshold. It follows that H4 is approved.

Table 11. Structural relation in model

	Hypotheses Testing	Sig./Non-Sig.
H_1	Perceived Ease of Use and Availability has a significant impact on users' Intension to use Cloud Computing.	Sig.
H_2	Security and Privacy have a significant impact on users' Intension to use Cloud Computing.	Sig.
H_3	Reliability has a significant impact on users' Intension to use Cloud Computing.	Sig.
H_4	Relative Advantage has a significant impact on users' Intension to use Cloud Computing.	Sig.

RECOMMENDATIONS AND SUGGESTIONS

- Establish the function of cloud computing resources in a product or service, taking into account the impact on numerous product and process areas.
- Use a risk-based strategy to ascertain whether the cloud computing resources are a good fit for the product or organisation.
- Learn how frequently the cloud computing resources are routinely updated so that you may create a revalidation approach and a set of standards that are both long-lasting and offer sufficient control.
- The risk and the proximity of any potential injury influence the frequency.
- Based on the likelihood that the vendor may use cloud computing resources to negatively impact its products and operational procedures, determine how closely one should examine the vendor and its operations.

CONCLUSION

While many benefits of cloud computing have been discussed, it is interesting to note that each company has unique circumstances, such as the sector of health care, where data privacy is a big concern. In addition, service providers like educational institutions and SMEs place a strong emphasis on information accessibility and simplicity of use. Hence, earlier research on cloud computing adoption and adoption determinants has a substantial impact on how academics and decision-makers study these issues. The factors discovered serve as indicators and manuals for businesses looking to embrace and use cloud computing services in a secure manner. Cloud computing helps companies stay competitive by reducing their IT costs and providing better service. At the European level, the market for cloud computing would already be worth 6 billion euros and expand by almost 20% annually. There are many challenges that businesses wishing to employ cloud computing services must overcome in order for those services to comply with French data protection laws. Particularly problematic in cloud computing transactions are matters pertaining to the determination of the service provider's legal qualification, the applicable law, the transmission of data, and security. There are numerous advantages to cloud computing, but it also has certain drawbacks. Each firm must choose the combination of cloud technologies and configurations that best suits its needs. The choice to switch to cloud computing should take into account all relevant criteria, including but not limited to Perceived Ease of Use and Availability, Security and Privacy, Reliability and Relative Advantage in influencing the intention of user's towards the usage of cloud computing.

FUTURE RESEARCH DIRECTIONS

Around 53.2% of the variation in user satisfaction with cloud computing services in the educational setting could be explained by the four parameters that were employed in the study. Further insights into the relative impact of other variables on user satisfaction may be gained. Our research model's explanatory power is strong, yet there is still potential for improvement. Our study model can be used as the foundation for discovering other relevant elements that may assist researchers better understand the behaviours associated with cloud computing adoption. This will increase the prediction potential of cloud computing adoption.

REFERENCES

Adjei, J. K. (2015). Explaining the role of trust in cloud computing services. *Info*, *17*(1), 54–67. doi:10.1108/info-09-2014-0042

Aleem, A., & Ryan Sprott, C. (2012). Let me in the cloud: Analysis of the benefit and risk assessment of cloud platform. *Journal of Financial Crime*, *20*(1), 6–24. doi:10.1108/13590791311287337

Alghushami, A. H., Zakaria, N. H., & Aji, Z. M. (2020). Factors Influencing Cloud Computing Adoption in Higher Education Institutions of Least Developed Countries: Evidence from Republic of Yemen. *Applied Sciences, 10*(22), 8098. doi:10.3390/app10228098

Anderson, J. Q., & Rainie, L. (2010). The future of cloud computing. *Pew Research Center's Internet & American Life Project An Initiative of the Pew Research Center*. https://pewinternet.org/Reports/2010/The-future-of-cloud-computing.aspx

Arias, C. A., Monroy, C. R., & Guerrero, Y. M. N. (2012). *The New Cloud Computing Paradigm: The Way To It Seen As A Utility.*

Armbrust, M., Fox, A., Griffith, R., Joseph, A. D., Katz, R., Konwinski, A., Lee, G., Patterson, D., Rabkin, A., Stoica, I., & Zaharia, M. (2010). A view of cloud computing. *Communications of the ACM*, *53*(4), 50–58. doi:10.1145/1721654.1721672

Asadi, Z., Abdekhoda, M., & Nadrian, H. (2019). Cloud computing services adoption among higher education faculties: development of a standardized questionnaire. *Education and Information Technologies, 25*(1), 175–191. doi:10.1007/s10639-019-09932-0

Azure, M. (2021). *What is cloud computing? A beginner's guide*. Microsoft. https://azure.microsoft.com/en-in/resources/cloud-computing-dictionary/what-is-cloud-computing/#benefits

Buyya, R., Yeo, C. S., Venugopal, S., Broberg, J., & Brandic, I. (2009). Cloud computing and emerging IT platforms: Vision, hype, and reality for delivering computing as the 5th utility. *Future Generation Computer Systems*, *25*(6), 599–616. doi:10.1016/j.future.2008.12.001

Changchit, C. (2014). Students' perceptions of cloud computing. *Issues in Information Systems*, *15*, 312–322. doi:10.48009/1_iis_2014_312-322

Churchill, G. A. Jr. (1979). A Paradigm for Developing Better Measures of Marketing Constructs. *JMR, Journal of Marketing Research*, *16*(1), 64–73. doi:10.1177/002224377901600110

Davis, F. D. (1987). *User acceptance of information systems : the technology acceptance model (TAM)*. Deep Blue. https://deepblue.lib.umich.edu/handle/2027.42/35547

Davis, F. D. (1989). Perceived usefulness, perceived ease of use, and user acceptance of information technology. *Management Information Systems Quarterly*, *13*(3), 319–339. doi:10.2307/249008

Evans, D. S., Schmalensee, R., Noel, M. D., Chang, H. H., & Garcia-Swartz, D. D. (2011). *Platform Economics: Essays on Multi-Sided Businesses*. SSRN. https://papers.ssrn.com/abstract=1974020

Gefen, D., Karahanna, E., & Straub, D. W. (2003). Trust and tam in online shopping: AN integrated model. *Management Information Systems Quarterly*, *27*(1), 51–90. doi:10.2307/30036519

Islam, P. T., Manivannan, D., & Zeadally, S. (2016). *A Classification and Characterization of Security Threats in Cloud Computing*. Undefined.

Jain, A., Bansal, S., & Bhardwaj, S. (2022). *COVID-19 Outbreak: A Paradigm Shift in Food and Beverage Industry with Context to Delhi-NCR*. 329–339. doi:10.1007/978-981-19-0357-1_28

Kim, H., Lee, D.-S., & Ham, S. (2013). Impact of hotel information security on system reliability. *International Journal of Hospitality Management*, *35*, 369–379. doi:10.1016/j.ijhm.2012.06.002

Lin, A., & Chen, N. C. (2012). Cloud computing as an innovation: Percepetion, attitude, and adoption. *International Journal of Information Management*, *32*(6), 533–540. doi:10.1016/j.ijinfomgt.2012.04.001

Marston, S., Li, Z., Bandyopadhyay, S., Zhang, J., & Ghalsasi, A. (2011). Cloud computing — The business perspective. *Decision Support Systems*, *51*(1), 176–189. doi:10.1016/j.dss.2010.12.006

Mell, P., & Grance, T. (2011). *The NIST Definition of Cloud Computing. Computer Security Division*. Information Technology Laboratory, National Institute of Standards and Technology Gaithersburg.

Mohammed, F., Ibrahim, O., & Ithnin, N. (2016). Factors influencing cloud computing adoption for e-government implementation in developing countries: Instrument development. *Journal of Systems and Information Technology*, *18*(3), 297–327. doi:10.1108/JSIT-01-2016-0001

Moore, G. C., & Benbasat, I. (1991). Development of an instrument to measure the perceptions of adopting an information technology innovation. *Information Systems Research*, *2*(3), 192–222. doi:10.1287/isre.2.3.192

Oliveira, T., Thomas, M., & Espadanal, M. (2014). Assessing the determinants of cloud computing adoption: An analysis of the manufacturing and services sectors. *Information & Management*, *51*(5), 497–510. doi:10.1016/j.im.2014.03.006

Opitz, N., Langkau, T. F., Schmidt, N. H., & Kolbe, L. M. (2012). Technology acceptance of cloud computing: Empirical evidence from German IT departments. *Proceedings of the Annual Hawaii International Conference on System Sciences*, 1593–1602. 10.1109/HICSS.2012.557

Oye, N. D., A.Iahad, N., & Ab.Rahim, N. (2014). The history of UTAUT model and its impact on ICT acceptance and usage by academicians. *Education and Information Technologies 2012*, *19*(1), 251–270. doi:10.1007/s10639-012-9189-9

Pańkowska, M., Pyszny, K., & Strzelecki, A. (2020). Users' Adoption of Sustainable Cloud Computing Solutions. *Sustainability 2020, Vol. 12, Page 9930, 12*(23), 9930. doi:10.3390/su12239930

Raj, M., & Bansal, S. (2019). Customer satisfaction in banking sector-a case study of h.D.F.C bank. *International Journal of Research and Analytical Reviews*. http://ijrar.com/

Raj, M., Jain, A., Bansal, S., & Verma, T. (2018). Non-Performing Assets: A Comparative Study of SBI & ICICI Bank from 2014-2017. *IOSR Journal of Business and Management (IOSR-JBM), 20*(9), 78–84. https://doi.org/doi:10.9790/487X-2009077884

Raj, M., Verma, T., Bansal, S., & Jain, A. (2018). Performance Of Mutual Funds In India : A Comparative Analysis Of SBI Mutual Funds And HDFC Mutual Funds. *IOSR Journal of Business and Management (IOSR-JBM), 20*, 36–43. https://doi.org/ doi:10.9790/487X-2010013643

Ratten, V. (2014). A US-China comparative study of cloud computing adoption behavior: The role of consumer innovativeness, performance expectations and social influence. *Journal of Entrepreneurship in Emerging Economies, 6*(1), 53–71. doi:10.1108/JEEE-07-2013-0019

Sabi, H. M., Uzoka, F. M. E., Langmia, K., & Njeh, F. N. (2016). Conceptualizing a model for adoption of cloud computing in education. *International Journal of Information Management, 36*(2), 183–191. doi:10.1016/j.ijinfomgt.2015.11.010

Stieninger, M., & Nedbal, D. (2014). Diffusion and Acceptance of Cloud Computing in SMEs: Towards a Valence Model of Relevant Factors. *2014 47th Hawaii International Conference on System Sciences (HICSS)*, 3307–3316. 10.1109/HICSS.2014.410

Sultan, N. (2010). Cloud computing for education: A new dawn? *International Journal of Information Management, 30*(2), 109–116. doi:10.1016/j.ijinfomgt.2009.09.004

Taylor, S., & Todd, P. A. (1995). Understanding Information Technology Usage: A Test of Competing Models. Https://Doi.Org/10.1287/Isre.6.2.144, *6*(2), 144–176. doi:10.1287/isre.6.2.144

Tehrani, S. R., & Shirazi, F. (2014). Factors influencing the adoption of cloud computing by Small and Medium size Enterprises (SMEs). Lecture Notes in Computer Science (Including Subseries Lecture Notes in Artificial Intelligence and Lecture Notes in Bioinformatics), 8522 LNCS(PART 2), 631–642. https://doi.org/doi:10.1007/978-3-319-07863-2_60/COVER

Truong, D. (2010). *How cloud computing enhances competitive advantages: A research model for small businesses*. The Business Review, Cambridge. https://www.researchgate.net/publication/273447113_How_cloud_computing_enhances_competitive_advantages_A_research_model_for_small_businesses

Walterbusch, M., & Teuteberg, F. (2012). Vertrauen im Cloud Computing. *HMD Praxis Der Wirtschaftsinformatik*, *49*(6), 50–59. doi:10.1007/BF03340757

Chapter 5
Sustainability of Mobile Wallets in the Era of Low Cost Data Usage in India

Khem Chand
Raffles University, India

Sapna Jangra
Institute of Management Studies and Research, Maharshi Dayanand University, India

Pravin Chandra Singh
https://orcid.org/0000-0002-6002-0703
Alabbar School of Management, Raffles University, India

Ravi Shekhar Tiwari
SRM Institute of Science and Technology, India

Rajesh Tiwari
Graphic Era University (Deemed), India

ABSTRACT

The present chapter explores the sustainability of mobile payment wallets amid low-cost data usage. To evaluate sustainability, the chapter evaluates the association between perception and satisfaction of m-Wallet. The chapter examines 506 m-Wallet users' perception and satisfaction. A self-administrated questionnaire was used to collect responses using an online survey. Five factors were extracted after exploratory factor analysis. Perception comprised of usefulness, self-efficacy, and ease of use. Structural equation modeling was employed on perception, satisfaction, and security. It was discovered that perception has a direct and indirect impact on satisfaction. Security has a direct impact on satisfaction. Security was utilized as a partial mediating factor between perception and satisfaction.

DOI: 10.4018/978-1-6684-7568-3.ch005

INTRODUCTION

Mobile technology has affected people across the world. A large number of consumers are using mobile, due to the extension of new services such as mobile wallet. The monthly data usage on mobile is expected to be 19 GB in 2023 and will increase to 46 GB in 2028 (Ericsson, 2022). Mobile data usage has increased in India from 1.24 GB in 2017-18 to 14.1 GB in 2021-22. There were only 32.8% broad band connections in India in 2015. Now there are 96% broad band connections (Mankotia, 2022) in 2022. The incentive package of USD 10 billion to promote manufacturing of semi-conductor will drive the domestic production of smart phones in India. The launch of 5G will create demand for 840 million 5G devices (Business Standard, 2022).

By 2023, the Indian digital payment market is expected to exceed $1 trillion. Indian government is working on reducing the corruption by digital transactions (Niti Aayog, 2020). With 18.3 transactions per inhabitant, India has the lowest number of digital payment transactions among the BRICS countries (RBI, 2020a). Under Mr. Narendra Modi's leadership, India has a lot of room to expand in terms of digital transactions. In 2016, the Modi government launched a demonetization campaign and a number of measures to strengthen the digital economy. After India's demonetization, the development and uptake of alternative payment systems, commonly known as e-money, accelerated. In India, the share of e-money transactions has increased from 0.9% in 2012 to 21.5% in 2017 (RBI, 2020b). The cost of data has significantly decreased in India from INR 268.9 in 2014 to INR 6.6 in 2021 (Sharma, 2021).

M-Wallet is a fund transfer or payment application that is part of the mobile data service (MDS). Banks, non-bank financial service providers, e-commerce enterprises, and technology companies are all now offering mobile wallets. Mobile wallet usage and growth has been aided by the widespread use of smartphones. Oxigen was the first non-bank organization to be integrated with the National Payments Corporation of India for instant money transfers utilizing the IMPS service, which was established in 2008 (Dataquest, 2014). Mr. Vijay Shekhar Sharma established the Paytm mobile wallet in 2010 (Paytm, 2020). Customers were forced to consider non-cash payment solutions at the time of demonetization in 2016. Covid-19 was another reason which pushed cashless payments in India.

M-wallet has gained popularity due to ease of use for payments, cash back, a wide range of bill payments, recharge, and shopping without the need for cash (Singh, 2011; Praiseye, and John 2018; Kumar and Seri, 2014; Paripunyapat and Kraiwanit, 2018; Nandhini and Girija, 2019). The growth in mobile is driven by rural areas now in India. Rural sector in expected to grow at 6%, as compared to urban sector which will grow at 2.5% (Business Standard, 2022). The demand for smart phones will increase to 400 million in 2026 (Business Standard, 2022). Mobile wallets have reduced dependence on banks for financial transactions in offline format and cash. Citizens are not required to go to bank for withdraw and payment. There is no waiting line in banks in current scenario (Patnam and Yao, 2020). The central government is promoting digital payment system and reducing corruption, so that farmers can take the benefits (Tiwari, 2019). M-wallet has finished the middlemen role in the payment system (Mohan, 2020).

Mobile wallet has enhanced ease of payments. On the other hand, users of mobile wallets have also got exposed to vulnerability of cyber-security. There has been sudden increase in cases of cyber-attacks in India. In 2021 it was observed that cyber-attacks have increased 845% (The Tribune, 2021). In the period between April-May-June 2022, eighteen million attacks per day and two hundred thousand threats per day from cyber criminals were done in India (Sur, 2022). According to a report by Microsoft, there are 921 password cyber-attacks occurring per second in the world, accounting for 74% increase in just one year. Microsoft stopped 34.7 billion identity attacks and 37 billion email attacks in the period between July, 2021 and June 2022 (The Statesman, 2022). Sujith and Julie (2017) identified data theft as a barrier for mobile wallet adoption in India.

Mobile wallets have given a boost to digital transactions. Unified Payment Interface (UPI) constitute 40% of all digital payments in India. UPI transactions have increased from 0.007 billion worth INR 0.02 lakh crores in April 2017 to 6.58 billion in August 2022 worth INR 10.73 lakh crores (Press Information Bureau, 2022). Digital transactions provide opportunity to increase the size of formal economy. In India only 6.25% people pay direct taxes, as compared to 45% in United States (Income Tax India, 2022). The tax collections have increased 303% from INR 6.2 lakh crore in financial year 2010 to INR 25.2 lakh crore in financial year 2022 (Tyagi, 2022). Joseph and Ramalingam (2022) found a significant positive impact of digital payments on GST collection in India. Digital payment is supporting economic growth in India. However, rise in cyber frauds amid rise in cash in circulation raises concerns on sustainability of mobile wallets. Reducing the cost of mobile data is not sufficient to drive usage of mobile wallets in India.

Objective

Although the users of mobile wallet have increased many fold in India, but there is need to dive deep into factors influencing mobile wallet usage and satisfaction (Chawla & Joshi, 2021). Digital transactions led by mobile wallets have led to increase in urban mobile transactions, but rural India lags behind in digital transactions. Despite digital push by government, cash in circulation reached an all time high of INR 30.18 lakh crore in March 2022, driven by rural India (Chadha, 2022). 66% population lives in rural part of India (Tandon, 2019). Reliance on cash for transactions in rural India, poses a challenge for the digital payment industry. There is need to investigate the factors determining perception, satisfaction of users. Cyber frauds have reduced faith of rural people on mobile wallets. Rural people have safety concerns about use of digital transactions (Reji, 2021). In 2018, digital wallet firms, lost 45% of its user base in India (Choudhury, 2018). Chand et al. (2022) found that preference of using m-wallet is directly and indirectly affected by user's perception. Various studies have been conducted on digital payments but there is a gap in studies on adaptation and determinates of m-wallet (Al-Qudah, 2022) and post adoption behavior. Preference, perception and satisfaction significantly influence mobile wallet users' in North India (Singh et al., 2017). This chapter will provide insights about the association between perception, security and satisfaction.

FACTORS INFLUENCING MOBILE WALLET USAGE

Security

Chandrasekhar and Ghosh (2018) argued that data theft and weak regulatory mechanism for regulating data theft is a concern for growth of electronic payments in India. Singh and Srivastava (2020) also found that data theft, spyware and phishing attacks has an adverse impact on long term usage and sustainability of mobiles. Saluja (2022) identified identity theft as significant weakness of fintech industry. It was suggested that the industry should adopt preventive measures to overcome the weakness. Confidentiality, integrity and availability of resources to manage cyber security is crucial (Jadey et al. 2022). Hoehle et al. (2022) argued that compensation to the customers in case of data theft influences the perception of justice. India needs detailed analysis of data security concerning mobile transactions (Uloli et al, 2022). India needs a comprehensive cyber security policy (Mishra et al. 2022).

Usefulness

Expectation confirmation theory was developed by Bhattacharjee (2001); Oliver and Westbrook (1993), examined TAM in combination with the information system. Customers make a disconfirmation assessment after judging the performance based on expectations. Model of expectation confirmation (ECM) can be used to track post-purchase behavior as well as promote technological products and services. Grover and Kar (2020) described a social media engagement model that was used to examine how users in India perceive mobile payments. According to Talwar et al. (2020) the service quality has a favorable effect on first-time mobile wallet users' initial trust, and initial trust has a positive influence on perceived usefulness and confirmation.

Kaur et al. (2020) adopted innovation resistance theory to investigate mobile payment acceptance. Value barriers, risk, and usage had a negative impact on adoption of mobile payment. In a study of retail mobile payment acceptance in India, Singh and Sinha (2020) discovered that perceived value and usefulness of the merchant's product encouraged m-wallet acceptance. Kumar, Adlakha, and Mukherjee (2018) investigated how perceived usefulness, perceived security, perceived ease of use and satisfaction influence the desire to use mobile wallet on a regular basis. The perceived usefulness was found to have a significant impact on m-Wallet satisfaction. The resolution of grievances has a mediating influence on perceived security. On Zhou's (2013) model, the authors incorporated grievance redressal and perceived security. There is a link between a customer's impression of a payment method and acceptance (Abbas and Hamdy, 2015; Hayashi, 2012).

Singh et al. (2017) developed an empirical model on m-Wallet. Three factors have been included in this model as consumer perception, preference, and satisfaction. They also discovered that perception and satisfaction had a substantial positive link. Customers that are happy with the service will use it again in the future. Rust and Oliver (1994) found that product quality and convenience, influences consumer satisfaction for m-wallet. According to Dahlberg et al. (2008), preference and satisfaction are closely associated in case of mobile wallets. According to Lin and Wang (2006), perceived value has a direct impact on customer satisfaction. Chand et al. (2022) found that preference is significantly influenced by perception. Satisfaction has a mediation role between the two.

Perception and Satisfaction

Perception of consumer significantly influences satisfaction of users' of mobile wallet (Rowland & Shrauger, 2013). Experience of using m-wallet indicates satisfaction of consumers. According to Yap and Ng (2019), the convenience and social features of the m-wallet have a substantial impact on perceived usefulness. It was also discovered that consumer perceived usefulness was unaffected by confidentiality. According to Ogonowski et al. (2014), social presence has an impact on perceived usefulness and enjoyment while shopping online from unfamiliar organisations. Perceived usefulness was studied by Davis et al. (1992) and Khayati & Zouaoui (2013) as a relationship between the consumer's perception and their experience with the technology. Will of policy makers influences well-being of stakeholders (Tiwari et al. 2021). Davis (1993) described that perceived usefulness is a consumer's attitude toward new technology that can help them perform better at work. The adoption and acceptance of peer-to-peer mobile payments were investigated by Kalinic et al. (2019). The usefulness of peer-to-peer mobile payment was discovered to be a crucial determinant of acceptability. The degree to which a user perceives a system to be painless and user friendly is described as ease of use. It has an impact on the user's intention to utilize m-wallets. If users can easily operate m-wallet functions, they will use it. Financial transactions that are free of errors improve the usability of mobile wallets (Flavian et al., 2020). The simplicity of use of e-wallets has an impact on the decision to utilise them (Chawla & Joshi, 2021). Self-efficacy is defined as "people's judgments of their capacities to organise and execute courses of action required to achieve specified sorts of performances." Users' self-efficacy is linked to their willingness to utilize mobile wallets (Bandura, 1997).

Consumer satisfaction is closely correlated to the simplicity of use, convenience, social influence, security, and user-friendliness (Singh, (2014). Marinkovic et al. (2020) discovered that m-wallet users' satisfaction can be predicted based on the performance of m-Wallet's expectancy. Active engagement of stakeholders is crucial for long term success. Good products can fail due to poor user satisfaction and weakness in transparency (Tiwari et al. 2020). According to Liao and Yang (2020), mobile payments improve the customer buying experience and will encourage online businesses to expand through offline channels.

Security and Satisfaction

Agus et al. (2007) explained that there is a significant positive relationship between security service and satisfaction. Abdulrahaman et al. (2018) found that high level security measures in m-wallet provide the safety from hackers. Bosamia, Mansi (2018) explained that mobile wallet is affected by various threats and vulnerabilities. It was also argued that high level of understanding is required for security measures towards m-wallet.

Significance of the Chapter

Several research studies have been conducted to explain the factors that impact customer adoption of technology, however there is a gap in the post adoption impact of M-wallet users' perceptions on satisfaction. No research has been conducted in North India, to determine the post adoption impact of perception on m-wallet users' satisfaction. The review of literature on technology adoption provides insights on the determinants of adoption of mobile wallet. It is observed that impact of satisfaction post adoption is ignored in previous studies. Ram and Chand (2015) described that satisfaction is significantly affected by perception. Singh et al. (2017) examined the significance of perception, satisfaction and preference of m-wallet. A strong relationship was found between perception and satisfaction. The study on post-adoption satisfaction looked at cross-cultural differences as well as national geographic limits (Venkatesh and Zhang, 2010; Olga, 2018). The chapter explores security, as a mediating factor between satisfaction and perception. Chapter attempts to fill the gap of post adoption behavior of users by adopting a survey method of data collection from users of mobile wallet.

Proposed Conceptual Model

The impacts of the m-Wallet users' perception on satisfaction are highlighted in the research review. The satisfaction of m-Wallet users is influenced by perception both directly and indirectly. As a result, as illustrated in Figure 1, this chapter conceptualizes the impact of m-Wallet users' perception on satisfaction both directly and indirectly. The security of the m-Wallet has been employed as a mediating factor between satisfaction and perception.

Figure 1. The effect of m-Wallet user's perception on their satisfaction

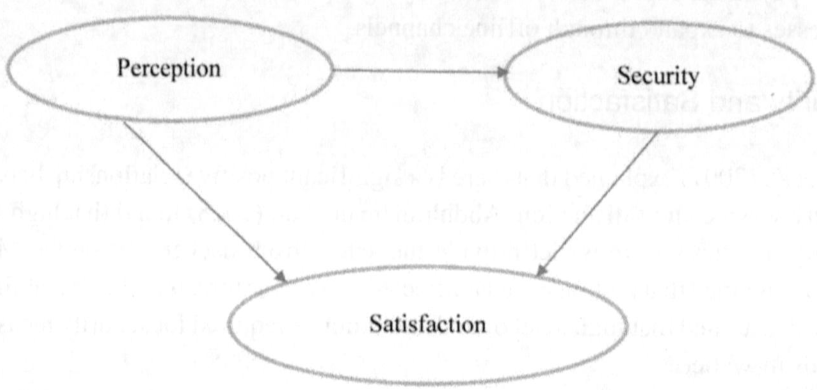

METHOD

The present chapter is exploratory cum descriptive in nature. North India has been selected due to highest digital payment transactions of users in India. North Inia constitute 50.90% of digital transactions in India till 2021 (Satista, 2021). Data was collected through questionnaire. A self-administrated questionnaire was developed. 31 statements (excluding demographic information) have been included in a questionnaire. Simple random sampling was used for the survey. Responses of 506 respondents were used for the analysis. The data was collected from North India. With five replies per parameter and 10 cases, the sample size was considered sufficient (Little and Rubin, 1989). A minimum sample size of 155 was necessary because the questionnaire comprised 31 items. The comments were tabulated on a five-point likert scale ranging from strongly disagree (1) to strongly agree (5). Young m-Wallet users between the ages of 15 and 30 were included in the survey. The age group of 15 to 30 years produces consistent results in research on technology adoption (Roberts and DelVecchio, 2000). Five factors were explored as described in Appendix-A table by applying the exploratory factor analysis (EFA). Three factors were comprised into perception of m-wallet users namely ease of use, self-efficacy and usefulness. Satisfaction and security comprised of 8 items. Perception comprised of 15 items. Four items in ease of use, four items in usefulness and seven items in self-efficacy were included. Second order confirmatory factor analysis (CFA) has been performed on these three factors of perception for validation. The impact of perception directly and indirectly on satisfaction of m-wallet users has been observed through structural equation modeling (SEM). Security had a mediating role between satisfaction and perception. Satisfaction was directly affected by security. Data was analysed using SPSS and AMOS 20.0 version. Following hypothesis were framed after review of literature.

Hypothesis

H1: Satisfaction is directly affected by perception of users' of mobile wallet
H2: Satisfaction is significantly affected by security of users' of mobile wallet
H3: Satisfaction is indirectly affected by perception of users' of mobile wallet
H4: Security plays mediation role between satisfaction and perception of users' of mobile wallet

Exogenous and Endogenous Variables

The users' perception and security of m-wallet has been considered as an exogenous variable for satisfaction. The satisfaction and security of m-wallet users are considered as endogenous variables for perception. Perception was associated with self-efficacy (SLCY), ease of use (EOUS) and usefulness (UFLS) (Singh et al. 2017).

Reliability of the Perception, Satisfaction, and Security

Reliability and consistency of the scale has been checked through the Cronbach's alpha (Hair et al., 1998). Cronbach's alpha of satisfaction was 0.875. The range of loading (8 items) was from 0.509 (Q57) to 0.853 (Q62). Reliability coefficient of security was 0.838. The loadings ranged from 0.557 (Q41) to 0.712 (Q35). Seven items have been included in self-efficacy which show reliability coefficient of 0.770 with factor loading range from 0.791 (Q17) to 0.403 (Q26). Five factors have been described in table 1.

Table 1. Items factor loadings and construct reliability

Factors (Cronbach's alpha)	Items	Sources	Factor Loading
	Please give your satisfaction rating in five point likert scale		
Satisfaction (0.875)	Banking services can be performed from anywhere (62)	Faulkner (2000), Koivisto (2008)	0.839
	Transfer money can be transferred to anyone from anywhere (60)		0.853
	I am using m-Wallet (55)		0.785
	Money security in m-Wallet (58)		0.568
	Need of current scenario (57)		0.509
	Suitability offer (61)		0.533
	Low fees charged (56)		0.556
	The persuasive offer (63)		0.751
Security (0.838)	Security of information (37)	Rao and Troshani (2007),Mathew et al. (2014), Singh (2011),Dahlberg et al. (2008)	0.652
	Security of banking details (35)		0.712
	Secured banking details in database (40)		0.629
	It is safe (33)		0.706
	Virus free (34)		0.613
	Secured form unauthorized third party (41)		0.557
	Protected from data leakages/theft (39)		0.592
	Security code not visible to other party (36)		0.559
Self-efficacy (0.770)	Easy to handle (17)	Dewan et al. (2009)	0.791
	I can easily perform all the functions of m-Wallet (24)		0.657
	Normal banking (20)		0.579
	Comfortable (18)		0.577
	Familiar with m-Wallet technology (25)		0.526
	New technology (28)		0.436
	All service in single app (26)		0.403
Ease of use (0.683)	Beneficial (7)	Riquelme and Rios (2010), and Mathew et al. (2014), Davis (1989), Illia et al. (2015)	0.749
	Faster service (5)		0.699
	Understandable (2)		0.570
	I am dependent on m-Wallet for financial transactions (13)		0.364
Usefulness (0.622)	Banking become easier (3)	Mathew et al. (2014), Samudra and Phadtare (2012)	0.629
	All banking service can be performed in seconds (16)		0.559
	Effectively (4)		0.433
	User- Friendly (6)		0.549

Factor loading value of ease of use with reliability coefficient 0.683, ranged from 0.749 (Q7) to 0.364 (Q13). The factor loading ranged from 0.629 (Q3) to 0.433 (Q4), and the reliability coefficient of four usefulness items was 0.622. (Q4). The factor loading ranged from 0.853 (Q62) to 0.364 (Q13), and Cronbach's alpha ranged from 0.875 (satisfaction) to 0.622 (usefulness), indicating that all dimensions were reliable.

ANALYSIS OF SURVEY DATA

Three factors have been identified after applying the exploratory factor analysis with principal components analysis. These factors represented perception of m-wallet. The perception construct was validated using second order confirmatory factor analysis.

Perception of m-Wallet Users

Second-order confirmatory analysis revealed 32 regression weights, 1 covariance, 17 variances, and a total of 50 parameters. The hypothesized model was fitted, but the model was adjusted for better fit, according to the comparison model (table 2). In the original model, the error terms e5 (Q18) and e7 (Q24) were correlated for better fit, with modification indices (MI) of 23.262 as shown in table 3. When comparing the modified model-1 to the original model, the improved model had higher values, indicating a better fit. The improved model is better fitted than the original model.

Two statements; I am independent on m-wallet for financial transaction (0.364 standard regression weights, Q13) and all service in single app (0.395 standard regression weights, Q26) have been removed due to low standard regression weight. Modified model-2 was compared with modified model-1 for better fit as shown in table 2.

Table 2. Comparison of models

Fit Statistics	TLI Model	IFI Model	RFI Model	NFI Model	CFI Model	GFI Model
Original Model						
Chi-square (χ^2) = 295.716, P = 0.000, CMIN/DF = 3.399, DF = 87, RMSEA = 0.069,						
Value	0.848	0.875	0.797	0.832	0.874	0.928
Modified Model -1						
Chi-square = 264.935, P = 0.000, CMIN/DF = 3.081, DF = 86, RMSEA = 0.064,						
Value	0.868	0.893	0.816	0.849	0.892	0.934
Modified Model -2						
Chi-square = 185.323, P = 0.000, CMIN/DF = 3.038, DF = 61, RMSEA = 0.064,						
Value	.893	.917	.848	.881	.916	.947

Sources: survey data

The result of above table shows chi-square (χ^2) = 185.323 and degree of freedom = 61, p>0.000, Chi-square-minimum/degree of freedom = 3.038. Chi-square value difference was 79.162 (264.935-185.323). The value of the baseline comparisons fit indices was NFI=0.881, RFI=0.848, IFI=0.917, TLI=0.893 and CFI=0.916 for modified model.

Table 3. Covariances of perception

Error term	Relation	Error term	M.I.	Par Change
e5	<-->	e15	4.189	-.050
e5	<-->	e11	4.476	.066
e5	**<-->**	**e7**	**23.262**	**-.140**
e1	<-->	e22	10.706	-.082
e1	<-->	e18	15.391	-.113

Source: survey data

Validating Perception, Security, and Satisfaction Construct

The construct of perception was validated using second-order confirmatory factor analysis. Structural equation modeling with perception has been used to validate security and satisfaction. Perception has a direct and indirect impact on m-Wallet users' satisfaction. There were 105 parameters in the measurement model, 69 regression weights, 1 covariance, and 35 variances. As demonstrated in table 5, the RMSEA of the original model was as high as 0.063, which was unacceptable. In the original model, e37 (Q57), e36 (Q58) terms of error were associated by a two-headed arrow, indicating that the modification indices (MI) were 98.837, as shown in table 4. The adjusted model's values were higher than the original model's, indicating that perception influences m-Wallet users' satisfaction both directly and indirectly. Security influences satisfaction by acting as a mediator between perception and satisfaction.

In case of perception the standard regression weight varied from 0.80 (Q17) to 0.425 (Q28) as shown in Appendix-A. The values of standard regression weight indicate three sub-constructs of perception which covers thirteen measurement variables. Figure 2 shows the squared multiple correlations of the observed items, which ranged from 0.18 (Q28) to 0.64 (Q17). The thirteen measurement variables of three sub-construct; usefulness, ease of use, self-efficacy and 8 measurement variables of security and satisfaction have been shown in table 1 after removing the two statements; I am independent on m-wallet for financial transaction Q13) and all service in single app (0.395).

Table 4. Covariances of satisfaction

Error Terms	*Relation*	*Error Terms*	*M.I.*	*Par Change*
e36	<-->	e43	11.317	.054
e36	<-->	e38	7.431	.033
e36	**<-->**	**e37**	**98.837**	**.124**
e35	<-->	e53	9.877	.060
e35	<-->	e51	7.199	-.054

Sources: survey data

The standard regression weights for three items for ease of use (Appendix-A) ranged from 0.558 (Q2) to 0.732 (Q5). Three items had squared multiple correlations ranging from 0.32 (Q2) to 0.54 (Figure 2). (Q5). Self-efficacy standard regression weights ranged from 0.425 (Q28) to 0.802 (Q17). For six items, the squared multiple correlations (Figure 2) varied from 0.18 (Q28) to 0.64 (Q17). As demonstrated in Appendix-A, standard regression weights of usefulness ranged from 0.432 (Q4) to 0.640 (Q3). Range of three items, the squared multiple correlations (Fig. 2), was from 0.19 (Q4) to 0.41 (Q3). Eight items comprise security construct which showed the standard regression weight (Appendix-A) between 0.557 (Q41) and 0.711 (Q35) respectively. The squared multiple correlations (Figure 2) for eight items lie between 0.31 (Q41) and 0.51 (Q35). Satisfaction included eight items which show the standardized regression weight (Appendix-A) between 0.508 (Q57) and 0.854 (Q60). The squared multiple correlation MCs (Figure 2) for eight items were 0.26 (Q57) and 0.73 (Q60).

Table 5. Comparison of baselines models

Fit Statistics	TLI Model	IFI Model	RFI Model	NFI Model	CFI Model	GFI Model
Original Model						
Chi-square (χ^2) = 1117.846, DF = 370, P = 0.000, CMIN/DF = 3.021, RMSEA = .063						
Value	.836	.852	.773	.793	.850	.858
Modified Model 1						
Chi-square = 1009.688, DF = 369, P = 0.000, CMIN/DF = 2.736, RMSEA = .059						
Value	.859	.873	.795	.813	.872	.873

Sources: survey data

In this model, there were 31 measurement variables, 435 different sample moments, 69 regression weights, 2 covariance, and 35 variances. There are a total of 106 parameters that have been calculated. The proposed model has a good fit statistic [χ^2 (Chi-square) = 1009.688, number of distinct parameters estimated = 66, and degree of freedom (DF) (435-66) =369, p>0.000, CMIN/DF= 2.736].

For the proposed model, the baseline comparative fit indices are NFI=0.813, RFI=0.795, IFI=0.873, TLI=0.859, and CFI=0.872. For the proposed model, the GFI and RMSEA are 0.873 and 0.059, respectively. The standard regression weight of observable items ranged between 0.425 and 0.854 (p<0.1).

Structural Equation Model

Figure 2. Perception effect on satisfaction

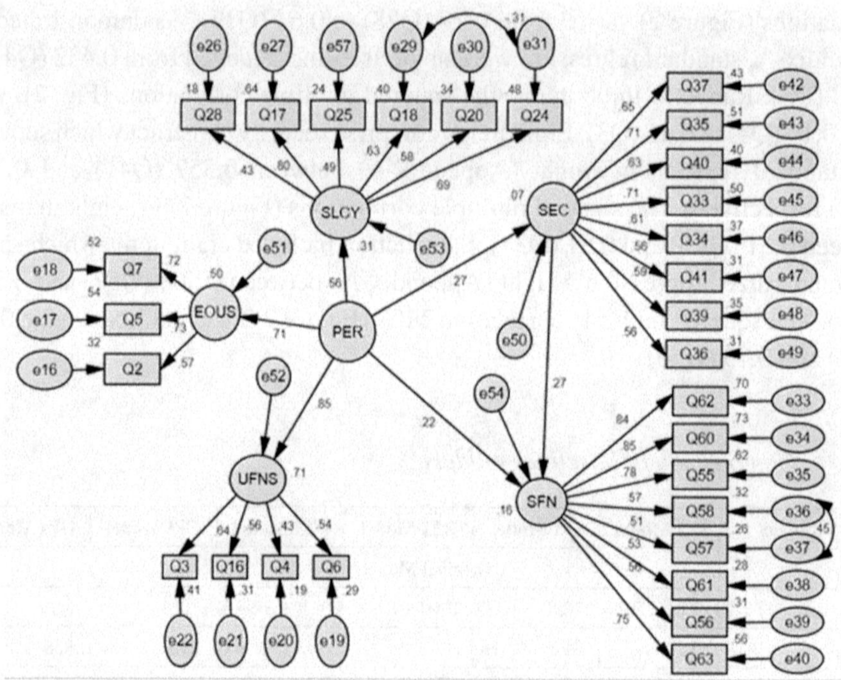

Effect of perception of users' of mobile wallet on the satisfaction ($\chi 2$/df =2.736, RMSEA = .059, CFI = .872, GFI = .873, AGFI = .850)

Note: EOUS=Ease of Use, SLCY= Self-Efficacy, PER = Perception, UFNS = Usefulness, SFN = Satisfaction, SEC = Security

Description of Model

In comparison to the direct model (369), the indirect model has three times the degree of freedom (372). The direct model was estimated utilizing the direct paths from m-Wallet users' perception to satisfaction. Without the meditation factor, the influence of perception and security on satisfaction has been assessed directly. The satisfaction was influenced by the perception, which was mediated by the security of the m-Wallet. Chi-square value of indirect model (N = 506, df = 372) = 1089.022, p<05, CMIN/DF (1089.022/372) = 2.927; Chi-square value of direct model (N = 506, df = 369) = 1009.688, p<05, CMIN/DF (1009.688/369) = 2.736.

The direct model, with a lower AIC (Akaike Criterion Information) value (1141.688), is much better fit than the indirect model, which has a higher AIC value (1215.022). The model's RMSEA is 0.059 for direct model. The effect of perception on m-Wallet users' satisfaction is presented in table 6.

Table 6. Standardized effect

Factors		Factors	Estimate
SEC	<---	PER	.273
SFN	<---	PER	.219
SFN	<---	SEC	.273
EOUS	<---	PER	.706
SLCY	<---	PER	.561
UFNS	<---	PER	.845

The satisfaction of m-Wallet users is said to be influenced both directly and indirectly by perception. The standardized regression weight of the direct model is 0.273 (p <0.05), according to the direct model. Overall, perception has a 0.294 effect on satisfaction. The indirect effect of perception on satisfaction was obtained as 0.074. Partial mediation is appropriate. In summary, perception influences the satisfaction of m-Wallet users both directly and indirectly.

Table 7. Standardized regression weight

Model	Direct Effect			Total Effect			Indirect Effect	
	Factors	Estimate	P	Factors	Estimate	P	Estimate	P
Model-1	PER-SFN	0.219	.000	PER-SEC-SFN	0.294	0.000	.074	0.000

Developing Data Driven Decisions

The chapter discovered that perception had both direct and indirect implications on m-Wallet user satisfaction. The sustainability of mobile is influenced by satisfaction, data safety. By reducing the odds of risk, M-Wallet security improves the satisfaction of its users. The perception of utilizing the m-Wallet is mediated by security. The simplicity of use, utility, and self-efficacy of m-Wallet are three elements that influence its perception. Suls and Wallston (2008) studied several factors (ease of use, security, trust and efficacy) that influence the consumer adaptation and usage of m-Wallet. Consumer's perception influences the preference and usage of new technology. M-Wallet users show their perception towards ease to handling, familiarity with the functions, improving banking service as compared to traditional mode of banking, comfort and ease of executing financial transactions. Three factors of perception significantly affect the satisfaction while using m-Wallet. High perception of users shows more satisfaction towards m-Wallet. Clark (2005) explained that preference of m-Wallet depends on consumer's satisfaction. Amin (2009) described that security and social identity affects the satisfaction significantly. Yang and Lee (2010) identified that there is a significant relationship between perception and satisfaction. Security of m-Wallet significantly affects the satisfaction of users. High security of m-Wallet provides enhanced satisfaction.

Security features and an SMS model were proposed by Nyamtiga et al. (2013) to improve data security across mobile networks. The satisfaction with mobile banking is influenced by m-Wallet customers' high perception. The perception of m-Wallet users has an impact on user satisfaction both directly and indirectly. The security of m-Wallet is beneficial in increasing customer happiness. Security was discovered to be a partial mediator between m-Wallet users' perceptions and satisfaction.

This chapter has added security as a mediating factor between satisfaction and perception of mobile wallet users. The mobile firms need to focus on satisfaction of users and safety features to prevent cyber-attacks. The findings support the model of perception and satisfaction (Singh et al., 2017). Studies have been done on impact of users' perception on satisfaction of m-Wallet (Venkatesh and Davis, 2000) but in this chapter post adoption behavior of mobile wallet users has been examined in North India. Perception influences satisfaction of m-wallet users. M-wallet firms and banks offering m-Wallet need to consider these factors for enhancing satisfaction of mobile wallet users. The present chapter adds to the existing literature on adoption of technology in India, by providing insights on variables affecting satisfaction of mobile wallet users. The findings of the chapter have implications for brand managers to enhance satisfaction of the customers of m-wallet. The findings have implications for government agencies involved in pushing digital payments through mobile to build perception into their approach of enhancing satisfaction of users by monitoring security. Sustainability of Mobile can be ensured by enhancing satisfaction of users of mobile wallets.

The government, regulatory agencies and corporates have to focus on security framework of mobile wallets to increase adoption and continuous usage of mobile wallets. Security influences the satisfaction of mobile users. Failure to address security and satisfaction of users will fail the digital push of the government and industry. Highest cash in circulation in 2022, six years after demonetization drive in 2016 is an eye opener for the policy makers. Supply driven mobile wallets ecosystem will not sustain in a diverse country like India, with 66% people living in rural areas. Demand driven mobile wallet ecosystem is the need of the hour. Security assurance for the rural users will create sustainable demand for mobile wallets.

CONCLUSION

The chapter explored the sustainability of mobiles by examining the satisfaction, security and perception. Sustainability will be ensured by continuous usage of mobiles for payments using mobile wallets and safety of the data usage. After initial euphoria, the rise in cyber-attacks and subsequent losses will reduce the satisfaction from the usage of mobile wallet and will become a constraint for growth of mobiles, once the initial stage of adoption is over. The satisfaction of m-wallet users is directly influenced by perception. Users are more satisfied with m-wallet because of its high perception and security. It is discovered that the users' perception has a substantial impact on satisfaction. The satisfaction of users is also influenced by the security of the m-wallet. The m-wallet security is a mediator between perception and satisfaction. Low-cost data alone will not lead to sustainability of mobile wallets. Satisfaction from the continuous usage will drive the sustainability of mobile wallets.

REFERENCES

Abbas, H. A., & Hamdy, H. I. (2015). Determinants of continuance intention factor in Kuwait communication market: Case study of Zain-Kuwait. *Computers in Human Behavior*, *49*, 648–657. doi:10.1016/j.chb.2015.03.035

Abdulrahaman, M. D., Alhassan, J. K., Ojeniyi, J. A., & Abdulhamid, S. M. (2018). Security risk analysis management in mobile wallet transaction: A case study of Pagatech Nigeria Limited. *International Journal of Computer Network and Information Security*, *10*(12), 21. doi:10.5815/ijcnis.2018.12.03

Agus, A., Barker, S., & Kandampully, J. (2007). An exploratory study of service quality in the Malaysian public service sector. *International Journal of Quality & Reliability Management*, *24*(2), 177–190. doi:10.1108/02656710710722284

Al-Qudah, A. A., Al-Okaily, M., Alqudah, G., & Ghazlat, A. (2022). Mobile payment adoption in the time of the COVID-19 pandemic. *Electronic Commerce Research*. doi:10.100710660-022-09577-1

Amin, H. (2009). An analysis of online banking usage intentions: An extension of the technology acceptance model. *International Journal of Business and Society*, *10*(1), 27–40.

Bandura, A. (1997). *Self-efficacy: The exercise of control*. W. H. Freeman and Company.

Bhattacharjee, A. (2001). Understanding information systems continuance: An expectation confirmation model. *Management Information Systems Quarterly*, *25*(3), 351–370. doi:10.2307/3250921

Bosamia, M. (2018). *Mobile wallet payments recent potential threats and vulnerabilities with its possible security measures.*

Business Standard. (2022). India to have 1 billion smartphone users by 2026: Deloitte report. *Business Standard.* https://www.business-standard.com/article/current-affairs/india-to-have-1-billion-smartphone-users-by-2026-deloitte-report-122022200996_1.html

Chadha, S. (2022). Why cash circulation in economy hit all-time high in March 2022 despite surge in digital payments, *The Times of India*. https://timesofindia.indiatimes.com/business/india-business/why-cash-circulation-in-economy-hit-all-time-high-in-march-2022-despite-surge-in-digital-payments/articleshow/90562209.cms

Chand, K., Tiwari, R., & Sapna. (2022). Effect of Perception and Satisfaction on Preference for Mobile Wallet. *FIIB Business Review*. https://doi.org/doi:10.1177/23197145221077365

Chandrasekhar, C. P., & Ghosh, J. (2018). The financialization of finance? Demonetization and the dubious push to cashlessness in India. *Development and Change*, *49*(2), 420–436. doi:10.1111/dech.12369

Chawla, D., & Joshi, H. (2021). *Degree of awareness and the antecedents of the digital media platform: The case of mobile wallets*. FIIB Business Review., doi:10.1177/23197145211023413

Choudhury, K. (2018). Fearing worst, mobile wallets plan to diversify; loses 45% of user base. *Business Standard*. https://www.business-standard.com/article/companies/fearing-worst-mobile-wallets-plan-to-diversify-loses-45-of-user-base-118033100711_1.html

Clark, L. (2005). Shopping without cash: The emergence of the e-purse. *Economic Perspectives*, *29*(4), 34–51.

Dahlberg, T., Mallat, N., Ondrus, J., & Zmijewska, A. (2008). Past, present and future of mobile payments research: A literature review. *Electronic Commerce Research and Applications*, *7*(2), 165–181. doi:10.1016/j.elerap.2007.02.001

Dataquest. (2020). *Oxigen launches India's first mobile wallet.* DQ India. https://www.dqindia.com/oxigen-launches-india-s-mobile-wallet/#:~:text=Oxigen%20Wallet%2C%20launch%20ed%20India's%20the,Transfers%20anytime%2C%20anywhere%20using%20IMPS

Davis, F. D. (1989). Perceived usefulness, perceived ease of use, and user acceptance of information technology. *Management Information Systems Quarterly*, *13*(3), 319–340. doi:10.2307/249008

Davis, F. D. (1993). User acceptance of information technology system characteristics, user perceptions and behavioral impacts. *International Journal of Man-Machine Studies*, *38*(3), 475–487. doi:10.1006/imms.1993.1022

Davis, F. D., Bagozzi, R. P., & Warshaw, P. R. (1992). Extrinsic and intrinsic motivation to use computers in the workplace. *Journal of Applied Social Psychology*, *22*(14), 1111–1132. doi:10.1111/j.1559-1816.1992.tb00945.x

Dewan, S., Low, G., & Land, L. (2009). Consumer choice model of mobile banking. *Proceedings of the 20th Australasian Conference on Information Systems*. Monash University, Melbourne. 2-4.

Ericsson. (2022). *Mobile Data Traffic Outlook*. Eric's Son. https://www.ericsson.com/en/reports-and-papers/mobility-report/dataforecasts/mobile-traffic-forecast#:~:text=The%20global%20monthly%20average%20usage,to%20grow%20to%2069%20percent

Faulkner, X. (2000). *Usability Engineering*. Palgrave.

Flavian, C., Guinaliu, M., & Lu, Y. (2020). Mobile payments adoption: Introducing mindfulness to better understand consumer behavior. *International Journal of Bank Marketing*, *38*(7), 1575–1599. doi:10.1108/IJBM-01-2020-0039

Grover, P., & Kar, A. (2020). User engagement for mobile payment service providers introducing- the social media engagement model. *Journal of Retailing and Consumer Services, 53*, 101718. doi:10.1016/j.jretconser.2018.12.002

Hair, J. F., Anderson, R. E., Tatham, R. L., & Black, W. C. (1998). *Multivariate Data Analysis*. Prentice Hall International.

Hayashi, F. (2012). Mobile payments: What's in it for consumers? *Economic Review-Federal Reserve Bank of Kansas City, 35*.

Hoehle, H., Venkatesh, V., Brown, S. A., Tepper, B. J., & Kude, T. (2022). Impact of customer compensation strategies on outcomes and the mediating role of justice perceptions: A longitudinal study of target's data breach. *Management Information Systems Quarterly, 46*(1), 299–340. doi:10.25300/MISQ/2022/14740

Illia, A., Ngniatedema, T., & Huang, Z. (2015). A conceptual model for mobile banking adoption. *Journal of Management Information and Decision Sciences, 18*(1), 111–122.

Income Tax India. (2022). *Why should I pay tax?* Income Tax India. https://incometaxindia.gov.in/Charts%20%20Tables/Why%20should%20I%20pay%20tax.htm#:~:text=a)%20It%20is%20an%20admitted,too%20small%20for%20our%20country.

Jadey, S., Girish, S. C., Raghavendra, K., Srinidhi, H. R., & Anilkumar, K. M. (2022). Introduction to cyber security. In *Methods, Implementation, and Application of Cyber Security Intelligence and Analytics* (pp. 1–24). IGI Global. doi:10.4018/978-1-6684-3991-3.ch001

Joseph, J., & Ramalingam, N. (2022). Digital Payments and GST Revenue. NIPFP. https://nipfp.org.in/media/medialibrary/2022/12/JJ.pdf.pdf

Kalinic, Z., Marinkovic, V., Molinillo, S., & Libanas, F. (2019). A multi-analytical approach to peer-to-peer mobile payment acceptance prediction. *Journal of Retailing and Consumer Services, 49*, 143–153. doi:10.1016/j.jretconser.2019.03.016

Kaur, P., Dhir, A., Singh, N., Sahu, G., & Almotairi, M. (2020). An innovation resistance theory perspective on mobile payment solutions. *Journal of Retailing and Consumer Services, 55*, 102059. doi:10.1016/j.jretconser.2020.102059

Khayati, S., & Zouaoui, S. K. (2013). Perceived usefulness and use of information technology: The moderating influences of the dependence of a subcontractor towards his contractor. Journal of Knowledge Management. *Economics and Information Technology., 3*(6), 68–77.

Koivisto, M. (2008). Acceptance of mobile communication technologies in student communities, to appear in special issue on dynamic virtual communities in the information society: Technologies, methodologies, and tools. *International Journal of Web Based Communities*, *4*(3), 21–32.

Kumar, A., Adlakha, A., & Mukherjee, K. (2018). The effect of perceived security and grievance redressal on continuance intention to use M-wallets in a developing country. *International Journal of Bank Marketing*, *36*(7), 1170–1189. doi:10.1108/IJBM-04-2017-0077

Kumar, A., & Seri, S. P. (2014). *Banking on mobile wallet-achieve significant benefits through proactive involvement in mobile wallet*. Infosys.

Liao, S., & Yang, L. (2020). Mobile payment and online to offline retail business models. *Journal of Retailing and Consumer Services*, *51*, 102230. doi:10.1016/j.jretconser.2020.102230

Lin, H., & Wang, Y. (2006). An examination of the determinants of customer loyalty in mobile commerce contexts. *Information & Management*, *43*(3), 271–282. doi:10.1016/j.im.2005.08.001

Little, R. J., & Rubin, D. B. (1989). The analysis of social science data with missing values. *Sociological Methods & Research*, *18*(2-3), 292–326. doi:10.1177/0049124189018002004

Mankotia, A. (2022). Massive data usage growth in India: Economic survey. *The Economic Times*. https://economictimes.indiatimes.com/industry/telecom/telecom-news/massive-data-usage-growth-in-india-economic-survey/articleshow/89245236.cms?utm_source=contentofinterest&utm_medium=text&utm_campaign=cppst

Marinkovic, V., Đorđević, A., & Kalinić, Z. (2020). The moderating effects of gender on customer satisfaction and continuance intention in mobile commerce: A UTAUT-based perspective. *Technology Analysis and Strategic Management*, *32*(3), 306–318. doi:10.1080/09537325.2019.1655537

Mathew, M., Sulphey, M. M., & Prabhakaran, J. (2014). Perceptions and intentions of customers towards mobile banking adoption. *The Journal Contemporary Management Research.*, *8*(1), 83–101.

Mishra, A., Alzoubi, Y. I., Anwar, M. J., & Gill, A. Q. (2022). Attributes impacting cybersecurity policy development: An evidence from seven nations. *Computers & Security*, *120*, 102820. doi:10.1016/j.cose.2022.102820

Mohan, N. (2020). Electronic Payment: Arhtiyas threaten to launch stir in Haryana. *Hindustan Times*. https://www.hindustantimes.com/chandigarh/ electronic-payment-arhtiyas-threaten-to-launch-stir-in-haryana-from-march-30/story-okbVm0amzc1b3Lb0yYUmNN.html/

Nandhini, M., & Girija, K. (2019). Customer perception regards e-wallets. *International Journal of Recent Technology and Engineering.*, *8*(4), 4061–4067.

Niti Aayog. (2020). *Digital Payments: Trends, Issues and Opportunities*. Niti Aayog. http://niti.gov.in/writereaddata/files/documentpublication/DigitalPaymentBook.pdf.

Nyamtiga, B. W., Sam, A., & Laizer, L. S. (2013). Enhanced security model for mobile banking systems in Tanzania. *International Journal of Technology Enhancements and Emerging Engineering Research.*, *1*(4), 20.

Ogonowski, A., Montandon, A., Botha, E., & Reyneke, M. (2014). Should new online stores invest in social presence elements? The effect of social presence on initial trust formation. *Journal of Retailing and Consumer Services. 21*(4), 482-491. https://doi.org/ conser.2014.03.004 doi:10.1016/j.jret

Olga, S. (2018). *Determinants of customer satisfaction on Chinese and Russian m-commerce markets.* DSpace. https://dspace.spbu.ru/bitstream/11701/12520/1/SharkoMaster Thesis.pdf/

Oliver, R. L., & Westbrook, R. A. (1993). Profiles of consumer emotions and satisfaction in ownership and usage. *Journal of Consumer Satisfaction, Dissatisfaction & Complaining Behavior*, *6*(1), 12–27.

Paripunyapat, D., & Kraiwanit, T. (2018). Financial technology acceptance in Bangkok metropolis and vicinity. *Review of Integrative Business and Economics Research*, *8*(3).

Patnam, M., & Yao, W. (2020). The Real Effects of Mobile Money: Evidence from a Large-Scale Fintech Expansion. *IMF working Paper*, 20/138.

Paytm. (2020). *About Paytm India*. Paytm. https://care.paytm.ca/hc/en-us/articles/360004846313-About-Paytm-India

Praiseye, T., & John, F. (2018). A study on consumer preference towards mobile wallet. *International Journal of Research and Analytical Reviews.*, *5*(3), 185–189.

Press Information Bureau. (2022). *Transforming India's Digital Payment Landscape*. Press Information Bureau. https://pib.gov.in/FeaturesDeatils.aspx?NoteId=151163&ModuleId%20=%202

Ram & Chand. (2016). Effect of drivers' risk perception and perception of driving tasks on road safety attitude. *Transportation Research Part F: Traffic Psychology and Behaviour*, *42*(1), 162–176. 10. 1016/j.trf.2016.07.012

Rao, S., & Troshani, I. (2007). A conceptual framework and propositions for the acceptance of mobile services. *Journal of Theoretical and Applied Electronic Commerce Research*, *2*(2), 61–73. doi:10.3390/jtaer2020014

Reji, R. (2022). The complexity of payments in rural India, available https://www.cnbctv18.com/views/the-complexity-of-payments-in-rural-india-10742161.htm

Reserve Bank of India. (2020b). *Drivers of Digital Payments: A Cross Country Study*. RBI Bulletin. https://www.rbi.org.in/scripts/BS_ViewBulletin.aspx?Id=18409

Reserve Bank of India (RBI). (2020a). *Benchmarking India's Payment Systems*. RBI. https://m.rbi.org.in/Scripts/PublicationReportDetails.aspx?UrlPage=&ID=923/

Riquelme, H. E., & Rios, R. E. (2010). The moderating effect of gender in the adoption of mobile banking. *International Journal of Bank Marketing*, *28*(5), 328–341. doi:10.1108/02652321011064872

Roberts, B. W., & DelVecchio, W. F. (2000). The rank-order consistency of personality traits from childhood to old age: A quantitative review of longitudinal studies. *Psychological Bulletin*, *126*(1), 3–25. doi:10.1037/0033-2909.126.1.3 PMID:10668348

Rowland, K., & Shrauger, S. (2013). *The coming new way to pay*. Aba Bank Marketing.

Rust, R. T., & Oliver, R. L. (1994). *Service quality: Insights and managerial implications from the frontier*. Scientific Research.

Saluja, S. (2022). Identity theft fraud-major loophole for FinTech industry in India. *Journal of Financial Crime*.

Samudra, M. S., & Phadtare, M. (2012). Factors influencing the adoption of mobile banking with special reference to Pune city. *ASCI Journal of Management.*, *42*(1), 51–65.

Sharma, N. (2021). Reliance Jio's cheap data turned India's internet dreams into reality. *Quartz*. https://qz.com/india/2055771/reliance-jios-cheap-data-turned-indias-internet-dreams-into-reality

Singh, K. (2011). Innovated technology in banking services. *Journal of Internet Banking and Commerce*, *16*(2), 1–16.

Singh, N., & Sinha, N. (2020). How perceived trust mediates merchant's intention to use a mobile wallet technology. *Journal of Retailing and Consumer Services*, *52*, 101894. Advance online publication. doi:10.1016/j.jretconser.2019.101894

Singh, N., Srivastava, S., & Sinha, N. (2017). Consumer preference and satisfaction of m-wallets: A study on north Indian consumers. *International Journal of Bank Marketing*, *35*(6), 944–966. doi:10.1108/IJBM-06-2016-0086

Singh, S. (2014). Customer perception of mobile banking: An empirical study in national capital region Delhi. *Journal of Internet Banking and Commerce*, *19*(3), 2–23.

Singh, S., & Srivastava, R. K. (2020). Understanding the intention to use mobile banking by existing online banking customers: An empirical study. *Journal of Financial Services Marketing*, *25*(3), 86–96. doi:10.105741264-020-00074-w

Sujith, T. S., & Julie, C. D. (2017). Opportunities and Challenges of E-payment System in India. *International Journal of Scientific Research and Management*, *5*(9), 6935–6943.

Suls, J., & Wallston, K.A. (2008). Social Psychological Foundations of Health and Illness. *John Wiley & Sons*. http://dx.doi.org/ doi:10.1002/9780470753552

Sur, A. (2022). India saw 18 million cyber-attacks in first quarter of 2022: Google's Royal Hansen. *Money Control*. https://www.moneycontrol.com/news/business/india-saw-18-million-cyber-attacks-in-first-quarter-of-2022-google-executive-royal-hansen-9084911.html

Talwar, S., Dhir, A., Khalil, A., Mohan, G., & Islam, A. (2020). Point of adoption and beyond. Initial trust and mobile-payment continuation intention. *Journal of Retailing and Consumer Services*, *55*, 102086. doi:10.1016/j.jretconser.2020.102086

Tandon, S. (2022). Millennials in Rural India Shaping Consumption patterns in the hinterland. *Mint*. https://www.livemint.com/industry/retail/millennials-in-rural-india-shaping-consumption-patterns-in-the-hinterland-1553026089886.html

The Statesman. (2022). Password attacks rise to 921 per second: Microsoft. *The Statesman*. https://www.thestatesman.com/technology/password-attacks-rise-to-921-per-second-microsoft-1503128467.html

The Tribune. (2022). Mobile cyber-attacks on Indian firms up 845% in last 5 months. *The Tribune*. https://www.tribuneindia.com/news/delhi/mobile-cyber-attacks-on-indian-firms-up-845-in-last-5-months-238994

Tiwari, R. (2019). August 15. Direct payment system for grain farmers of Punjab, Haryana soon. *The Economic Times*. https://economictimes.indiatimes.com/news/economy/agriculture/direct-payment-system-for-grain-farmers-of-punjab-haryana-soon/ articleshow/70686123. cms?from=mdr

Tiwari, R., Chand, K., & Anjum, B. (2020). Crop Insurance in India: A Review of Pradhan Mantri Fasal Bima Yojana (PMFBY). *FIIB Business Review.*, *9*(4), 249–255. doi:10.1177/2319714520966084

Tiwari, R., Chand, K., Bhatt, A., Anjum, B., & Thirunavukkarasu, K. (2021). Agriculture 5.0 in India: Opportunities and Challenges of Technology Adoption. *A Step Towards Society 5.0*, 179-198. https://www.taylorfrancis.com/chapters/edit/10.1201/9781003138037-10/agriculture-5-0-india-rajesh-tiwari-khem-chand-arvind-bhatt-bimal-anjum-thirunavukkarasu

Tyagi, P. (2022). A whopping 303% jump! India's tax collection growth in last 12 years. *Business Today*. https://www.businesstoday.in/latest/economy/story/a-whopping-303-jump-indias-tax-collection-growth-in-last-12-years-357310-2022-12-22?onetap=true

Uloli, T., Sadasivam, G. S., & Arthi, R. (2022). Requirements analysis of security and privacy of mobile payments-Indian context. *International Journal of Mobile Communications*, *20*(6), 639–658. doi:10.1504/IJMC.2022.125923

Venkatesh, V., & Davis, F. D. (2000). A theoretical extension of the technology acceptance model: Four longitudinal field studies. *Management Science*, *46*(2), 186–204. doi:10.1287/mnsc.46.2.186.11926

Yang, K., & Lee, H. J. (2010). Gender differences in using mobile data services: Utilitarian and hedonic value approaches. *Journal of Research in Interactive Marketing*, *4*(2), 142–156. doi:10.1108/17505931011051678

Yap, C. M., & Ng, B. A. (2019). Factors influencing consumers perceived usefulness of m-wallet in Klang Valley, Malaysia. *Review of Integrative Business and Economics Research.*, *8*(4), 1–23.

Zhou, T. (2013). An empirical examination of continuance intention of mobile payment services. *Decision Support Systems*, *54*(2), 1085–1091. doi:10.1016/j.dss.2012.10.034

APPENDIX A

Standardized regression weights

Factors	Items	Standard Regression Weight
Ease of Uses(EOUS)	Understandable (Q2)	.558
	Faster service (Q5)	.732
	Beneficial (Q7)	.724
Usefulness (UFNS)	User- friendly (Q6)	.542
	Effectively (Q4)	.432
	All banking service can be performed in seconds (Q16)	.556
	Banking become easier (Q3)	.640
Self-Efficacy (SLCY)	New technology (Q28)	.425
	Easy to handle (Q17)	.802
	Comfortable (Q18)	.629
	Normal banking (Q20)	.582
	I can easily perform all the functions of m-Wallet Q24	.697
	Familiar with m-Wallet technology (Q25)	.488
Satisfaction (SFN)	Transfer money can be transferred to anyone from anywhere (Q60)	.854
	I am using m-Wallet (Q55)	.785
	Money security in m-wallet (Q58)	.567
	Need of current scenario (Q57)	.508
	Suitability offer (Q61)	.533
	Low fees charged (Q56)	.555
	Banking services can be performed from anywhere (Q62)	.839
	The persuasive offer (Q63)	.751
Security(SEC)	Security of banking details (Q35)	.711
	Secured banking details in database (Q40)	.629
	It is safe (Q33)	.706
	Virus free (Q34)	.612
	Secured from unauthorized third party (Q41)	.557
	Protected from data leakages/theft (Q39)	.592
	Security of information (Q37)	.652
	Security code not visible to other party (Q36)	.559

Sources: survey data

Chapter 6
Sustainable Business, Economic, and Environmental Practices:
An Introduction to Environmental Accounting

Vyomkesh Bhatt
https://orcid.org/0000-0001-7456-4149
G L Bajaj Institute of Technology and Management, India

Ram Singh
https://orcid.org/0000-0002-6565-3091
MM Institute of Management, Maharishi Markandeshwar (Deemed), Mullana-Ambala, India

Rohit Bansal
https://orcid.org/0000-0001-7072-5005
Vaish College of Engineering, Rohtak, India

ABSTRACT

Industrialization, urbanisation, and globalisation, all of which are essential to the contemporary industrialised economy, have come at a high cost in terms of environmental degradation. Over the years, the influence on the environment due to the adoption of these practices has been understood and accepted by many. However, it is also very apparent that these practices are necessary in order to raise the living standards of citizens in any nation whether developed or developing or underdeveloped. Due to increased public knowledge of environmental hazards,

DOI: 10.4018/978-1-6684-7568-3.ch006

customers are now more openly supporting environmentally beneficial actions in the present era. The notion of environmental accounting is one of the most crucial aspects to consider in order to assure that businesses, governments, and society as a whole are taking proactive actions to protect the environment and incorporate it into their business models. This article delves into the notion of environmental accounting, its core approach, concepts, and present situation in India.

1. INTRODUCTION

Environmental accounting was developed first in a number of European nations. Norway was one of the first countries to develop environmental accounting practices. Environmental accounting is the discipline of accounting that analyses and reports a country's economic impact on the environment or the cost of an organization's activities to the environment. Environmental accounting is the act of identifying, quantifying, and assigning environmental information costs, as well as incorporating these costs into management decisions and disseminating information to organizational stakeholders. Environmental accounting is a branch of accounting that analyses, measures, and communicates the costs of a company's environmental economic consequences.

As a result of increased environmental awareness and a crusade for long-term economic and social development, businesses throughout the world have become more conscious of the importance of environmental stewardship. In recent years, this has captivated the interest of the public at large, business organisations, and global institutions even more. In the 1990s, it became a prominent subject being addressed by nations and corporations all over the world, with varying levels of attention emanating from both within and outside of the business community. (Okoye et al., 2004)

The need for environmental accounting is founded on the principle that it will not only assist shareholders in making economic judgments regarding a firm's sustainability capabilities, but will also improve the firm's performance, strengthen its competitiveness, and promote protracted success and a good reputation, which is even a main issue for current and prospective investors. (Anazonwu et al., 2018)

For a better understanding of how nature affects the economy, green accounting is a valuable resource. It is possible to have diverse aims and opinions when it comes to environmental accounting. For example, the conservation of natural assets and the change in well-being as a result of environmental effects are simply two examples of what environmental accounting is all about (Serafy, S., 1997). Accordingly, environmental accounting may be described as a way to communicate an organization's social and environmental repercussions to relevant groups in society as well as society as a whole (Deegan, 2002).

The Kyoto Protocol is the best-known and most widely implemented instance of environmental accounting in the world. As part of the Kyoto Protocol, developed and industrialized nations signed a legally binding accord to eliminate six greenhouse emissions that are viewed as contributing to global warming. It is an example of global environmental accounting in action, as exemplified by the Kyoto Protocol. The Kyoto Protocol analyses changes in carbon emissions by referring to measurements defined by the United Nations. As a result of these collaborations, national governments bear responsibility for establishing and implementing legislation that facilitates compliance with greenhouse gas emission regulations, such as those for automobiles. (Arowoshegbe et al., 2016)

Enterprises that are subject to Kyoto Protocol inspection have embraced the active adoption of environmental accounting, not just to establish systems and implement decision-making that assures that companies remain solvent during a cycle of changes in manufacturing and air quality monitoring, which nearly invariably result in an increase in production costs. Sustainable environmental accounting systems were used by countries that decided to participate proactively in the Protocol.

Numerous significant firms, including Formosa, the British Petroleum Company, and Volkswagen's largest automotive producers, have gone belly up as a result of EA information disclosure fraud (Nguyen, 2019). It is a cautionary tale for companies to raise their level of environmental protection awareness. In recent years, there has been a growing concern regarding organizations' responsibility to report environmental data. Companies are expected to share information about EA in their reports in order to improve their performance and reputation. The firm is under pressure to improve reporting accountability as a result of investor and consumer requests, as well as European Union (EU) requirements (Spasic & Stojanovic, 2013).

Accountability for a company's environmental effects is a key component of sustainable business practices, and environmental accounting and monitoring are key components of this. Measurement of sustainability practices provides a quantitative foundation for supervision of sustainability practices. Environment Accounting plays a greater role in ensuring that companies are adhering to practices that helps in promoting sustainable development.

Data from environmental accounting may be used to account for the economic implications of ecological asset depletion and deterioration in economic strategies. If economic or revenue sustainability is an issue, economic policies can be devised to make consumers of natural resource base pay for the decline in ecological assets.

If the policy issue is ecological sustainability, or maintaining a specific standard of natural assets, then the maintenance cost technique, is used to figure out the suitable payment by users of these assets. For example, the cost of emitting 1,000 metric tonnes of SO2 is calculated to be 0.907. 396. A variety of market instruments employ similar valuation notions in the creation of policy measures intended to compel families and businesses to internalise their environmental costs and contribute to sustainability in both the economy and the environment. Users fees, effluent charges, and tradable pollution licences are examples of such devices, as are reductions or eliminations of ecologically detrimental handouts.

In course, the initial costs assessed by economic actors are not always endured by the identical entities. The eventual occurrence of environmental consequences would have to be estimated using suitable hypotheses about manufacturing and consumption of technology, as well as economic behavior (Bartelmus, 1998, p. 22). These types of modelling would indicate the consequent shift in manufacturing and consumption patterns, as well as the consequences for policy goals, distribution of income and structural transformation. Depending on the goals of the policy, the proceeds from the use of market tools might be applied in various ways. The money ought to be put in assets that support at least maintaining the level of present national income if the objective is to accomplish macro economic sustainability.

In theory, investments in human resources and capital assets might likewise be undertaken exactly as these unconventional but crucial assets contribute to revenue creation. If ecological sustainability is the primary goal, tax rates should be set to recoup the cost of maintenance, and revenues should be spent to maintain the overall stock of natural assets or to safeguard their economic and ecological functions.

Structural and sectoral changes, advocated by global financial and development agencies, are a significant tool for macroeconomic stability in many developing nations. These programmes can employ environmental accounting to incorporate natural sustainable management into financial, macroeconomic, exchange-rate, and trade policy reform.

Economic policies should be created with a set of underlying environmental and social variables, as well as the macroeconomic functions of natural capital, in mind to accomplish the broad societal sustainability objective. Policy makers should take into consideration data from the physical accounts of non-produced natural assets, industrial emissions, and asset distribution data that may be obtained when industrial categorization is connected to the generated and non-produced assets in both physical and financial terms.

Such data gives insight on the core problems of ecological sustainability and intergenerational justice, laying the groundwork for policy decisions on how much natural resources should be entrusted to future generations. The calculation of environmental costs is intended to guarantee that future generations have had access to enough capital to receive at least the benefits achieved during the present accounting period.

Sustainable Development has often been referred to as the use of resources to fulfil the economic, social, and environmental requirements of people in such a way that the interests of both the present and future generations are met as a corollary. The goal of sustainability is to ensure long-term company success while also contributing to economic and social progress, a healthy environment, and a stable society. It is about making a good difference in society while also safeguarding the communities and environment where the business operates. In this reference the important pillars of sustainability are environment, society and economy. (Johnson et al, 2021)

2. ENVIRONMENT ACCOUNTING AND INDIA

An economic momentum that was lacking in India's previous quasi-socialist system has been built over the recent decades now. The reform process appears to be producing growth, but it is also crucial to observe and channel the forces of development and economic growth in order to ensure that they significantly improve the quality of life for present and future generations. In order to manage the economy sustainably, it should also be assessed through the perspective of sustainability.

In India, yearly conferences of central and state statistics bodies explored the development of an adequate environmental statistical system for the country. The UN Foundation for the Development of Environmental Accounts was designed in the 1990s as a framework for environmental statistics. The Compendium of Environmental Statistics was originally published in 1997. In the years that followed, the Compendium was published on a yearly basis. In the year 2020, EnviStats-India 2020: Vol.I: Environment Statistics by National Statistical Office, Ministry of Statistics & Programme Implementation, Government of India was issued. Some jurisdictions have also begun to publish state-specific compendiums of environmental statistics.

Environment Accounting and conservation management of natural resources is still in its adolescent stage of practice in India. Environment Accounting consist of threefold framework comprising of Physical Accounting, Monetary Valuation and assimilation of results with the economic reports of the nation. Partha Dasgupta of Cambridge University, a distinguished environmental economist, was appointed to develop a framework of green national accounts in the year 2011 and the committee's report was submitted in 2013.

The true wealth of a nation, according to the report, is found in the number of people in a country and their structure, their level of education, the quality of their health care, and the amount of natural resources a country possesses. Net Domestic Product is computed by subtracting Gross Domestic Product with the depreciation of tangible assets such as building and equipment's, corrosion of quantity and quality of natural capital and intangible assets such as loss of human capital. The social value of the change in per capita asset stocks, not only the aggregate investment divided by the population, is the change in aggregate investment per capita.

The report further makes three critical propositions:

a. If wealth grows, an economy's development is sustainable over any small period of time.
b. In case of a favorable per capita net aggregate investment, cross generational development welfare will increase over the period of time.
c. If the National Domestic Product per capita is more than the total consumption per capita the cross generational welfare will have a progressive impact.

In India, green accounting and reporting are inadequate. There are no basic regulations regulating environmental costs and responsibilities, with the exception of the Companies Act of 2013, which allows companies to seek options for resource and environmental protection sustainability, except in their status and financial results. However, this does not imply that India does not have environmental protection rules in place; rather, it indicates that environmental accounting has yet to gain traction as a tool for environmental protection in India. (Saxena, A., 2020)

3. PROCESS OF ENVIRONMENTAL ACCOUNTING

The System of Environmental-Economic Accounting is the most comprehensive system for assessing a society's environmental imprint (SEEA). At its forty-third session in 2012, the United Nations Statistical Commission (UNSC) adopted the SEEA Central Framework as an international standard. It is the first worldwide statistical standard for accounting for environmental and economic factors. Using the SEEA Central Framework, users can better comprehend the economic and environmental ramifications of human activities as well as how environmental assets are held and how they develop over time.

Concepts, classifications, and accounting methods accepted across the globe form the basis of the Central Framework. When used as an accounting system, it allows for data integration and conceptual integrity in the tables and accounts. For a number of purposes, this data may be used to develop coherent indications that aid in decision-making as well as reports and aggregates. The SEEA framework comprises of additional twofold mechanism, i.e. SEEA Experimental Ecosystem (SEEAEE) and SEEA Extensions and Applications (SEEAEA).

No statistical standard will be established by these SEEA Experiment Ecosystem Accounts, but rather they will provide an assessment of the state of the art in applying a systems approach to ecosystem measurement in a broad framework that builds on the SEEA Central Framework. SEEAEA will provide wide range of information which can be then used for systematic decision making and analysis of previous decisions impacts.

Environmental assets and changes in their stock are included in the central framework together with economic activity and transactions that have an impact on those assets, all of which fall under the broad umbrella of the central framework.

Figure 1. SEEA central framework (SEEA UN)

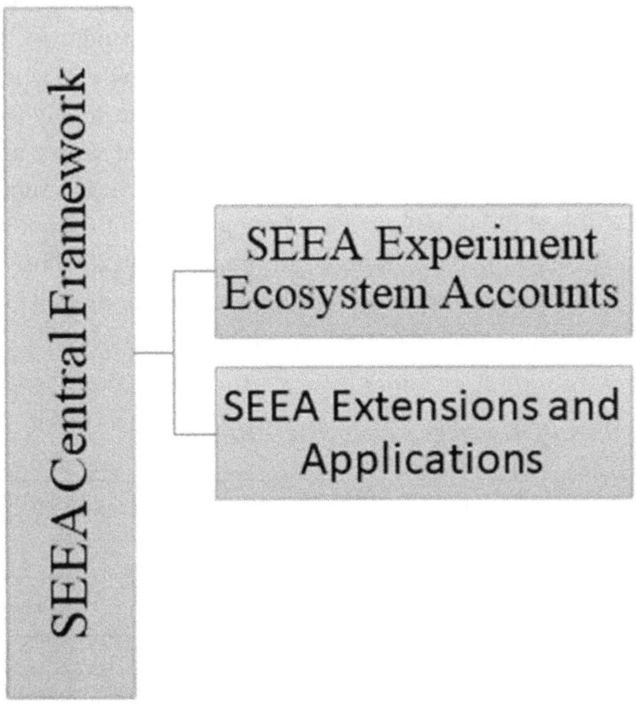

The SEEA Central Framework uses different tables and accounts to convey information about the stock, the flows in the economy and the environment. Listed below are the tables and accounts included in the Central Framework:

i. Monetary supply and usage tables(MSUT) and Physical supply and use tables (PSUT)
ii. In each accounting period, assets accounts are created for each environmental asset to record their flow i.e., the asset status quo at start of the period and

changes occurred in the assets during the period in both the physical and monetary terms

iii. SEEA framework also comprises of different economic accounts that convey information specially focused upon the economy values arrived after making adjustment for depletion during the stipulated period of time.

iv. Operating accounts related to environmental assets.

The monetary supply and usage tables keep track of all the monetary exchanges of goods and services inside a country's economy. Natural contributions from the environment, such as wood manufacturing, or activities and expenditures related to the environment, such as environmental protection expenditures, account for a large portion of product flows measured in monetary terms.

MSUT is broadly classified into two different heads, i.e supply and usage. The focus in MSUT is to have an equivalence between the total supply and total usage of any given commodity over the stipulated period of time.It is a fundamental part of both the MSUT and PSUT tables. Each commodity's entire supply is shown in the supply table by its output and imports. In simple terms, total use is the sum of consumption expenditures by households and governments, as well as gross capital formation and exports, according to the row in the table of use.

Table 1. Basic form of monetary supply and use table

	Manufacturing/ Service Industry	Household	Government	Accumulation	Rest of the world	Total
Supply Table						
Products	Output				Imports	Total Supply
Use Table						
Products	Intermediate consumption	Household final consumption expenditure	Government final consumption expenditure	Gross capital formation (including changes in inventories)	Exports	Total Use
	Value Added					

Source: SEEA UN

PSUT convey information about the supply and its subsequent usage of natural resources, products, etc. in measurable units in an economy over a specific period of time.PSUTs are used to study alterations in consumption and production patterns through time, as well as to evaluate how an economy sources and uses energy, water, and materials. Because government activity is totally documented inside the first column, Industries, the column for government is deleted to generate the PSUT. That is, the intermediate consumption linked with operations carried out by government entities is included in estimations of the industry's flow. The Households column in the PSUT is solely concerned with household consumption activities.

Table 2. Basic form of a physical supply and use table

	Manufacturing/Service Industry	Household	Accumulation	Rest of the world	Environment	Total
Supply Table						
Natural Inputs					Flows from the Environment	Total supply of natural inputs
Products	Output			Imports		Total supply of product
Residuals	Residuals generated by industry	Residuals generated by final household consumption	Residuals from scrapping and demolition of produced assets			Total supply of residual
Use Table						
Natural inputs	Extraction of natural inputs					Total use of natural inputs
Products	Intermediate consumption	Household final consumption	Gross capital formation	Exports		Total use of product
Residuals	Collection & treatment of waste and other residuals		Accumulation of waste in controlled landfill sites		Residual flows direct to environment	Total use of residual

Source: SEEA UN

Asset Accounts

Assets accounts are created to specifically convey information about the opening and closing stock levels, and the flow of stock during the accounting period of the environmental assets. Assessing whether present economic patterns deplete and degrade environmental assets is one reason for accounting for environmental assets. A more complete picture of national wealth may be gleaned from asset account data by combining environmental resource and land value estimates with other types of asset evaluations, such as production and finance. There are two stages to this process: the initial environmental asset inventory and the final environmental asset inventory. If it is possible, the nature of the rise or decrease in stock is mentioned if it can be documented. An additional word has been added to the monetary entries to indicate the revaluation of environmental assets. It takes into account the asset price movements during the stipulated period of time to specify the information about the change in asset value.

In Table 3, reclassification of stock is only applicable for asset accounts in monetary terms.

Table 3. Basic form of an asset account

Opening stock of environmental assets	
Additions to stock	
	Growth in stock
	Discoveries of new stock
	Upwards reappraisals
	Reclassifications
	Total additions to stock
Reductions in stock	
	Extractions
	Normal loss of stock
	Catastrophic losses
	Downwards reappraisals
	Reclassifications
	Total reductions in stock
Reclassification of the stock*	
Closing stock of environmental assets	

Source: SEEA UN

The relationships between environment data, physical, combined tangible, and financial accounts are depicted in Figure 2. Environment statistics primarily give fundamental data to physical accounts, which serve as the foundation for appraisal in monetary accounting. Statistics on financial environmental protection, which are immediately included in financial statements, are an exception. The graph differentiates between physical and combined physical-monetary accounting. This is in acknowledgement of the growing interest in tying actual movements of residuals to the causal economic activity as well as in simply physical material flow accounting (MFA), which offers an indicator of economic environmental constraints.

Figure 2. Environmental data relationship framework (SEEA UN)

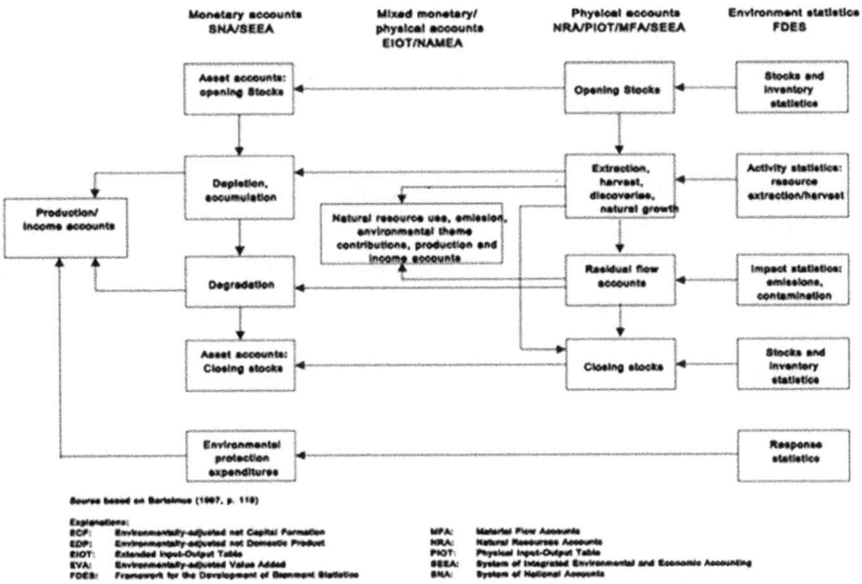

4. ACCOUNTING PRINCIPLES IN ENVIRONMENT ACCOUNTING

Some of the important accounting principles that is to be followed while practicing environment accounting are:

Double and quadruple entry accounting

In the double entry system, there must be two records for each transaction. Financial assets and debts are therefore recorded in connection with production, consumption, investment, and property income or transfer. They may have risen or been reduced. In order to maintain the integrity of the statements it is of vital importance that both parties rather than one party only to a transaction record and maintain in their respective books accurately. This is known as "quadruple entry accounting." Purchases of raw materials such as wood result in increased demand from households, decreasing cash flow and decreasing stocks, all while increasing cash flow for the timber industry. All the transactions specified in the above example needs to be recorded and maintained by all the entities for environment accounting to arrive at accurate valuation.

Time of recording

Documenting transactions when ownership shifts and a claim or liability emerges or is cancelled is the basic norm in financial accounting. Transactions are documented whenever economic value is created, altered, or deleted within a single unit. When using the accrual method, physical flows should be recorded at the same time as monetary flows. When it comes to environmental processes, the conventional calendar and financial years used in monetary accounting may have quite distinct cycles and lengths. Depending on the underlying cycles, physical and monetary adjustments should be made.

Measurement

Accounting records has to be made in monetary terms and as a result every transaction recorded and maintained needs to be measured in monetary terms. Depending on the type of asset involved, the unit of measurement for accounting in physical terms will be different. The flow of energy is frequently measured in terms of joules, the stock and flow of water in terms of cubic metres, and the flow of other materials in terms of mass, such as tonnes.

5. CHALLENGES IN ENVIRONMENT ACCOUNTING

Given that both economic growth and environmental conservation are equally vital but diametrically opposed issues, a rigorous evaluation of the benefits and costs of environmental damage is required in order to determine the tolerance limit for environmental damage and the required degree of development. It is also obvious that the majority of the environmental information given by firms is deemed to be non-financial in nature. Such material is only a description of the company's efforts.

The information on the amount of spending on such efforts and their meaningful impact on financial performance is glaringly absent. Again, there is significant variance in the reporting style and topics chosen by the firms. This can exacerbate the problem of a lack of comparison and verification. As a result, it is believed that such information should be connected with financial accounting information in order to be reliable. The monetary measurement of environmental costs and benefits is required for integration. However, all environmental costs and benefits cannot be adequately evaluated in monetary units, at least at the micro level.

In addition, there is the matter of a lack of rules pertaining to environmental accounting practices. There are no basic regulations controlling environmental costs and duties, with the exception of the Companies Act of 2013, which allows companies to seek options for resource and environmental protection sustainability, except in their status and financial performance.

6. CONCLUSION

Traditional cost accounting methodologies have become insufficient because traditional accounting processes have neglected significant environmental expenses and activities with environmental repercussions. Financial statements cannot be expected to show the condition of a "true and fair picture of operations" if essential environmental concerns and actions are not revealed.

There is no denying that progress improves people's lives and boosts the economy, but it comes at a cost. One of the biggest difficulties of the 21st century is achieving essential development without inflicting irreversible environmental damage. Over the years, social and environmental issues have been and continue to be major concerns for countries all over the world. The environment faces several issues as a result of human and industrial activity. Environmental conditions are worsening with every decade apart from ozone layer depletion which saw a positive momentum in conserving it wide range of environmental problems though known are largely being overlooked.

Environmental accounting can range from a basic tweak to current accounting systems to a more comprehensive environmental accounting strategy that connects traditional, physical, and financial information systems. "Environmental accounting" entails more than just keeping track of environmental benefits and expenditures. Environment accounting is a concrete mechanism that takes into the account environment impacts as a direct result of any entity decisions. This accounting mechanism for non-environmental costs and advantages like input pricing, customer demand, and so on will lead to favorable change in the decision making. (Goswami, M.2014)

Organisations with a longer track record of strong environmental performance were less likely to fail (Lin & Dong, 2018). Better environmental performance among companies lowers risk and demonstrates a positive relationship between value and environmental performance (Cai et al., 2016). Environmental performance may be viewed as a method in venture processes that has significant ties with many stakeholders (Oikonomou et al.,2014). (Yeh et al. 2019) claim that because Chinese businesses are more environmentally conscious, their cost of borrowed financing is lower. While investing in improving environmental responsibility performance, it will make a significant commitment to lowering companies' equity financing costs (Xu et al., 2015).

Oikonomou et al. (2014) and Salvi et al. (2018) both claim that environmental responsibility and performance strength can lower the cost of equity capital. Moreover, (Jha and Cox 2015) state that reducing the cost of loan capital is possible, and that excellent environmental responsibility performance will result in a reduction in credit availability (Ghoul et al., 2011). The amount to which EA facts are disclosed does have a beneficial effect on the financial success of businesses currently as well as in the foreseeable future (Nguyen & Tran, 2019).

Traditional accounting gives even less information on how business actions affect the environment or how high the social cost is than environmental accounting. The primary reason for this is that natural resources are not held by t he corporation and, as such, are not included in the statement of financial condition; hence, their depreciation cannot be demonstrated. In order to conserve environment it is of paramount importance that changes should be made in the legal environment of the country incorporating the environmental accounting standards, and in the same breadth the corporate sector should also focus on creating policy and guidelines focusing upon the environment conservation wherever possible in order to minimize the impact. These measures though are an arduous task but are vital for environment accounting to archive its objectives.

REFERENCES

Anazonwu, H. O., Egbunike, F. C., & Gunardi, A. (2018). Corporate Board Diversity and Sustainability Reporting: A Study of Selected Listed Manufacturing Firms in Nigeria. *Indonesian Journal of Sustainability Accounting and Management*, *2*(1), 65–78. doi:10.28992/ijsam.v2i1.52

Arowoshegbe, A., & Uniamikogbo, E. (2016). Accounting for Social and Environmental Challenges: A Theoretical Perspective. *Saudi Journal of Business and Management Studies*, *1*(3), 143–148.

Bartelmus, P. (1998). The value of nature: valuation and evaluation in environmental accounting. In K. Uno & P. Bartelmus (Eds.), *Environmental Accounting in Theory and Practice*. Kluwer. doi:10.1007/978-94-017-1433-4_16

Cai, L., Cui, J., & Jo, H. (2016). Corporate environmental responsibility and firm risk. *Journal of Business Ethics*, *139*(3), 563–594. doi:10.100710551-015-2630-4

Das, P. K. (2016). Environmental Accounting: A Conceptual Study of Indian Context. *International Journal of Social, Behavioral, Educational, Economic, Business and Industrial Engineering*, *10*(8), 2914–2920.

Deegan, C. (2002). The legitimizing effect of social and environmental disclosures – a theoretical foundation. *Accounting, Auditing & Accountability Journal, 15*(3), 282–311. doi:10.1108/09513570210435852

Enyi, P. E. (2012). Environmental and Social Accounting as an Alternative Approach to Conflict Resolutions In A Volatile and E-Business Environment. *Journal of Sustainable Development and Environmental Protection*, *4*(2), 1–7.

Ghoul, S. E., Guedhami, O. C. Y., Kwok, C., & Mishara, D. R. (2011). Does corporate social responsibility affect the cost of capital? *Journal of Banking & Finance*, *35*(9), 2388–2406. doi:10.1016/j.jbankfin.2011.02.007

Goswami, M. (2014). Corporate Environmental Accounting: the issue, its practices and challenges: A study on Indian corporate accounting practices. *IOSR Journal of Business and Management*, *16*(5), 36–42. doi:10.9790/487X-16533642

Jha, A., & Cox, J. (2015). Corporate social responsibility and social capital. *Journal of Banking & Finance*, *60*(2), 252–270. doi:10.1016/j.jbankfin.2015.08.003

Johnson, E., & Festus, A. (2021). Environmental Accounting Practices and Environmental Capacity for Sustainable Economy. *International Journal of Business and Management*, *9*(4), 225–232.

Lin, K. C., & Dong, X. (2018). Corporate social responsibility engagement of financially distressed firms and their bankruptcy likelihood. *Advances in Accounting*, *43*(1), 32–45. doi:10.1016/j.adiac.2018.08.001

Nguyen, L. S. (2019). Relationship between environmental financial accounting practices and corporate financialrisk: Evidence from listed companies in Vietnam's securities market. *Asian Economic and Financial Review*, *9*(2), 285–298. doi:10.18488/journal.aefr.2019.92.285.298

Nguyen, L. S., & Tran, M. D. (2019). Disclosure levels of Environmental Accounting information and financial performance: The case of Vietnam. *Management Science Letters*, *9*(4), 557–570. doi:10.5267/j.msl.2019.1.007

Oikonomou, I., Brooks, C., & Brooks, C. (2014). The effects of corporate social performance on the cost of corporate debt and credit ratings. *Financial Review*, *49*(1), 49–75. doi:10.1111/fire.12025

Okoye, A. E., & Ngwakwe, C. C. (2004). Environmental Accounting: A convergence of antecedent divergence. Accountancy; Management Companion. Nigerian Accounting Association (NAA).

Salvi, A., Petruzzella, F., & Giakoumelou, A. (2018). Does sustainability foster the cost of equity reduction? The relationship between corporate social responsibility (CSR) and riskiness worldwide. *African Journal of Business Management*, *12*(12), 381–395. doi:10.5897/AJBM2018.8562

Saxena, A. (2020). Environmental Accounting Practices in India. *International Journal of Scientific Research*, *9*(2), 1014–1016.

Serafy, S. (1997). Green Accounting and Economic Policy. *Ecological Economics*, *21*(3), 217–229. doi:10.1016/S0921-8009(96)00107-3

Spasi, D., Stojanovi, (2013). Sustainability reporting - theoretical framework and practice in the serbian oilindustry, *Economics and Organization*, *10*(3).

Yeh, C. C., Lin, F., Wang, T. S., & Wu, C. M. (2019). *Does corporate social responsibility affect cost of capital in China?* Asia Pacific Management Review.

ADDITIONAL READING

1Library. (n.d.). *Inland Waters - 5.3: Appendix C system of environmental-economic accounting*. 1Library. https://1library.net/article/inland-waters-appendix-c-environmental-economic-accounting.y879n6wz https://unstats.un.org/unsd/publication/seriesf/seriesf_78e.pdf

Business Doc Box. (n.d.). *SEEA Central Framework*. BDB. https://businessdocbox.com/Green_Solutions/126523986-Seea-central-framework.html

United Nations. (n.d.). *Ecosystem Accounting | System of Environmental Economic Accounting*. United Nations. https://seea.un.org/ecosystem-accounting/ https://documents1.worldbank.org/curated/en/716841468196144823/text/103743-WP-PUBLIC-central-framework.txt

Waves Partnership. (2023). *Wealth Accounting and the valuation of Ecosystem Services*. Waves Partnership. https://www.wavespartnership.org/

Chapter 7
Analyzing Artificial Intelligence From Social Science Perspectives:
Artificial Intelligence and Human Intelligence

Govind Srivastava
https://orcid.org/0000-0001-5098-9564
Jaipuria Institute of Management, India

ABSTRACT

Artificial intelligence is the most burning concept of the 21st century, and it has changed the way companies operate, governments serve, and people lead their lives. Artificial intelligence is used in various areas, such as robotics, natural language, comprehension, medical diagnosis, defense, public transportation, etc.. AI is challenging the superiority of human brains, and it is having a severe impact on human rights, family life, employment, human value, and ethics. As there are tremendous implications of artificial intelligence, it is high time to investigate the relationship between human beings and intelligent machines. On one hand, artificial intelligence produced several benefits in terms of better analysis, categorization of groups, and future prediction; on the other hand, it is impacting the right to privacy, family life, employment, freedom of expression and association. The policymakers must take a call to make a trade-off between human beings and intelligent machines.

DOI: 10.4018/978-1-6684-7568-3.ch007

INTRODUCTION

Artificial intelligence works like an intelligent machine which can think and take decisions promptly. It operates on the basis of an algorithm which instructs the machine to perform a particular type of task. The use of AI may reduce the risk associated with human life in the case of dangerous tasks. Moreover, it can work continuously without any breaks with a minimum defection rate. Artificial intelligence offers multiple benefits; it improves the shopping experience, predicts behavioural patterns, and automates communication between companies and customers through mail, chats, and social media. It is estimated that 85% of all customer interactions will take place through the intelligent machine. AI also provides real-time information as it is needed by various industries such as the public transport industry, manufacturing industry etc. Real-time data is used to track the location of public transport facilities. It is also extensively used for data mining as the extraction of relevant data is very important, keeping in mind the huge volume of the data. Klassner (2002), in his interesting work, integrated robotics with artificial intelligence.

There is various sub-area of artificial intelligence associated with robotics, natural language, comprehension, and medical diagnosis. Robots are mainly associated with mechanical engineering, and it is extensively used in various industry. AI may solve complex problems, predicts the future and can take prompt decision within a fraction of a second. AI demonstrated all its abilities in smartphones, laptops, self-operating vehicles, robots and drones. AI uses algorithms which can execute any required task provided it has access to data with adequate speed. *Most interestingly, artificial intelligence can do almost everything that we do; It suggests better holiday destinations, recommends movies which can give better enjoyment, suggest the right job, and it can drive the car more safely than us.* More importantly, it can advise whether it is sensible to be the parent, and it can also suggest whether it is wise to stay with the person for a better future or not. AI uses machine learning to draw inferences on the basis of patterns/trends. An algorithm does a better job than a human being and is free from human biases. The human brain also contains complex algorithms, but AI can do a better job than the human brain. Big data complement artificial intelligence which is used to increase the effectiveness of the algorithm. Big data is a large chunk of the data which is collected from various sources. In consumer research, Big data analytics is a very important intervention because it analyzes the preference of customers based on past trends, diagnose the reason behind particular kind of behaviour and predict future behaviour. Now a day's, big data is used in a variety of industries such as manufacturing, transportation, education, retailing, health care and financial services.

AI is challenging the superiority of human beings, and this leads to multiple consequences. This is high time to investigate the relationship between human beings and machines. AI is increasingly impacting our life ranging from household support to companionship to policing and warfare.

In the future, the distinction between human beings and machines might erode, and machines may also express emotional attachment and anxiety. A humanoid robot named Sophia was developed by Hanson Robotics. Sophia has the capability to participate in the interview. Later on, Sophia became a citizen of Saudi in the year 2017.

Innovation is continued, and Jeff Bezos recently adopted a versatile robotic pet. This robotic pet can open the door and is capable of loading the dishwasher. Human beings developed a machine which is smarter than them; such a machine contains singularity and superintelligence. As computational power is increasing day by day at an exponential pace so it is beyond the imagination what kind of challenges and threats humanoid robots will impose on human civilization. We are living in a world where a lot of intelligent machines are operating. There is a need for rules and policies so that intelligent machines can respect human rights despite the fact that machines are more intelligent than human beings. Artificial intelligence is impacting human rights and value, and it is having short, medium and long-term perspectives.

DEFINING ARTIFICIAL INTELLIGENCE

There is no acceptable definition of AI around the world. Different scholars tried to define AI based on their experience and knowledge. Some of the most accepted definition is given by Marvin Minsky and John McCarthy. Marvin Minskey defined AI as "the science of making machines do things that would require intelligence if done by men". John McCarthy, defined AI as "the science and engineering of making intelligent machines". A recent Stanford University report defines AI as "a science and a set of computational technologies that are inspired by but typically operate quite differently from the ways people use their nervous systems and bodies to sense, learn, reason, and take action".

Stuart Russell and Peter Norvig, who authored a popular book on AI, classified AI into broader categories such as AI, which thinks like a human being; AI, which acts like a human being; AI, which thinks rationally and AI, which acts rationally.

AI is classified into various sub-fields such as machine learning, robotics, neural network, neuroscience, cognitive science, computer science, probability etc. Neuroscience analyzes the brain pattern of the person using neuroimaging techniques such as FMRI, PET, TMR etc. Artificial intelligence helps to predict the behavioural pattern of the person based on the data collected through brain mapping.

Figure 1. Artificial Intelligence
Sources: https://www.gettyimages.in/photos/artificial-intelligence Sos

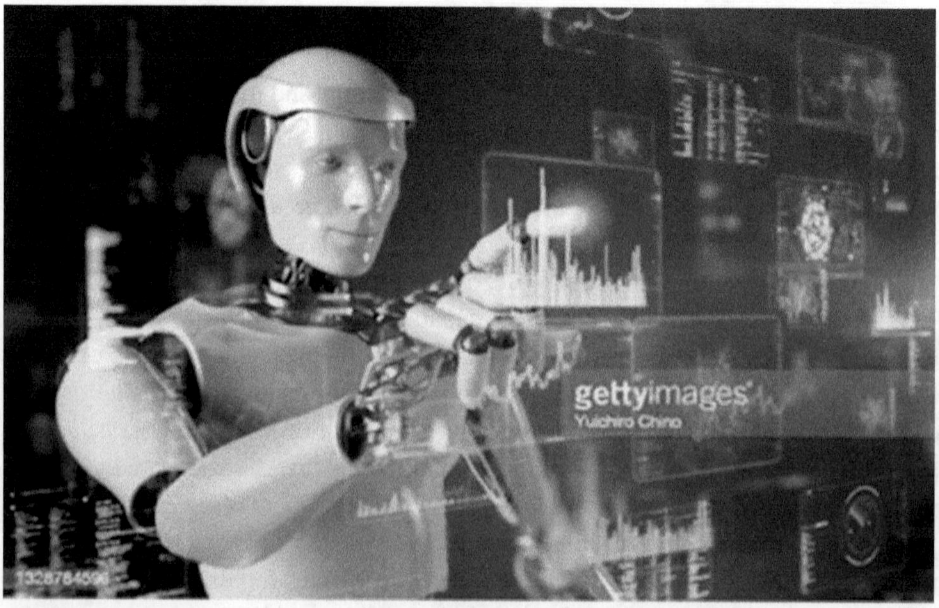

APPLICATION OF AI IN BIG DATA, MACHINE LEARNING AND DATA MINING

Almost all companies are using Big data to customize their offer and to offer better experiences to their customers. Big data contains a huge volume of data; these data are collected from various touch points such as social media websites, contests, online promotional campaigns, shopping malls etc. These data provide very important insight regarding how customers define, select, purchase and dispose of goods and services. These data are used to devise an effective marketing mix strategy. Li *et al.*(2018) discussed different types of roles in all kinds of artificial intelligence.

In the present context, data mining is the need of the hour, as a huge volume of data is available on POS and different social media websites (O'Leary,2013). Alrahhal and Abi Sen (2018) attempted to understand several research questions and emphasized on clustering and neural network. Data mining play an important role as it deals with the huge volume of complex data.

We found prominent studies on the application of artificial intelligence in drug discovery and public health (Zhu,2020; Benke,2018). Das *et al.*, (2015) also discussed the vast application of artificial intelligence. Artificial intelligence and machine learning can be used for future prediction (Alimadadi *et al.*,2020).

Figure 2. Neural network

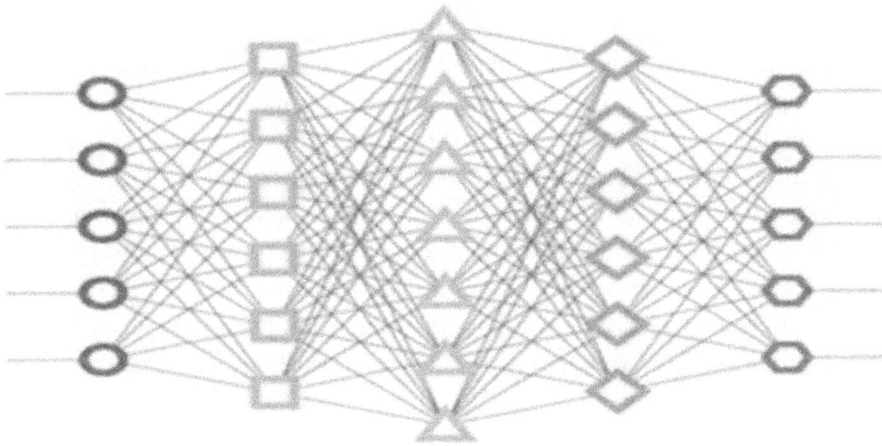

shutterstock.com · 484275202

Figure 3. Machine learning

shutterstock.com · 422669446

Khanzode and Sarode (2020) presented a comprehensive review of the advantages and disadvantages of artificial intelligence and machine learning. Riedl(2019) brought new perspectives using human-centred AI. He attempted to understand AI from sociocultural perspectives. Artificial intelligence and machine learning can be used to investigate the adverse impact of nanomaterials. Artificial intelligence and machine learning can be used in a variety of fields; Now it is extensively used in radiology for diagnosis purposes (Thrall et al.,2018)

Data mining is used to extract significant and relevant information from a huge volume of data. It is used in data visualization, machine learning and statistics. In the era of big data, data mining is felicitated by machine learning. Machine learning is the subfield of artificial intelligence. Machine learning learns from the data over a period of time. This learning is through "a statistical process that starts with a body of data and tries to derive a rule or procedure that explains the data or can predict future data." In machine learning, the output of the result is called the model. In most AI applications, researchers are using machine learning as it is more accurate and reliable. Machine learning also uses deep learning, which is based on the neural network and brain structure of the human being. Some of the important application of machine learning is machine vision, natural language processing and speech recognition. These are used by Google and Facebook.

ANALYZING THE RELATIONSHIP BETWEEN ARTIFICIAL INTELLIGENCE, HUMAN RIGHTS, AND ETHICS

Human rights are universal and binding. There are national and international laws to protect human rights. The impact of AI on human rights is a debatable and controversial issue. Ethics is a set of moral principles and it is associated with justice, fairness, transparency, accountability and privacy etc. The ethical and societal impact of AI needs to be analyzed. The major players of AI, such as Google, Face book formulated ethical principles to deal with artificial intelligence. Human rights are more well-defined and structured than ethics. Human rights and ethical principles are mutually reinforcing.

Donahoe and Metzger (2019) discussed how artificial intelligence is impacting human rights. Other significant studies on artificial intelligence and ethics were conducted by Livingston and Risse (2019); Kriebitz and Lütge (2020) ; Fernandez-Aller *et al.*, (2021).

Bostrom and Yudkowsky (2018), in their remarkable study, analyzed how artificial intelligence is different from a human being in the context of ethical assessment. Ethics have multiple perspectives; an ethical dilemma occurs when AI interact with a human being and when it takes a decision in adverse situations (Etzioni & Etzioni,2017; Dignum, 2018; Russell *et al.*,2015; Shaw, 2019; Geis *et al.*, 2019).

In the information era, everything depends on the communication network and the quality of information and in that context, ICT plays an important role in smart cities. Intelligent transport system minimizes the accident rate and traffic congestion. Artificial intelligence, deep learning and machine learning algorithms can be used for the efficient management of resources and to improve the quality of the services in smart cities (Ullah *et al.*, 2020).

A huge volume of private data is available on social media, and it can be misused. *The Cambridge Analytica scandal is a wake-up call for all of us. The company like Facebook also admitted that the private data of millions of users were stolen by hackers.*

The right to privacy and data protection is also a very important issue. It is very essential for the dignity of the person. The right to privacy is also essential for other human rights, such as freedom of expression. Now people are using digital life; they are using the internet of things, so data analysis using AI can track the data from various important touch points. Researchers have developed the ML model, which can detect age, gender, and marital status using the location of the mobile. The future location of the person can also be predicted based on past trends. Such data are private in nature. Social media is also influencing the result of the election. Analysts are using AI to analyze the information obtained from social media. Such analysis helps to predict the behaviour of users. *Monitoring and surveillance of the general population are impacting the freedom of expression and association of the general public; China invested huge capital in face recognition technology.* In the US, more than 50% of adults are covered under the face recognition system. Such type of surveillance is not needed as it cannot control crime. Moreover, it is impacting the natural behaviour of large no of people as they always feel that they are being observed all the time (24*7). Such security measure violates the fundamental right to privacy.

HOW TO MAKE VALUE ALIGNMENT BETWEEN AI AND HUMAN BEINGS

Value alignment between artificial intelligence and human beings is a big and complex issue; there is a possibility that super-intelligent machines may have different value commitments than human beings. Their priority and commitment might be different from human beings, and this may lead to different courses of action. The designer of AI must ensure that the value system of AI is aligned with the value system of human beings. Artificial stupidity is another side of the coin of AI. Few researchers are drawing attention to bias in AI. Bias in AI may occur intentionally or unintentionally. The researcher may include those parameters that he gives much importance. Moreover, data is collected by human beings, and there are always chances of natural human bias in the collection/ selection of the data. Research is still continued to address bias in AI systems. There is a possibility of error in machine learning; even if the error rate is very low, this may impact the lives of millions of people.

In the year 2015, Google photo image recognition software created chaos, and it impacted millions of users. Due to the complex ML model, an analyst could not understand why this happened. In such circumstances, a narrow error rate may produce severe consequences.

If AI is used in the judiciary without proper scrutiny and transparency, it can produce an inaccurate result. UN principles on human rights and business can be applied to AI to integrate human rights with AI.

UNDERSTANDING THE IMPACT OF AI ON FAMILY AND SOCIAL LIFE

The family is the fundamental unit of society. AI can be used for health and reproductive screening. Some people could not have children as per the result of the screening test. As AI gives the more accurate result and is widely used for diagnostics purposes so it may prevent people from marrying with those people who cannot produce a child. AI-powered testing can be also used to produce a child of desired qualities. AI is going to impact family life, marriage, and relationship significantly, and this will create an abiding impact on human emotion, personal and social life.

USE OF AI IN HEALTH CARE INDUSTRY AND ETHICAL PREDICAMENT

AI is also extensively used in the healthcare industry. It gives better diagnosis results and recommends a better treatment plan. Lio et al.,(2015) stressed on the role of artificial intelligence in diagnosis. IBM, S Watson is more accurate than Human doctors in diagnosing diseases, but sometimes it also gives the wrong result. It is the question of choosing between human doctor's advice Vs AI-recommended advice. The fact should not be forgotten that it is the question of the life and death of the patient. The policymakers must decide the right interface between Doctors and automation. The Doctors must be in the loop while using automation, and the degree of the usage of automation should be also decided in advance. AI can be also misused by Insurance companies for profiling of customers based on food habits, illness, and past trends, and these companies may charge high premiums from those customers who are vulnerable to disease.

AI also impact freedom of movement; any person can leave the country based on his wish, provided there are no legal restrictions. The person also holds the right to settle at any place based on his convenience. AI, along with satellite imagery, face recognition technology, and cell phone location, can be used by the government to restrict the movements of individuals. If AI is used by the government to decide "Who can travel", it can influence the lives of thousands of travellers if a small error occurs in the system. AI can be also used to create discrimination among the group/ communities if the government treats different groups differently.

Internationally, various international human rights laws are available; these are the Universal Declaration of Human Rights (UDHR), the International Covenant on Civil and Political Rights (ICCPR), and the International Covenant on Economic, Social and Cultural Rights (ICESCR).

IMPACT OF AI ON THE JOB MARKET

Technology has a mixed impact on society and employment. On the one hand, it creates a window of new opportunities for skilled employees, improves efficiency, and reduces operational costs and defects; at the same time, it makes people jobless due to the disruption of technology. Every new technology is a destructive force for existing technology; it makes those employees obsolete who do not upgrade their skills. Few economists stated that technological waves created more jobs than they destroyed.

Philip Alston, in his study, pointed out that automation and robotization are already throwing many middle-aged workers out of the job, even in much safer jobs.

AI created a mixed impact on the job market. Automation is being used in various industries across the world. The combination of AI with automation is creating a severe impact on the labour market. In order to address this threat imposed by AI and automation, governments are using a Universal basis income scheme for the people. The countries like Canada and Finland are testing this scheme. *The government of India is also planning to introduce such scheme to remove poverty and uplift the living standard of the people.*

The value of AI is increasing exponentially. AI industry value is projected to increase by over 13x over the next 7 years. 83% of companies claim that AI is a top priority in their business plans. It is noteworthy to mention that the global AI market is valued at over $136 billion.

IMPLICATIONS OF THE STUDY

Artificial intelligence is drawing the attention of industries and governments across the globe as it is minimizing the defection rate and increasing productivity. AI can be very much useful in a variety of the fields, such as agriculture, critical manufacturing activity, medical diagnosis, satellite engineering etc. Moreover, the government can devise the policy for the deprived section of society based on the accurate analysis done by AI. It can be also used for weather forecasting and to predict a natural disaster which can save the lives of millions of people. By 2025, as many as 97 million people will work in the AI space. According to Tech Jury: 97% of mobile users are using AI-powered voice assistants. More than 4 billion devices already work on AI-powered voice assistants. 40% of people use the voice search function at least once every day.

CONCLUSION

AI is only one decade old, so there are many unknown possibilities which are about to come. Due to excellent analytical capability, it helps to solve various problems in medical science, transportation, manufacturing, retailing and numerous fields. AI is very much helpful to visually impaired people; it can mitigate climate change and predicts natural disaster. At a slow pace, the government is also using AI in smart cities and several other projects to improve the performance of governance.

If not used wisely and ethically, AI may lead to severe negative consequences. Surveillance and face recognition technology hurt privacy, and this can be used to discriminate between groups/ communities. AI may lead to perceptual bias and it can be used to spread fake news, forged audio/video and for spreading propaganda among the targeted groups. Fake news/rumours on social media have become very sensitive issues for society/ government. It is dividing society, impacting harmony and peace and creating severe law and order issues. The application of AI can be used to spoil the image and integrity of any individual/ institution. Artificial intelligence is increasing power distance in society as financial companies are using an algorithm based on the area of residence, creditworthiness, browsing history and consumption of goods. Most importantly, some countries are developing autonomous weapons. Fully autonomous weapons are a threat to human civilization as all the decisions are taken by machines, and there is no human intervention.

REFERENCES

Alimadadi, A., Aryal, S., Manandhar, I., Munroe, P. B., Joe, B., & Cheng, X. (2020). Artificial intelligence and machine learning to fight COVID-19. *Physiological Genomics*, *52*(4), 200–202. doi:10.1152/physiolgenomics.00029.2020 PMID:32216577

Alrahhal, M. S., & Abi Sen, A. (2018). *Data mining, big data, and artificial intelligence: An overview, challenges, and research questions.*

Benke, K., & Benke, G. (2018). Artificial intelligence and big data in public health. *International Journal of Environmental Research and Public Health, 15*(12), 2796. doi:10.3390/ijerph15122796 PMID:30544648

Bostrom, N., & Yudkowsky, E. (2018). The ethics of artificial intelligence. In *Artificial intelligence safety and security* (pp. 57–69). Chapman and Hall/CRC. doi:10.1201/9781351251389-4

Das, S., Dey, A., Pal, A., & Roy, N. (2015). Applications of artificial intelligence in machine learning: Review and prospect. *International Journal of Computer Applications, 115*(9), 31–41. doi:10.5120/20182-2402

Dignum, V. (2018). Ethics in artificial intelligence: Introduction to the special issue. *Ethics and Information Technology, 20*(1), 1–3. doi:10.100710676-018-9450-z

Donahoe, E., & Metzger, M. M. (2019). Artificial intelligence and human rights. *Journal of Democracy, 30*(2), 115–126. doi:10.1353/jod.2019.0029

Etzioni, A., & Etzioni, O. (2017). Incorporating ethics into artificial intelligence. *The Journal of Ethics, 21*(4), 403–418. doi:10.100710892-017-9252-2

Fernandez-Aller, C., de Velasco, A. F., Manjarres, A., Pastor-Escuredo, D., Pickin, S., Criado, J. S., & Ausin, T. (2021). An inclusive and sustainable artificial intelligence strategy for europe based on human rights. *IEEE Technology and Society Magazine, 40*(1), 46–54. doi:10.1109/MTS.2021.3056283

Geis, J. R., Brady, A. P., Wu, C. C., Spencer, J., Ranschaert, E., Jaremko, J. L., Langer, S. G., Borondy Kitts, A., Birch, J., Shields, W. F., van den Hoven van Genderen, R., Kotter, E., Wawira Gichoya, J., Cook, T. S., Morgan, M. B., Tang, A., Safdar, N. M., & Kohli, M. (2019). Ethics of artificial intelligence in radiology: Summary of the joint European and North American multisociety statement. *Radiology, 293*(2), 436–440. doi:10.1148/radiol.2019191586 PMID:31573399

Khanzode, K. C. A., & Sarode, R. D. (2020). Advantages and Disadvantages of Artificial Intelligence and Machine Learning: A Literature Review. [IJLIS]. *International Journal of Library and Information Science, 9*(1), 3.

Klassner, F. (2002, February). A case study of LEGO Mindstorms'™ suitability for artificial intelligence and robotics courses at the college level. In *Proceedings of the 33rd SIGCSE technical symposium on Computer science education* (pp. 8-12). 10.1145/563340.563345

Kriebitz, A., & Lütge, C. (2020). Artificial intelligence and human rights: A business ethical assessment. *Business and Human Rights Journal*, *5*(1), 84–104. doi:10.1017/bhj.2019.28

Li, L., Lin, Y. L., Zheng, N. N., Wang, F. Y., Liu, Y., Cao, D., Wang, K., & Huang, W. L. (2018). Artificial intelligence test: A case study of intelligent vehicles. *Artificial Intelligence Review*, *50*(3), 441–465. doi:10.100710462-018-9631-5

Liao, P. H., Hsu, P. T., Chu, W., & Chu, W. C. (2015). Applying artificial intelligence technology to support decision-making in nursing: A case study in Taiwan. *Health Informatics Journal*, *21*(2), 137–148. doi:10.1177/1460458213509806 PMID:26021669

Livingston, S., & Risse, M. (2019). The future impact of artificial intelligence on humans and human rights. *Ethics & International Affairs*, *33*(2), 141–158. doi:10.1017/S089267941900011X

O'Leary, D. E. (2013). Artificial intelligence and big data. *IEEE Intelligent Systems*, *28*(2), 96–99. doi:10.1109/MIS.2013.39

Riedl, M. O. (2019). Human-centred artificial intelligence and machine learning. *Human Behavior and Emerging Technologies*, *1*(1), 33–36. doi:10.1002/hbe2.117

Russell, S., Hauert, S., Altman, R., & Veloso, M. (2015). Ethics of artificial intelligence. *Nature*, *521*(7553), 415–416. doi:10.1038/521415a PMID:26017428

Shaw, J. (2019). Artificial intelligence and ethics. *Harvard Magazine*, 30.

Thrall, J. H., Li, X., Li, Q., Cruz, C., Do, S., Dreyer, K., & Brink, J. (2018). Artificial intelligence and machine learning in radiology: Opportunities, challenges, pitfalls, and criteria for success. *Journal of the American College of Radiology*, *15*(3), 504–508. doi:10.1016/j.jacr.2017.12.026 PMID:29402533

Ullah, Z., Al-Turjman, F., Mostarda, L., & Gagliardi, R. (2020). Applications of artificial intelligence and machine learning in smart cities. *Computer Communications*, *154*, 313–323. doi:10.1016/j.comcom.2020.02.069

Winkler, D. A. (2020). Role of artificial intelligence and machine learning in nanosafety. *Small*, *16*(36), 2001883. doi:10.1002mll.202001883 PMID:32537842

Zhu, H. (2020). Big data and artificial intelligence modeling for drug discovery. *Annual Review of Pharmacology and Toxicology*, *60*(1), 573–589. doi:10.1146/annurev-pharmtox-010919-023324 PMID:31518513

Chapter 8
Data Democratization:
Empowering Employees for Data-Driven Innovation

Sasari Samarasinghe
University of Southern Queensland, Australia

Sachithra Lokuge
https://orcid.org/0000-0003-4558-687X
University of Southern Queensland, Australia

ABSTRACT

The exponentially growing usage and its benefits of digitizing data, as well as changes in data management practices, are continuously moderating the global economy and how organizations perform business operations. While data security is at its prime importance, organizations tend to move from traditional data silo models to inter-organizational data openness and sharing models where everyone who needs access to data is empowered to find, access, interoperate, and reuse (FAIR) data without gatekeepers. The phenomenon of 'data democratization' has gained attention among practitioners and scholars in recent years as a process of managing inter-organizational open data and empowering employees to develop their innovative, creative, and decision-making skills. Thus, the objective of this book chapter is to focus on this new phenomenon of data democratization and understand how it can support the development of data-driven innovative skills among employees to generate social and economic values based on the results of an in-depth systematic literature review.

DOI: 10.4018/978-1-6684-7568-3.ch008

INTRODUCTION

The value of the data depends on the context of use, use of data analytics and the extent to which data can be reused (Adikari et al. 2021; Smet et al. 2021). With the fourth industrial revolution (Industry 4.0), real-time operations with data-driven practices have gained more attention as an enabler for a fast and efficient way of resolving issues and improving the operations (Harland et al. 2022; Sedera et al. 2016; Sedera et al. 2022). According to NewVantagePartners (2022) "Data and artificial intelligence (AI) Executive Survey 2022," among 94 Fortune 1000 companies who participated in the survey, 97% of organizations claimed that they are investing in data initiatives, which is an increasing trend compared to previous years (Lokuge and Sedera 2018). The advancement of technologies and the value of data have led to exponential growth to empower business leaders and decision-makers to make decisions based on facts, trends, and statistics by accessing the right information at the right time (Leonard 2018; Lokuge and Duan 2021; Lokuge et al. 2018). With this move, industries realized the importance of openness of data for decision-makers by removing data silos (Lokuge and Sedera 2020; Lokuge et al. 2020a). The necessity for this transformation has been further encouraged with the recent pandemic and the nature of business moving to a decentralized hybrid form such as "working from home." As such, democratization of data has gained attention as a novel process of broadening access to data, using data, interacting, and sharing appropriate data for employees that are required to perform their job and make decisions with the help of data and analytics tools within the boundaries of legal, confidentiality and security limitations (Samarasinghe et al. 2022). In the traditional information technology (IT)-ownership model, for managing organizational data, usually limited access is provided for technical data users such as IT team, data engineers etc. However, with the introduction of novel concepts such as data democratization, both technical data users as well as non-technical users who work on the front-line of the business will have access to data and empowered for efficient and accurate decision-making, collaboration, and will enable to become a contributor of the knowledge-sharing culture (Awasthi and George 2020; Labadie et al. 2020; Lefebvre et al. 2021; Lokuge et al. 2020b; Lokuge et al. 2018).

One of the key benefits of data democratization is to empower employees to make decisions based on digitalization and digitization to achieve competitive advantage over traditional data management practices (Sedera et al. 2021; Török 2020). Empowerment fosters creativity and innovation by offering true ownership to employees for their work and contribution. Data in raw format is less informative and time consuming to sort, analyze, and make decisions. With the help of analytical solutions, both data and analytics together help organizations and employees for accurate decision-making and to optimize their performance (Lokuge and Sedera

2014b; Lokuge et al. 2019; Sedera and Lokuge 2019b; Sedera and Lokuge 2019c; Su et al. 2022).

Data-driven innovation (DDI) is the application of data and analytics to support the discovery and execution of innovation to deliver business value (OECD 2015). According to Gartner (2022), based on their analysis of data and analytics trends, data literacy, analytics talent, and addressing the scarcity of data through appropriate strategies are considered as the key drivers for accurate decision-making with the help of data and analytics (Gartner 2022). Therefore, when data is democratized, and appropriate analytical tools are provided for employees (data consumers) with continuous learning and training to improve data literacy and skills would empower employees to use data and analytics for decision-making and uplift their capabilities (Ghasemaghaei and Calic 2019; Lefebvre et al. 2021; Lokuge and Sedera 2014a; Lokuge et al. 2016a). Thus, it is assumed that data democratization fosters the innovative capabilities of employees, but there is a lack of studies that discuss the link between these two phenomena. Thus, the objective of this book chapter is to investigate, through a systematic literature review, the association between data democratization and data-driven innovation. Thereby, this book chapter attempts to provide future research areas for researchers in both management and information systems (IS) disciplines.

The remainder of the book chapter proceeds as follows. First, the methodology followed during the literature review process is provided. The analysis section provides the outcomes of the analysis and the summary of the literature considered for the study. Further, an overview of data democratization and data-driven innovation is provided. Finally, this chapter concludes by providing future research directions to both management and IS scholars.

RESEARCH BACKGROUND

Data Democratization

The objective of the core concept of data democratization attempts to provide inter-organizational open data access to both technical and non-technical employees who need access to data, analyze data, and share data within the appropriate legal and security boundaries with the help of analytical tools and appropriate data literacy (Awasthi and George 2020; Lefebvre et al. 2021). Rather than a one-time change, data democratization is considered as an "ongoing process" (Awasthi and George 2020). However, data democratization does not mean that every employee in the organization is given access to all data that is not relevant to perform their job; yet data democratization establishes grounds to provide access to find, use, interact, and share data that is required to perform their job without waiting for pre-authorization and obstacles that delay the decision-making and operational processes. Therefore, as in Figure 1, the essence of data democratization consists of several attributes such as enabling access to digital data for both technical and non-technical employees, providing continuous training to uplift their data literacy and analytical skills, implementing necessary confidentiality, legal and security limitations to prevent data misuse, transferring data ownership and responsibility to employees to ensure the accountability of accessing and using data and the actions they take etc. In addition, promoting a collaborating and knowledge-sharing culture is also important as organizational culture is a key element to drive this change positively within the organization, and this entails providing appropriate analytical tools that serve data and analytics needs of data consumers as well (Gable et al. 2008; Samarasinghe et al. 2022; Sedera and Gable 2010).

Figure 1. Attributes of data democratization

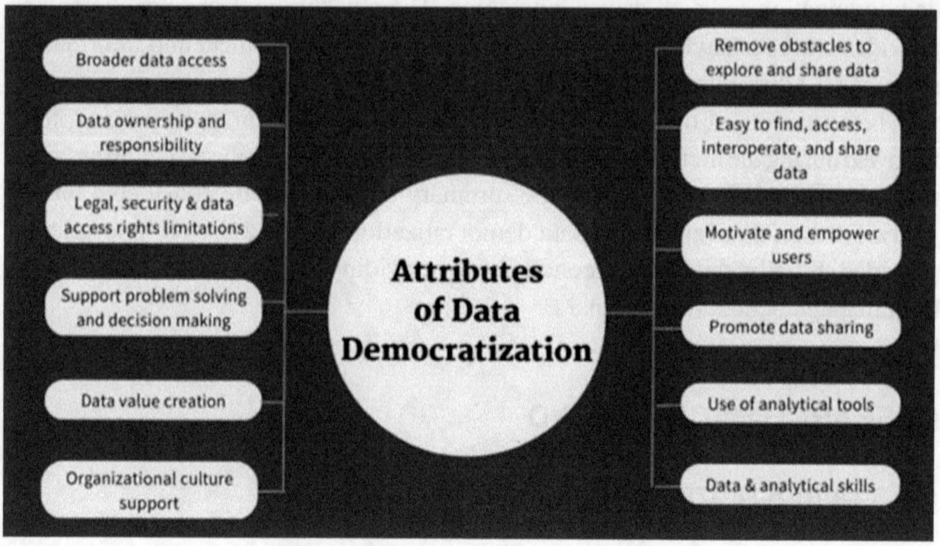

The role of the citizen data scientist (i.e., an individual who has a contextualized vision of the organization and his/her individual business area and, performs data analytics tasks and draws conclusions related to his/her job but is not a data scientist in a profession nor does not have a formal knowledge of data analytics and statistics) is prominent in data democratization, as it empowers every employee irrespective of their technical knowledge on data and analytics to use self-service analytical tools to prepare data, solve problems, and justify business value with the help of data (Awasthi and George 2020; Sedera and Dey 2013). Thus, to build successful citizen data scientists, the organization should build and promote collaborative culture between citizen data scientists and expert data scientists, who are technically capable of handling data analytics and statistics (Awasthi and George 2020; Lefebvre et al. 2021).

The goal of data democratization is to support problem-solving and empower data consumers to make fast and accurate decisions using data and analytics (Awasthi and George 2020; Hinds et al. 2021; Lefebvre et al. 2021; Shamim et al. 2021), to achieve a competitive advantage with improved operations and reducing response time (Awasthi and George 2020), and develop individual innovativeness through data value creation (Awasthi and George 2020; Lefebvre et al. 2021; Shamim et al. 2021; Zotoo et al. 2021). The future of democratized data enables employees within an organization to access explicit and data-driven insights which could be used to resolve operational issues, offer solutions, and unlock new capabilities for employees through simplification and empowerment.

Open Data and Data Democratization

In both management and IS literature, "open data" is often defined as data which is free to use, reuse, and redistribute (Awasthi and George 2020; Doctor and Joshi 2021). It benefits citizens, governments, and businesses by increasing the quality and transparency of information dissemination cost-effectively (Doctor and Joshi 2021; EuropeanCommission 2020). At the same time, open government data (OGD) is gaining more popularity due to its benefits to both the public and government by promoting transparency and accountability and providing access to government data to all citizens to empower them to contribute and engage with government initiatives (EuropeanCommission 2020). Open data creates its economic value by being a driver for economic growth and contributing to the development of innovative business models and services (EuropeanCommission 2020). It also offers social value by empowering citizens to contribute to policymaking and maintain engaging relationships with the government.

However, data democratization differentiates from 'open data' and 'open government data' as in data democratization, it considers providing inter-organizational open data for employees with several other attributes described above as it is not only giving access to data (Awasthi and George 2020).

Data Security and Data Governance

With the growing demand for data and analytics, organizations are more focused towards becoming data driven (NewVantagePartners 2021). However, proliferation of both data consumers and the volume of data organization has impelled data security issues to forefront. Data security ensures that data is accessed, used, and shared withing appropriate legal, confidentiality and security boundaries (Awasthi and George 2020). Data democratization mandates inter organizational open data access and self-service model, which intersects the data democratization and data security. Therefore, it is important to design and implement privacy at the data level as a part of data governance framework. The data producers should understand the needs of data consumers (i.e., both technical and non-technical employees), as well as data consumers should understand the requirements and restrictions of data production and usage processes to avoid data misuse (Wells 2021). Having a strong data governance with well-defined and internally consistent data is essential to ensure data security and privacy (Hinds et al. 2021; Samarasinghe and Lokuge 2022). Therefore, it is important to ensure that employees are well-aware and ethically responsible of how to use data within accepted legal, confidentiality and security guidelines defined by data governance framework (Hinds et al. 2021; Marinakis et al. 2021). Also, the data governance framework should ensure (1) data lifecycle is governed in a controlled and secure manner, (2) establishing organization-wide rules and policies to enforce data governance, data quality and data security, (3) improve collaborations between data governance and security teams and data stewards, and (4) use proactive controls to identify and protect from threats in real-time (Daruwalla 2020).

Moving to the Cloud

Data is the most important material for data democratization and data-driven innovation (Awasthi and George 2020; Hossain et al. 2022). Trillions of data being produced daily by a firm and to ensure secure storage, real-time backups with cost-effective server maintenance, organizations move from their on-premises (on-prem) physical servers to cloud-based servers such as Amazon Web Services (AWS), Microsoft Azure, Google cloud (Sedera et al. 2002; Walther et al. 2013). Most organizations eventually settle on a hybrid cloud setup, where there are on-prem servers as well as multiple cloud servers to deploy workloads. However, it is important to store, secure and govern all data distributed among those hybrid environments (Moorhead 2023). These technology and cloud infrastructure investments are to be done in a more proactive approach where data is democratized and available for all users, so that it is possible for them to make data-driven decisions. Self-service is essential so that data consumers – especially non-technical employees who are referred to as citizen data scientists can find, access, explore and visualize information in their job to make data-driven decisions (Moorhead 2023). However, it is important to have a strong data governance framework that ensures data security and privacy are not violated by employees.

Role of Data Analytics in Data Democratization

Self-service analytics tools are important in data democratization as they allow data consumers to analyze data and derive data-driven decisions. Technologies such as artificial intelligence (AI) and machine learning models help organizations to make data usable and turn data into insights rapidly (Alsheibani et al. 2018). While analytics requires specific skillset in general, in data democratization, by using AI, machine learning, natural language querying and data transformation techniques offer producing and delivery insights directly to data consumers based on their requirements.

While technology strengthens the data democratization efforts, analytical tools strengthen data democratization opportunities (Lefebvre et al. 2021). They empower data consumers to self-analyse data according to their data needs (Lefebvre et al. 2021; Zotoo et al. 2021). However, organisations should increase awareness among employees to use right tool to find data (Samarasinghe and Lokuge 2022).

Data-Driven Innovation

Data-driven innovation (DDI) helps organizations to improve and promote their products and processes, discover new market models, as well as to introduce process improvements for organizational growth and sustainability (Lokuge et al. 2021; Zillner 2021). The advancement of technologies and data digitization support organizations to empower employees and develop their innovation capabilities through data value creation (Jetzek et al. 2014). Data can be used and reused within the space they have been developed for using data-enabled innovation (Trabucchi and Buganza 2019). Thus, data-driven innovation is referred to organizations using data and analytics to empower employees at all levels to improve and develop their innovative capabilities to improve and promote products, services, processes, and business models to achieve competitive advantage (Granell et al. 2022; Zillner 2021). Technological advancements, cost-effective data storage and processing options, and advanced analytical self-service tools have made organizations realize the benefits and value of using data and analytics by converting into a data-driven organization and promoting data-enabled innovations (Chatterjee et al. 2021).

The success of data-driven innovation depends on the organization-level and individual-level factors (Babu et al. 2021; Bhatti et al. 2022; Janssen et al. 2017). At the organization-level, it is important that the organization has robust analytical capabilities, technological capabilities, top management support, strong data governance practices, as well as, most importantly a data-driven culture (Babu et al. 2021; Janssen et al. 2017; Shi et al. 2022). At the individual level, the knowledge, and capabilities of employees in using data and analytics, as well as the willingness to upskill data literacy, and use data and analytics on the job is vital (Ahmad et al. 2013; Sedera et al. 2004; Shi et al. 2022).

Based on DDI literature, transforming from traditional and digital innovation to data-driven innovation requires providing access to data for employees at every level (i.e., removing data silos), data literacy and analytical capabilities of the employees, strong data governance framework and importantly a supporting data-driven culture (Cronholm et al. 2017; Lokuge and Duan 2023). These factors are related to data access, analytics, and security, which are associated with the data democratization process. Thus, this study analyses the existing literature on both data democratization and data-driven innovation to theoretically support evidence to assess how data democratization can empower employees for data-driven innovation.

Digital Transformation and Data-Driven Innovation

Digital transformation enables organizations to use digital technologies to create new or modify existing processes, customer experience, and culture to meet changing business and market requirements (Adhikari Egodawele et al. 2022; Egodawele et al. 2023; Tabrizi et al. 2019). Digital transformation can vary from organization to organization. To enable data-driven digital transformation, it requires to overcome data fragmentation and to minimize data gaps. By implementing a comprehensive data strategy to assist the organization to consolidate, analyze, synchronize data, digital transformation can help organizations to overcome data fragmentation and reduce gaps in data. In data-driven approach, organizations gain unique insights into their operations that improve their business strategy, operations, and embrace digital transformation (Forbes 2022). Digital technologies allow organizations to look at their business through the lens of data without the lens of process (Forbes 2022). Use of digital technologies facilitates innovation within the organization (Wong and Ngai 2022).

To facilitate DDI, data, analytics and use of digital technologies are important to create value from data to produce meaningful insights (Sultana et al. 2022). While both digital transformation and data-driven innovation are crucial parts of data-driven business, organizations find it challenging due to various reasons. These challenges include lack of necessary resources and tools, poor leadership support, lack of capabilities and skills withing the organization, absence of clear vision etc., that drop the organization readiness to accept the transformation. Therefore, it is important to ensure the organizational readiness so that the data-driven digital transformation can build and maintain the right infrastructure and culture to facilitate DDI, ensuring that organization can stay at the forefront of their market.

Data-Driven Innovation Process

According to the literature, a seven-steps process has been introduced by scholars Babu et al. (2021) and Sultana et al. (2021). The DDI process begins with conceptualising the needs of the market and developing further steps to introduce products addressing the market needs (Babu et al. 2021). After conceptualising new data products catering to customer needs, the next step is data acquisition, in which data are captured from all data sources. In the data refinement stage, structured and unstructured data will be refined to create an implementable data structure (Akter et al. 2021b). A robust data management platform is important under the storage and retrieval step to deal with the velocity, variety and volume of unstructured data (Wang et al. 2018). The data distribution model is essential to foster learning and problem-solving through collaborative problem-solving mechanisms (Sultana et al. 2021). To facilitate the presentation and monetization of data, organisations should integrate unique models supported by analytics capabilities (Akter et al. 2021b; Sultana et al. 2021). This is supported by having a unified data platform that can share data across organisational boundaries for a better presentation of data products to target stakeholders (Sultana et al. 2021). The final step is market feedback. Customer feedback is important in DDI because it helps to improve products and services as well as to measure customer satisfaction and create a better customer experience (Sultana et al. 2021). The below Figure 2 represents the stages of data-driven innovation process adopted from the literature.

Figure 2. Steps in DDI process

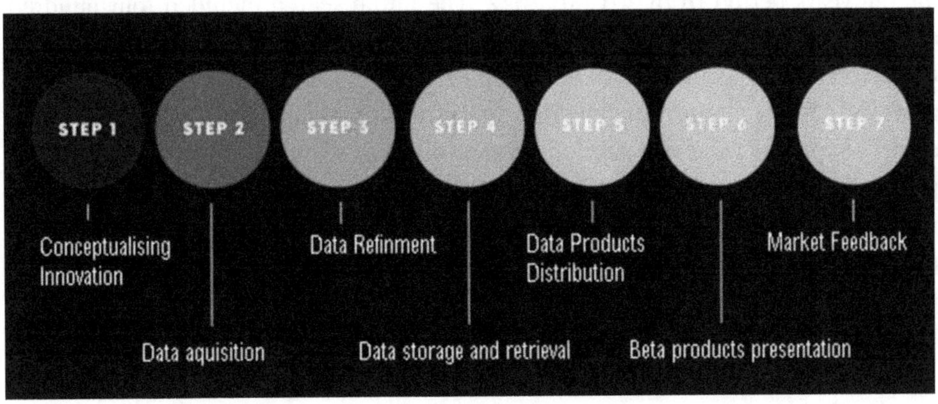

RESEARCH METHODOLOGY

This section of the book chapter elaborates on the methodology detailing the search strategy, IS and Management journals reviewed for the analysis, synthesizing literature, and analyzing the results related to data democratization and data-driven innovation literature. For the analysis, the study included published research articles from 2013 to 2022. The study followed the systematic literature review model of Levy and Ellis (2006). The study considered nine (09) online databases - AIS virtual library, Wiley online library, Taylor & Francis online library, Emerald insight, Springer, ScienceDirect, IEEE, ACM digital library, and Scopus – for the analysis. The analysis included both journals and IS conference articles related to the topic, as both data democratization and data-driven innovation research areas are still growing.

When searching for the literature, the search strategy was spanned to cover literature published on both data democratization and data-driven innovation, without limiting the search strategy specific to filter research that discussed both areas together. These two areas of related research are still understudied in-depth and reviewing the literature in a wide scope of both phenomena allowed the researchers to canvass a substantial body of developing literature related to data democratization and data-driven innovation. The search strategy included a range of keywords such as "data democratization" OR "data democratisation" OR "data-driven innovation" OR "data-enabled innovation" OR "big data innovation" OR "data-infused innovation" OR "data innovation" OR "data-based innovation" AND "empower*." Due to the language fluency limitation of the researchers, the study considered articles published in the English language.

The initial search highlighted that most of the articles had been published within the ten years period from 2013 to 2022. The initial search included four hundred and four (404) papers. After screening and reviewing each article, articles unrelated to the research objective or not matching the study's topic were excluded from the analysis. After applying the exclusion criteria and removing duplicate articles, forty-eight (48) papers were selected for the analysis of this study. The authors read each paper carefully, analyzed them individually and documented essential information identified as important for this study. Table 1 lists the references for the IS and management articles used for the systematic literature review.

Table 1. Summary of literature used for the analysis

Year	References	No. of Papers
2022	(Bhatti et al. 2022), (Eichler et al. 2022), (Fadler and Legner 2022), (Hertzano and Mahurkar 2022), (Hopf et al. 2022), (Lefebvre and Legner 2022), (Liang et al. 2022), (Samarasinghe et al. 2022), (Shi et al. 2022), (Su et al. 2022), (Wang et al. 2022), (Zhao and Kamioka 2022)	12
2021	(Akter et al. 2021a), (Babu et al. 2021), (Belhadi et al. 2021), (Bresciani et al. 2021), (Chatterjee et al. 2021), (Chaudhuri et al. 2021), (Hinds et al. 2021), (Kanbara and Shaw 2021), (Kozak et al. 2021), (Lefebvre et al. 2021), (Marinakis et al. 2021), (Ostern and Perscheid 2021), (Visvizi et al. 2021), (Saura et al. 2021), (Shamim et al. 2021), (Sitar-Tăut 2021), (Zotoo et al. 2021)	17
2020	(Awasthi and George 2020), (Hyun et al. 2020), (Labadie et al. 2020), (Rizk and Elragal 2020)	04
2019	(Bharati and Chaudhury 2019), (Ghasemaghaei and Calic 2019), (Hyun et al. 2019), (Trabucchi and Buganza 2019)	04
2018	(Zeng and Glaister 2018)	01
2017	(Chandy et al. 2017), (Cronholm et al. 2017), (Dwivedi et al. 2017), (Janssen et al. 2017), (Keller et al. 2017), (Sorescu 2017), (Troilo et al. 2017)	07
2015	(Bosch-Sijtsema and Bosch 2015)	01
2014	(Jetzek et al. 2014)	01
2013	(Provost and Fawcett 2013)	01

FINDINGS

This section provides the findings of the analysis. First, an overview of the main concepts is provided below. The objective of this study was to investigate how the democratization of data would lead to empowering employees for data-driven innovation through data value generation. Despite the potential significance of data democratization, based on existing research and anecdotal evidence, data democratization is still growing and far from its true potential. Many existing studies have discussed the attributes, success factors, and industrial applications of data democratization, but the spectrum of innovation and value creation is still understudied. Based on the analysis, it was evident that data and analytics are two key inputs for data democratization and data-driven innovation. A common assumption is that when data can be freely accessed and available in more informative formats, it will lead to value creation and support innovation (Jetzek et al. 2014). However, empirical research studies in this area have the potential for growth.

The three main phases of the innovation process are idea generation, idea conversion, and idea diffusion (Jetzek et al. 2014). Several research studies have pointed out various factors that support data-driven innovation. The most commonly identified key requirements are; (i) broader access to data for employees, (ii) comprehensive data governance and privacy policy, (iii) data validity and complete data, (iv) use of appropriate analytical tools and sufficient data analytics skills among employees, (v) motivation of employees to accept the change (Babu et al. 2021; Bhatti et al. 2022; Cronholm et al. 2017; Ghasemaghaei and Calic 2019).

These key requirements are the key attributes of the data democratization process that ensure employees are given access to data to use, analyze, interact, and share within the appropriate legal boundaries and empower them to make decisions, develop innovative thinking and derive conclusions using data and self-service analytics (Figure 3). Therefore, based on the analysis, this study attempts to identify how data democratization would help organizations empower employees to participate in the innovation process by using data and analytics.

Figure 3. Innovations driven by data and analytics

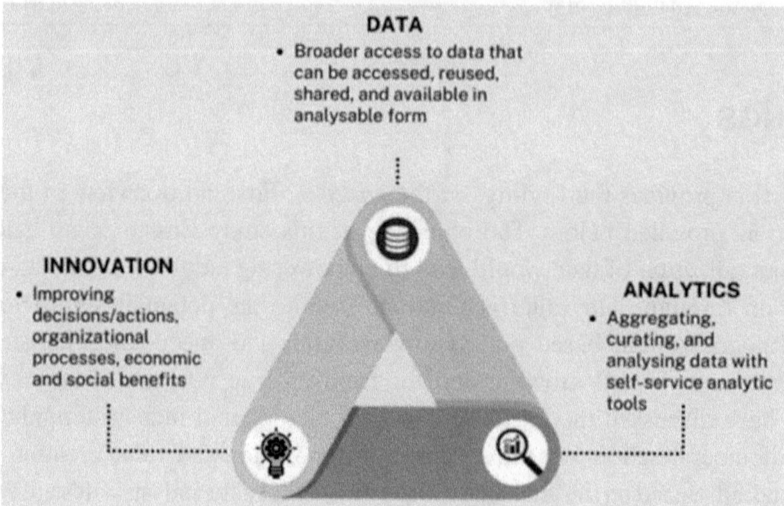

Data Democratization for Promoting Data-Driven Innovation

The following benefits of implementing data democratization can help organizations to promote and practice data-driven innovation as explained below.

1. Increase Data Access and Data Usage for Employees

Data silos are segregated groups of data that provide access to a limited or one group of people and are stored in different multiple applications, and often managed by gatekeepers assigned by the organization (Lokuge et al. 2016b; Patel 2019). The main aim of data democratization is to broaden the inter-organizational openness to data for both technical and non-technical employees to access, use, analyze and share data appropriately for performing their job (Awasthi and George 2020; Labadie et al. 2020; Lefebvre et al. 2021). Increasing data access and data mobility allows employees to access the information they need when they want to perform their job (Babu et al. 2021; Lokuge and Sedera 2016). While providing data access is important, the data should also be explored to determine whether the envisioned value proposition can be realized and whether the data is of high quality to ensure the accuracy of decisions and the idea generation process (Zillner 2021).

Data democratization unlocks the potential for employees to create organizational value with access to the data (Awasthi and George 2020), which is important for the data-driven innovation (Bhatti et al. 2022). In order to form ideas using data and analytics, therefore having access to data, use data and interact data without bottlenecks is important. Thus, democratization of data can support data access and idea generation among every employee to empower them to become data-driven innovators in the organization.

2. Comprehensive Data Governance Framework

When broadening data access, data-driven innovation requires trustworthy governance and data privacy to prevent data misuse, inaccurate data access or outdated decisions (Chatterjee et al. 2022). According to a 2021 survey of Fortune 1000 companies, 48.5% of respondents had claimed that they use data as the basis for their innovation, and implement a data governance framework to facilitate consistently, compact, and clean data for employees to support their innovative thinking is important (NewVantagePartners 2021). Thus, the absence of quality governance not only loses data-driven opportunities; but also wastes resources.

In data democratization, having strong data governance and privacy policy is one of the key attributes to ensure both technical and non-technical employees access data that is accurate, current, and valid and ensures that data ownership is a shared responsibility of both employees who access data and the organization (Samarasinghe et al. 2022). In traditional data management practices, the main issue is that top management is often unaware of the potential for data value creation by having strong data governance. Therefore data-driven initiatives and innovation efforts often become ineffective (Trabucchi and Buganza 2019). Data democratization strategy ensures that the organization implements a strong governance framework and empowers employees to become data native and to create data acumen (Marinakis et al. 2021). Thus, data democratization offers a more reliable data foundation and mitigates the risk of data misuse with good governance to enable new innovative ideas to flourish.

3. Increase Data Validity, Data Accuracy and Data Completeness

To empower employees for data-driven innovation, the accuracy of data, quality and completeness of data is essential. Inaccurate and incomplete data may result in wrong decisions and ideas that might create a risk for business operations (Jetzek et al. 2014). Inaccurate and incomplete data will not only impact emerging new ideas enabled by data and analytics but also, the conversion or development of ideas into an outcome such as a product or service, as well as the idea diffusion phase where it is adopted by and used to ensure customization, individualization, and continuous delivery (Rizk and Elragal 2020).

Data democratization ensures that the organization create rigorous standards to evaluate data for its completeness, accuracy, timeliness and consistency by formatting, cleaning, and processing unstructured data that is understandable to both technical and non-technical employees (Lefebvre et al. 2021). With data democratization organizations educate non-technical employees about data quality management so that they can identify inconsistencies and errors to raise them or fix those by themselves (Awasthi and George 2020; Marinakis et al. 2021). Thus, data democratization empowers employees to not only access and interpret data, but also to act on the intelligence they glean from the job-relevant data they deal with to develop data-driven insights and ideas that can help for the betterment of the organization.

4. Improve Data Analytical Skills and Data Literacy Among Employees

Data-driven innovation requires employees to use analytical tools to assess and develop insights for making data-driven decisions and developing ideas. Providing access to data is not sufficient for employees, especially non-technical employees, to develop data-driven innovative insights (Zillner 2021). Employees should be able to easily find, retrieve, understand, and analyze data. With the help of self-service analytical tools, data can be displayed in readable, user-friendly formats and data visualization tools to easily identify data trends and patterns to derive insights (Lefebvre et al. 2021; Rizk and Elragal 2020).

Continuous training on developing data analysis skills and improving data literacy is another important attribute of the data democratization process (Awasthi and George 2020; Lefebvre et al. 2021; Samarasinghe et al. 2022; Zotoo et al. 2021). Especially, when expanding the data access and data analytics to non-technical employees, the knowledge and skills levels are not equally distributed within the organization. If employees are unaware and lack data skills, it can lead to employee demotivation due to information overload and changes in their job tasks. With data democratization, employees' normal job function is included with the data analytics tasks as well which were earlier done by technical employees (Lefebvre et al. 2021). Therefore, the data democratization process includes organization-wide training and education to encourage and create opportunities to practice and use data comfortably can increase employee confidence in using data and analytics (Lefebvre et al. 2021; Sedera and Lokuge 2019a). Thus, it will empower employees to make informed and data-driven decisions. Data democratization provides more freedom and empowers employees to have more responsibility for the data they use, process, manage and share, which will reduce errors. Thus, employees are empowered and build confidence to promote developing new ideas and data-driven innovative insights.

5. A Data-driven Culture to Motivate and Empower Employees to use Data and Analytics to Develop their Innovative Capabilities

Having a data-driven culture is a key pillar for successfully implementing a data-driven environment in an organization. According to a 2022 survey of Fortune 1000 companies, even more than 98% responded that they invest in data initiatives, but only 21% responded that they could create a data-driven culture (NewVantagePartners 2022). Therefore, data-driven culture highly influences the innovation process and makes the pathway for organizations to become more competitive in the industry (Chatterjee et al. 2021). The main essence of a data-driven culture is to empower employees to make decisions based on analytics and insights obtained from the data (Lefebvre et al. 2021). To promote data utilization in daily operations among employees at every level of the organization conventional decision-making strategy based on strong beliefs and assumptions should be discontinued and develop trust and commitment among all employees to empower them to use data and analytics for daily operations (Lokuge and Sedera 2019).

The data democratization process ensures the organizational culture readiness to promote data utilization among both technical and non-technical employees to make decisions based on analytics and insights (Awasthi and George 2020; Labadie et al. 2020; Lefebvre et al. 2021). A positive work culture promotes employee engagement, productivity, and experience, and reduces the resistance for accepting new changes to work processes and organizational procedures (Labadie et al. 2020). Therefore, in an organization where data democratization is being practiced, the organizational culture can accelerate the application of data and analytics and motivate and empower employees to develop new insights using data and analytics to improve products, services, and processes.

FUTURE RESEARCH DIRECTIONS

When analyzing the literature related to identifying how data democratization empowers employees for data-driven innovation, the following future research areas were identified which has potential importance and contribution to IS body of knowledge.

- **Data value generation through data democratization to promote innovativeness**: Promoting innovativeness through data value creation is one of the benefits of data democratization that has been mentioned by several authors in their studies. However, case analysis or an empirical study on this area is still untouched. Therefore, as a future research area, considering the findings of this book chapter literature analysis, the study can extend to validate findings with real-world data.
- **Economic and social value generation through inter-organizational open data – "data democratization"**: The literature on open data and open government data (OGD) has discussed the economic and social value created for both citizens and government. However, a study on this area of inter-organizational open data in a democratized data setting for employees and the organization is still not studied. Therefore, this could be another future research area as identifying economic and social value generation is important to empower both employees and organizations to move from traditional data management practices to data-driven practices.
- **Contribution of data democratization in the innovation mechanism – idea generation, idea conversion and idea diffusion**: Identifying data-driven innovation mechanism and how it influences the impact of data democratization by broadening access to inter-organizational open data for employees and empowering them to use data and analytics would be another interesting area of study for future research. Further, the study can extend to analyze economic values and the social impact of data-driven innovation, as in innovation literature, social values are less discussed and analyzed.
- **Data-driven innovation strategies**: Using digital innovation strategies, resource-based view, dynamic capability theory and management literature, IS researchers can identify data-driven innovation strategies in a data-driven

context. Digital innovation literature has been established over the period, and a comparison of how innovation strategies change from digital innovation to data-driven innovation would be an interesting area of study for future research.

CONCLUSION

In the global digital economy, the true power of data and analytics has motivated organizations to shift their interest in investing in data-driven initiatives to support business growth and thrive in market challenges. The primary goal of an organization is to transform themselves into data-driven entities and empower employees to use data and analytics in decision making, problem solving, idea generation, and in return to increase profitability and business growth. The legacy data management practices such as IT-ownership model restricted data access only to a selected individual or group of individuals in the organization creating data silos. With the growing demand of data and market pressure created from pandemics such as COVID-19 has changed this legacy practices and data silo models to reduce response time, derive accurate decisions, and draw conclusions by empowering employees who are non-technical but more knowledgeable about the organization vision and the business function they are involved in. Data democratization is a data management practice that helps organizations to remove data silos and empower both technical and non-technical employees to access, use, interact, share, and reuse data with the help of self-service analytic tools to produce efficient and effective decisions. It ensures employees (also known as citizen data scientists) are given access to data and use data within the appropriate legal boundaries to empower them using data and value generating from data. In data democratization literature, it is discussed that data democratization helps to create data value and support innovation, but however, a thorough investigation into this phenomenon is still limited. While data-driven innovation is gaining more attention with organizations transferring to data-driven practices, it is timely to study how data-driven practices such as data democratization empower data-driven innovation. Thus, this book chapter attempted to summarize the findings of the existing academic publications and to further the understanding of how data democratization support data-driven innovation.

In reviewing the academic publications on data democratization and data-driven innovation, it was evident that the innovation aspect of data democratization has not yet received its due diligence and there are several areas where academics need to pay attention to. The objective of this book chapter was to examine the literature to support how data democratization can empower employees to data-driven innovation. After analyzing 48 papers related to data democratization and data-driven innovation, the authors identified five key benefits of the data democratization process that could resolve the key barriers towards data-driven innovation and promote data-driven innovation within the organization.

The findings of this study contribute to the academic body of knowledge by providing IS scholars with future directions for studying the notion of data-driven innovation with democratized data. It also contributes to the data democratization and DDI body of knowledge as both research areas are still growing. Also, the study contributes to innovation literature by identifying how inter-organizational open data management practices can empower people and facilitate innovations. There are practical implications as well. The study helps practitioners to empower employees to develop their innovative capabilities of using data and analytics. Also, the findings of this book chapter can be used by organizations to identify new capabilities and new skills within the organization that can support successful implementation of data democratization and data-driven innovation. As the future research areas, this book chapter identified several areas such as value generation through data democratization, promotion of data-driven innovation through data democratization, promoting innovation, economic, and social value generation through inter-organizational open data, the contribution of data democratization in the innovation process, and data-driven innovation strategies.

REFERENCES

Adhikari Egodawele, M. H., Sedera, D., & Bui, V. (2022). A Systematic Review of Digital Transformation Literature (2013–2021) and the Development of an Overarching a-Priori Model to Guide Future Research. In *Australasian COnference on Information Systems*. AIS.

Adikari, A., Burnett, D., Sedera, D., de Silva, D., and Alahakoon, D. (2021). Value Co-Creation for Open Innovation: An Evidence-Based Study of the Data Driven Paradigm of Social Media Using Machine Learning. *International Journal of Information Management Data Insights* (1-2), 100022.

Ahmad, M. N., Zakaria, N. H., & Sedera, D. (2013). Ontology-Based Knowledge Management for Enterprise Systems. In *Competition, Strategy, and Modern Enterprise Information Systems* (pp. 184–212). IGI Global. doi:10.4018/978-1-4666-2464-1.ch010

Akter, S., McCarthy, G., Sajib, S., Michael, K., Dwivedi, Y. K., D'Ambra, J., & Shen, K. N. (2021a). *Algorithmic Bias in Data-Driven Innovation in the Age of Ai*. Elsevier. doi:10.1016/j.ijinfomgt.2021.102387

Akter, S., McCarthy, G., Sajib, S., Michael, K., Dwivedi, Y. K., D'Ambra, J., & Shen, K. N. (2021b). *Algorithmic Bias in Data-Driven Innovation in the Age of Ai.* Elsevier. doi:10.1016/j.ijinfomgt.2021.102387

Alsheibani, S., Cheung, Y., & Messom, C. (2018). Artificial Intelligence Adoption: Ai-Readiness at Firm-Level.

Awasthi, P., & George, J. J. (2020). A Case for Data Democratization. In *Americas Conference on Information Systems*. Virtual: AIS Library.

Babu, M. M., Rahman, M., Alam, A., & Dey, B. L. (2021). Exploring Big Data-Driven Innovation in the Manufacturing Sector: Evidence from Uk Firms. *Annals of Operations Research, 21*(April), 1–28. doi:10.100710479-021-04077-1 PMID:33897083

Belhadi, A., Mani, V., Kamble, S. S., Khan, S. A. R., & Verma, S. (2021). Artificial Intelligence-Driven Innovation for Enhancing Supply Chain Resilience and Performance under the Effect of Supply Chain Dynamism: An Empirical Investigation. *Annals of Operations Research*, 1–26. doi:10.100710479-021-03956-x PMID:33551534

Bharati, P., & Chaudhury, A. (2019). Assimilation of Big Data Innovation: Investigating the Roles of It, Social Media, and Relational Capital. *Information Systems Frontiers 21*(6), 1357-1368.

Bhatti, S. H., Hussain, W. M. H. W., Khan, J., Sultan, S., & Ferraris, A. (2022). Exploring Data-Driven Innovation: What's Missing in the Relationship between Big Data Analytics Capabilities and Supply Chain Innovation? *Annals of Operations Research*, 1–26. doi:10.100710479-022-04772-7

Bosch-Sijtsema, P., & Bosch, J. (2015). User Involvement Throughout the Innovation Process in High-Tech Industries. *Journal of Product Innovation Management, 32*(5), 793-807.

Bresciani, S., Ciampi, F., Meli, F., & Ferraris, A. (2021). Using Big Data for Co-Innovation Processes: Mapping the Field of Data-Driven Innovation, Proposing Theoretical Developments and Providing a Research Agenda. *International Journal of Information Management, 60*, 1–15. doi:10.1016/j.ijinfomgt.2021.102347

Chandy, R., Hassan, M., & Mukherji, P. (2017). Big Data for Good: Insights from Emerging Markets. *Journal of Product Innovation Management, 34*(5), 703-713.

Chatterjee, S., Chaudhuri, R., Shah, M., & Maheshwari, P. (2022). Big Data Driven Innovation for Sustaining Sme Supply Chain Operation in Post Covid-19 Scenario: Moderating Role of Sme Technology Leadership. *Computers & Industrial Engineering, 168*, 168. doi:10.1016/j.cie.2022.108058 PMID:36569991

Chatterjee, S., Chaudhuri, R., & Vrontis, D. (2021). Does Data-Driven Culture Impact Innovation and Performance of a Firm? An Empirical Examination. *Annals of Operations Research*, 1–26. doi:10.100710479-020-03887-z

Chaudhuri, R., Chatterjee, S., Vrontis, D., & Thrassou, A. (2021). Adoption of Robust Business Analytics for Product Innovation and Organizational Performance: The Mediating Role of Organizational Data-Driven Culture. *Annals of Operations Research*, 1–35. doi:10.100710479-021-04407-3

Cronholm, S., Göbel, H., & Rittgen, P. (2017). Challenges Concerning Data-Driven Innovation. *The 28th Australasian Conference on Information Systems*, (pp. 1-11). Hobart Australia: Australasian Conference on Information Systems

Daruwalla, B. (2020). Data Democratization: Balancing Risk Vs Reward through Data Governance. *Data Protection*. Security Intelligence. https://securityintelligence.com/posts/data-democratization-governance/

Doctor, G., & Joshi, P. (2021). Empowering Cities through Open Data-Open Government Data Initiatives in India. *14th International Conference on Theory and Practice of Electronic Governance*, India. 10.1145/3494193.3494241

Dwivedi, Y.K., Janssen, M., Slade, E.L., Rana, N.P., Weerakkody, V., Millard, J., Hidders, J., & Snijders, D. (2017). Driving Innovation through Big Open Linked Data (Bold): Exploring Antecedents Using Interpretive Structural Modelling. *Information systems frontiers, 19*(2), 197-212.

Egodawele, M., Sedera, D., Grover, V., Seneviratne, D., & Sooriyapperuma, B. (2023). "Shooting 'Yohani'to Global Stardom: A Teaching Case of Social Media Strategy of a Top-10 Youtuber," *Communications of the Association for Information Systems, 52*(1), p 21.

Eichler, R., Gröger, C., Hoos, E., Schwarz, H., & Mitschang, B. (2022). Data Shopping—How an Enterprise Data Marketplace Supports Data Democratization in Companies. *International Conference on Advanced Information Systems Engineering*, (pp. 19-26). Springer. 10.1007/978-3-031-07481-3_3

EuropeanCommission. (2020). *The Benefits and Value of Open Data*. EC. https://data.europa.eu/en/publications/datastories/benefits-and-value-open-data

Fadler, M., & Legner, C. (2022). Data Ownership Revisited: Clarifying Data Accountabilities in Times of Big Data and Analytics. *Journal of Business Analytics, 5*(1), 123-139.

Forbes. (2022). Why Data-Driven Insights Are Critical to Digital Transformation. *Forbes.* https://www.forbes.com/sites/forbesbusinessdevelopmentcouncil/2022/05/10/why-data-driven-insights-are-critical-to-digital-transformation/?sh=67b34fad78c2

Gable, G.G., Sedera, D., & Chan, T. (2008). Re-Conceptualizing Information System Success: The Is-Impact Measurement Model. *Journal of the Association for Information Systems 9*(7), 377-408.

Gartner. (2022). *Gartner Identifies Three Imperatives Driving the Top Trends in Data and Analytics for 2022.* Gartner. https://www.gartner.com/en/newsroom/press-releases/2022-03-29-gartner-identifies-three-imperatives-driving-the-top-trends-in-data-and-analytics-for-2022

Ghasemaghaei, M., & Calic, G. (2019). Does Big Data Enhance Firm Innovation Competency? The Mediating Role of Data-Driven Insights. *Journal of Business Research, 104*, 69–84. doi:10.1016/j.jbusres.2019.07.006

Granell, C., Mooney, P., Jirka, S., Rieke, M., Ostermann, F., Van Den Broecke, J., Sarretta, A., Verhulst, S., Dencik, L., & Oost, H. (2022). *Emerging Approaches for Data-Driven Innovation in Europe: Sandbox Experiments on the Governance of Data and Technology*, 93-97.

Harland, T., Hocken, C., Schröer, T., & Stich, V. (2022). Towards a Democratization of Data in the Context of Industry 4.0. *Sci 4*(3), 29.

Hertzano, R., & Mahurkar, A. (2022). Advancing Discovery in Hearing Research Via Biologist-Friendly Access to Multi-Omic Data. *Human Genetics, 141*(3-4), 1–4. doi:10.100700439-022-02445-w PMID:35235019

Hinds, T.L., Floyd, N.D., & Ueland, J.S. (2021). Policy and Praxis in Data Democratization Efforts: A Case Study of Minnesota State's Equity 2030. *New Directions for Institutional Research 189*(192), 53-70.

Hopf, K., Weigert, A., & Staake, T. (2022). Value Creation from Analytics with Limited Data: A Case Study on the Retailing of Durable Consumer Goods. *Journal of Decision Systems*, 1–37. doi:10.1080/12460125.2022.2059172

Hossain, M. A., Quaddus, M., Hossain, M. M., & Gopakumar, G. (2022). Data-Driven Innovation Development: An Empirical Analysis of the Antecedents Using Pls-Sem and Fsqca. *Annals of Operations Research*, 1–43. doi:10.100710479-022-04873-3 PMID:36570556

Hyun, Y., Hosoya, R., & Kamioka, T. (2019). The Moderating Role of Democratization Culture: Improving Agility through the Use of Big Data Analytics. In *Pacific Asia Conference on Information Systems*. Virtual: AIS Library.

Hyun, Y., Kamioka, T., & Hosoya, R. (2020). Improving Agility Using Big Data Analytics: The Role of Democratization Culture. *Pacific Asia Journal of the Association for Information Systems, 12*(2), 35-63.

Janssen, M., Konopnicki, D., Snowdon, J.L., & Ojo, A. (2017). Driving Public Sector Innovation Using Big and Open Linked Data (Bold). *Information Systems Frontiers 1*(2), 189-195.

Jetzek, T., Avital, M., & Bjorn-Andersen, N. (2014). Data-Driven Innovation through Open Government Data. *Journal of theoretical and applied electronic commerce research, 9*(2), 100-120.

Kanbara, S., & Shaw, R. (2021). Disaster Risk Reduction Regime in Japan: An Analysis in the Perspective of Open Data, Open Governance. *Sustainability, 14*(1), 19.

Keller, S., Lancaster, V., & Shipp, S. (2017). Building Capacity for Data-Driven Governance: Creating a New Foundation for Democracy. *Statistics and Public Policy, 4*(1), 1-11.

Kozak, J., Kania, K., Juszczuk, P., & Mitręga, M. (2021). Swarm Intelligence Goal-Oriented Approach to Data-Driven Innovation in Customer Churn Management. *International Journal of Information Management*, *60*, 1–16. doi:10.1016/j.ijinfomgt.2021.102357

Labadie, C., Legner, C., Eurich, M., & Fadler, M. (2020). Fair Enough? Enhancing the Usage of Enterprise Data with Data Catalogs. *2020 IEEE 22nd Conference on Business Informatics (CBI)*, (pp. 201-210). IEEE. 10.1109/CBI49978.2020.00029

Lefebvre, H., & Legner, C. (2022). How Communities of Practice Enable Data Democratization inside the Enterprise. In *ECIS 2022 Proceedings*. AIS Virtual Library.

Lefebvre, H., Legner, C., & Fadler, M. (2021). Data Democratization: Toward a Deeper Understanding. *Forty-Second International Conference on Information Systems*, (pp. 1-17). AIS Library, .

Leonard, K. (2018). The Role of Data in Business. *Small Business*. https://smallbusiness.chron.com/role-data-business-20405.html

Levy, Y., & Ellis, T. J. (2006). A Systems Approach to Conduct an Effective Literature Review in Support of Information Systems Research. *Informing Science*, 9. doi:10.28945/479

Liang, X., Li, G., Zhang, H., Nolan, E., & Chen, F. (2022). Firm Performance and Marketing Analytics in the Chinese Context: A Contingency Model. *Journal of Business Research*, *141*, 589–599. doi:10.1016/j.jbusres.2021.11.061

Lokuge, S., & Duan, S. X. (2021). Towards Understanding Enablers of Digital Transformation in Small and Medium-Sized Enterprises. *Australasian Conference on Information Systems*. AIS.

Lokuge, S., & Duan, S. X. (2023). Exploring the Enablers of Digital Transformation in Small and Medium-Sized Enterprises. Handbook of Research on Business Model Innovation Through Disruption and Digitalization), pp 136-156.

Lokuge, S., & Sedera, D. (2014a). Deriving Information Systems Innovation Execution Mechanisms. *Australasian Conference on Information Systems*, Auckland, New Zealand.

Lokuge, S., & Sedera, D. (2014b). Enterprise Systems Lifecycle-Wide Innovation Readiness. *Pacific Asia Conference on Information Systems*. AIS.

Lokuge, S., & Sedera, D. (2016). Is Your It Eco-System Ready to Facilitate Organizational Innovation? Deriving an It Eco-System Readiness Measurement Model. *International Conference on Information Systems*, AIS.

Lokuge, S., & Sedera, D. (2018). The Role of Enterprise Systems in Fostering Innovation in Contemporary Firms. *Journal of Information Technology Theory and Application (JITTA), 19*(2), 7-30.

Lokuge, S., & Sedera, D. (2019). Attaining Business Alignment in Information Technology Innovations Led by Line-of-Business Managers. *Australasian Conference on Information Systems*, Perth, Australia.

Lokuge, S., & Sedera, D. (2020). Fifty Shades of Digital Innovation: How Firms Innovate with Digital Technologies. *Pacific Asia Conference on Information Systems*, AIS.

Lokuge, S., Sedera, D., Ariyachandra, T., Kumar, S., & Ravi, V. (2020a). The Next Wave of Crm Innovation: Implications for Research, Teaching, and Practice. *Communications of the Association for Information Systems, 46*(1), 560-583.

Lokuge, S., Sedera, D., Atapattu, M., & Samaranayaka, D. (2016a). Exploring the Role of Is in Agriculture: Creating an Agenda Towards Agri-Informatics. *Pacific Asia Conference on Information Systems*, AIS.

Lokuge, S., Sedera, D., Cooper, V., & Burstein, F. (2021). Digital Transformation: Environmental Friend or Foe? Panel Discussion at the Australasian Conference on Information Systems 2019. *Communications of the Association for Information Systems* (48), 47. 10.17705/1CAIS.04846

Lokuge, S., Sedera, D., & Grover, V. (2016b). Thinking inside the Box: Five Organizational Strategies Enabled through Information Systems. *Pacific Asia Conference on Information Systems*, AIS.

Lokuge, S., Sedera, D., Grover, V., & Xu, D. (2019). Organizational Readiness for Digital Innovation: Development and Empirical Calibration of a Construct. *Information & Management, 56*(3), 445-461.

Lokuge, S., Sedera, D., & Palekar, S. (2020b). The Clash of the Titans: Cio and Lob Engagement in It Innovation. In K. Sandhu (Ed.), *Leadership, Management, and Adoption Techniques for Digital Service Innovation* (pp. 86–102). IGI Global. doi:10.4018/978-1-7998-2799-3.ch005

Lokuge, S., Sedera, D., & Perera, M. (2018). The Clash of the Leaders: The Intermix of Leadership Styles for Resource Bundling *Pacific Asia Conference on Information Systems*, AIS.

Marinakis, V., Koutsellis, T., Nikas, A., & Doukas, H. (2021). AI and Data Democratisation for Intelligent Energy Management. *Energies, 14*(14), 43-41.

Moorhead, P. (2023). Data Democratization in a Hybrid World. *Forbes*. https://www.forbes.com/sites/patrickmoorhead/2023/02/23/data-democratization-in-a-hybrid-world/?sh=12b63b192a9c

NewVantagePartners. (2021). Newvantage Partners Releases 2021 Big Data and Ai Executive Survey. The Journey to Becoming Data-Driven. *Data And AI Executive Survey 2021*. Business Wire. https://www.businesswire.com/news/home/20210104005022/en/NewVantage-Partners-Releases-2021-Big-Data-and-AI-Executive-Survey

NewVantagePartners. (2022). The Quest to Achieve Data-Driven Leadership: A Progress Report on the State of Corporate Data Initiatives. *Data And AI Executive Survey 2022*. https://www.newvantage.com/_files/ugd/e5361a_ad5a8b3da8254a71807d2dccdb0844be.pdf

OECD. (2015). Data-Driven Innovation: Big Data for Growth and Well-Being, 1-456. OECD.

Ostern, N. K., & Perscheid, G. (2021). Solve for Blockchain: Toward a Framework for Navigating Blockchain Tensions. In *ICIS 2021 Proceedings* (pp. 1–9). AIS Virtual Library.

Patel, J. (2019). Bridging Data Silos Using Big Data Integration. *International Journal of Database Management Systems, 11*(3), 01-06.

Provost, F., & Fawcett, T. (2013). Data Science and Its Relationship to Big Data and Data-Driven Decision Making. *Big data, 1*(1), 51-59.

Rizk, A., & Elragal, A. (2020). Data Science: Developing Theoretical Contributions in Information Systems Via Text Analytics. *Journal of Big Data, 7*(7), 1-26.

Samarasinghe, S., & Lokuge, S. (2022). Exploring the Critical Success Factors for Data Democratization. In *ACIS 2022 Proceedings*. ACIS.

Samarasinghe, S. S. U., Lokuge, S., & Snell, L. (2022). Exploring Tenets of Data Democratization. PACIS 2022 Proceedings, (pp. 1-5). Virtual: AIS Electronic Library (AISeL).

Saura, J. R., Ribeiro-Soriano, D., & Palacios-Marqués, D. (2021). From User-Generated Data to Data-Driven Innovation: A Research Agenda to Understand User Privacy in Digital Markets. *International Journal of Information Management, 60*, 102331. doi:10.1016/j.ijinfomgt.2021.102331

Sedera, D., & Dey, S. (2013). User Expertise in Contemporary Information Systems: Conceptualization, Measurement and Application. *Information & Management, 50*(8), 621–637.

Sedera, D., Gable, G., & Palmer, A. (2002). Enterprise Resources Planning Systems Impacts: A Delphi Study of Australian Public Sector Organisations. *Pacific Asia Conference on Information Systems*, AIS.

Sedera, D., & Gable, G.G. (2010). Knowledge Management Competence for Enterprise System Success. *The Journal of Strategic Information Systems, 19*(4), 296-306.

Sedera, D., Gable, G. G., & Chan, T. (2004). Knowledge Management as an Antecedent of Enterprise System Success. N.C. Romano (ed.), *Americas Conference on Information Systems*. AIS.

Sedera, D., & Lokuge, S. (2019a). Do We Put All Eggs in One Basket? A Polynomial Regression Study of Digital Technology Configuration Strategies. *International Conference on Information Systems*. AIS.

Sedera, D., & Lokuge, S. (2019b). Does It Get Better over Time? A Longitudinal Assessment of Enterprise System User Performance. *Information Technology & People, 33*(4), 1098-1123.

Sedera, D., & Lokuge, S. (2019c). From Punctuation to Equilibrium: A Longitudinal Assessment of Enterprise Systems User Performance. Academy of Management Proceedings. Academy of Management Briarcliff Manor.

Sedera, D., Lokuge, S., Grover, V., Sarker, S., & Sarker, S. (2016). Innovating with Enterprise Systems and Digital Platforms: A Contingent Resource-Based Theory View. *Information & Management, 53*(3), 366–379.

Sedera, D., Tan, C.-W., & Xu, D. (2022). Digital Business Transformation in Innovation and Entrepreneurship. *Information & Management, 59*(3), 103620.

Sedera, D. D., Lokuge, S., & Nugawela, S. (2021). How Status Quo Bias Affects Digitalization of Agriculture: A Mixed-Method Study of Agri-Business Ceos. *International Conference on Information Systems*. AIS Library.

Shamim, S., Yang, Y., Zia, N. U., & Shah, M. H. (2021). Big Data Management Capabilities in the Hospitality Sector: Service Innovation and Customer Generated Online Quality Ratings. *Computers in Human Behavior, 121*, 106–777. doi:10.1016/j.chb.2021.106777

Shi, Y., Cui, T., & Liu, F. (2022). Disciplined Autonomy: How Business Analytics Complements Customer Involvement for Digital Innovation. *The Journal of Strategic Information Systems, 31*(1), 1. doi:10.1016/j.jsis.2022.101706

Sitar-Tăut, D.A. (2021). Mobile Learning Acceptance in Social Distancing During the Covid-19 Outbreak: The Mediation Effect of Hedonic Motivation. *Human Behavior and Emerging Technologies, 3*(3), 366-378.

Smet, A. D., Gagnon, C., & Mygatt, E. (2021). *Organizing for the Future: Nine Keys to Becoming a Future-Ready Company.* McKinsey. https://www.mckinsey.com/capabilities/people-and-organizational-performance/our-insights/organizing-for-the-future-nine-keys-to-becoming-a-future-ready-company

Sorescu, A. (2017). Data-Driven Business Model Innovation. *Journal of Product Innovation Management, 34*(5), 691-696.

Su, X., Zeng, W., Zheng, M., Jiang, X., Lin, W., & Xu, A. (2022). Big Data Analytics Capabilities and Organizational Performance: The Mediating Effect of Dual Innovations. *European Journal of Innovation Management, 25*(4), 1142-1160.

Sultana, S., Akter, S., & Kyriazis, E. (2022). How Data-Driven Innovation Capability Is Shaping the Future of Market Agility and Competitive Performance? *Technological Forecasting and Social Change, 174*, 121–260. doi:10.1016/j.techfore.2021.121260

Sultana, S., Akter, S., Kyriazis, E., & Wamba, S.F. (2021). Architecting and Developing Big Data-Driven Innovation (Ddi) in the Digital Economy. *Journal of Global Information Management (JGIM), 29*(3), 165-187.

Tabrizi, B., Lam, E., Girard, K., & Irvin, V. (2019). Digital Transformation Is Not About Technology. Harvard business review, 13, 1-6.

Török, L. (2020). Industry 4.0 from a Few Aspects, in Particular in Respect of the Decision Making of the Management: /Will the New Industrial Revolution Change the Traditional Management Functions? *International Review of Applied Sciences and Engineering*.

Trabucchi, D., & Buganza, T. (2018, September). Data-Driven Innovation: Switching the Perspective on Big Data. *European Journal of Innovation Management, 5*(22), 23–40.

Troilo, G., De Luca, L.M., & Guenzi, P. (2017). Linking Data-Rich Environments with Service Innovation in Incumbent Firms: A Conceptual Framework and Research Propositions. *Journal of Product Innovation Management, 34*(5), 617-639.

Visvizi, A., Troisi, O., Grimaldi, M., & Loia, F. (2021). Think Human, Act Digital: Activating Data-Driven Orientation in Innovative Start-Ups. *European Journal of Innovation Management, 25*(6), 452-478.

Walther, S., Sarker, S., Sedera, D., & Eymann, T. (2013). Exploring Subscription Renewal Intention of Operational Cloud Enterprise Systems-a Socio-Technical Approach. *European Conference on Information Systems*, AIS.

Wang, Y., Blobel, B., & Yang, B. (2022). Reinforcing Health Data Sharing through Data Democratization. *Journal of Personalized Medicine, 12*(9), 1380.

Wang, Y., Kung, L., & Byrd, T. A. (2018). Big Data Analytics: Understanding Its Capabilities and Potential Benefits for Healthcare Organizations. *Technological Forecasting and Social Change, 126*, 3–13. doi:10.1016/j.techfore.2015.12.019

Wells, J. (2021). The Intersection of Data Democratization and Security. DBTA. https://www.dbta.com/BigDataQuarterly/Articles/The-Intersection-of-Data-Democratization-and-Security-146091.aspx

Wong, D. T., & Ngai, E. W. (2022). Linking Data-Driven Innovation to Firm Performance: A Theoretical Framework and Case Analysis. *Annals of Operations Research*, 1–20. doi:10.100710479-022-05038-y PMID:36407941

Zeng, J., & Glaister, K.W. (2018). Value Creation from Big Data: Looking inside the Black Box. *Strategic Organization, 16*(2), 105-140.

Zhao, Y., & Kamioka, T. (2022). Understanding the Role of Chief Data Officers: Insights from Japanese Companies. PACIS 2022 Proceedings. AIS Virtual Library.

Zillner, S. (2021). Innovation in Times of Big Data and Ai: Introducing the Data-Driven Innovation (Ddi) Framework. In E. Curry, A. Metzger, S. Zillner, J. C. Pazzaglia, & A. García Robles (Eds.), *The Elements of Big Data Value* (p. 289). Springer. doi:10.1007/978-3-030-68176-0_12

Zotoo, I.K., Lu, Z., & Liu, G. (2021). Big Data Management Capabilities and Librarians' Innovative Performance: The Role of Value Perception Using the Theory of Knowledge-Based Dynamic Capability. *The Journal of Academic Librarianship, 47*(2), 102-272.

ADDITIONAL READING

Adikari, A., Burnett, D., Sedera, D., de Silva, D., & Alahakoon, D. (2021). Value co-creation for open innovation: An evidence-based study of the data driven paradigm of social media using machine learning. *International Journal of Information Management Data Insights, 1*(2), 100022. doi:10.1016/j.jjimei.2021.100022

Marr, B. (2017). *Data strategy: How to profit from a world of big data, analytics and the internet of things* (1st ed.). Kogan Page Publishers.

Marr, B. (2018). *Data-driven HR: how to use analytics and metrics to drive performance* (1st ed.). Kogan Page Publishers.

Ramamurthy, A. (2019). Follow a Data-Driven Road Map for Enterprise Decision-Making. *Journal-American Water Works Association, 111*(6), 78-81.

Zillner, S. (2021). Innovation in Times of Big Data and AI: Introducing the Data-Driven Innovation (DDI) Framework. In E. Curry, A. Metzger, S. Zillner, J. C. Pazzaglia, & A. García Robles (Eds.), *The Elements of Big Data Value* (pp. 289). Springer, Cham. https://doi.org/https://doi.org/10.1007/978-3-030-68176-0_12 (Springer)

KEY TERMS AND REFERENCES

Citizen Data Scientist: In an organization which practices data democratization, a citizen data scientist is an individual who performs data analytics work but who does not necessarily have formal knowledge of data analytics or statistics or is not a data scientist in the profession.

Data Democratization: A process of providing inter-organizational, open data access to both technical (i.e., data scientists, IT specialists etc.) and non-technical (i.e., marketing specialists, product teams etc.) employees to find, access, interoperate, share, and reuse data in their job within the appropriate legal, security, and confidentiality boundaries and using self-service analytic tools to make decisions and develop ideas to support business functions and resolve problems.

Data: Data is a raw form of information and knowledge that can be available in formats such as texts, figures, numerals, symbols, or observations. It is also considered as a strategic asset to the organization.

Data-driven Innovation: A form of developing and implementing new ideas with the use of data and analytics to develop or improve new products, services, processes, business models, and markets, by empowering employees at every level to use data and analytics to improve their innovative capabilities.

Innovation: Discovery and implementation of a new idea related to a product, service, process, or organization policy that is new or an improvement to the organization.

Literature review: A form of academic writing demonstrating an overview of the knowledge and understanding of previously published academic publications related to a specific topic.

Open data: Data that is free to use, reuse and share with anyone to empower their engagement and contribution.

Open Government Data: Government data that is free to use, reuse and re-distribute with any citizen to empower them to engage and contribute to policy decisions.

Chapter 9
Financial Literacy and Perceived Risk Attitudes as Drivers of Investment Intentions in the Digital Era:
A Case Study of Delhi-NCR

Priyanka Tyagi
SRM Institute of Science and Technology, India

Ajay Jain
https://orcid.org/0000-0002-6087-0206
SRM Institute of Science and Technology, India

ABSTRACT

Financial markets all over the world offer a wide range of financial products. Financial instruments such as equity, mutual funds, bonds, government securities, gold, fixed deposits, and many other options are available in financial markets to investors. The purpose of this research study is to analyze the influence of the independent factors of financial literacy and perceived risk attitudes on investment intentions. The population of the study is from the area of Delhi-NCR. Researchers used a descriptive research design and convenient sampling method in the current study. The data of 223 respondents was collected through an online survey via Google form link. The researchers used a PLS-SEM to analyze the research data. The results of the study indicated financial literacy and perceived risk attitudes have a significant impact on investment intentions.

DOI: 10.4018/978-1-6684-7568-3.ch009

1. INTRODUCTION

In India, the unorganized sector is huge, and the government has withdrawn pension schemes even in the organized sector. Moreover, lack of social security schemes and major instability after COVID-19 may impact the financial well-being of the people. The Concept of financial literacy helps people to understand personal finance in a better way and lack of financial literacy may cause financial crises. In the current study financial literacy means knowledge about financial services, products, and risk-reward relationships in terms of usage of financial products and services. (Hung et al., 2011) mentioned financial literacy as basic knowledge of financial and economic principles, and the capacity to apply that knowledge and other financial skills to efficiently manage the financial resources.

In this regard some research studies showed that, financial literacy is required to understand complex financial information (Nalini et al., 2016), and it is a key element for investment-related matters as affects the lives of individuals and their financial well-being (Amari & Jarboui, 2015). The economy needs to increase investors to boost liquidity and growth. So, researcher realized strong need to know the effect of financial literation and, perceived risk attitude on investment intentions.

Because, financial literacy impacts decision making regarding personal finances of individuals (Lusardi, 2019), and also impacts individuals' intentions to invest, save and purchase insurance products and services (Lin et al., 2019). The present study is crucial as financial literacy is essential to understand these complex investment instruments and also helps to predict risks associated with these complex financial products (Rodrigues et al., 2019). Many researchers have used social psychological theories (Ajzen, 2011), indicated that TBP has importance in predicting the investment intentions. There are so many researches on three individual-level antecedents of Theory of Planned Behavior namely attitudes, subjective norms and perceived behavioral control. The present study intended to assess the influence of financial literacy and perceived risk attitudes on investment intentions with different approach. Researchers in current study asked directly investment related question instead of measuring subjective and objective financial literacy.

Additionally, investors must concentrate on wise investment and must take educated financial decisions (Ahmed et al., 2017). The present study will deeply investigate the combined effect of financial literation and, perceived risk attitudes on investment intentions. In view of this current study, it would be helpful in looking for the concerned areas for improvement and, that in turn, would provide the person with the information needed to make a sound investment decision for future stability, thereby contributing to the growth and development of the country. The remaining part of the article is structured as follows: researchers start with a brief explanation of the literature that has already been published on the significance of financial literacy, the research gap in the existing literature, the methodology applied, and the in-depth analysis followed by conclusion, Limitations.

2. LITERATURE REVIEW AND HYPOTHESIS DEVELOPMENT

The following section discusses the literature related to financial literacy, perceived risk attitude and investment intentions.

2.1 Financial Literacy

The previous research proved that the consumer financial literacy is required to select and decide among various investment alternatives. The results of the research study showed that financial literacy – both subjective and objective significantly influences the intentions while only objective financial literacy observed to impact behaviour (Sivaramakrishnan et al., 2017). Interestingly, consumer behaviour is dominated by knowledge and risks. The research presents and evaluates an unique conceptual model that demonstrates how consumers' objective financial knowledge and investing experience influence their future investment intentions, which are mediated by perceived risks and attitudes toward investing. Structural equation modelling was used for data analysis. Researchers showed that objective financial knowledge and investing experience significantly impacts investment intentions (Munnukka et al., 2017).

According to (Shehata et al., 2021), in financial decision making behavioral finance has a vital role. Previous researchers revealed that the effect of subjective knowledge was higher than objective knowledge. (Haslem, 2014) noted that financial literacy and financial education help investors in various financial decisions, retirement planning, saving aspects, and financial literacy also impact investment intentions. (Njuguna, n.d.), revealed that especially in the investment related decision-making processes, financial and economic theories presume that individual as a rational person. But limited knowledge about the investment process can lead to losses. Results of the study revealed that investment knowledge (subjective), investment value (expected), perceived-behavioral control positively impact investment intentions. A study conducted by (Cristofaro et al., 2022), to identify the factors that influence potential bit coin investors in Malaysia. The findings of the research study showed that an investor's perceived risk attitude, and perceived behavioural control have a considerable beneficial impact on their crypto-currency investment decisions. A survey of 2,532 crypto-currency users in the United States and China was conducted to gather information on their behavioural tendencies and cultural characteristics. The findings showed that while attitude, subjective norms, perceived behavioural control, and herding behaviour all have significant impact on the desire to use crypto-currencies for electronic commerce, financial knowledge had no effect. It shows different perspective.

The decision-making process of investors has been advocated by different researchers from a social psychological viewpoint, results indicated past behavior has no direct effect on investment intentions. Social pressure and financial literacy found to have a direct and, positive impact on the investment intentions of Indian investors (Raut, 2020). It is found that product knowledge significantly impacts investment intentions (Lim et al., 2013).

The review of relevant literature has been providing supporting evidence that financial literacy impacts the investment intentions of individuals.

2.2. Perceived Risk Attitudes

According to (Poeteri et al., 2021), there is a growth in financial sectors and new trends are coming in this area. Peer to Peer lending applications are gaining more attention as investment alternatives among millennials. Results of the research revealed that perceived risk and, trust found to impact investment intentions significantly. Another finding of the study was that; the perceived risk was more important in mediating investment intentions via peer-to-peer lending than the trust. In other study, researchers highlighted that financial literation levels of the individuals have a positive association with complex and diversified portfolios (Koh et al., 2020) and stock choices of investors frequently change from time to time as a result of information and perceived risk (Weber, 2010).

Researchers argued that the risk preference and, perceived behavioral control positively impacts intentions to invest (Mahastanti & Hariady, 2014). Further, risk tolerance plays an important role in a variety of household financial decisions. According to the findings of the study, investors may be interested in investing in a particular company only if they have the time and talent to investigate it, as well as money to invest. Individual investors typically begin formulating an investment intention by evaluating the financial positions of several companies using objective criteria such as return on equity, dividend payout ratio, and beta. Then, as individuals continue to justify their investment decisions to invest the companies' stocks, their emotional views of such judgments may come into the equation (Samsuri et al., 2019).

Similarly, digital currency investing has grown because of the global shift toward technology driven life. Malaysia is one of Asia's early adopters of bitcoin with high awareness. The findings of the research study indicated that risk attitude and, perceived behavioural control have a strong influence on crypto-currency investment decision (Veerasingam & Teoh, 2022).

Where as (Reza et al., 2017), noted that, while making the investment decisions perceptions of risk are critical. Researchers found Self-efficacy, trust, perceived quality, risk inclination, and investor knowledge were found to be the most important predictors of perceived risks in the Tehran Stock Exchange. Furthermore, data shown that perceived risks have a detrimental impact on investment intent. Lastly, findings demonstrated that individual investors' perceived risk was indirectly impacting the investment intention via information seeking and, attitude.

Previous literature has shown risk tolerance and perceived risk attitude assumes significant role in influencing investment intentions (Ostrovsky-Berman & Litwin, 2019; Li & Qian, 2018). Moreover, financial decisions have grown increasingly essential to researchers, personal financial planners, investment consultants, and policymakers, especially as the economic landscape has become more complex. In the realm of financial decision-making, a person's willingness to take a risk is critical in making financial decisions and reaching financial goals. Therefore, researcher included Perceived risk attitudes in the present study.

2.3. Investment Intentions

Previous research proved that the investment intentions influenced by financial literacy and risk aversion (Canikli & Aren, 2019). Further, shareholders' decisions to buy and sell stocks are influenced by internal and external psychological factors, according to financial behaviour theories. The psychological factors significantly impacted the perceived risk and rewards, according to the findings. Moreover, the findings revealed that product literacy moderates the association between social characteristics and perceived risk and return. The perception of risk had a favourable impact on brand perception (Asgarnezhad Nouri et al., 2017). Since, capital market development is essential for economic growth (Natsir & Arifin, 2021), revealed that product knowledge and social influence has a significant positive impact on investment intentions. Besides, (Anubha et al., 2019) have revealed online consumer engagement has significant impact on purchase intentions.

After the literature review, it is logical to expect that financial literacy and perceived risk attitude have a positive impact on the investment intention of individuals.

H_1- Investment intentions are directly impacted by financial literacy.

H_2-Investment Intentions are significantly positively impacted by perceived risk attitude.

Researchers have gathered strong evidence after literature review to consider Financial Literacy and Perceived Risk Attitude as independent variables that influence Investment Intentions (Dependent variable) of individual investors.

3. RESEARCH GAP

In several studies Intentions are studied as a motivating factor that affects efforts or behaviour to carry out specific action or behaviour. Many studies have found a link between financial literacy and a variety of behaviours, including saving, wealth, and portfolio selection. There is plenty of literature available where Intention is considered as an independent variable. In the current study, researchers have taken intention as a dependent variable. Many of the studies only focused (TBP) Theory of planned behaviour or the (TRA) Theory of Reasoned Action. There are few other studies that have only focused on the source side of intentions or consequences. Thus, to fill this research gap researchers asked investment intentions related questions instead of measuring objective and subjective financial literacy. However, there are few researches on how consumers perceive risks in decision-making scenarios, as well as the impact of objective knowledge and experience on risk perceptions, attitudes, and behavioural intentions. Clearly it is important to study the combined impact of financial literacy and perceived risk attitude on the dependent variable Investment Intentions.

4. OBJECTIVES

The first objective of the study is to assess the impact of financial literation on investment intentions. The second objective of study is to assess the impact of perceived risk attitude on investment intentions of investors.

5. METHODOLOGY

Sampling and Data Collection

Researcher conducted an online survey via Google form link, that was circulated on various whatsApp numbers and email addresses. The current research study adopted descriptive research design and a convenient sampling method for data collection. The researchers collected data from 223 respondents. The data of 200 were accepted after removing outliers and analyzed to assess the impact of financial literacy levels and, perceived risk attitude on investment intentions of individuals. In the current study partial least square used structural equation modelling (PLS-SEM) for data analysis.

Figure 1. Research framework

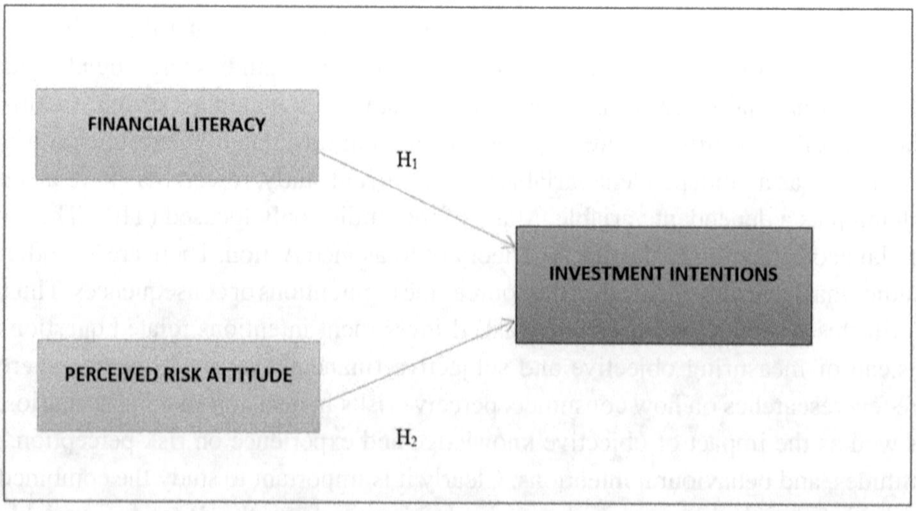

Measures

Since, measurement of constructs through the measurement scale is crucial part in research (Ringle & Sarstedt, 2016). Here, goodness of a measurement scale can be evaluated on the basis of reliability and validity. The details of measurement scale are given below in the table no 1.

Table 1. Constructs and sample items

Constructs	Number of Items	Items	Source
Financial Literacy	7	"I have awareness about different investment avenues".	(Sivaramakrishnan et al., 2017).
		"I stay informed on financial planning developments by reading newspapers and magazines".	(Sivaramakrishnan et al., 2017).
Perceived Risk Attitude	10	"I am prepared to take risk from borrowed money when making an investment".	(Lim et al., 2013) modified by the researcher
		"I can visualize the outcomes of my investments, and am willing to accept high risk".	(Lim et al., 2013) modified by the researcher
Investment Intentions	6	I believe to invest in early life as I will bring financial wealth.	(Lim et al., 2013) modified by the researcher
		"I am highly intended to invest my money in financial and other investment alternatives"	(Lim et al., 2013) modified by the researcher

6. DATA ANALYSIS

The researcher performed descriptive data analysis by using SPSS version 22. Further analysis was done by two step methods (measurement model and structural model) proposed by (Henseler et al., 2009), to report and evaluate generated results. A measurement model has been used to evaluate the appropriateness of the scale items. In the study researcher retained only the items with good factor loadings and removed the items with low factor loading, as per (Chin, 1998). Additionally, CR (Construct reliability) was measured by using Fornell and Larcker (1981) criterion, Where CR value should be equal to (0.7) or above reflect acceptable level of reliability. Here, AVE (average variance extracted) values should be above 0.50. Further, cross loading values in corresponding variables should be higher than other constructs.

Table 2. Parameter values of factor loadings, average variance extracted, composite reliability

Constructs	Items	Loadings	AVE	CR
Financial Literacy	FL1	0.972		
	FL2	0.986		
	FL3	0.972	0.949	0.987
	FL4	0.975		
	FL5	0.966		
Perceived Risk Attitude	VART1	0.917		
	VART2	0.959		
	VART3	0.978	0.940	0.984
	VART4	0.968		
	VART5	0.970		
	VART6	0.975		
Investment Intention	VARI1	0.983		
	VARI2	0.955		
	VARI3	0.964	0.924	0.984
	VARI4	0.972		
	VARI5	0.974		

Analysis of the Measurement Model

The researchers evaluated the measurement model to examine the convergent and discriminant validity of the observed variables. Where loading value of specific indicators must be above 0.6, AVE value should be above 0.5 and, CR value should be above 0.7, according to (F. Hair Jr. et al., 2006). Therefore fitness of a model is assured by fulfilment of these prescribed criterions. Here, details of measurement properties of the constructs are given in the Table 2 and Table 3.

Table 3. Discriminant validity

Financial Literacy	0.974		
Investment Intention	0.788	0.970	
Perceived Risk Attitude	0.731	0.905	0.961

Figure 2. Results of measurement model

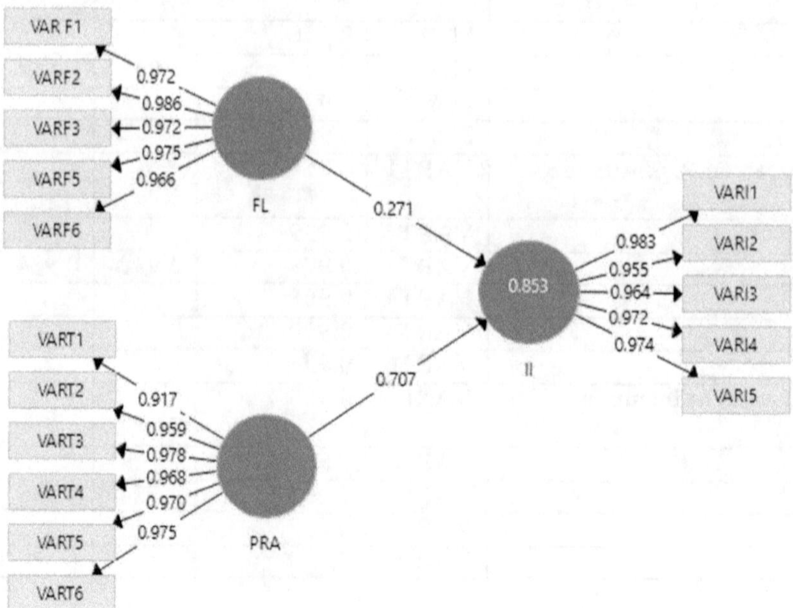

Analysis of Structural Model

Estimation of structural model was performed after analysing validity and reliability of constructs by using measurement model. Researcher used refined items in hypothesis testing. In figure 3, a full structural regression model is presented. Hypothesis testing summary is shown by the researchers in Table 4. The researcher found a positive impact of financial literacy and perceived risk attitude on investment intentions ($\beta = 0.271$, $p < 0.01$). Furthermore, results indicated that Perceived Risk Attitude has a significant impact on the individual's investment intentions ($\beta = 0.707$, p is less than 0.01).

Table 4. Testing of hypothesis

Hypotheses	Beta	p values	Outcome
H_1:FL ——→ II	2.404	0.000	Accepted
H_2:PRA ——→ II	6.024	0.000	Accepted

FL (Financial Literacy), PRA (Perceived Risk Attitude), II (Investment Intentions)

Figure 3. Results of structural regression model

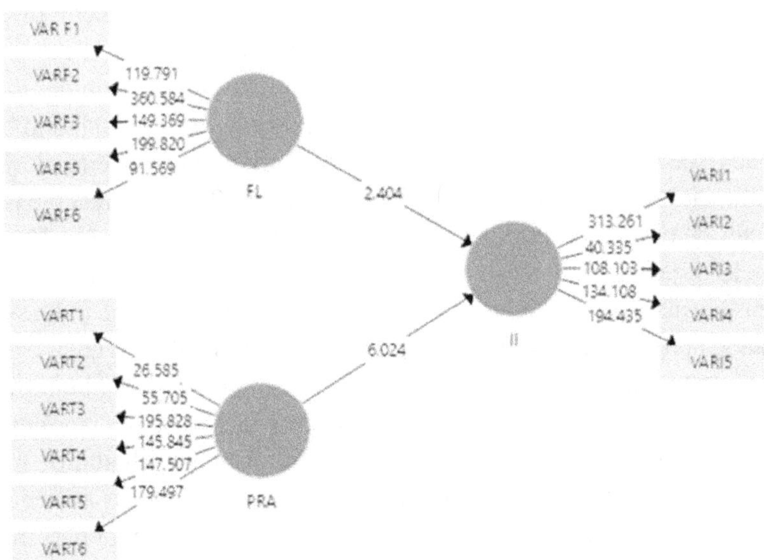

Based on the results of structural model, researcher found that financial literacy and perceived risk attitude have significant impact on the investment intentions. Financial literacy level has significant positive impact on investment intentions, results of the study are supported by the findings of (Yang et al., 2021), where researchers found that financial literacy enables individuals to assess the investment avenues and select the option that can offer best. Increasing financial literacy levels result in higher investment intentions. In current study, perceived risk attitude was found to be a strong factor that influences investment intentions of individuals. This specific finding supported by the findings of (Thai et al., 2017), researchers found direct and indirect impact of perceived risk attitude on investment intentions. Individuals with high risk perception are more intended to invest. In the present study, financial literacy and the presence of perceived risk attitude, there are higher chances that an individual will invest.

7. CONCLUSION

Studying the impact of Financial Literacy and Perceived Risk Attitude on investment intentions was the main objective of this study. Results of the research revealed that, financial literation and perceived risk attitude have significant impact on investment intentions of individuals. Furthermore, increasing financial literacy levels and perceived risk attitude will result into increased investment intentions. The results of the research study are beneficial to financial advisors as financial advisors deal with people from different literacy levels and attitudes related to investment. Investment decisions depend on the literacy level and perceived risk attitude of the investors. Where there is increased financial literacy and perceived risk attitude, there is a higher probability of investing. Those who are new to stock market should be made aware of advisors and policy makers. Sufficient attention can be given to develop the financial literacy levels of individuals. (Bayar et al., 2020) argued that the financial literacy can be developed through educational programs to increase the demand for financial products and services with an understanding of varied risks. With the increased financial literacy people could easily know about the risk associated with financial products and services Thus, in the early life of individuals, financial education can be introduced. Financial literation can be increased by introducing educational programs. Where, important concepts like risks and reward, return on investment, Investment alternatives, time value of money should be included. Financial understanding helps individuals to understand the risk associated with the investment avenues. The findings are useful to investors and practitioners interested in the financial markets. The implication of the research study is that capital markets, government and related authorities need to take steps to improve financial literacy level of the general public.

Limitations

In the present study respondents residing in urban areas were taken, and rural area respondents may be considered for future studies with large sample sizes. An in-depth analysis of investors according to geographical areas can be performed in future studies. Additionally, to find better results research variables can be expanded in further research, for example other variables like behavioural factors and personality factors can be included. Moreover, mixed methods can be applied like perceived risk attitude may be studied through qualitative research in further studies.

REFERENCES

Ahmed, Z., Ramakrishnan, S., & Noreen, U. (2017). Financial literacy as competitive advantage for individual investors' decision making. *Advanced Science Letters, 23*(9), 8988–8993. doi:10.1166/asl.2017.10009

Ajzen, I. (2011). The theory of planned behaviour: Reactions and reflections. In Psychology and Health, 26(9), 1113–1127. https://doi.org/ doi:10.1080/08870446.2011.613995

Amari, M., & Jarboui, A. (2015). Financial Literacy and Economics Education Among Young Adults: An Observation From Tunisia. *Journal of Business & Finance Librarianship, 20*(3), 209–219. Advance online publication. doi:10.1080/08963568.2015.978834

Anubha, J. A., & Hooda, M. (2019). Consumer engagement towards travel websites and purchase intentions. *Journal of Advanced Research in Dynamical and Control Systems, 11*(8 Special Issue).

Asgarnezhad Nouri, B., Motamedi, S., & Soltani, M. (2017). Empirical analysis of the financial behavior of investors with brand approach (case study: Tehran stock exchange). *Scientific Annals of Economics and Business, 64*(1), 97–121. doi:10.1515aeb-2017-0007

Bayar, Y., Sezgin, H. F., Öztürk, Ö. F., & Şaşmaz, M. Ü. (2020). Financial Literacy and Financial Risk Tolerance of Individual Investors: Multinomial Logistic Regression Approach. *SAGE Open, 10*(3). Advance online publication. doi:10.1177/2158244020945717

Canikli, S., & Aren, S. (2019). *Effect Of Financial Literacy And Risk Perception On Individual Investors' Investment Choices*. EPSBS. doi:10.15405/epsbs.2019.01.02.68

Chin, W. W. (1998). The partial least squares approach to structural equation modeling. *Modern methods for business research, 295*(2), 295-336.

Cristofaro, M., Giardino, P. L., Misra, S., Pham, Q. T., & Hiep Phan, H. (2022). Behavior or culture? Investigating the use of cryptocurrencies for electronic commerce across the USA and China. *Management Research Review*. doi:10.1108/MRR-06-2021-0493

Hair, F., Jr., Black, W., Babin, B., & Anderson, R. (2006). 2010 Hair et al.pdf. In Clemson International Institute for Tourism.

Haslem, J. A. (2014). Selected topics in financial literacy. *The Journal of Wealth Management, 17*(3), 47–57. doi:10.3905/jwm.2014.17.3.047

Henseler, J., Ringle, C. M., & Sinkovics, R. R. (2009). The use of partial least squares path modeling in international marketing. *Advances in International Marketing, 20*, 277–319. doi:10.1108/S1474-7979(2009)0000020014

Hung, A., Parker, A. M., & Yoong, J. (2011). Defining and Measuring Financial Literacy. SSRN *Electronic Journal*. https://doi.org/ doi:10.2139/ssrn.1498674

Koh, B. S. K., Mitchell, O. S., & Rohwedder, S. (2020). Financial knowledge and portfolio complexity in Singapore. *The Journal of the Economics of Ageing, 17*, 100179. doi:10.1016/j.jeoa.2018.11.004

Li, N., & Qian, Y. (2018). The Impact of Educational Pairing and Urban Residency on Household Financial Investments in Urban China. *Journal of Family and Economic Issues, 39*(4), 551–565. doi:10.100710834-018-9579-2

Lim, K. L., Soutar, G. N., & Lee, J. A. (2013). Factors affecting investment intentions: A consumer behaviour perspective. In Journal of Financial Services Marketing, 18(4). https://doi.org/ doi:10.1057/fsm.2013.23

Lin, X., Bruhn, A., & William, J. (2019). Extending financial literacy to insurance literacy: A survey approach. *Accounting and Finance, 59*(S1), 685–713. doi:10.1111/acfi.12353

Lusardi, A. (2019). Financial literacy and the need for financial education: Evidence and implications. *Swiss Journal of Economics and Statistics, 155*(1), 1. doi:10.118641937-019-0027-5

Mahastanti, L. A., & Hariady, E. (2014). Determining the factors which affect the stock investment decisions of potential female investors in Indonesia. *International Journal of Process Management and Benchmarking*, *4*(2), 186. doi:10.1504/IJPMB.2014.060407

Munnukka, J., Uusitalo, O., & Koivisto, V. J. (2017). The consequences of perceived risk and objective knowledge for consumers' investment behavior. *Journal of Financial Services Marketing*, *22*(4), 150–160. doi:10.105741264-017-0033-6

Nalini, R., Alamelu, R., Amudha, R., & Cresenta Shakila Motha, L. (2016). Financial literacy and its contributing factors in investment decisions among urban populace. *Indian Journal of Science and Technology*, *9*(27). doi:10.17485/ijst/2016/v9i27/97616

Natsir, K., & Arifin, A. Z. (2021). The Effect of Product Knowledge and Influence of Society on Investment Intention of Stock Investors with Perceived Risk as Mediation. *Estudios de Economía Aplicada*, *39*(12). doi:10.25115/eea.v39i12.6022

Njuguna, P. K. (n.d.). *Determinants Of Investment Intentions: An Individual Retail Investor's Perspective From Nairobi Securities Exchange*. Research Gate. https://www.researchgate.net/publication/341089225

Ostrovsky-Berman, E., & Litwin, H. (2019). Social Network and Financial Risk Tolerance Among Investors Nearing and During Retirement. *Journal of Family and Economic Issues*, *40*(2), 237–249. doi:10.100710834-018-9592-5

Poeteri, N. A., Simanjuntak, M., & Hasanah, N. (2021). The Investment Intention Among Indonesian Millennials via Peer-to-Peer Lending Applications. *Peer-Reviewed Article Jurnal Keuangan Dan Perbankan*, *25*, 2443–2687. doi:10.26905/jkdp.v25i4.6352

Raut, R. K. (2020). Past behaviour, financial literacy and investment decision-making process of individual investors. *International Journal of Emerging Markets*, *15*(6), 1243–1263. doi:10.1108/IJOEM-07-2018-0379

Reza, A., Monfared, K., Fathi, S., & Ranjbarian, B. (2017). Perceived risks of individual investors in the capital market: the antecedences and consequences. In Int. J. Business Innovation and Research, 14(2).

Ringle, C. M., & Sarstedt, M. (2016). Gain more insight from your PLS-SEM results the importance-performance map analysis. In Industrial Management and Data Systems, 116(9). https://doi.org/ doi:10.1108/IMDS-10-2015-0449

Rodrigues, L. F., Oliveira, A., Rodrigues, H., & Costa, C. J. (2019). Assessing consumer literacy on financial complex products. *Journal of Behavioral and Experimental Finance*, *22*, 93–104. doi:10.1016/j.jbef.2019.02.005

Samsuri, A., Ismiyanti, F., & Narsa, I. M. (2019). Effects of risk tolerance and financial literacy to investment intentions. *International Journal of Innovation. Creativity and Change*, *10*(9), 40–54.

Shehata, S. M., Abdeljawad, A. M., Mazouz, L. A., Aldossary, L. Y. K., Alsaeed, M. Y., & Sayed, M. N. (2021). The moderating role of perceived risks in the relationship between financial knowledge and the intention to invest in the Saudi Arabian stock market. *International Journal of Financial Studies*, *9*(1), 1–16. doi:10.3390/ijfs9010009

Sivaramakrishnan, S., Srivastava, M., & Rastogi, A. (2017). Attitudinal factors, financial literacy, and stock market participation. *International Journal of Bank Marketing*, *35*(5), 818–841. doi:10.1108/IJBM-01-2016-0012

Thai, P., Trang, M., & Tho, N. H. (2017). International Journal of Economics and Financial Issues Perceived Risk, Investment Performance and Intentions in Emerging Stock Markets. *International Journal of Economics and Financial Issues*, *7*(1), 269–278. http:www.econjournals.com

Veerasingam, N., & Teoh, A. P. (2022). Modeling cryptocurrency investment decision: Evidence from Islamic emerging market. *Journal of Islamic Marketing*. doi:10.1108/JIMA-07-2021-0234

Weber, E. U. (2010). Risk attitude and preference. In Wiley Interdisciplinary Reviews: Cognitive Science, 1(1), 79–88. https://doi.org/ doi:10.1002/wcs.5

Yang, M., al Mamun, A., Mohiuddin, M., Ali Al-Shami, S. S., & Zainol, N. R. (2021). Predicting stock market investment intention and behavior among malaysian working adults using partial least squares structural equation modeling. *Mathematics*, *9*(8), 873. doi:10.3390/math9080873

Chapter 10
A Study on Oil Price Volatility Exposure to Stock Market Return:
Evidence From China

Gopal Bihari Saraswat
https://orcid.org/0000-0001-6985-1952
Department of Management Studies, SRM Institute of Science and Technology, Ghaziabad, India

Madhav Saraswat
https://orcid.org/0000-0002-1075-2869
Ch. Charan Singh University, Meerut, India

ABSTRACT

The objective of this chapter is to find the impact of crude oil price fluctuations on the stock market return of China. Further, the study extended to find the magnitude and the level of exposure to stock market return from the exchange rate. The study used quarterly time series data from 2008 to 2022 to measure the exposure magnitude to the stock market return from variability in crude oil price, exchange rate, interest rate, and GDP. The study used the ARDL bound test and VDC analysis as methodology and checked for multiple breakpoints. The study findings suggested a long running cointegration among crude oil price, exchange rate, interest rate and stock market return. Results indicated that disequilibrium in the short run to stock market return would converge back itself. The investigation concluded that oil and exchange rates transmit shocks to the stock market return. But the oil exposure to the stock market return is the highest, whereas the GDP causes the least volatility.

DOI: 10.4018/978-1-6684-7568-3.ch010

INTRODUCTION AND THEORETICAL FRAMEWORK

According to (Prasad Bal & Narayan Rath, 2015) energy is a crucial aspect of a country's development, and crude oil plays a significant role in economic prosperity. As stated by (Alamgir & Amin, 2021), oil is an essential energy source and a strong indicator of financial stability. Crude oil is primarily used in various sectors of an economy, such as transportation, industry, and electricity generation. The availability and affordability of crude oil can significantly impact a country's economic growth (Prasad Bal & Narayan Rath, 2015). Countries that are net exporters of crude oil can generate significant revenue from crude oil exports, which can contribute to their economic growh. For example, Middle East countries, like Saudi Arabia and the UAE, rely heavily on crude oil exports to generate revenue and drive economic growth. The crude oil industry can also create job opportunities, which can contribute to a country's economy. This includes jobs in exploration, drilling, refining, transportation etc. On the contrary, oil-importing developing countries heavily rely on crude oil imports to meet their energy demand, and securing a steady supply of crude oil is essential for their energy security. Disruptions in the crude oil supply can cause power outages, transportation disruption, and economic loss (Jamil, 2016). Crude oil imports are a significant source of expenditure for oil-importing developing countries. The foreign exchange reserves needed for crude oil imports can significantly impact a country's economy. Additionally, oil price fluctuations can cause an impact on foreign exchange reserves and exchange rate.

Past studies have demonstrated that the fluctuation in crude oil prices can serve as a paradigm for global market shocks, and future price volatility could severely impact the global economy, especially the oil importing countries. Empirical studies from the early 1970s and 1990s have concluded that shocks in oil demand and supply can lead to price fluctuations and may impact the cost of transportation, which can have a ripple effect on the prices of goods and services. Further, oil price fluctuations cause an impact on inflation and consumer spending (Alamgir & Amin, 2021). However, crude oil impact is not limited to the energy sector but extends to other areas of the economy, particularly for countries that are net oil importers.

China is the world's largest crude oil importer, followed by USA and India. Oil accounts for around 20% of total energy consumption (International Energy Agency, 2021) of the countrys total energy needs. China's crude oil import bill in 2022 is around US $229.3 billion, almost 200% more than India's crude oil needs and 75 per cent more than the USA. China's growing need for energy consumption is due to its large population and industrialization. In the last decade, the country witnessed an upliftment of the people from poverty to the middle class, making oil demand ubiquitous across emerging countries. China comprises 16 per cent of the world's middle class, and another 350 million people are estimated to join by 2030. Thus, as China continues to industrialize and urbanize, an upsurge in crude oil demand for transportation and other energy requirements is inevitable. As such, securing a steady supply of crude oil is essential for China's energy security.

China is also part of the trade block called BRICS and is a significant contributor to energy demand of the group. Due to the high crude oil import bill, China is exposed to global oil price volatility. Such volatility could further lead to shocks to China's stock market (Cong et al., 2008). This is evident from the countries' dependence on crude oil imports which compelled them to rely on the US $ as import bills to be paid in foreign currency. Therefore, fluctuating oil prices may transmit volatility to the exchange rate of the country as well as the demand for foreign currency increase in the oil-importing country. There is a strong link between crude oil prices and exchange rates in the long-run, and the relationship is time-varying (Beckmann et al., 2020). The impact of crude oil price also relies on the fact that a country is oil-exporting or importing. The export country's oil prices increase leads to a rise in the price of relative commodities. The rapid fluctuation of exchange rate prices can cause importing countries to be vulnerable to volatility (Chaudhuri & Daniel, 1998). Hence, exchange rate exposure due to crude oil price volatility is inevitable. Further, companies in the energy sector, such as oil and gas producers, tend to be sensitive to fluctuations in crude oil prices. When prices of oil rise, the stock prices of these companies may also increase as companies stand to benefit from higher profits. However, if the crude oil prices drop, then these companies' stock prices may decline. Therefore, the risk of exposure to currency exchange rates and the country's stock market due to variability in crude oil prices is inevitable. The present study investigates the risk exposure of the relationship among exchange rate, crude oil price, interest rate, and stock market return. The study is significant for traders, policymakers, and researchers to formulate strategies amid future uncertainties.

Previous research has employed diverse techniques to explore and examine the relationship between the price of oil and the exchange rate. Some studies used the simple regression method and formed various long-run models to assess the impact of fluctuation of one variable over other. Later, models based on non-linear relationships like ARDL (Asaad, 2021; Jalal & Gopinathan, 2022; Kumar et al., 2022a; Mroua & Trabelsi, 2020; Zhang & Baek, 2022) and NARDL were used. These models also evaluated the asymmetric relationship and analyzed the transmission of shocks to the exchange rate from the crude oil prices, through the use of NARDL-based methods (Ameur et al., 2022; Karim et al., 2022; Odugbesan et al., 2021; Pal & Mitra, 2019). These non-linear methods become essential because they capture the frequently changing price of oil from positive to negative and captures the shock transmissions. However, some studies used the Wavelet-based Coupla model (Benhmad, 2012; Boubaker & Raza, 2017; He et al., 2021; Jiang & Yoon, 2020; Karim et al., 2022; Khraief et al., 2021; Mensi et al., 2018; Tiwari et al., 2013; Tiwari & Albulescu,

2016) and (Karim et al., 2022; Mensi et al., 2014; Tiwari et al., 2019) to understand the speed of transmission and adjustment of system variables. Finally, studies also used Vector Auto Regression (VAR) (Balcilar et al., 2017; Beckers & Beidas-strom, 2015; Boldanov et al., 2016; Ceylan et al., 2020; Ji et al., 2019; Lv, 2019; Nouira et al., 2018; Raju & Marathe, 2020; Singhal & Ghosh, 2016; Syed, 2021; Wen et al., 2019; Yin & Ma, 2018), Error Correction Method, and causality test to evaluate and determine the causal effect and direction of the transmission of shocks.

The present study uses the ARDL, causality and VDC methods to investigate the impact of volatility in the crude oil prices on the currency exchange rate and stock market returns in China. Further, the study also showcases the evolution of time series-based linear regression. The present study highlights the use of linear/symmetrical methods like ARDL, variance decomposition, and Granger causality test. The study provides a robust econometric methodology to investigate the issue and aims to provide results which could be used by investors, policymakers and traders. The present chapter is structured as follows: (i) Introduction and theoretical Framework (ii) Literature Review (iii) Methodology (iv) Conclusion (V) References.

LITERATURE REVIEW

The Chinese economy is vulnerable to variability in the oil prices, meaning that when the price rises, the effect on general commodity prices and the influence of monetary policy becomes less important in the short run (Degiannakis et al., 2018). On the contrary, the study (Bagchi, 2017) revealed that China's stock market return is more affected by positive shocks in oil prices than negative information. Therefore, the price of oil is a powerful indicator of the prospective returns in the Chinese stock market (Adu et al., 2015); (Chen et al., 2017) but not the other way around (Fang & You, 2014). Nonetheless, a nation's economic position as either an importer or exporter of oil can significantly affect its stock market (Doko Tchatoka et al., 2019). A positive shock in oil prices is inversely proportional to an emerging country's stock market (Basher et al., 2012);. On the contrary, the study of (Robert D. Gay, 2008) suggested that there is no impact of fluctuations in the exchange rate and oil prices on stock market return because stock market returns fluctuate due to regional microeconomic exposures and macro-economic factors (Lim & Sek, 2014) and there is a positive effect between oil and the exchange rate. In contrast, the interest rate negatively affect the exchange rate (Alenzi, 2015).

Studies used various methods to analyze the oil and exchange relationship (Khraief et al., 2021; Zhang & Baek, 2022) by applying the NARDL methodology to calculate a non-linear association between crude oil and exchange rate. The study concluded that oil price asymmetrically affects the exchange rate. (Lv, 2019) used the vector autoregression (VAR) and impulse response method to investigate the oil price rise and its impact on China's economy. Additionally, the research employs the Granger causality analysis to evaluate the spillover effect of crude oil prices on economic metrics.

Further, the study of (Nouira et al., 2018) used exchange rates and thee crude oil prices for 18 years and conducted study for eight countries. The study highlighted the relationship between exchange rates and the crude oil prices and the causality in variance. This explains the spillover relation between the variables. The study used the ARCH/GARCH method to examine the clustering of volatility and its causal effect on the exchange rate. The study determined that when there is a rise in crude oil prices by the oil exporting countries, the exchange rate of importing countries depreciates, and the USD value increases. The study (Kisswani & Elian, 2021; Saidu et al., 2021) based on-linear autoregressive distributed lags model (NARDL) and ARDL model examined the asymmetry for five countries as Canada, China, Japan, the Republic of Korea, and the UK. The study used oil prices and five countries' exchange rates to find the asymmetry due to volatility in global oil prices and its effect on the local currencies. The results revealed that fluctuations in global oil prices casue asymmetric impacts on the exchange rate. On the contrary, (Alqaralleh, 2020) used the ARDL method and concluded that a slower depreciation rate follows a high rate of appreciation of the exchange rate. Further, the study revealed that exchange rates react differently to negative and positive crude oil prices shocks in the long and short-run.

(Ajala et al., 2021; Saraswat et al., 2022) research conducted using the ARDL methodology showed that fluctuations in oil prices lead to variations in exchange rates and stock market returns, indicating a relationship between the three variables. The correlation between oil price and the currency exchange rate is robust, and the impact varies depending on the timeframe (Beckmann et al., 2020). The studies (Aali-Bujari et al., 2018; Alamgir & Amin, 2021; Bagchi, 2017; Cong et al., 2008; He et al., 2021; Kumar et al., 2022b; Li & Giles, 2015; Mensi et al., 2014; Papapetrou, 2001; Sahu et al., 2014; Srinivasan, 2015) focused on the relationship of the currency exchange rate, oil and market return in the past but failed to capture the long term behaviour of such relationship. The present study focuses on the long-term behaviour from the financial crisis of 2008 to late 2017 to capture the long-term outlook and behaviour of crude oil prices with China's stock market and exchange rate. The research utilized data analysis models based on ARDL and ECM and a causality test to determine the behaviour of crude oil prices and their influence on study variables.

Data Description and Methodology

The study used Brent crude oil price, exchange rate, interest rates, Shanghai Stock Exchange of China (SSEC) return and GDP as study variables. The interest rate is the proxy variable for a 10-year long-term Chinees government bond (10-GBYC). The study covers daily time series data for ten years, from Jan 2008 to Dec 2022. The daily time series data of variables are collected from www.investing.com and St. Louis Fred online database. The research spans 15 years, which is significant as it encompasses critical events like the 2008 financial crisis, the 2014 oil price crash, the post-2014 global market turbulence, and the 2020 global pandemic.

The descriptive statistic is calculated in the methodology section to develop a profound understanding of data. Additionally, the study utilized Bai-Perron multiple breakpoint tests to identify any structural breaks in the time series data. The stationarity test ADF was also estimated to confirm the stationarity order and ascertain the appropriate level of variable integration. However, the stock market return is an I(0)[1]; therefore, after applying the ADF unit root test, the cointegration estimated for the long-run among the variables using Auto-Regressive Distribution Lag (ARDL) Bound test. ARDL test could only be used if all variables under study are a combination of I(1) and I(0) variables. The unit root test result suggests that stock market return is I(0) and other variables are I(1) therefore use of ARDL is most suitable. Furthermore, the study employed the Granger Causality test and Variance Decomposition to determine the causal relationship and measure the impact of one variable's one standard deviation innovation shock on the other variable.

Model Specification

The study followed the model proposed by (Alenzi, 2015). The study formulated an expanded model to determine the effect of variability in oil price, exchange rate and interest rate on the market returns. The model is outlined below:

$$\textit{Stock Market Return}_t = \beta_1 + \beta_2 \textit{Brent Crude} + \beta_3 \textit{Exchange Rate} + \beta_4 \textit{Interest Rate} + u_i \tag{1}$$

The response variable is stock market return, and the experimental variable are the Brent oil prices, interest rate and exchange rate. The is the white noise distribution error term. To ensure reliable and consistent empirical results, all variables were converted into natural logarithms in the model transformation process.

The ARDL Model

The ARDL (Autoregressive Distributed Lag) model is a valuable tool for econometric analysis, particularly when the variables under investigation are non-stationary. Non-stationary variables refer to those that exhibit trends or patterns that change over time and can be difficult to analyze using traditional econometric methods. The ARDL model can handle both I(0) (stationary) and I(1) (non-stationary) variables without requiring differentiation or transformation of the variables. This makes it a versatile tool that can be used to analyze a wide range of economic phenomena.

One significant benefit of using the ARDL model is its ability to estimate the variables' short-term and long-term relationships. This is important because economic phenomena often exhibit dynamic relationships that change over time. For example, the impact of fiscal or monetary policies on the economy may have short-term and long-term effects. The Autoregressive model can help researchers understand the nature of these relationships and how they change over time.

The ARDL model has been used to study various economic phenomena, including price and income elasticities and the impact of monetary and fiscal policies. It is a highly effective tool for econometric analysis in many cases. For example, (Pesaran et al., 2001) argue that the ARDL model is more efficient and reliable than other popular methods, such as the Vector Error Correction Model (VECM), when the data sample is small. Similarly, (Narayan & Narayan, 2010) demonstrate the superiority of the ARDL model over the Johansen cointegration approach when dealing with small samples.

Another advantage of the ARDL model is its flexibility in allowing for the inclusion of both lagged and contemporaneous variables. This feature makes the ARDL model suitable for investigating dynamic relationships between variables. For example, it can be used to analyze the effect of monetary policy on inflation and output in the short-run and the long-run. This flexibility makes the ARDL model a powerful tool for econometric analysis, particularly when dealing with complex economic phenomena.

The ARDL model is a flexible method for econometric analysis that can handle variables that exhibit trends over time, estimate relationships between variables in both the short and long term, and consider variables that have an impact in the past and present. Various studies have shown that the ARDL model is more effective than other popular methods when working with small data samples. Additionally, the ARDL bound test is particularly helpful for testing long-term relationships between variables that are not stationary. This test can handle small sample sizes and can include both I(1) and (0) variables in the same model.

Primary Results

The primary result of the graph plots is presented in Figure 1 below, where the plot of the oil price shows a volatile trend over the period. The oil price touched a high of 123 $/barrel in 2008q2 but also crashed to the bottom of 46 $/barrel by 2009q1 amidst the global financial crisis. However, the oil price sustained between 110 $/barrel to 117 $/barrel from 2011 to early 2014 due to the financial bailouts and government expenditures to support the global economies and market. In 2014, the global oil market collapsed, which caused oil prices to fall sharply to 35 $/barrel by 2016q1. Similarly, oil prices also went through a nightmare in early 2020 due to the global pandemic, which compelled the countries to lockdown and economic activities to come to a standstill. Post-lockdown, as the countries had eased out the lockdown regulations and opened the economies for trade, the oil prices had witnessed a skyrocketing trend and touched as high as 112 $/barrel. The span of the past 15 years had a volatile phase for oil markets worldwide as markets faced the financial crisis, the oil price collapse and the pandemic.

The Chinees stock market price indicated that the global recession significantly impacted the Chinese stock market. The market faced a bloodbath in 2007 when it touched a high of 4430 points and fell to a low of 1723 points. Further, the recession caused China's market to lose around 200%, perplexing investors and traders and causing succumbing to volatility. But the market recovered from 2009 onwards and sustained between 3125 and 2000 points until 2014. However, the stock market touched a 4450-point level by 2015. The boom in the Chinees stock market was also evident because, during 2015, oil prices were falling due to the global oil price collapse. Still, an oil importer, China benefited from the low crude oil prices which led investors to cheered up. However, the euphoria of the stock market boom started to fade away post-2016. The pandemic accelerated the pace of the market to fall as the Chinees city the Wuhan was declared the pandemic's epicentre.

The Chinees currency is one of the few currencies in the world which had appreciated against the US $ post the global financial crisis. The Chinese currency had seen sharp appreciation against the US $ during 2008 and 2014, which was caused by the Chinees productivity increment and resource mobilization, which made it the world manufacturing facility where most of the MNCs started either manufacturing or assembling their product resulting in impetus to Chinese GDP and so as the local currency demand. On the contrary, China's currency lost its shine gradually amid global uncertainty and the crude oil price collapse of 2014. The crude price collapse gave the US $ impetus to grow against the yuan from 6.05/USD in 2014 to 6.95/USD by 2016. In 2020, the pandemic caused a severe impact on the yuan, and the currency lost its shine against the US $. Further, the global market uncertainty amidst the pandemic continued the free fall in the Chinees currency.

The graph of the crude oil prices and the currency exchange rate also suggests that the exchange rate and the oil prices had a negative correlation relationship. This is also evident as the country being the largest crude oil importer, pays higher oil import bills in the US $, when oil prices rise and vice versa.

The instability in global markets had a considerable effect on oil prices, exchange rates, and the stock market, resulting in risk exposure to interest rates. The interest rate was unstable amid the rise and fall of oil prices and the China's stock market. Further, the GDP of the country also witnessed a gradual but significant rise during the previous period amidst China ambition to being the global manufacturer and exporter, given impetus to the GDP growth. GDP contracted amidst the 2020 pandemic due to forced lockdown in the country and further extension of lockdown amidst stringent measures to curb the pandemic in the country.

Figure 1. Growth on oil, stock market price, exchange, interest, and GDP

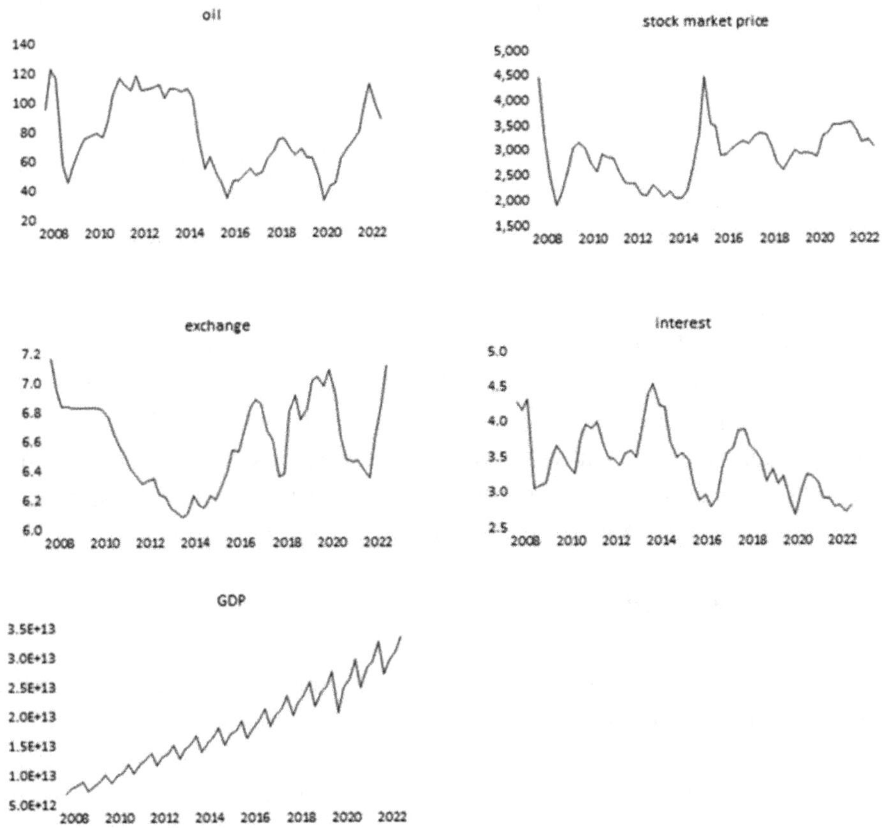

The Chinees stock market and the price of the crude oil had a long-term negative correlation, as indicated by the graph plot of both series. Further, the graph plot indicates that the Chinees stock market is exposed to fluctuations in crude oil price because when the China's stock market depreciates, crude oil price increases. The negative correlation seems sustained throughout the study sample period from 2008 to 2022. Similarly, the oil price, exchange rate and the stock market and interest rates also have a long-term negative correlation relationship. Additionally, a negative correlation is observed in both crude oil prices and the stock market, indicating that an upsurge in oil prices significantly affects the market return.

Descriptive Statistics

The descriptive statistics in **Table 1** below revealed that the average price of crude oil was US $ 78.29/barrel, whereas the stock market average level was 2912.544 points. Further, the average rate of exchange rate was 6.59, interest was 3.44 per cent, and GDP size was US $ 18.1 trillion. The results also indicated that the oil price maximum and the minimum range were US $ 122.7855 and 33.38922 per barrel. However, the maximum and minimum value for the exchange rate was between 7.163637 and 6.090685. The stock market remained volatile during the study period, as the standard deviation was 550.0816, indicating higher volatility. Further, oil prices' standard deviation was around 25.63, which made this black commodity highly volatile. However, the stock market remained the most volatile, and the standard deviation was the highest among the other variables in the study. On the contrary, the exchange and interest rates were the least volatile compared to crude and stock markets.

Furthermore, the descriptive statistics revealed that all-time series were positively skewed, except for the exchange rate, and the kurtosis outcomes showed that all-time series were platykurtic (kurtosis<3), except for the stock market, which was leptokurtic (kurtosis>3). Finally, the normality test results of the Jarque-Bera test indicated that no variable in system was normally distributed because test statistics for normal distribution were rejected at a 5% significance level.

Multiple Break Point Test

The field of time-series analysis has given great importance to the detection of structural breaks in common economic data sets. The significance of such breaks has been emphasized particularly when examining unit root processes (Bai & Perron, 2003; Onel, 2005; Perron, 1989). Consequently, the study employed the Bai-Perron multiple breakpoint test to detect any structural breaks in the time series data, as ignoring a break in the time series could lead to spurious results (Onel, 2005; Perron,

1989). The breakpoint test results **Table 2** suggested one breakpoint in time series linear model at 2015q3 because the break test rejected the 0 vs 1 hypothesis at 5% significance. Therefore, results statistics concluded that null hypothesis of no break point has rejected at a 5% significance level.

Table 1. Descriptive statistics

	oil	stock market	exchange	interest	gdp
Mean	78.29662	2912.544	6.594960	3.445870	1.81E+13
Median	75.25623	2931.860	6.612032	3.465117	1.73E+13
Maximum	122.7855	4484.293	7.163637	4.529742	3.36E+13
Minimum	33.38922	1921.697	6.090685	2.684415	6.94E+12
Std. Dev.	25.68316	550.0816	0.298434	0.464911	7.19E+12
Skewness	0.147014	0.366305	-0.018076	0.391485	0.310850
Kurtosis	1.690791	3.469074	1.810259	2.425121	2.086478
Jarque-Bera	4.501202	1.891865	3.541977	2.358820	3.052583
Probability	0.105336	0.388317	0.170165	0.307460	0.217340
Sum	4697.797	174752.6	395.6976	206.7522	1.09E+15
Sum Sq. Dev.	38917.87	17852794	5.254700	12.75237	3.05E+27
Observations	60	60	60	60	60

Table 2. Multiple break point test

Sequential F-statistic determined breaks:			**1**
Break Test	F-statistic	F-statistic	Value**
0 vs. 1 *	6.163646	30.81823	18.23
1 vs. 2	1.559291	7.796456	19.91
Break dates:			
	Sequential	Repartition	
1	2015Q3	2015Q3	
* Significant at the 0.05 level.			
* Bai-Perron (Econometric Journal, 2003) critical values.			

Unit Root Test

The ADF test for unit root results in **Table 3** below indicated that oil price, interest rate, exchange rates and GDP have unit root (Non-stationary) at intercept and trend intercept levels. And the unit root statistics p-values failed to reject the null hypothesis. However, p-value statistics of first-difference on intercept and trend and intercept levels suggested that variables are free from the unit root. Therefore, oil price, exchange rate, interest rate and GDP variables are I(1) as all are first difference stationary. On the contrary, China's stock market returns unit root test p-value indicated that it is stationary at levels because the p-value rejected the null hypothesis. Further, when the return variable was tested on the first difference, unit root results suggested that the variable is also stationary at the first difference. Therefore, unit root test statistics concluded that oil, interest rate, exchange rate and GDP are the first difference stationary I(1), but the variable return is I(0) level stationery. The study comprises I(1) and I(0) variables and emphasizes to use ARDL method for further analysis.

Table 3. Unit root test result

	Levels		First Difference	
Variable	**Intercept**	**Trend & Intercept**	**Intercept**	**Trend & Intercept**
Log(oil)	-2.0365	-1.9421	-6.3042	-6.3289
P-Value	0.2708	0.6200	0.0000	0.0000
Log(return)	-5.5283	-5.4242	-9.7816	-9.7763
P-Value	0.00000	0.00002	0.00000	0.00000
LOG(interest)	-2.7558	-3.3389	-6.8444	-6.7833
P-Value	0.0710	0.0702	0.00000	0.00000
LOG(exchange)	-2.0943	-2.1686	-4.8742	-5.0135
P-Value	0.2477	0.4975	0.0002	0.0007
Log(GDP)	-2.5318	-2.4080	-2.7099	-3.4803
P-Value	0.1137	0.3715	0.0454	0.0416

Linear Autoregressive ARDL Model

The stationary test statistics suggested that variables have no unit root at different integration orders I(1) and I(0). The ARDL test is a robust test for small sample sizes and allows for including both I(0) and I(1) variables in the same model. The ARDL model is a versatile tool for econometric analysis that can handle non-stationary variables, estimate both short-run and long-run relationships between variables, and includes lagged and contemporaneous variables. Several studies have established its superiority over other popular methods in small sample sizes. Meanwhile, the ARDL bound test is useful for testing relationships between variables, especially when the variables are non-stationary.

The study used the ARDL model to identify the long-term relationship between crude oil prices, interest rates, exchange rates, and stock market returns. The ARDL model equation is presented in equation 2 below using ARDL (4, 1, 0, 0, 1) lag based on constant trend and Akaike Info Criterion (AIC) as lag specification method. The constructed ARDL model has a variable return as a dependent variable and is regressed on its 4 lags. Further, the oil is regressed on 1 lag, the exchange on 0 lag, interest on 0 lag and GDP on 1 lag, respectively. The ARDL long-run model is given in Table 4 below:

Table 4. Long-run ARDL.

Variable	Coefficient	Std. Error	t-Statistic	Prob.*
log(return(-1))	-0.089927	0.111171	-0.808904	0.4230
log(return(-2))	0.017438	0.093526	0.186448	0.8530
log(return(-3))	-0.180311	0.096397	-1.870514	0.0682
log(return(-4))	-0.245857	0.094199	-2.609967	0.0124
log(oil)	-0.057857	0.068787	-0.841112	0.4049
log(oil(-1))	-0.221302	0.067739	-3.266956	0.0021
log(exchange)	0.142409	0.276444	0.515144	0.6091
log(interest)	-0.012255	0.095195	-0.128735	0.8982
log(gdp)	0.105557	0.081220	1.299645	0.2006
log(gdp(-1))	0.205135	0.081351	2.521611	0.0155
dum2015q3	-0.345446	0.054797	-6.304129	0.0000
C	-8.336797	1.926556	-4.327307	0.0001

The long-run ARDL model coefficient is negative and significant at 5%. Similarly, the breakpoint variable introduced in the model is also significant, indicating that the dummy variable dum2015q3 break in time series significantly affects the model specification. Further, the long-run estimated model suggests that the dependent variable return's lag 4 is significant. However, the independent variables oil and gdp are significant at lag 1, suggesting a long-run correlation in both the variables with the return.

ARDL Cointegration and Bound Test

In addition, the study employed the ARDL model using the bound test cointegration technique to examine the long-term cointegration relationship. To improve its performance, the ARDL bound test approach was used, and an ECM model was estimated to measure the short and long-term effects. Given equation (1) above is reparametrized with the following specifications:

$$\Delta logreturn_t = \alpha + \lambda_1 logreturn_{t-1} + \lambda_2 logoil_{t-1} + \lambda_3 logexchange_{t-1} + \lambda_4 loginterest_{t-1} + \lambda_5 loggdp_{t-1} + \sum_{k=1}^{n}\beta_k \Delta logreturn_{t-k} + \sum_{k=1}^{n}\delta_k \Delta logoil_{t-k} + \sum_{k=1}^{n}\varphi_k \Delta logexchange_{t-k} + \sum_{k=1}^{n}\pi_k \Delta loginterest_{t-k} + \sum_{k=1}^{n}\vartheta_k \Delta loggdp_{t-k} + \varepsilon_t \quad (2)$$

Where Δ is the first difference operator and εt is the white-noise error term. The equation (2) provides the single equation framework to measure long- and short-run estimates. The short-run effects are estimates using a coefficient of each first difference i.e. β_k, δ_k, φ_k, π_k and, while the long-run effect is estimated using λ_1 to λ_5, which is normalized on λ_1.

The ARDL Bound test results are presented in Table 5 below; the bound test estimated F statistics is 16.95, greater than the significant value at 5% for I(0) and I(1). Therefore, the null hypothesis of no cointegration relationship is rejected. The model estimation results indicated a long-run cointegration relationship among return, oil, exchange, interest and gdp. Thus, model estimation using a bound test concluded that there is a significant long-run cointegration relation at 5%.

The estimated cointegration relationship model is presented in Table 6, which shows that the coefficient of the cointegration equation is negative and significant at the 5% level. This suggests that approximately 149.86% of disequilibrium movement is corrected within one quarter.

Table 5. Bound test result

F-Bounds Test		Null Hypothesis: No levels relationship		
Test Statistic	**Value**	**Signif.**	**I(0)**	**I(1)**
			Asymptotic: n=1000	
F-statistic	16.95140	10%	2.2	3.09
k	4	5%	2.56	3.49
		2.5%	2.88	3.87
		1%	3.29	4.37
Actual Sample Size	55		Finite Sample: n=55	
		10%	2.345	3.28
		5%	2.763	3.813
		1%	3.738	4.947

Table 6. Cointegration equation model

Variable	Coefficient	Std. Error	t-Statistic	Prob.
D(LRETURN(-1))	0.408730	0.095213	4.292789	0.0001
D(LRETURN(-2))	0.426168	0.093847	4.541104	0.0000
D(LRETURN(-3))	0.245857	0.080130	3.068217	0.0037
DLOG(OIL)	-0.057857	0.060940	-0.949417	0.3477
DLOG(GDP)	0.105557	0.069871	1.510753	0.1382
DUM2015Q3	-0.345446	0.032556	-10.61070	0.0000
CointEq(-1)*	-1.498657	0.140649	-10.65528	0.0000

The Error Correction Model

The ARDL ECM is required to be tested if variables are integrating at various levels, and this gives optimum results instead of using Vector Error Correction Model (VECM)(Mishra, 2015; Seng & Hook, 2001). However, the cointegration relationship is further confirmed by estimating the linear long-run ECM model in Table 7. Therefore, the ARDL ECM model below is estimated based on (4, 1, 0, 0, 1) lags of return, oil, exchange, interest and gdp. The ECM model suggested that the equation coefficient is -8.336797, negative and significant at a 5% significance level, suggesting a long term cointegration relationship among the variables. Further, the result identifies a long-run relationship and a persistent effect on stock market return.

Table 7. ARDL ECM model based on (4, 1, 0, 0, 1) lags

Panel-A				
Variable	**Coefficient**	**Std. Error**	**t-Statistic**	**Prob.**
C	-8.336797	1.926556	-4.327307	0.0001
Log(return(-1))*	-1.498657	0.185421	-8.082474	0.0000
log(oil(-1))	-0.279159	0.043783	-6.375930	0.0000
log(exchange)**	0.142409	0.276444	0.515144	0.6091
log(interest)**	-0.012255	0.095195	-0.128735	0.8982
log(gdp(-1))	0.310693	0.057332	5.419140	0.0000
d(log(return(-1)))	0.408730	0.127323	3.210192	0.0025
d(log(return(-2)))	0.426168	0.118291	3.602700	0.0008
d(log(return(-3)))	0.245857	0.094199	2.609967	0.0124
dlog(oil)	-0.057857	0.068787	-0.841112	0.4049
dlog(gdp)	0.105557	0.081220	1.299645	0.2006
dum2015Q3	-0.345446	0.054797	-6.304129	0.0000
* p-value incompatible with t-Bounds distribution.				
** Variable interpreted as Z = Z(-1) + D(Z).				
Panel-B				
R-Square: 0.762104 Serial Correlation LM Test LM Test: 0.3032 (p-value) [4 lags]				
Adjusted R-square: 0.732367 Heteroskedasticity Test: 0.4970 (p-value)				
Jarque-Bera normality test: 0.8411 (p-value)				

Notes: The statistical significance is tested at a significance level of 5%. The variable "dum2015q3" represents the breakpoint date. The LM test refers to the Breusch-Godfrey test for serial correlation, the Breusch-Pagan-Godfrey is the test for heteroskedasticity, and the JB stat represents the Jarque-Bera test for normality, with the number of lags given in the parentheses.

The short-run ECM estimation results also indicated a relationship between the stock market return with other variables. The diagnostic tests are applied to the ECM model to test the model's optimization and stability. The results of the diagnostics tests given in Panel-B of Table 7 above indicate the ECM model is free from serial cointegration as p-value is greater than 5%. The LM test of serial correlation is tested using 4 lags to estimate the test and provides confirmatory evidence of no serial correlation. The Durbin-Watson statistics presented in the long-run model is at 2.0 further confirms that the model is free from serial correlation (Gujarati, 2011). Further, the Breusch-Pagan-Godfrey is heteroskedasticity test is also used to test the homoscedasticity of the residuals; the calculated p-value, which is greater than 5%, suggests that model is homoskedastic and residuals are free from heteroskedasticity. Finally, Jarque-Bera test was used to test whether residuals are normally distributed. The calculated p-value of the test is more than 5% indicating that residuals are normally distributed.

To test the ARDL ECM model stability model, residuals are plotted using the CUSUM test Figure 2, suggesting that the residuals plot is within the upper and lower critical bound of 5 per cent, Thus, the plot provides confirmatory evidence that the ECM model is stable.

Figure 2. CUSUM v. 5% significance

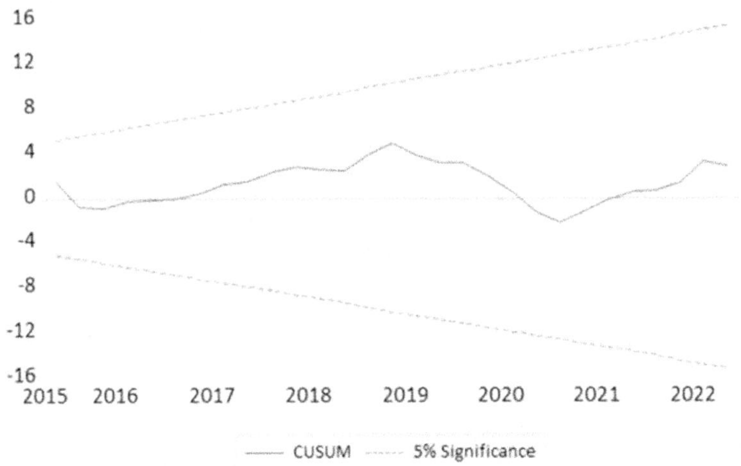

Figure 3. CUSUM of squares v. 5% significance

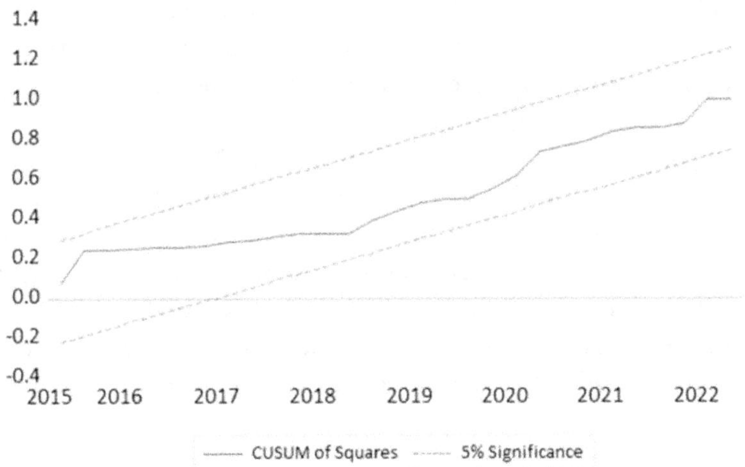

Further, to confirm the stability and best fit of the model, residuals are plotted using the cusum square plot in Figure 3. The plot suggested that residual squares are within the 5% significance level, indicating that the model is optimum, stable, and provides the best fit for residuals.

Granger Causality Test

The causality test statistics in Table 8 below suggest that oil price granger causes a change in return but not the other way around. The p-value for the null hypothesis of no causal relationship between oil price and the stock market return is less than 5%, leading to the rejection of the null hypothesis at a 5% significance level. However, the other hypothesis that the exchange rate does not cause a change in return is accepted. The Granger causality result indicates no causality from the stock market return to the exchange rate. On the contrary, the hypothesis that interest rate does not cause a change in return is rejected at 5% significance as the p-value is less than 5%. But the hypothesis that returns cause a change in return is rejected. This means that the relationship between interest rate and return is unidirectional. The Granger causality test could not reject the rest of the other hypotheses as p-values are more than 5%. Hence, it could be concluded that fluctuation in crude oil prices and interest rates causes a change in China's stock market return, and this relationship is unidirectional.

Variance Decomposition Result

The variance decomposition is estimated for 10 quarters to assess the long-run impact among the variables. The VDC results of the decomposition of stock market return presented in Table 9 suggested that fluctuation in return may cause a long-run change of 11.38% in oil price and 14.33% in exchange rates. Further, volatility in stock market return could contribute to a 5.47% fluctuation in the interest rate and 4.25% in GDP. On the contrary, return also causes a fluctuation from its past lags in the long-run, which is around 65%.

The fluctuation in crude oil price could cause a 12.85% per cent shock to the stock market return and 44.86 per cent to itself. However, the shock in crude oil prices may cause a significant shock to China's exchange rate and interest rate, which are 20.65% and 8.35%, respectively. Further, a shock in oil causes a fluctuation of 13.26% to GDP in long-run. The results display the impact of oil price fluctuation on all the study variables in long-run. Where an exchange is the most affected variable as China imports most of its country's crude oil requirements.

Table 8. Granger causality test

Null Hypothesis:	Obs	F-Statistic	Prob.
d(log(oil)) does not Granger cause log(return)	57	7.79554	0.0011
log(return) does not Granger cause d(log(oil))		1.91718	0.1573
d(log(exchange)) does not Granger cause log(return)	57	0.36177	0.6982
log(return) does not Granger cause d(log(exchange))		0.10966	0.8963
d(log(interest)) does not Granger cause log(return)	57	3.65578	0.0327
log(return)does not Granger cause d(log(interest))		2.67934	0.0781
d(log(gdp)) does not Granger cause log(return)	57	0.10856	0.8973
log(return)does not Granger cause d(log(gdp))		0.96007	0.3895
d(log(exchange)) does not Granger cause d(log(oil))	57	0.43695	0.6484
d(log(oil)) does not Granger cause d(log(exchange))		0.45496	0.6370
d(log(interest)) does not Granger cause d(log(oil))	57	0.21053	0.8108
d(log(oil)) does not Granger cause d(log(interest))		2.33936	0.1065
d(log(gdp)) does not Granger cause d(log(oil))	57	0.05238	0.9490
d(log(oil)) does not Granger cause d(log(gdp))		1.04422	0.3592
d(log(interest)) does not Granger cause d(log(exchange))	57	0.66851	0.5168
d(log(exchange)) does not Granger cause d(log(interest))		0.31426	0.7317
d(log(gdp)) does not Granger cause d(log(exchange))	57	2.24624	0.1160
d(log(exchange)) does not Granger cause d(log(gdp))		0.83649	0.4390
d(log(gdp)) does not Granger cause d(log(interest))	57	2.24624	0.1160
d(log(interest)) does not Granger cause d(log(gdp))		0.83649	0.4390

The exchange decomposition result indicated that the currency exchange rate fluctuation could transmit a 5.50% shock to stock market return and 2.91% to oil prices. Further, the result suggested that a shock to the exchange rate also caused a change of 71.39% from its lagged values. The interest rate and GDP shocks are exposed to 11.14% and 9.03%, respectively, to the fluctuations in exchange. The VDC of exchange indicated that shock in the exchange rate causes a major exposure to the interest rate and GDP thereafter.

The VDC of interest shock revealed that return is exposed to 4.36% from such shocks. Further, a major shock in oil prices of 25.91% comes from interest rate fluctuations, but GDP is affected by 3.63% only in long-run. The exchange is affected by 12.41%, which may cause a spillover impact on the country's import bills.

Finally, VDC results of GDP indicate that China's economy affects oil prices by and large. The shock from GDP caused 20.85% in oil prices and has the power to change the global landscape for the oil demand. However, the shock in GDP failed to cause any major impact on the return and exchange. The VDC result summarizes that fluctuation in oil prices causes a major shock to return and exchange. Further, returns could also affect the major shock to the exchange rate. This indicates a bidirectional relationship between the variables. However, the exchange rate may cause a spillover effect on the interest and GDP of the country to some extent. Therefore, the relationship between exchange and interest is also bidirectional because both cause shocks to each other in long-run.

Table 9. Variance decomposition results

Period	S.E	log (return)	d(log (oil))	d(log (exchange))	d(log (interest))	d(log (gdp))
VDC of log(return):						
1	0.084296	100.0000	0.000000	0.000000	0.000000	0.000000
2	0.090601	86.62110	12.38591	0.345988	0.300596	0.346406
3	0.093688	82.11078	12.26268	1.959495	2.876878	0.790160
4	0.098966	76.62800	11.99557	6.820146	2.884730	1.671554
5	0.105839	70.34878	10.71584	12.75626	2.640745	3.538370
6	0.108003	68.03271	11.49432	12.30376	4.029265	4.139942
7	0.108513	67.48407	11.61044	12.77923	4.013364	4.112896
8	0.109299	66.62187	11.44429	13.74911	4.127931	4.056797
9	0.110725	65.29850	11.34107	14.15935	5.204911	3.996162
10	0.111193	64.74950	11.38252	14.13357	5.476590	4.257822
VDC of d(log(oil)):						
1	0.125238	7.009727	92.99027	0.000000	0.000000	0.000000
2	0.145594	7.917615	69.77526	9.028655	0.692831	12.58564
3	0.159157	8.103515	58.41601	16.56028	2.153656	14.76655
4	0.176019	13.48225	48.77411	21.21613	3.369144	13.15836
5	0.179368	13.08651	47.21039	20.59253	5.584124	13.52645
6	0.183322	12.57275	45.19567	20.35221	8.361221	13.51815
7	0.184289	12.45664	45.25114	20.49555	8.419957	13.37671
8	0.184791	12.47473	45.17184	20.56770	8.380812	13.40492
9	0.185319	12.71649	45.10399	20.45944	8.376289	13.34379
10	0.185875	12.85892	44.86360	20.65517	8.355476	13.26683

continues on following page

Table 9. Continued

Period	S.E	log (return)	d(log (oil))	d(log (exchange))	d(log (interest))	d(log (gdp))
VDC of d(log(exchange)):						
1	0.018080	8.355169	2.141101	89.50373	0.000000	0.000000
2	0.020596	6.549365	1.844696	83.69021	2.243617	5.672109
3	0.021411	6.072172	2.095390	78.44291	5.647407	7.742122
4	0.021903	5.904938	2.028212	74.96200	9.315007	7.789839
5	0.022212	5.771759	2.867275	73.28478	9.538660	8.537522
6	0.022786	5.544989	2.770585	74.11386	9.432103	8.138460
7	0.023031	5.519640	2.711996	74.45458	9.240746	8.073039
8	0.023249	5.599774	2.968875	73.08160	9.751800	8.597949
9	0.023434	5.524670	2.924385	72.00423	11.07365	8.473065
10	0.023541	5.504104	2.913929	71.39602	11.14813	9.037822
VDC of d(log(interest)):						
1	0.066634	0.558531	33.45970	1.481103	64.50066	0.000000
2	0.067863	0.557047	32.46841	1.883555	63.56631	1.524677
3	0.069984	0.565925	30.78588	3.683495	63.53055	1.434154
4	0.070602	1.247494	30.52651	3.642637	62.53281	2.050552
5	0.074838	4.130324	27.28070	7.751004	58.88908	1.948893
6	0.075320	4.139364	27.24693	8.464094	58.14859	2.001025
7	0.075855	4.122421	27.64438	8.808181	57.45191	1.973105
8	0.077175	4.085718	26.77392	10.95342	56.08477	2.102178
9	0.078583	4.400999	26.03870	12.22224	54.10919	3.228880
10	0.078909	4.365644	25.91314	12.41860	53.66748	3.635129
VDC of d(log(gdp)):						
1	0.032537	0.044613	18.52503	1.305584	0.648392	79.47638
2	0.034607	0.186409	19.04592	2.370369	0.672743	77.72456
3	0.035707	0.809660	20.36782	2.673017	0.647530	75.50198
4	0.037054	1.029969	25.64023	2.594419	0.602061	70.13332
5	0.045278	0.953851	21.98973	2.970417	1.403696	72.68231
6	0.047892	1.212698	20.12920	2.723321	1.279493	74.65529
7	0.049054	2.143069	20.26900	2.628124	1.936378	73.02343
8	0.050160	2.068745	23.44946	2.693249	1.929644	69.85890
9	0.055561	1.786262	22.02471	2.394323	1.691296	72.10340
10	0.057767	1.821026	20.85341	2.938282	1.760573	72.62671
Cholesky Ordering: log(return) d(log(oil)) d(log(exchange)) d(log(interest)) d(log(gdp))						

CONCLUSION

The objective of this chapter was to find the influence of crude oil price fluctuation on the market returns in China. Further study also included other macroeconomic variables such as exchange, interest and GDP to explore the impact of volatility on return. Initially, the study tested stationary tests using an ADF test to confirm the order of integration for the variable in the system. The data comprises time series data from 2008 to 2022 with quarterly frequency ranging from the financial crisis to the recent pandemic across the world. As large time series data is most likely to suffer from the economic events of depression and crisis; therefore, structural breaks in data are unavoidable. Hence, the study used a Bai-Peron multiple breakpoint test, which suggested one break in time series data. The study has used the combination of different order integration variables such as I(1) and I(0) therefore, the ARDL test is applied to bring a robust methodology and model fit. Additionally, the ARDL bound test is utilized to determine the cointegration relationship, and an ECM model is estimated to evaluate the importance of the short-term and long-term connections between the variables within the system. Finally, causality and VDC tests are applied to provide a confirmatory and precise understanding of volatility shock from one variable to another.

The ADF test suggested that the return is I(0) level stationery, but other variables in the system are I(1) first difference stationary. Further, Bai-perron multiple breakpoint test indicated a structural break in the model at 2015q3, which was significant at 5% significance and cause a major challenge to the model stability. The ARDL bound suggested a long-run cointegration between the return, oil, exchange, interest and gdp. The cointegration coefficient was negative and significant at 5%, implying that 149.86% movement of any disequilibrium is corrected within one quarter. The long-run model provides confirmatory evidence of the spillover effect on the returns, and the short-run model indicates a connection between oil and the gdp to the market return. The analysis results confirm that return is affected by the volatility spillover from oil, exchange, interest and gdp.

The Granger causality test statistics concluded that oil and interest cause fluctuations in return, and investors expected returns have exposed the shock from the oil market fluctuations. However, the causality test further failed to reject other hypotheses of Granger causality. The causality results also revealed a unidirectional causality on the stock market return from oil prices and interest rates.

On the other hand, VDC results concluded that the fluctuations in crude oil prices could transmit a 12.85% shock to the stock market return. Further, oil price fluctuations could cause a shock of 20.65% to exchange rates. The VDC findings revealed that the interest rate could cause only 25.91% to oil and 12.41% to exchange rates. However, interest rate shock to the return and gdp is marginal in long-run.

Moreover, the return could also cause a shock of 11.38% and 14.13% to the oil and exchange rate, respectively. Finally, findings revealed that China's stock market return is highly exposed to oil price shock but moderately affected exposed to GDP fluctuation. The findings are essential to disclose that China's stock market return is highly volatile to oil prices, and both have a bidirectional relationship over the period. The returns cointegrate in the long-run and expose themselves to shocks from the currency exchange rate, oil price, interest rates and GDP. The chapter explains to researchers and students the various econometric methods in time series analysis, especially with different stationery integration orders. Further, the chapter illustrates the profound methodology of ARDL short and long-run models and estimation diagnostics. In conclusion, the study's robust methodology-based results can benefit traders, investors, and policymakers seeking to comprehend the connection between crude oil price fluctuation and market returns.

REFERENCES

Aali-Bujari, A., Venegas-Martínez, F., & Santillán-Salgado, R. J. (2018). On the stock market-electricity sector nexus in Latin America: A dynamic panel data model. *International Journal of Energy Economics and Policy*, *8*(6), 148–154. doi:10.32479/ijeep.7120

Adu, G., Alagidede, P., & Karimu, A. (2015). Stock return distribution in the BRICS. *Review of Development Finance*, *5*(2), 98–109. doi:10.1016/j.rdf.2015.09.002

Ajala, K., Sakanko, M. A., & Adeniji, S. O. (2021). the Asymmetric Effect of Oil Price on the Exchange Rate and Stock Price in Nigeria. *International Journal of Energy Economics and Policy*, *11*(4), 202–208. doi:10.32479/ijeep.10977

Alamgir, F., & Amin, S. (2021). The nexus between oil price and stock market: Evidence from South Asia. *Energy Reports*, *7*, 693–703. doi:10.1016/j.egyr.2021.01.027

Alenzi, M. (2015). *The Impact of Exchange Rate, Interest Rate and Oil Price Fluctuations on Stock Returns Of GCC Listed Companies* [Thesis, University of Plymouth].

Alqaralleh, H. (2020). On the asymmetric response of the exchange rate to shocks in the crude oil market. *International Journal of Energy Sector Management*, *14*(4), 839–852. doi:10.1108/IJESM-10-2019-0011

Asaad, Z. A. (2021). Oil Price, Gold Price, Exchange Rate and Stock Market in Iraq Pre-During Covid19 Outbreak: An Ardl Approach. *International Journal of Energy Economics and Policy*, *11*(5), 562–571. doi:10.32479/ijeep.11552

Bagchi, B. (2017). Volatility spillovers between crude oil price and stock markets: Evidence from BRIC countries. *International Journal of Emerging Markets*, *12*(2), 352–365. doi:10.1108/IJoEM-04-2015-0077

Bai, J., & Perron, P. (2003). Computation and analysis of multiple structural change models. *Journal of Applied Econometrics*, *18*(1), 1–22. doi:10.1002/jae.659

Balcilar, M., van Eyden, R., Uwilingiye, J., & Gupta, R. (2017). The Impact of Oil Price on South African GDP Growth: A Bayesian Markov Switching-VAR Analysis. *African Development Review*, *29*(2), 319–336. doi:10.1111/1467-8268.12259

Basher, S. A., Haug, A. A., & Sadorsky, P. (2012). Oil prices, exchange rates and emerging stock markets. *Energy Economics*, *34*(1), 227–240. doi:10.1016/j.eneco.2011.10.005

Beckers, B., & Beidas-strom, S. (2015). Forecasting the Nominal Brent Oil Price with VARs — One Model Fits All? *IMF Working Paper, 15/251.*

Beckmann, J., Czudaj, R. L., & Arora, V. (2020). The relationship between oil prices and exchange rates: Revisiting theory and evidence. *Energy Economics*, *88*, 104772. doi:10.1016/j.eneco.2020.104772

Ben Ameur, H., Ftiti, Z., & Louhichi, W. (2022). Revisiting the relationship between spot and futures markets: Evidence from commodity markets and NARDL framework. *Annals of Operations Research*, *313*(1), 171–189. doi:10.100710479-021-04172-3 PMID:34334864

Benhmad, F. (2012). Modeling nonlinear Granger causality between the oil price and U.S. dollar: A wavelet based approach. *Economic Modelling*, *29*(4), 1505–1514. doi:10.1016/j.econmod.2012.01.003

Boldanov, R., Degiannakis, S., & Filis, G. (2016). Time-varying correlation between oil and stock market volatilities: Evidence from oil-importing and oil-exporting countries. *International Review of Financial Analysis*, *48*, 209–220. doi:10.1016/j.irfa.2016.10.002

Boubaker, H., & Raza, S. A. (2017). A wavelet analysis of mean and volatility spillovers between oil and BRICS stock markets. *Energy Economics*, *64*, 105–117. doi:10.1016/j.eneco.2017.01.026

Ceylan, R., Ivrendi, M., Shahbaz, M., & Omay, T. (2020). Oil and stock prices: New evidence from a time varying homogenous panel smooth transition VECM for seven developing countries. *International Journal of Finance and Economics, September 2018*, 1–16. doi:10.1002/ijfe.2202

Chaudhuri, K., & Daniel, B. C. (1998). Long-run equilibrium real exchange rates and oil prices. In Economics Letters (Vol. 58). doi:10.1016/S0165-1765(97)00282-6

Cong, R. G., Wei, Y. M., Jiao, J. L., & Fan, Y. (2008). Relationships between oil price shocks and stock market: An empirical analysis from China. *Energy Policy*, *36*(9), 3544–3553. doi:10.1016/j.enpol.2008.06.006

Da Chen, C., Cheng, C. M., & Demirer, R. (2017). Oil and stock market momentum. *Energy Economics*, *68*, 151–159. doi:10.1016/j.eneco.2017.09.025

Degiannakis, S., Filis, G., & Arora, V. (2018). Oil prices and stock markets: A review of the theory and empirical evidence. *The Energy Journal (Cambridge, Mass.)*, *39*(5), 85–130. doi:10.5547/01956574.39.5.sdeg

Doko Tchatoka, F., Masson, V., & Parry, S. (2019). Linkages between oil price shocks and stock returns revisited. *Energy Economics*, *82*, 42–61. doi:10.1016/j.eneco.2018.02.016

Fang, C. R., & You, S. Y. (2014). The impact of oil price shocks on the large emerging countries' stock prices: Evidence from China, India and Russia. *International Review of Economics & Finance*, *29*, 330–338. doi:10.1016/j.iref.2013.06.005

Gay, R. D. Jr. (2008). Effect Of Macroeconomic Variables On Stock Market Returns For Four Emerging Economies: Brazil, Russia, India, And China. *Applied Economics*, *40*(11), 1363–1372. doi:10.1080/00036840600820663

Gujarati, D. (2011). []. Palgrave macmillan.]. *Econometrics By Example*, *I*, 101–102.

He, X., Gokmenoglu, K. K., Kirikkaleli, D., & Rizvi, S. K. A. (2021). Co-movement of foreign exchange rate returns and stock market returns in an emerging market: Evidence from the wavelet coherence approach. *International Journal of Finance & Economics, August 2020*, ijfe.2522. doi:10.1002/ijfe.2522

International Energy Agency. (2021). *International Energy Agency*. IEA. https://www.iea.org/countries/china

Jalal, R., & Gopinathan, R. (2022). Time-Varying and Asymmetric Impact of Exchange Rate on Oil Prices in India: Evidence from a Multiple Threshold Nonlinear ARDL Model. *Finance Research Letters*, *103297*, 103297. doi:10.1016/j.frl.2022.103297

Jamil, F., & G. E. K. (2016). The impact of crude oil prices on the economy of developing countries. *International Journal of Economics, Commerce, and Management*, *IV*(11), 11–20.

Ji, Q., Liu, B. Y., & Fan, Y. (2019). Risk dependence of CoVaR and structural change between oil prices and exchange rates: A time-varying copula model. *Energy Economics*, *77*, 80–92. doi:10.1016/j.eneco.2018.07.012

Jiang, Z., & Yoon, S. M. (2020). Dynamic co-movement between oil and stock markets in oil-importing and oil-exporting countries: Two types of wavelet analysis. *Energy Economics*, *90*, 104835. doi:10.1016/j.eneco.2020.104835

Karim, M. M., Kawsar, N. H., Ariff, M., & Masih, M. (2022). Does implied volatility (or fear index) affect Islamic stock returns and conventional stock returns differently? Wavelet-based Granger-causality, asymmetric quantile regression and NARDL approaches. *Journal of International Financial Markets, Institutions and Money*, *77*, 101532. doi:10.1016/j.intfin.2022.101532

Khraief, N., Shahbaz, M., Mahalik, M. K., & Bhattacharya, M. (2021). Movements of oil prices and exchange rates in China and India: New evidence from wavelet-based, non-linear, autoregressive distributed lag estimations. *Physica A*, *563*, 125423. doi:10.1016/j.physa.2020.125423

Kisswani, K. M., & Elian, M. I. (2021). Analyzing the (a)symmetric impacts of oil price, economic policy uncertainty, and global geopolitical risk on exchange rate. *Journal of Economic Asymmetries*, *24*, e00204. doi:10.1016/j.jeca.2021.e00204

Kumar, S., Kumar, A., & Singh, G. (2022a). Gold, crude oil, bitcoin and Indian stock market: Recent confirmation from nonlinear ARDL analysis. *Journal of Economic Studies (Glasgow, Scotland)*. doi:10.1108/JES-01-2022-0007

Kumar, S., Kumar, A., & Singh, G. (2022b). Gold, crude oil, bitcoin and Indian stock market: Recent confirmation from nonlinear ARDL analysis. *Journal of Economic Studies (Glasgow, Scotland)*. doi:10.1108/JES-01-2022-0007

Li, Y., & Giles, D. E. (2015). Modelling volatility spillover effects between developed stock markets and Asian emerging stock markets. *International Journal of Finance & Economics*, *20*(2), 155–177. doi:10.1002/ijfe.1506

Lim, S. Y., & Sek, S. K. (2014). Exploring the Inter-relationship between the Volatilities of Exchange Rate and Stock Return. *Procedia Economics and Finance*, *14*, 367–376. doi:10.1016/S2212-5671(14)00725-4

Lv, Q. (2019). The Influence of International Oil Price Fluctuations on Chinese Economy Based on VAR Model. *IOP Conference Series. Earth and Environmental Science*, *371*(5), 052007. doi:10.1088/1755-1315/371/5/052007

Mensi, W., Hammoudeh, S., Reboredo, J. C., & Nguyen, D. K. (2014). Do global factors impact BRICS stock markets? A quantile regression approach. *Emerging Markets Review*, *19*, 1–17. doi:10.1016/j.ememar.2014.04.002

Mensi, W., Hkiri, B., Al-Yahyaee, K. H., & Kang, S. H. (2018). Analyzing time–frequency co-movements across gold and oil prices with BRICS stock markets: A VaR based on wavelet approach. *International Review of Economics & Finance*, *54*, 74–102. doi:10.1016/j.iref.2017.07.032

Mishra, S. (2015). An Econometric Investigation of Long and Short Run Relationship among Global Crude Oil Price, Exchange Rate and Stock Price in India : *XIMB. Journal of Management*, *12*(2), 1–19.

Mroua, M., & Trabelsi, L. (2020). Causality and dynamic relationships between exchange rate and stock market indices in BRICS countries: Panel/GMM and ARDL analyses. *Journal of Economics, Finance and Administrative Science*, *25*(50), 395–412. doi:10.1108/JEFAS-04-2019-0054

Narayan, P. K., & Narayan, S. (2010). Carbon dioxide emissions and economic growth: Panel data evidence from developing countries. *Energy Policy*, *38*(1), 661–666. doi:10.1016/j.enpol.2009.09.005

Nouira, R., Hadj Amor, T., & Rault, C. (2018). Oil price fluctuations and exchange rate dynamics in the MENA region: Evidence from non-causality-in-variance and asymmetric non-causality tests. *The Quarterly Review of Economics and Finance*. doi:10.1016/j.qref.2018.07.011

Odugbesan, J. A., Sunday, T. A., & Olowu, G. (2021). Asymmetric effect of financial development and remittance on economic growth in MINT economies: An application of panel NARDL. *Future Business Journal*, *7*(1), 39. doi:10.118643093-021-00085-6

Onel, G. (2005). Testing for Multiple Structural Breaks: An Application of Bai-Perron Test To the Nominal Interest Rates and Inflation in Turkey. *Dokuz Eylül Üniversitesi İktisadi İdari Bilimler Fakültesi Dergisi*, *20*(2), 81–94.

Pal, D., & Mitra, S. K. (2019). Asymmetric oil price transmission to the purchasing power of the U.S. dollar: A multiple threshold NARDL modelling approach. *Resources Policy*, *64*, 101508. doi:10.1016/j.resourpol.2019.101508

Papapetrou, E. (2001). Oil price shocks, stock market, economic activity and employment in Greece. *Energy Economics*, *23*(5), 511–532. doi:10.1016/S0140-9883(01)00078-0

Perron, B. Y. P. (1989). The Great Crash, the Oil Price Shock, and the Unit Root Hypothesis Author. *The Econometric Society Stable, 57*(6), 1361–1401. https://www.jstor.org/stable/1913712

Pesaran, M. H., Shin, Y., & Smith, R. J. (2001). Bounds testing approaches to the analysis of level relationships. *Journal of Applied Econometrics, 16*(3), 289–326. doi:10.1002/jae.616

Prasad Bal, D., & Narayan Rath, B. (2015). Nonlinear causality between crude oil price and exchange rate: A comparative study of China and India. *Energy Economics, 51*, 149–156. doi:10.1016/j.eneco.2015.06.013

Raju, G. A., & Marathe, S. R. (2020). Relationship between crude oil prices and macro-economic variables: Evidence from brics countries. *International Journal of Energy Economics and Policy, 10*(5), 264–271. doi:10.32479/ijeep.9755

Sahu, T. N., Bandopadhyay, K., & Mondal, D. (2014). Crude oil price, exchange rate and emerging stock market: Evidence from India. *Jurnal Pengurusan, 42*, 75–87. doi:10.17576/pengurusan-2014-42-07

Saidu, M. T., Naseem, N. A. M., Law, S. H., & Yasmin, B. (2021). Exploring the asymmetric effect of oil price on exchange rate: Evidence from the top six African net oil importers. *Energy Reports, 7*, 8238–8257. doi:10.1016/j.egyr.2021.07.037

Saraswat, G. B., Saraswat, M., Singh, S. K., & Tiwari, R. S. (2022). The Fluctuation in Interest Rate, Exchange Rate and Crude Oil Price and its impact on Stock Market. *YMER Digital, 21*(01), 484–52. doi:10.37896/YMER21.01/44

Seng, W. K., & Hook, L. S. (2001). *Part a Cointegration Test – Ardl Bounds Test*. 1–32.

Singhal, S., & Ghosh, S. (2016). Returns and volatility linkages between international crude oil price, metal and other stock indices in India: Evidence from VAR-DCC-GARCH models. *Resources Policy, 50*, 276–288. doi:10.1016/j.resourpol.2016.10.001

Srinivasan, P. (2015). Modeling and Forecasting of Time-Varying Conditional Volatility of the Indian Stock Market. *IUP Journal of Financial Risk Management, 12*(1), 49–64. http://0-search.ebscohost.com.wam.city.ac.uk/login.aspx?direct=true&db=bth&AN=109099697&site=ehost-live

Syed, A. A. (2021). Symmetric and Asymmetric Influence of Macroeconomic Variables on Stock Prices Movement: Study of Indian Stock Market. *New Challenges for Future Sustainability and Wellbeing*, 319–339. https://doi.org/ doi:10.1108/978-1-80043-968-920211017/FULL/HTML

Tiwari, A. K., & Albulescu, C. T. (2016). Oil price and exchange rate in India: Fresh evidence from continuous wavelet approach and asymmetric, multi-horizon Granger-causality tests. *Applied Energy*, *179*, 272–283. doi:10.1016/j.apenergy.2016.06.139

Tiwari, A. K., Dar, A. B., & Bhanja, N. (2013). Oil price and exchange rates: A wavelet based analysis for India. *Economic Modelling*, *31*(1), 414–422. doi:10.1016/j.econmod.2012.11.043

Tiwari, A. K., Trabelsi, N., Alqahtani, F., & Hammoudeh, S. (2019). Analysing systemic risk and time-frequency quantile dependence between crude oil prices and BRICS equity markets indices: A new look. *Energy Economics*, *83*, 445–466. doi:10.1016/j.eneco.2019.07.014

Wen, D., Wang, G., Ma, C., & Wang, Y. (2019). Risk spillovers between oil and stock markets: A VAR for VaR analysis. *Energy Economics*, #pagerange#. https://doi.org/S0140988319300568

Yin, L., & Ma, X. (2018). Causality between oil shocks and exchange rate: A Bayesian, graph-based VAR approach. *Physica A*, *508*, 434–453. doi:10.1016/j.physa.2018.05.064

Zhang, X., & Baek, J. (2022). The role of oil price shocks on exchange rates for the selected Asian countries: Asymmetric evidence from nonlinear ARDL and generalized IRFs approaches. *Energy Economics*, *112*, 106178. doi:10.1016/j.eneco.2022.106178

ENDNOTE

1 Level stationary variable: which means that if variable is difference in first order it is found to be a stationary variable at levels.

Chapter 11
Data Analysis on Weaving Productivity of a Jute Industry in West Bengal, India

Satya Narayan Bag
AMA College of Polytechnic, Kolkata, India

ABSTRACT

The target efficiency of the Hessian shuttle loom was much lower than the Sacking loom due to the lighter construction of the Hessian fabric and lower yarn count. It was found that variation of actual CV% of efficiency percentage of Hessian Shuttle loom was comparatively higher than Sacking loom. It is due to the high variation of the number of loom running /day and the lighter construction of the Hessian fabric. In the case of Victor loom, there is a positive co-relationship between Kgs/loom/shift and machine efficiency. Here the value of R is positive. In the case of the S 4 loom, there is a strong positive co-relationship between machine efficiency and kgs/loom/shift. Here the value of R is 0.98 which indicates a strong positive relationship between the two variables. The relationship is statistically significant at a 95% confidence level. In the case of sacking quality narrow shuttle loom, it is found that kgs/loom/shift is positively correlated with loom efficiency %.

INTRODUCTION

KJL is a pioneer jute industry in West Bengal, India. Jute yarn, Fabrics, Bag, wide hessian cloths etc. are the major finished products of this unit. Raw Jute is the input material of such products. The unit is gradually converted its production process, machinery into modern machines and processing. As a result, the quality

DOI: 10.4018/978-1-6684-7568-3.ch011

of the finished goods has been enhanced. The demands of customers in domestic and international market are now gradually increasing. The technically skill and competent people are now trying to enrich the finished goods into international standard. The present study is to look back at the productivity status of various department of weaving section. Weaving is the most important area in Jute industry. Here, two sets of yarn are interlaced, forming fabric. So, productivity status of such department is very urgent for planning of meeting of customer's requirement in-time. Various productivity parameters and their inter relation is studied and statistical analysis were performed based on data obtained during study. Various findings are then tabulated to find out the suitable corrective measures for timely delivery of finished goods to the customers.

OBJECTIVES OF THE STUDY

The objectives of the study are represented here.

- To study the various productivity parameters, their targets, achievement over certain period of weaving department.
- To study the interrelation of various production parameters.
- To achieve suitable corrective measures for improvement in various areas of weaving department.

RESEARCH METHODOLOGY

Productivity of various areas of weaving department is monitored, studied for 15 to 17 days. The data so collected in various shifts and days, are primary in nature. After collecting of data, tabulation is performed in proper ways. Statistical analyses are performed by online statistical calculator, software. Various conclusions are then drawn based on analysis.

RESULTS AND DISCUSSION

We have studied 15 days production data of weaving department. Table 1, explained the productivity parameters of Hessian Shuttle loom. Table 2 explained the productivity parameters of sacking loom. Target efficiency of Hessian shuttle loom was much lower than Sacking loom due to lighter construction of the Hessian fabric and lower yarn count. It is found that variation of actual CV% of efficiency % of Hessian Shuttle loom was comparatively higher than Sacking loom. It is due to high variation of number of loom running /day and lighter construction of Hessian fabric.

Table 1. Day wise production details of Hessian weaving department

Date	Production in Kg		Production /loom/shift in kg		Total Looms	Efficiency	
	Target	Actual	Target	Actual		Target	Actual
18.6.22	6531	4075	39.58	24.7	165	65	40.78
17.6.22	6536	4269	40.59	26.32	161	65	41.14
15.6.22	8203	4925	45.82	27.51	179	65	39.60
14.6.22	7671	4326	47.93	27.21	159.0	65	36.71
13.6.22	8791	5141	49.5	28.4	181	65	39.16
12.6.22	1741	1056	54.4	33.0	32.0	65	37.26
11.6.22	9095	5395	50.52	29.97	180.0	65	39.78
10.6.22	9897	5673	51.81	29.7	191.0	65	38.67
9.6.22	10316	5876	51.58	29.38	200.0	65	37.89
8.6.22	9872	5782	53.65	31.42	184	65	39.32
7.6.22	9848	5598	53.81	30.59	183	65	38.79
6.6.22	10420	5975	54.84	31.45	190	65	39.45
5.6.22	3298	1724	56.86	29.72	58	65	34.19
4.6.22	10415	6022	53.96	31.2	193	65	38.87
3.6.22	10721	6517	53.33	32.42	201	65	41.5
2.6.22	10675	6309	53.375	31.55	200	65	40.19
1.6.22	9456	5648	55.29	33.03	171	65	39.47
Average	8440.353	4959.471	50.99088	29.85706	166.3529	65	38.98647
Max. Value	10721	6517	56.86	33.03	201	65	41.5
Min. Value	1741	1056	39.58	24.7	32	65	34.19
S.D.	2604.2	1518.72	4.95	2.38	47.68	0	1.763
CV%	30.85%	30.62%	9.7%	7.97%	28.66%	0	4.52%

Source: Production registered book of the Mill

Total number of Hessian loom running was comparatively less than the Sacking loom. This is due to variation of Hessian quality product order, availability of weavers. Day wise production of Sacking quality was much higher compare to Hessian quality, due to higher number of loom and heavier fabric at sacking weaving machine Kg / loom/shift of Hessian loom was much lower compare to sacking quality, due to the lighter construction of cloth . CV % of Kg/loom/shift in Hessian quality loom was much higher compare to Sacking quality, due to the high CV % of actual day wise production of Hessian quality loom.

Table 2. Day wise production details of sacking weaving department

Date	Production in Kg		Production /loom/shift in kg		Total Looms	Efficiency	
	Target	Actual	Target	Actual		Target	Actual
18.6.22	14033	13457	63.21	60.62	222	80	76.72
17.6.22	13590	12953	63.20	60.25	215	80	76.25
15.6.22	16434	15707	63.2	60.41	260	80	76.46
14.6.22	13463	12837	63.2	60.27	213	80	76.28
13.6.22	14853	14194	63.20	60.4	235.0	80	76.45
12.6.22	6510	6011	63.20	58.36	103.0	80	73.87
11.6.22	14412	13729	63.21	60.210	228	80	76.21
10.6.22	13527	12876	63.21	60.17	214.0	80	76.15
9.6.22	13336	12759	63.20	60.13	211	80	76.54
8.6.22	13401	12759	63.21	60.180	212	80	76.17
7.6.22	13589	12953	63.20	60.250	215	80	76.26
6.6.22	12894	12371	63.20	61.64	204	80	76.76
5.6.22	6511	5934	63.21	57.61	103	80	72.91
4.6.22	13906	13225	63.20	60.11	220	80	76.08
3.6.22	13273	12643	63.20	60.2	210	80	76.2
2.6.22	13969	13302	63.20	60.19	221	80	76.18
1.6.22	14412	13729	63.21	60.21	228	80	76.21
Average	13065.47	12437.59	63.20353	60.07118	206.7059	80	75.98235
Min Value	6510	5934	63.2	57.61	103	80	72.91
Max Value	16434	15707	63.21	61.64	260	80	76.76
S.D.	2594.9	2552.57	0.0049	0.872	41.05	0	1.009
CV%	19.86%	20.52%	0	1.45%	19.85%	0	1.32%

Source: Production registered book of the Mill

Figure 1 explained the variation of actual and target machines efficiency % over different day . It is found that variation of day wise efficiency % of Hessian quality loom was much higher compare to sacking quality loom. The target and actual efficiency % of sacking quality machines are higher compare to Hessian quality loom. All are shuttle loom in both the quality.

Figure 1. Variation of weaving efficiency % over different date in the month of June 2022
Source: Production registered book of the Mill

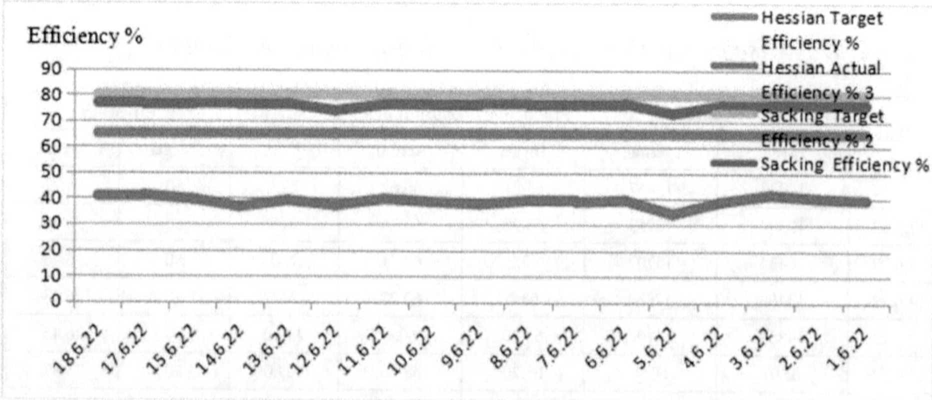

Figure 2. Variation of weaving Kg/loom/shift over different date in the month of June 2022
Source: Production registered book of the Mill

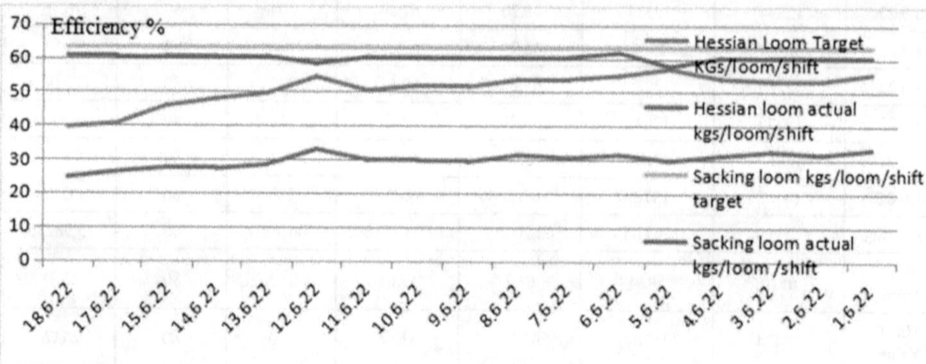

Figure 2 explained the production parameters of Kg. /loom/shift of both the hessian and sacking quality loom. Here both are shuttle loom. It is found that due to heavier construction of the sacking quality fabrics, the kg /loom/shift of sacking quality are much higher compare to hessian type of cloth .It is found that variation of Kg./loom/shift of hessian loom is much higher compare to sacking loom. It is due to higher number of looms in sacking loom and lower CV5 of number of loom running in each days compare to hessian shuttle loom.

Figure 3. Variation of target and actual efficiency % of Victor and S4 loom in the month of June 2022

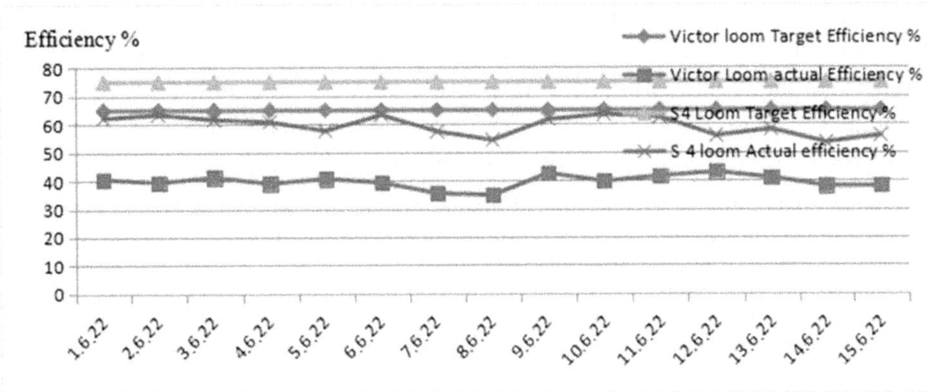

Table 3. Production parameters of Victor & S4 loom in June 22[Average /day]

Date	Efficiency % Victor loom		Kg/loom /shift Victor loom	Efficiency % S4 loom		Kg/loom/shift S4 loom
	Target	Actual		Target	Actual	
1.6.22	65	40.44	33	75	62.20	81
2.6.22	65	39.36	32	75	63.38	80
3.6.22	65	41.12	33	75	61.69	81
4.6.22	65	38.99	32	75	60.80	79
5.6.22	65	40.60	32	75	57.56	75
6.6.22	65	39.28	32	75	63.32	83
7.6.22	65	35.47	27	75	57.27	75
8.6.22	65	34.87	32	75	54.26	71
9.6.22	65	42.46	30	75	61.58	80
10.6.22	65	39.64	28	75	63.4	83
11.6.22	65	41.4	27	75	62.42	82
12.6.22	65	42.87	36	75	55.65	73
13.6.22	65	40.80	25	75	57.91	76
14.6.22	65	37.88	25	75	53.27	70
15.6.22	65	38.05	23	75	55.74	73
Average	65	39.5	29.8	75	59.3	77.4
Max . value	65	42.87	36	75	63.4	83
Min. value	65	34.87	23	75	53.27	70
S.D.	0	2.28	3.72	0	3.56	4.2
CV %	0	5.7%	12.4%	0	6.0%	5.42%

Source: Production registered book of the Mill

From table 3, it is found that Kg/loom/shift of S4 loom was much higher compare to Victor loom. This is due to fabric construction at S4 loom. Lighter cloth is running at Victor loom, which gives lower values of Kg/loom/shift. Target efficiency of S4 loom was much higher compare to Victor loom, due to the heavier fabric structure and heavier yarn count of both the warp and weft yarn compare to Victor weaving machine .CV % of Kg/loom /shift of Victor loom is much higher compare to S4 loom., due to higher value of mean of S4 loom compare to Victor loom.

Figure 3 explained the variation of target and actual efficiency of Victor and S4 loom in the month of June 22. It is found that Target and actual efficiency of S4 loom were quite higher compare to Victor loom, due to heavier fabric of S4 loom. Yarn count of the S4 loom was higher than Victor loom. Finer yarn count of Victor loom, leads to breakages of warp and weft yarn resulting higher yarn breakage during weaving operation. This leads to lower loom efficiency of Victor loom. From Figure 3 and Table 3, it is found that CV% of day wise actual Efficiency of S4 loom was much higher compare to Victor loom. Higher variation of actual efficiency was not desirable .Higher the variation of actual efficiency %, higher will be the variation of production between machines and production variation in day wise manner too.

Table 4. Statistical analysis of production parameter and finding out relationships

Sl No .	Variable X	Variable Y	Value of R	Value of R²	Value of P and comments
1	Victor loom Actual Production in Kg/ loom/shift	Victor loom Actual efficiency /day	0.3118.	0.0972.	The P value is 0.2579. The result is not significant at p< 0.05. It is found that from value of R, technically positive correlation observed between two variables. It is weaker relation
2	S 4 loom Actual Production in Kg/ loom/shift	S 4 loom Actual efficiency /day	0.9854	0.971	The value of R indicates that this is a strong positive co relation, which means that high X variable scores go with high Y variable scores. The P value is <0.00001. The result is significant at P<0.05.
3	Production /loom/shift in Kg Sacking loom	Production in Kg [actual]/day of Sacking loom	0.8429.	0.7105.	This is a strong positive correlation, which means that high X variable scores go with high Y variable scores. The P-Value is .000022. The result is significant at p < .05.
4	Production /loom/shift in Kg Sacking loom	Actual Efficiency % Sacking loom	0.9555.	0.913.	This is a strong positive correlation, which means that high X variable scores go with high Y variable scores. The P-Value is < .00001. The result is significant at p < .05.

continues on following page

Table 4. Continued

Sl No .	Variable X	Variable Y	Value of R	Value of R^2	Value of P and comments
5	Total Looms/day Sacking [NL]	Production in Kg [actual]/day of sacking loom [NL]	0.9999.	is 0.9998.	This is a strong positive correlation, which means that high X variable scores go with high Y variable scores. The P-Value is < .00001. The result is significant at p < .05.
6	Production /loom/shift in Kg Hessian loom	Production in Kg [actual] Hessian loom /day	0.163.	0.0266.	Although technically a positive correlation, the relation between our variables is weak . The P-Value is .53192. The result is not significant at p < .05.
7	Production /loom/shift in Kg Hessian loom	Actual Efficiency % Hessian loom	-0.0844.	0.0071.	Although technically a negative correlation, the relation between our variables is only weak. The P-Value is .760204. The result is not significant at p < .05.
8	Total Looms/day Hessian [NL]	Production in Kg [actual]/day of Hessian loom [NL]	0.9675.	0.9361.	This is a strong positive correlation, which means that high X variable scores go with high Y variable scores. The P-Value is < .00001. The result is significant at p < .05.

Table 4 explained the Pearson's correlation between two production parameters of weaving department. It exhibited the significant relationship between two production parameters of weaving area. The following points are to be results of the statistical test between two sets of data.

- In case of Victor loom there is a positive co relation between Kg/loom/shift and machine efficiency. Here value of R is positive. The relation is very weak. The relation is statistically not significant at 95% confidence level.
- In case of S 4 loom, there is a strong positive co relation present between machine efficiency and Kg/loom/shift. Here value of R is 0.98 which indicates strong positive relation between two variables. The relationship is statistically significant at 95% confidence level.
- In case of Sacking [NL], which is shuttle loom, observed that there is a positive co relation between Kg/loom/shift and actual production /day .The value of R is 0.84, which indicates strong relation between two variables. The relation is statistically significant.
- In case of sacking quality narrow shuttle loom it is found that Kg/loom/shift is positively co related with loom efficiency %. The value of R is 0.955, which indicates strong relation between two variables. It is found that the relation is statistically significant at 95% confidence level.

- Higher the number of loom of sacking quality shuttle loom, higher will be actual day wise production. This is true as the value of R is 0.999, which indicates strong positive relation between two parameters. The relation is statistically significant.
- In case of Hessian quality shuttle loom, it is found that actual production /day in Kg. is positively co related with Kg/loom /shift. The value of R is 0.163, which indicates positive relation but it is very weak and it is not statistically significant.
- In case of Hessian quality shuttle loom, it is found that Kg/loom/shift and loom efficiency are negative related. The value of R indicates that .This relation is very weak and not statistically significant.
- In case of Hessian quality shuttle loom, it is found that, number of loom is positively co related with total actual production/day in Kg . The value of R is 0.96, which indicates strong positive relation between the two variables. The relation is statistically significant at 95% confidence level.

CORRECTIVE MEASURES

It is found that in some cases the actual achievement is far behind from the target .Management has taken several initiatives for improvement in productivity and efficiency of the weaving department. The steps are stated below.

- Training of unskilled manpower and counseling them the target production of the machines..
- Recruitment of skilled manpower for machine operations.
- Weekly meeting with all level of production, maintenance officers relating to various problem of department and root cause analysis.
- Corrective route map for overcoming such problem.
- Discussion on day wise achievement of each department and requisite solution for achievement.
- Follow up maintenance schedule of machinery.
- Monitoring and reduction of process wastage and corrective measures.
- Timely delivery of finished goods to the customers and post-delivery activities.
- Proper batch mixing of raw Jute, so that spinning breakage will be as minimum as possible.

CONCLUSION

Present study is an important area of discussion on productivity analysis weaving department. Various productivity parameters are calculated, analyzed and finding out the interrelationship of various parameters. Based on statistical analysis, corrective measures are taken by Top Management. This study is an important for productivity parameters of various department of manufacturing organization.

REFERENCES

Bag, S. N. (2020). *Impact of COVID-19 Pandemic on Productivity of Jute Industry: A Case Study*. Fibre2Fashion. https://www.fibre2fashion.com/industry-article/8796

Bag, S. N., & Sinha, R. C. (2021). *Study on Weaving Performance of a Jute Mill in Pre- & Post-COVID Lockdown Periods.* Fibre2Fashion. https://www.fibre2fashion.com/industry-article/8923

Das, P. (2011, May). Productivity and Efficiency in the Jute Industry. *Economic and Political Weekly*, *46*(19), 74–76.

Kibria, M. G., & Tisdell, C. A. (1985, May- June). Operating capital and productivity patterns in jute weaving in Bangladesh. *Journal of Development Economics*, *18*(1), 133–152. doi:10.1016/0304-3878(85)90011-2

. Mohideen R K, & Muthuraju P. (2016). An analysis of Trend and growth rate of Textile Industry in India. *Shanlax International Journal of Commerce, 4*(3).

Tisdell, C. A. (1983). *Productivity Progress and Learning by Doing in Bangladesh Jute Weaving Industry.* Researcsh Gate. https://www.researchgate.net/publication/303447627

Chapter 12
Barriers:
Investigating the Factors Impacting the Sustainability of Students' Online Learning

Ajay Jain
https://orcid.org/0000-0002-6087-0206
SRM Institute of Science and Technology, India

Shruti Bansal
SRM Institute of Science and Technology, India

Shobha Bhardwaj
Institute of Management Studies, Ghaziabad, India

ABSTRACT

Online education is a technique in which students use internet-connected devices like computers or mobile to attend teacher's lectures. During the Corona pandemic time, all the educational institutions has globally adopted this technique. The researcher aimed to examine obstacles faced by students living in Delhi-NCR (National Capital Region) while using e-education. To accomplish these six barriers i.e., individual, technological, instructor's dimension, infrastructural, learning environment challenges, and miscellaneous barriers used in this study which are represented by total 25 items. These selected barriers were investigated by applying a multivariate statistical tool i.e., Partial Least Squares (PLS) approach. The outcomes revealed that besides technological barriers and learning environment challenges all other factors have significant impact on prolonged use of E-learning. This study has several benefits that can help educational institutions in developing strategies for teaching students in a much better way.

DOI: 10.4018/978-1-6684-7568-3.ch012

1. INTRODUCTION

The world is now moving towards the fourth industrial revolution i.e. technological revolution in which life has become dependent on technology that alters businesses, education and other sectors speedily. This change blurs the borders between personal and professional life (Agarwal et al., 2021).

Covid-19 has hampered almost all sectors of the economy. As a result of this major problem, the GDP and economic growth of the nation have decreased (Jain et al., 2022). A report stated that Covid-19 has been a major reason behind the closure of schools in 188 countries. All schools were not able to implement technology-based teaching methods due to which they had to close their institutions (OECD, 2020). For supporting this new methodology, learning providers by the use of Online Learning system can manage all the teaching activities from starting to end for betterment. These supporting parties can also assist the education instructors, schools, and colleges to provide education to their students during their sudden unforeseen closed down (Almaiah et al., 2020). But the students of those institutions that have suddenly applied the online learning method had to face a lot of problems such as mental health problems, learning issues, etc.(Barrot et al., 2021) .

A survey stated that the movement of traditional teaching towards online learning affected the students in various ways. Some students felt that the online mode of teaching is much more stressful as compared to the physical mode of classroom teaching. During the Covid pandemic starting days, the teachers were not much capable of delivering lectures and maintaining online classes confidently but now their performance improved from 68.9% to 77.1% (Chakraborty et al., 2021).

Online Learning through online education has a huge contribution to the educational development of the students in today's time. This online education was being used even in earlier days, but present needs and circumstances are making it more popular. In the last few years, it has been observed that there is a paradigm shift from Classroom Learning to Online Learning, but it has been widely popularized by its usage during the COVID-19 pandemic. Increasing client happiness in the era of globalization is a difficult undertaking, particularly in the service industry (Raj & Bansal, 2019). A Virginia-based study also identified that the student's performance becomes decreased from offline to online classes during the Covid pandemic by viewing year-to-year performance graphs (Bird et al., 2022).

For supporting this new methodology-online learning, learning providers by the use of an Online Learning system can manage all the teaching activities from starting to end for betterment. Therefore, understanding the basic problems of Online Learning is essential for successful Online Learning system implementation. However, each technology and technique has some advantages and disadvantages. But in this study, researcher have taken some selective variables by following some respective literatures and looked at their effect on students' online learning. Some selective variables have been taken in this study, but these are not enough to represent the whole impact on online learning of students. Apart from these, there are many other variables that will be part of any other future research study to see the impact on online learning. This research study helps to identify variables that are least and most impacting students Online Learning while using online education system collectively and individually.

2. LITERATURE REVIEW

Through a thorough evaluation of the available research, this section outlines how the study's hypotheses were developed.

For research and educational purposes, the Internet has emerged as one of the most crucial resources for teachers and students (Hartshorne & Ajjan, 2009). When referring to technology-based Online Learning, the internet and other crucial technologies are utilised to develop learning materials, instruct students, and manage courses in an organisation (Fry, 2001). Dispersed learning, online-distance learning, and hybrid learning are only a few examples of how the term "Online Learning" is applied. Online Learning as a concept comprises a variety of uses, instructional strategies, and procedures (Rossi, 2009). Taking the IT support in online learning and teaching mode of education is known as Online Learning. Any learning that is enabled electronically is referred to as Online Learning by taking into consideration digital instruments, according to a researcher (Abbad et al., 2009).

The application of Online Learning method by institutions especially for undergraduate and post graduate education, offers multiple advantages and benefits. In fact Online Learning is one of the best medium or a way of education due to various advantages. The application of Online Learning provides institutions and students with a great option to teach and learn from anywhere anytime without considering other factor (Smedley, 2010). Online Learning uses a digital platform, and through interactive video sessions, students may watch all activities just like they would in a classroom and communicate with instructors (Zhang et al., 2006).

Despite the benefits of utilising online learning in the classroom, there are also drawbacks. When numerous people use the same Online Learning platform frequently at once, the internet may get congested, which could result in unexpected costs and delays (Collins et al., 2002); (Klein & Ware, 2003). Online Learning results in a lack of student interaction. Due to the lack of in-person interactions with teachers or instructions, Online Learning may prove to be less effective than the contemporary form of education (Arkorful & Abaidoo, 2014).

Barriers

A study has been conducted to find out the obstacles faced by medical students in a developing nation while using an online learning mode of education. The study identified that the pandemic had produced mental stress and anxiety among students, which developed concentration issues in their academics (Baticulon et al., 2021). These medical students face technological, individual, household, institutional, and communal hurdles during online learning. Students felt anxious as a result of long online lectures (Rajab et al., 2020). Physical problems are also generated, such as eye strain due to the long-run use of online learning (Octaberlina & Muslimin, 2020). A supported study stated that stress, anxiety, loneliness, and depressive symptoms have increased among students after the Covid-19 pandemic (Elmer et al., 2020).

One of the factor that has significantly affects students' satisfaction with online learning is technical support (Nambiar, 2020). Although there are some benefits to online learning, such as convenience and flexibility (Aboagye & Jung, 2018); (Muhammad & Anwar, 2020); (Alchamdani et al., 2020); (Farooq et al., 2020); (Hussein et al., 2020), these advantages have been limited in absence of technological knowledge and experience (Rajab et al., 2020). According to a study, the absence of past experience taking online courses and expertise utilising and operating online technologies has contributed to technological hurdles (Muflih et al., 2020). Based on these reviews, the following hypothesis has been framed by researcher stated below:

Therefore, the hypothesis proposed by the researcher is as follows:

H_1-Individual Barriers have an effect on Online Learning of the students.
H_2-Technological Barriers have an effect on Online Learning of the students.

The rapid development of various activities in our everyday lives is being influenced by advances in digital technology because the Online Learning system has earned a competitive advantage over the traditional methods. It is also found that infrastructure and technology dimensions are the most important influencing factors among all the barriers considered for successful Online Learning system installation (Naveed et al., 2017). A study stated that there is a statistically significant pattern for the factors social contact, administrative/instructor issues, and learner motivation. The likelihood of using online courses has increased in future as the barriers reduced (Muilenburg & Berge, 2005).

Online instructors play the most important function in the Online Learning design outlook (Yengin et al., 2011). A study examined four critical success factors which have been measured by using student insight (Selim, 2007). Instructor and student qualities, technology organization, and university support are all elements to consider. The study's findings revealed that the most important aspect in Online Learning performance is instructor characteristics, followed by IT infrastructure and institution support while student attributes are the least important component in Online Learning's success.

Therefore, the hypothesis proposed by the researcher is as follows:

H_3-Instructor' Dimensions have an effect on Online Learning of the students.

The dominance of the English language, lack of research grants for Online Learning, and absence of proper training on Online Learning courses from the university were the most important barrier factors for the implementation of Online Learning (Lakbala, 2016). The massive investment in installing, administering, and maintaining the Online Learning system covered in Infrastructure and Technology category (Naveed et al., 2017). Inadequate training and institutional support have been reported to be key obstacles for medical students who are using online platform or mode of education for their medical study (Farooq et al., 2020). During ICT orientation programs, educational institutions can help students obtain abilities (Sharpe & Benfield, 2015).

Therefore, the hypothesis proposed by the researcher is as follows:

H_4-Infrastructure Barriers have an effect on Online Learning of the students.

A study has identified seven barriers which are: Self-regulation, Technological literacy and competency, Student isolation, Technological sufficiency, Technological complexity, Learning resource, and, Learning environment which are collectively represented by thirty-seven variables. The biggest problem for children who use online learning platforms at home is that they less knowledge of online learning platform technical proficiency.(Ganai et al., 2019).

Therefore, the hypothesis proposed by the researcher is as follows:

H_5- Learning Environment Challenges have an effect on Online Learning of the students.

After taking the expert opinion of academic professionals, the researcher has identified 7 variables to represent the Miscellaneous Barrier factor, which are affecting the online education of the students. These variables are- Unaware about online Ethical Code of Conduct, Comparison between classroom and online learning, Students followed unfair Practices, Lack of direct interaction, lack of personal counseling, Student life imbalanced and Impact of class size.

Based on the above details, the researcher has framed a hypothesis mentioned below:

H 6 - Miscellaneous Barriers have an effect on Online Learning of the students

3. RESEARCH METHODOLOGY

The researcher gathered detailed information regarding students' experiences in an online learning environment to comprehend their set assumption. The online survey was conducted among the students who have attended online classes through Google form. This study has collected 303 responses of the students who are studying in class 10th or above (Intermediate, Under graduation and Post Graduation). As it is the university's official learning management system, students can select MS teams for study.

3.1 Research Objective

The aim of this study is to examine the various barriers faced while using the Online Learning system from a student's perspective in **Delhi-NCR (National Capital Region).**

3.2 Sample Size

Priori sample size method has been used to identify the sample size (Soper, 2017). The required information consists of 0.3 anticipated effect sizes, 0.8 desired statistical power level, 0.05 probability level, 6 latent variables, and 25 observed variables. The received calculated minimum sample size value for model is 94, and the recommended minimum sample size is 161. The sample size of this study collected is 303, which sufficiently met the requirements to represent the total population.

3.3 Scale Development and Data Collection and Time Period of Study

The survey Link was shared on social media (WhatsApp, Facebook, and Instagram). The researcher reached out to organizations to ask them to share the information with students at their respective schools and colleges. Participation was entirely voluntary with complete anonymity assured and informed consent obtained. A five-point Likert scale-based questionnaire was designed to collect the data. The measurement scale has contained 25 items representing 7 factors that are detailed below in table no.1. To gain some insight knowledge, an open-ended question has been asked at the end of the questionnaire also. Around three months have been taken by researcher for data collection data and total six months for paper preparation.

3.4 Statistical Tool

Proposed model and hypothesis have been tested in this study by applying the Smart PLS tool by following their assumptions of data normality, sample size and constructs that are formatively measured (Joe F. Hair et al., 2014).

3.5 Research Framework

The researcher has framed a conceptual model to represent this study by taking the help from various literature reviews discussed above. This proposed model shows that there is an impact of selected six factors (independent variables) i.e. Individual Barrier, Technological Barrier, Instructor Dimension, Infrastructure barrier, Learning environment Challenges, and Miscellaneous Barrier over prolonged use of Online Learning. Six respective factors have been represented by 25 items to check their impact on the issues faced by prolonged use of Online Learning (single dependent variable) used in this study. In the data analysis part, the individual and collective impact of all factors will be seen on the dependent factor. The PLS-SEM multivariate statistical tool application was used to find out which factor has more impact on the dependent variable and which has the least impact.

Figure 1. Research framework

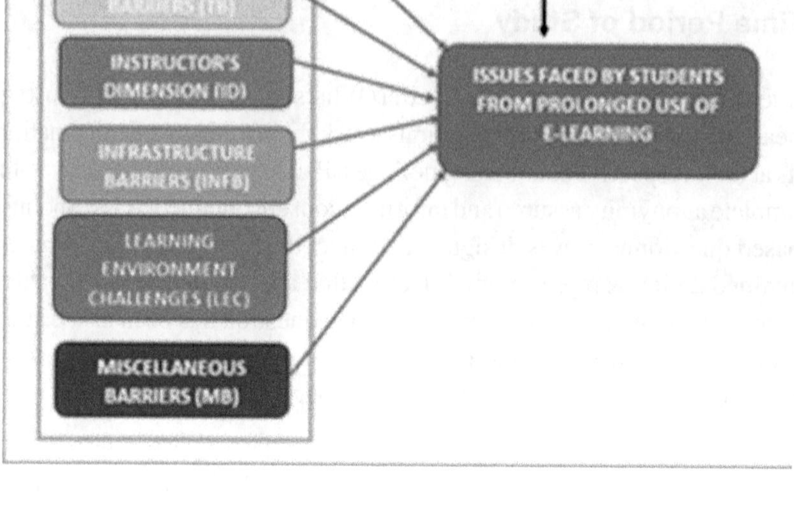

Barriers

Table 1. Factors and items with codes

Codes	**Items***All Were In Five-Point (1=Strongly Disagree To 5=Strongly Agree)*
IB	***Individual Barriers***
IB1	The use of Online Learning for a long time causes anxiety disorder, depression, and stress.
IB2	Staring at electronic devices for a long time causes backache, headache, and eyestrain.
IB3	Limited availability of study material for practical work such as laboratory tools, and printers at home.
TB	***Technological Barriers***
TB1	Non-availability of gadgets used to operate online learning at home creates a problem.
TB2	Frequently faces Internet issues while using Online Learning software that is due to location or limited data pack.
TB3	Due to not being technically sound, we have to face issues in using electronic devices and software.
TB4	Facing difficulties while using the Online Learning platform such as Security Issues, Privacy issues, etc.
INSB	***Instructor's Barriers***
INSB1	Lack of ICT* skills among teachers lead to communication and proper exchange of information problems. (ICT*- Information and communications technology)
INSB2	Most of the teachers are not having much knowledge of online teaching.
INSB3	Sometimes teachers appear uncomfortable while giving lectures online for a very long duration of time.
INSB4	Most of the teachers show resistance to learning or adopting anything new such as new technology.
INFB	***Infrastructure Barriers***
INFB1	Lack of sufficient infrastructure for proper online study to the students from the institutions.
INFB2	The college does not provide any training to the students before starting online education.
INFB3	Colleges do not expend much on new and better quality online teaching software for proper Online Learning education.
LEB	***Learning Environment Barriers***
LEB1	While Online Learning, most of the time we are distracted due to the sudden appearance of social media pop-ups or ads.
LEB2	Distractions are caused due to discussions held with family members unknowingly.
LEB3	It is not easy for everyone to find the right location and peaceful environment while studying online. Unable to complete certain projects and assignments at home with limited material.
MB	***Miscellaneous Barriers***
MB1MB2	Unawareness among students and teachers about following online education ethical code of conduct. Classroom learning is a better mode in comparison to online learning.
MB3	Short tricks or unfair practices are used to answer the teacher's question online.
MB4	Lack of direct interaction between teacher and students.
MB5MB6MB7	Lack of solution Personal query or counseling by teachers like classroom learning.Imbalances occur between student Personal life and college life.Merging of classes increases class size which impacts over effective learning of students.
EL	***Issues Faced By Students From Prolonged Use Of Online Learning***
EL1	The online class activities and discussions didn't allow me to gain knowledge.

4. DATA ANALYSIS

The data analysis has been broadly divided into two parts based on applying the PLS-SEM tool, i.e. Structural model and measurement model.

4.1 Goodness of Model Fit

At the initial level of model assessment, the goodness of model fit has been conducted before proceeding to other parts of data analysis such as measurement and structural evaluation (Henseler et al., 2016). The calculated SRMR (Standardised Root Mean Square Residuals) value in the above-stated table is 0.113, which is almost equal to its threshold value of 0.1. So, the SRMR value is also acceptable (Henseler et al., 2015); (Hu & Bentler, 1998). The calculated NFI value is 0.524 in the current study.

The value of R^2 is 0.20. It depicts that 20 percent of the independent factors selected in the study collectively impacted on the dependent variable and rest percentage may depend on other factors which are not taken in this study. So, our calculated R^2 value is also showing medium type of acceptable results, which stated that R^2 value between 0.13 to 0.25 is considered to be medium (Cohen, 1992).

4.2 Construct Reliability

The calculated Cronbach's alpha values of all the factors in this research are almost greater than the minimum acceptable range i.e. 0.61-0.70. Factor EL, IB, ID, MB, and INFB alpha values are above 0.7. But TB and LEC values are slightly on the lower side of the minimum acceptable range i.e. 0.5 and 0.6 (Konting et al., 2009). But in the present research, the composite reliability of all factors is greater than 0.70 in all the cases. So, satisfactory results have been achieved (Hair et al., 2014).

4.3 Convergent Validity

The received calculated AVE values are higher than the standard threshold value i.e. 0.50 in all cases except infrastructure barriers as shown in Table 2 below. It indicates that the questionnaire accurately reflects model's and each study variable's features.

To calculate discriminant validity, the Heterotrait-Monotrait Ratio of Correlations (HTMT) criterion has been used. In this method, all the received values are less than 0.90 threshold value, which means that discriminant validity has been acknowledged by following (Henseler et al., 2015) mentioned in Table 3.

Table 2. Construct reliability and validity

	Cronbach's Alpha	Rho_A	Composite Reliability	Average Variance Extracted (AVE)
EL	1.000	1.000	1.000	1.000
IB	0.786	0.792	0.903	0.823
ID	0.797	0.858	0.863	0.613
INFB	0.666	1.457	0.731	0.496
LEC	0.582	0.678	0.819	0.695
MB	0.833	0.850	0.875	0.505
TB	0.524	0.783	0.727	0.532

Table 3. Heterotrait-Monotrait ratio (HTMT)<Tbl_Large></Tbl_Large>

	EL	IB	ID	INFB	LEC	MB	TB
EL							
IB	0.111						
ID	0.364	0.074					
INFB	0.251	0.728	0.484				
LEC	0.290	0.205	0.626	0.480			
MB	0.406	0.122	0.686	0.517	0.805		
TB	0.238	0.481	0.758	0.588	0.676	0.605	

Multicollinearity is used to calculate Variance Inflation Factors (VIF) whose calculated values must lie between the range 4.0 or less than 0.2 tolerance (Hair et al., 2010). The Collinearity Statistics (outer VIF values) of all the aforementioned items have a value of less than four, indicating that the variables have no multicollinearity effect.

4.4 Final Structural Equation Modeling (SEM)

It is clearly shown in figure 2 that out of 25 items taken by the researcher for this study of selected six factors, only 21 items are remaining left in the optimised model after checking each indicator's outside weight and outer loadings by following the criteria that All the indicator loading exceeded the minimum threshold of 0.60 (Henseler et al., 2009).

Table 4. Collinearity statistics (VIF)

Table- Outer VIF Values	VIF	*Table- Outer VIF Values*	VIF
EL	**1.000**	**INFB2**	**1.559**
IB2	**1.722**	**INFB3**	**1.536**
IB3	**1.722**	**LEC3**	**1.203**
TB1	**1.020**	**LEC4**	**1.203**
TB3	**1.520**	**MB1**	**1.547**
TB4	**1.502**	**MB2**	**1.810**
ID1	**1.480**	**MB3**	**1.230**
ID2	**1.813**	**MB4**	**2.224**
ID3	**1.934**	**MB5**	**2.159**
ID4	**1.446**	**MB6**	**1.787**
INFB1	**1.138**	**MB7**	**1.773**

This means that the items that are least impacting over the online learning of the students' factors are automatically rejected by the structural model to achieve the model stability. After rejecting the least contributing items, the values of Chi-square, NFI and SRMR are also improved to some extent. Based on these received values, out of all six hypothetical assumptions set by the researcher, four hypotheses are accepted.

Table 5. Path coefficients values

Structural Paths	*Original Sample (O)*	*Sample Mean (M)*	*Standard Deviation (Stdev)*	*T Statistics |O/Stdev|*	*P-Values*	*Decision*
IB -> EL	-0.171	-0.173	0.038	4.477	**0.000**	**ACCEPTED**
TB -> EL	-0.010	-0.008	0.048	0.217	**0.829**	**REJECTED**
ID -> EL	0.125	0.120	0.058	2.155	**0.032**	**ACCEPTED**
INFB -> EL	0.181	0.180	0.066	2.750	**0.006**	**ACCEPTED**
LEC -> EL	0.020	0.028	0.049	0.405	**0.686**	**REJECTED**
MB -> EL	0.226	0.231	0.067	3.361	**0.001**	**ACCEPTED**

Figure 2. Structural equation modelling (SEM)

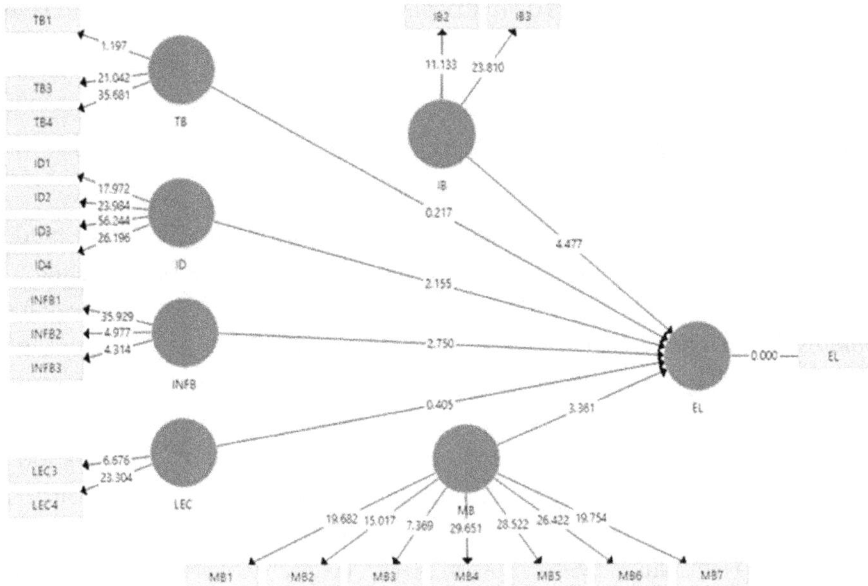

Table 6. Structural relation in model

	Hypothesis Significance	Sig./Non-Sig.
H_1	Individual Barriers have an effect on Online Learning of the students.	Sig.
H_2	Technological Barriers have an effect on Online Learning of the students.	Non-Sig.
H_3	Instructors' Dimensions have an effect on Online Learning of the students.	Sig.
H_4	Infrastructure Barriers have an effect on Online Learning of the students.	Sig.
H_5	Learning Environment Challenges have an effect on Online Learning of the students.	Non-Sig.
H_6	Miscellaneous Barriers have an effect on Online Learning of the students	Sig.

The hypothesis significance has been analysed by using the analytical bootstrapping step of PLS SEM statistical tool. The calculated p-value of first hypothesis ($H_{1)}$ is 0.000, which is less than 0.10 significance level at a 90% confidence level that means H_1 is accepted. The calculated p-value of H_2 is 0.829 is more than 0.10 significance level at a 90% confidence level that means Hypothesis second is rejected. The calculated p-value of H_3 is 0.032 which is less than 0.05 significance level at a 95% confidence level that means H_3 is accepted. The calculated p of H_4 is 0.006 that is very less from 0.10 value at 90% confidence level that means H_4 is accepted. The calculated p of H_5 is 0.686 which is more than 0.10 significance level at a 90% confidence level that means H_5 is rejected. The calculated p-value of H_6 is 0.001 which is less than the 0.10 significance level at a 90% confidence level that signifies that H_6 is accepted.

5. FINDINGS AND DISCUSSIONS

In this study, it has been checked that while using the online learning mode of study, what problems have the students faced during the time of pandemic? The results showed that students faced a variety of types and degrees of online learning problems. Their greatest challenge was linked to their individual barriers, while their least challenge was technological barriers. While the majority of research found that technology use and proficiency were the most frequent issues students encountered while taking online courses (Rasheed et al., 2020), the situation is a little bit different in developing nations during pandemic. This is hardly surprising given the abundance of data demonstrating the strong technology and digital literacy of Gen Z kids (born since 1996) (Barrot, 2018); (Ng, 2012); (Roblek et al., 2019). According to the students' responses, the pandemic has also been found to make their issues worse, particularly in terms of mental health, finances, interactions, and mobility. The finding reveals that health issues have been faced by students from long-run use of Online Learning such as anxiety, depression, eyesight issues, etc. The results indicate that the teaching and learning quality as well as the students' mental health were most impacted by COVID-19 on students' online learning experiences. Apart from COVID-19's direct threats, other factors contributing to students' anxiety included their physical and social limitations, and their worries about their financial stability. These results support those made by (Copeland et al., 2021) and (Fawaz et al., 2021) who detailed how the pandemic had a negative impact on students' mental and emotional health.

Learning Environment Challenges also has non-significant relationship with Online Learning. This can be supported by the fact that Online Learning mode of teaching pedagogy, the matter has been framed according to the respondents need (Normadhi et al., 2019). This type of online learning methodology provides the student a customised content based on the students requirements. (Kolekar et al., 2017); (Franzoni & Assar, 2009).

Overall results show that each student experienced obstacles and techniques to varying degrees. As a result, they should be seen as the result of numerous elements interacting. According to the students' comments, the resources at their disposal, their interactions with teachers and peers, and the institution's current regulations and norms for online learning (Fawaz et al., 2021) all played a role in mediating their online learning issues and techniques. The lockdowns that were mandated and the socioeconomic circumstances of the students made the difficulties that students faced throughout the pandemic worse. The third hypothesis acceptance stated that the instructor's dimension factor has an impact on the Online Learning of students. It means there is a lack of information and communication skills among teachers. The fourth hypothesis has also proved significant, which means infrastructure barriers have an impact on the Online Learning of the students. This means most of the institutions lack basic amenities that should be provided to the students. The sixth hypothetical assumption i.e. Miscellaneous barriers also have an impact on the Online Learning of the students.

5.1. Implications

Policymakers and government education related ministries should take appropriate initiatives based on the findings of this study for higher studies students (Under graduation and post graduations) studies development. By the implementation of these initiatives, learners would be able to join online learning and continue their studies during the pandemic in maximum numbers. This study has greatly increased our knowledge that what problems students have to face while using online learning, especially where these resources or infrastructure are very less available. Schools with similar learning environments could use the results of this study to develop and improve their respective learning continuity plans to lessen the negative effects of the pandemic. In fact application of suitable IT structure as well as giving adequate instruction on technological difficulties faced while using online platforms can encourage students to take online classes regularly. It will be helpful to prevent the collapse of university studies for undergraduates in a developing country like India.

5.2. Suggestions

Based on the results and findings, individual barriers, instructor's dimensions, infrastructure barriers, and miscellaneous barriers affecting Online Learning mode of learning of students. So, the following suggestions have been recommended by the researcher mentioned below:

- Colleges and institutions should focus on these barriers by adopting different strategies for making students' online learning more fruitful and knowledgeable.
- Instructors should be trained with proper ICT skills so that they don't face any trouble while teaching students.
- Schools and colleges should provide adequate infrastructure for proper online study to the students and also provide training to students before starting

the online study. Institutions should expend much on new and better quality online teaching software for proper Online Learning education.

- Moreover, awareness among students and teachers for following online education ethical code of conduct should be increased. Direct interaction between teacher and students should be there and personal query or counseling by teachers should be done from time to time during online Learning.

6. CONCLUSION

In the modern world, no region is untouched by technology. The idea of online learning is gradually being adopted in education as a result of this development. Although these modifications are positive, the researcher has demonstrated in this work that they also have significant drawbacks. Due to the lack of other study options available to students during the Corona pandemic, online education has also been widely adopted and used. However, it has now been adopted as the main teaching and learning method by the majority of educational institutions and students. A new era of education known as "Online Learning" has begun as a result of the COVID-19 epidemic, which has an impact on the entire educational system, notably colleges. Understanding the adoption drivers as well as the primary problems that existing Online Learning systems encounter is essential for successful Online Learning system utilization.

7. LIMITATIONS

In contrast to teachers in colleges and universities, students are the focus of this study's examination of online hurdles. As study participants, only enrolled undergraduate and graduate students have been taken into consideration. By focusing on regions outside of the Delhi-NCR, future study can leverage these challenges to investigate obstacles faced in the form of various barriers on the online learning process in more detail.

8. IMPLICATIONS OF THE STUDY

The question of whether online learning is more or less affordable than other options cannot be answered with a straightforward yes or no. Every level of educational stakeholders needs thorough information on efficient teaching techniques and strategies to increase educational output. It is important to pay attention to a variety of factors when comparing relative productivity, including the number of students served, the subject area, size, budget, and design considerations like the teacher's role and the degree of blending of online and in-person components. The framework provided in this report is meant to be a resource for stakeholders to use in evaluating the research that is currently available. It can also serve as a template for future study design. Education stakeholders must invest in productivity research that compares the cost-effectiveness of instructional options and advances understanding of the most effective ways to define and measure student, teacher, and system outcomes as online learning alternatives continue to proliferate. Teaching online has a wide range of effects on pedagogy, teacher-student interaction, grading, and other parts of the campus, like social life and administration. No matter where, when, or how an online course is taught, all of them share the fundamental notion that students will be studying away from campus, typically by themselves.

Cope's Best Practices for Authors

- *Author Contribution:* The work is based on identifying the factors that are seriously affecting the student's online learning. An application of PLS SEM proven helpful to find the significance level of all six hypothetical assumptions and out of which two has been clearly rejected based on the result received. This paper is prepared by the consideration of all three authors.
- *Conflict of Interest*: There is no conflict of interest associated with this paper
- *Funding Acknowledgements:* No funding agencies associated with this paper

REFERENCES

Abbad, M. M., Morris, D., & de Nahlik, C. (2009). Looking under the Bonnet: Factors affecting student adoption of Online Learning systems in Jordan. *International Review of Research in Open and Distance Learning*, *10*(2), 1–25. doi:10.19173/irrodl.v10i2.596

Aboagye, J., & Jung, J. Y. (2018). Debt holding, financial behavior, and financial satisfaction. *Financial Counseling and Planning*, *29*(2), 208–218. doi:10.1891/1052-3073.29.2.208

Afini Normadhi, N. B., Shuib, L., Md Nasir, H. N., Bimba, A., Idris, N., & Balakrishnan, V. (2019). Identification of personal traits in adaptive learning environment: Systematic literature review. *Computers & Education*, *130*, 168–190. doi:10.1016/j.compedu.2018.11.005

Agarwal, D. D. K., Bansal, S., Jain, A., & Jain, S. (2021). A Study on Investment Behavior of Individual Investors With Reference To Delhi-NCR. *International Journal of All Research Education and Scientific Methods (IJARESM)*. http://www.ijaresm.com/a-study-on-investment-behavior-of-individual-investors-with-reference-to-delhi-ncr

Alchamdani, A., Fatmasari, F., Anugrah, E. R., Sari, N. P., Putri, F., & Astina, A. (2020). The Impact of Covid19 Pandemic on Online Learning Process in the College at Southeast Sulawesi. *JURNAL KESEHATAN LINGKUNGAN, 12*(1si), 129–136. doi:10.20473/jkl.v12i1si.2020.129-136

Almaiah, M. A., Al-Khasawneh, A., & Althunibat, A. (2020). Exploring the critical challenges and factors influencing the Online Learning system usage during COVID-19 pandemic. *Education and Information Technologies, 25*(6), 5261–5280. doi:10.1007/s10639-020-10219-y

Arkorful, V., & Abaidoo, N. (2014). *The role of Online Learning, the advantages, and disadvantages of its adoption in Higher Education*. Undefined.

Barrot, J. S. (2018). Facebook as a learning environment for language teaching and learning: A critical analysis of the literature from 2010 to 2017. *Journal of Computer Assisted Learning, 34*(6), 863–875. doi:10.1111/jcal.12295

Barrot, J. S., Llenares, I. I., & del Rosario, L. S. (2021). Students' online learning challenges during the pandemic and how they cope with them: The case of the Philippines. *Education and Information Technologies, 26*(6), 7321–7338. doi:10.100710639-021-10589-x PMID:34075300

Baticulon, R. E., Sy, J. J., Alberto, N. R. I., Baron, M. B. C., Mabulay, R. E. C., Rizada, L. G. T., Tiu, C. J. S., Clarion, C. A., & Reyes, J. C. B. (2021). Barriers to Online Learning in the Time of COVID-19: A National Survey of Medical Students in the Philippines. *Medical Science Educator, 31*(2), 615–626. doi:10.1007/s40670-021-01231-z

Bird, K. A., Castleman, B. L., & Lohner, G. (2022). Negative Impacts From the Shift to Online Learning During the COVID-19 Crisis: Evidence from a Statewide Community College System. EdWorkingPapers.Com. https://doi.org/doi:10.26300/GX68-RQ13

Chakraborty, P., Mittal, P., Gupta, M. S., Yadav, S., & Arora, A. (2021). Opinion of students on online education during the COVID-19 pandemic. *Human Behavior and Emerging Technologies, 3*(3), 357–365. doi:10.1002/hbe2.240

Cohen, J. (1992). A new criterion for assessing discriminant validity in variance-based structural equation modeling. *Current Directions in Psychological Science*. doi:10.1111/1467-8721.ep10768783

Collins, J., Hammond, M., & Wellington, J. (2002). *Teaching and Learning with Multimedia*. Teaching and Learning with Multimedia. doi:10.4324/9780203441305

Copeland, W. E., McGinnis, E., Bai, Y., Adams, Z., Nardone, H., Devadanam, V., Rettew, J., & Hudziak, J. J. (2021). Impact of COVID-19 Pandemic on College Student Mental Health and Wellness. *Journal of the American Academy of Child and Adolescent Psychiatry*, *60*(1), 134–141.e2. doi:10.1016/j.jaac.2020.08.466 PMID:33091568

Elmer, T., Mepham, K., & Stadtfeld, C. (2020). Students under lockdown: Comparisons of students' social networks and mental health before and during the COVID-19 crisis in Switzerland. *PLoS One*, *15*(7), e0236337. doi:10.1371/journal.pone.0236337 PMID:32702065

Farooq, F., Rathore, F. A., & Mansoor, S. N. (2020). Challenges of online medical education in Pakistan during COVID-19 pandemic. *Journal of the College of Physicians and Surgeons—Pakistan*, *30*(1), S67–S69. doi:10.29271/jcpsp.2020.Supp1.S67 PMID:32723456

Fawaz, M., Al Nakhal, M., & Itani, M. (2021). COVID-19 quarantine stressors and management among Lebanese students: a qualitative study. *Current Psychology*, *41*(11), 7628–7635. doi:10.1007/s12144-020-01307-w

Franzoni, A. L., & Assar, S. (2009). *Student Learning Styles Adaptation Method Based on Teaching Strategies and Electronic Media*. JStor. https://www.jstor.org/stable/jeductechsoci.12.4.15

Fry, K. (2001). Online Learning markets and providers: Some issues and prospects. *Education + Training*, *43*(4/5), 233–239. doi:10.1108/EUM0000000005484

Ganai, A., Naveed Hamid, I., Sudhakar Dwivedi, I., Jyoti Kachroo, I., Manhas, I. J., Hamid, N., Dwivedi, S., Kachroo, J., & Manhas, J. (2019). Influence of packaging elements of ready to eat food products on buying behaviour. ~ *189* ~. *Journal of Pharmacognosy and Phytochemistry*, *8*(2), 189–194.

Hair, J. F. Black, W. C., & Babin, B. J. (2010). *Multivariate Data Analysis: A Global Perspective*. Google Books. https://books.google.co.in/books/about/Multivariate_Data_Analysis.html?id=SLRPLgAACAAJ

Hair, Joe F., & Sarstedt, Hopkins, M., Kuppelwieser, L., & G., V. (. (2014). Partial least squares structural equation modeling (PLS-SEM): An emerging tool in business research. *European Business Review*, *26*(2), 106–121. doi:10.1108/EBR-10-2013-0128

Hartshorne, R., & Ajjan, H. (2009). Examining student decisions to adopt Web 2.0 technologies: Theory and empirical tests. *Journal of Computing in Higher Education*, *21*(3), 183–198. doi:10.100712528-009-9023-6

Henseler, J., Hubona, G., & Ray, P. A. (2016). *Using PLS path modeling in new technology research: updated guidelines*. doi:10.1108/IMDS-09-2015-0382

Henseler, J., Ringle, C. M., & Sarstedt, M. (2015). A new criterion for assessing discriminant validity in variance-based structural equation modeling. *Journal of the Academy of Marketing Science*, *43*(1), 115–135. doi:10.100711747-014-0403-8

Henseler, J., Ringle, C. M., & Sinkovics, R. R. (2009). The use of partial least squares path modeling in international marketing. *Advances in International Marketing*, *20*, 277–319. doi:10.1108/S1474-7979(2009)0000020014

Hu, L., & Bentler, P. M. (1998). Fit indices in covariance structure modeling: Sensitivity to underparameterized model misspecification. *Psychological Methods*, *3*(4), 424–453. doi:10.1037/1082-989X.3.4.424

Hussein, E., Daoud, S., Alrabaiah, H., & Badawi, R. (2020). Exploring undergraduate students' attitudes towards emergency online learning during COVID-19: A case from the UAE. *Children and Youth Services Review*, *119*, 105699. doi:10.1016/j.childyouth.2020.105699

Jain, A., Bansal, S., & Bhardwaj, S. (2022). *COVID-19 Outbreak: A Paradigm Shift in Food and Beverage Industry with Context to Delhi-NCR*, 329–339. doi:10.1007/978-981-19-0357-1_28

Klein, D., & Ware, M. (2003). Online Learning: New opportunities in continuing professional development. *Learned Publishing*, *16*(1), 34–46. doi:10.1087/095315103320995078

Kolekar, S. V., Pai, R. M., & Manohara Pai, M. M. (2017). Prediction of Learner's Profile based on Learning Styles in Adaptive Online Learning System. [IJET]. *International Journal of Emerging Technologies in Learning*, *12*(06), 31–51. doi:10.3991/ijet.v12i06.6579

Konting, M., Kamaruddin, M., & Man, N. A. (2009). Quality Assurance in Higher Education Institutions: Exist Survey among Universiti Putra Malaysia Graduating Students. *International Education Studies*, *2*(1). doi:10.5539/ies.v2n1p25

Lakbala, P. (2016). Barriers in Implementing Online Learning in Hormozgan University of Medical Sciences. *Global Journal of Health Science*, *8*(7), 83. doi:10.5539/gjhs.v8n7p83 PMID:26925885

Muflih, S., Abuhammad, S., Karasneh, R., Al-Azzam, S., Alzoubi, K. H., & Muflih, M. (2020). *Online Education for Undergraduate Health Professional Education during the COVID-19 Pandemic: Attitudes, Barriers, and Ethical Issues*. Research Square., doi:10.21203/rs.3.rs-42336/v1

Muhammad, A., & Anwar, K. (2020). Online Learning amid the COVID-19 Pandemic: Students' Perspectives. *Online Submission, 2*(1), 45–51. https://www.doi.org/10.33902/JPSP.2020261309

Muilenburg, L. Y., & Berge, Z. L. (2005). *Student Barriers to Online Learning: A factor analytic study. 26*(1), 29–48. doi:10.1080/01587910500081269

Nambiar, D. (2020). The impact of online learning during COVID-19: students' and teachers' perspective. *The International Journal of Indian Psychology*. https://www.researchgate.net/publication/343229234_The_impact_of_online_learning_during_COVID-19_students%27_and_teachers%27_perspective

Naveed, Q. N., Muhammed, A., Sanober, S., Qureshi, M. R. N., & Shah, A. (2017). Barriers effecting successful implementation of Online Learning in Saudi Arabian Universities. *International Journal of Emerging Technologies in Learning*, *12*(6), 94–107. doi:10.3991/ijet.v12i06.7003

Ng, W. (2012). Can we teach digital natives digital literacy? *Computers & Education*, *59*(3), 1065–1078. doi:10.1016/j.compedu.2012.04.016

Octaberlina, L. R., & Muslimin, A. I. (2020). EFL Students Perspective towards Online Learning Barriers and Alternatives Using Moodle/Google Classroom during COVID-19 Pandemic. *International Journal of Higher Education*, *9*(6), 1. doi:10.5430/ijhe.v9n6p1

OECD. (2020). *The potential of Online Learning for adults: Early lessons from the COVID-19 crisis*. OECD. https://read.oecd-ilibrary.org/view/?ref=135_135358-ool6fisocq&title=The-potential-of-OnlinOnline Learning-for-adults-Early-lessons-from-the-COVID-19-crisis

Raj, M., & Bansal, S. (2019). Customer Satisfaction In Banking Sector-A Case Study Of H.D.F.C Bank. *International Journal of Research and Analytical Reviews*. http://ijrar.com/

Rajab, M. H., Gazal, A. M., & Alkattan, K. (2020). Challenges to Online Medical Education During the COVID-19 Pandemic. *Cureus*, *12*(7). doi:10.7759/cureus.8966 PMID:32766008

Rasheed, R. A., Kamsin, A., & Abdullah, N. A. (2020). Challenges in the online component of blended learning: A systematic review. *Computers & Education*, *144*, 103701. doi:10.1016/j.compedu.2019.103701

Roblek, V., Mesko, M., Dimovski, V., & Peterlin, J. (2019). Smart technologies as social innovation and complex social issues of the Z generation. *Kybernetes*, *48*(1), 91–107. doi:10.1108/K-09-2017-0356

Rossi, P. G. (2009). Learning Environment With Elements Of Artificial Intelligence. *Journal of Online Learning and Knowledge Society*, *5*(1), 191–199. doi:10.20368/1971-8829/306 PMID:33809696

Selim, H. M. (2007). Online Learning critical success factors: An exploratory investigation of student perceptions. *International Journal of Technology Marketing*, *2*(2), 157–182. doi:10.1504/IJTMKT.2007.014791

Sharpe, D. R., & Benfield, D. G. (2015). *Institutional strategies for supporting learners in a digital age.* Taylor and Francis. doi:10.11120/elss.2012.04020004

Smedley, J. (2010). Modelling the impact of knowledge management using technology. *OR Insight*, *23*(4), 233–250. doi:10.1057/ori.2010.11

Soper, D. S. (2017). *A-priori sample size calculator*. Google Scholar. https://scholar.google.com/scholar?hl=en&as_sdt=0%2C5&q=Soper%2C+D.+S.+%282017%29.+A-priori+sample+size+calculator+for+structural+equation+models+%5BSoftware%5D.+Available+at+www.+dan+ielsoper.+com%2Fstatcalc+%28accessed+28+October+2020%29.&btnG=

Yengin, I., Karahoca, A., & Karahoca, D. (2011). Online Learning success model for instructors' satisfactions in perspective of interaction and usability outcomes. *Procedia Computer Science*, *3*, 1396–1403. doi:10.1016/j.procs.2011.01.021

Zhang, D., Zhou, L., Briggs, R. O., & Nunamaker, J. F. Jr. (2006). Instructional video in Online Learning: Assessing the impact of interactive video on learning effectiveness. *Information & Management*, *43*(1), 15–27. doi:10.1016/j.im.2005.01.004

Chapter 13
Ethical Business Marketing:
The Practices to Compete Successfully in Business

Pradeep Reddy K.
https://orcid.org/0000-0003-0344-411X
SAGE University, Bhopal, India

Venkateswarlu Chandu
K.L. Business School, Vaddeswaram, India

Narendra Ryali
Koneru Lakshmaiah Education Foundation, India

Amala Gangula
IBPS, Mumbai, India

Debesh Mishra
https://orcid.org/0000-0003-2665-1365
Sri Polytechnic, Komand, India

Swagatika Mishra
VSSUT Burla, India

ABSTRACT

Organizations use a variety of strategies to acquire a competitive advantage in today's competitive environment. The question is whether these behaviours are consistent with our organization's beliefs and ideals. Ethical activities are thus the solution. Managers or the top management now have a moral obligation to embrace these methods, thus businesses must incorporate social responsibility into every marketing choice they make. This study emphasizes the significance of employing ethical marketing methods to achieve a competitive advantage over competitors. The significance of manufacturers acting in a socially responsible manner is also highlighted in the study.

DOI: 10.4018/978-1-6684-7568-3.ch013

INTRODUCTION

Marketing's goal is to surpass competitors in terms of effectively meeting the requirements of the intended consumer. This idea is occasionally conflicting with societal-welfare and -interest. Cigarettes and alcohol, for example, serve consumer requirements but cause harm, while even simple items, such as packing things in throwaway packaging materials, contribute significantly to deteriorating the ecosystem and causing climate changes. The environment reacts to all of the organization's actions. As a result, corporations should include social responsibility into every marketing choice. Marketing is a complex and dynamic job that requires taking risks and competing in a fiercely competitive industry. Market research operations are carried out in order to give critical information for accomplishing business objectives. Since ethical concerns are essential to marketing research activities due to performance demands, market research professionals are required to structure their efforts according to the foundation for ethical considerations.

Modern society expects businesses to be ethically accountable to their constituents in the competitive climate of today (Martin and Johnson, 2010; Olins, 2014). The "Societal Marketing Concept (SMC)" is a better conceptualization of the conventional marketing idea that strikes a balance between societal-expectations, human-requirements, and marketing-agencies (Kotler, 1972). According to this idea, all marketers must uphold social responsibility principles when promoting their goods and services. Specifically, they must meet the preferences as well as requirements of their targeted audiences for protecting and improving the customer's welfare- and societal-wellbeing, while achieving organizational goals. Ethical advertising is being developed in a way that protects the environment. Companies launching ethical advertisements employ only environmentally conscious and reusable materials, as well as non-polluting ways in nature. The advertising will also do all possible to minimize unnecessary resource usage (Drumwright and Murphy, 2009). Relationships maintaining with consumers and developing brand loyalty are important issues in today's marketing background (Melewar and Nguyen, 2017). In line with the SMC, the "food and restaurant industries" ought to create recipes with fewer fats and starches, but more nutrients. Marketers should also avoid using professional athletes in toxic product advertisements or promoting foods to children in a way that encourages overeating.

SCOPE OF WORK AND THE STUDY'S TARGET

The goal or scope of this research work is to highlight and comprehend the reasons for an organization's use of ethical practices to facilitate achieving a competitive advantage over competitors. The relevance of employing ethical marketing strategies is the study's goal. The following items may be clearly recognized as the study's targets:

a) To look for reasons why a company should embrace ethical procedures.
b) To determine the most recent-trend in the use of these techniques in businesses.

ADOPTED METHODOLOGY

To comprehend the aims of this study, secondary data is collected from literature on the related topic, including journals, essays, newspapers, novels, and more. Since numerous academics have worked on this area, there is an abundance of literature available. So, employing ethical practices is stressed together with its relevance and advantages. The study makes advice for managers on how to implement these practices.

REVIEW OF LITERATURE

Ethical Business Marketing (EBM)

Ethics, according to Taylor (1975), is an "insight into the source and causes of morals", where moral code is defined as "subjective judgments, values, and principles of behaviour. Vitell defined ethics in marketing as "an examination into the nature and reasons of moral judgments, norms, and rules of behaviour relevant to marketing decisions and marketing circumstances" in 1986, founded on Taylor's definition of business ethics. Similarly, based on the description by Thompson (2005), ethics represents what is good and wrong; of moral decisions and defending the choices individuals make. Ethics is preoccupied with the character of particular decisions that are chosen, as well as the morality in both the leader of such actions in terms of their repercussions (Chonko, 1995). Ethics aims to solve moral difficulties in humans. Ethical philosophy is connected to moral psychology, normative ethics, and value theory (Cooper, 1999). A collection of moral principles is indicated in the literature by the words "ethics" or "morals" (Resnik, 2011). Because social responsibility in ethics encompasses social interactions within society, in which companies function, ethics is also inextricably linked to social responsibilities (Goolsby and Hunt, 1982; Sen *et al.,* 2006; Stanaland *et al.,* 2011; Hur *et al.,* 2014).

According to the characterizations above, the terms ethics and morality can be interchangeably used. The phrases "ethics and ethical" relate to the study of moral-behaviour or the code that one adheres to. Corporations that appropriately establish and follow ethical-codes, usually are regarded as responsible demonstrating commitment to ethical-behaviour. A well-defined ethical-code that includes corporate relationships with its customers, staff-members, government-agencies, environmental-concerns, statutory-provisions, and strategy-implementation would present a regional- and global-business's clear vision-statement to a home-nation community while also inspiring a social-conscience and self-belief (Rodriguez-Dominguez *et al.,* 2009; Stohl *et al.,* 2009; Sevensson *et al.,* 2009; Godos-Diez *et al.,* 2011). According to Gaski (1999), the "ethical business marketing (EBM)" is a code of 'morality and behaviour' used in marketing-practices. The execution of EBM pushes firms making acceptable and ethical marketing-decisions. EBM is an important topic for both academicians and practitioners because ethical-principles demand businesses to adhere to basic-responsibility for social, and execute their marketing-operations in ways that make business "visible and acceptable" to everybody. Corporate-ethics call for establishing and maintaining of minimal responsibility standards and behaviours that businesses should adhere to, as well as an accountability-system for a company's ethical-roles executions (Donaldson and Werhane, 1983). In an added formal-setting, the marketing-ethics may be described in one of two ways: either including the systematic-study of the moral-assessment of marketing choices/practices, and as the 'criteria or norms' used in determining, if a promotional-activity is morally proper or unethical (Smith and Murphy, 2012).

Commodity-ethics, proximity-ethics, valuation-ethics, and branding-ethics, are all examples of ethical promotional strategies. Commodity ethics encompasses legal-rules such as good manufacturing practices, product responsibility, and product-imitation. Several scholars have explored the marketing-mix methods from ethical-considerations (Malhotra and Miller, 1998; Low and Davenport, 2005; Jeurissen and Van De Ven, 2006; Brubaker, 2007; Nill and Schibrowsky, 2007; Bretcu, 2013; Hur *et al.,* 2014; Ludlum and Johnson, 2015).

For marketing-mix strategy, ethical challenges are classified as commodity, valuation, proximity, and branding ethics (Camenisch, 1991; Aguilar, 1994; Ford and Richardson, 1994; Malhotra and Miller, 1998; Low and Davenport, 2005; Bretcu, 2013).

- Commodity ethical problems include safety and reliability, cleanliness, non-toxicity, labeling and brand, and service (i.e., Is consumer safety advice adequately disclosed on the container?).
- Valuation ethical difficulties include the use of deceptive business tactics, unlawful pricing, and misleading or inaccurate costing (i.e., Does the producer avoid utilizing a malicious cost structure of purposefully reducing prices to eliminate competition in the market?).

- The level of the partnership, the transparency of the operation, and the sales policies are all influenced by proximity ethical considerations (i.e., Does the company abstain from influencing activities by exploiting its social standing?).
- Under legal law, branding ethical concerns comprise promotion, as does the extent of deceptive or misleading characteristics (i.e., Do the manufacturers refrain to provide fraudulent, fake, and embellished adverts to customers?)

Other ethical concerns arise as a result of topics such as merchandising choices, direct-marketing, and supplying and distribution management. Privacy, secrecy, and interference are examples of ethical difficulties in direct-marketing (Chonko, 1995).

Significance of EBM

The fact that customers in contemporary cultures continue to want quality-based items and choose companies that are socially known, despite the fact that they may have to pay more for those things; which further emphasizes the significance of ethical-marketing (McGuire *et al.,* 1988). In a study, Islam *et al.* (2020) emphasized how businesses about their products/services cannot be told to customers; rather, they must also deliver excellent customer experiences to keep them loyal over-time. This dedicated client-base will provide a durable competitive-edge for businesses across industries. Managers and marketers are instructed through ethical-marketing techniques on how to handle a moral-dilemma (Reidenbach *et al.,* 1991). Corporate-executives and -suppliers have acknowledged the relevance of ethics in the progress of company's sustainability and wide-ranging challenges in marketing such as product-quality and -safety, price-tags, and promotion (Lee and Jin, 2019). Promotional ethical-concerns, for example, might be examined in marketing and direct-marketing. Marketing, selling, and corporate-communications are all topics covered under sales-promotion ethics (Dudiak, 2001). Ethical promotional-activities aim to highlight a company's ethical-ideals in order to entice customers to buy from them (Schlegelmilch and Berseder, 2010). It is worth noting in this regard that customers have been shown to respond favourably to socially-responsible businesses (Lämsä *et al.,* 2008).

However, it has been noticed that such enterprises have historically had a comparatively lesser market-shares (Boulstridge and Carrigan, 2000). Brenner and Molander (1977) provided several-examples of harmful-behaviours carried out by businesses in the traditional-sense. Ethical-marketing strategies allow addressing both the clients' bodily- and spiritual-requirements. This results in greater sales, which assists firms in building consumer loyalty. It also boosts the company's worth in the eyes of its personnel. It also serves as an extra motivation for self-development and increased workplace performance (Preston, 2010). Numerous studies have indicated that EBM procedures are the most viable parts of a company's numerous operations that a consumer watches when compared to "unethical business marketing (UBM)" tactics. Furthermore, EBM practices are significant aspects that impact and affect customer impression of a brand. According to F. Taylor, the creator of ethical-approaches to marketing, the social-issues solution not only does not contradict, however is in direct-association with the business-objectives. For instance, boosting population-welfare through resource-conservation increases consumption of goods and services (Kotler, 1972).

EBM and UBM

The principles of ethical and unethical marketing are not the same. All ethical advertising is concerned with the product's genuineness, the manufacturing process, and firm's working circumstances. Ethical-advertising does not seek to embellish genuine items or conceal flaws in those things (Keith *et al.,* 2008). Advertisements that promote products that are unclear or wholly dissimilar to what is provided, and what individuals already own, are not displayed (Drumwright and Murphy, 2009). Unethical- and ethical-advertising, both lead to product-disparities in the opposite manner. It is recommended to always produce individual-logos, -graphics, or commercials to show originality, whose purpose is to demonstrate the distinction between the goods and competitors. Each logo may be clearly distinguished and recognized. Buyers may identify a certain brand among dozens of items in the same specialist area by using images and logos. Unethical-advertising tries to seek in discovering a technique to provide goods in similar-appearance as other companies in the same-category. It will take advantage of client's confusion, since shoppers may not be able to distinguish between phoney- and authentic-products because they will all seem very-similar, if not the same. Companies with immoral-ideals would profit by deceiving and lying to a large-audience in this manner. According to studies, a lack of application and enforcement of ethical-codes in marketing research-sectors is seen to result in immoral-conduct (Yallop, 2012).

In contrast to unethical-advertising, ethical-advertising must be socially-sensitive. It does not play on normal human-emotions like jealousy, greed, or fear. He will try his utmost to create a cheerful- and upbeat-mood. We also oppose divisive stereotypes based on age, religion, gender, or ethnicity. Furthermore, many ethical firms recruit each one regardless of masculinity, ethnicity, colour, or sacred views. Minority difficulties and misconceptions are prioritized in ethical-advertising (Keith *et al.,* 2008). Whereas, an opposite effect is found in unethical-advertising, which tries to influence people's emotions and wants (Crane, 1999). The most important ethical-concerns surrounding consumer-marketing have been outlined by Smith and Murphy

(2012), and may be utilized to assess a company's marketing-strategies. Numerous studies have found that, despite views of ethically-manufactured items, customers are not necessarily prepared to pay-extra. In other-situations, though, customers may be ready to spend a little extra for such items, which are a continuing issue for marketers (Stanforth and Hauck, 2010). Furthermore, because consumers may lack the information and time to evaluate costs, firms may turn to unfair pricing tactics for immediate gains, which can have a severe influence on the long-term viability of these kinds of enterprises (Khandelwal and Bajpai, 2012).

EBM's Theories

According to Cavanagh *et al.* (1981), there are three main groups of ethical theories: utilitarian theories, which compare behaviour in terms of its effects; right theories, which emphasize the claim or rights of persons, such as right to due process, the privacy rights, right to liberty of religion, and right to unfettered expression; and theories of fairness, which concentrate on the distributional effects of behaviour. Ross (1930) emphasises that moral decision-making must take into account consequences, but that consequences alone do not render an act moral. According to Ross, there are obligations that tie us ethically. In order to make a moral decision, we must balance our options in light of the obligations they entail and choose which responsibility is the most pressing. Chonko and Hunt (1985) investigated the right standards of promotion executives. Findings show that: (a) bribe is the most frequently reported issue faced by marketing executives as viewed via fairness, truthfulness, and pricing policy; (b) As they try to strike a balance between the needs of the business and those of the customers, ethical conflict becomes most apparent; (c) marketing managers recognize many opportunities for their groups to engage in unethical behaviour, but such behaviour, generally does not result in success; and (d) the survival of moral norms isn't usually related with the measure of unethical conduct via marketing executives. We can see that unethical behaviours are more widespread in marketing and advertising, or that managers employ unethical techniques in marketing and marketing to achieve competitive advantage by luring customers. However, if ethical marketing tactics are employed, it is possible to serve the goal of recruiting clients more effectively. Many topics have emerged area of branding and sales ethics. According to Consoli (1976), advertisers today exhibit an exaggerated fashion for ethics while using marketing and competitive branding. There is another perspective to it, as stated by Simon et al., other than using moral behaviours for ethical reasons or ceasing to injure others (1972), is the affirmative obligation to combat societal problems like poverty, prejudice, or city deterioration. Businesses with broadly accepted moral standards outperform their competitors and have a higher reputation in society, which will allow them to establish more powerful stakeholder families in the long run. (Aydın, 2003; Burnaz *et al.*, 2009; Certo and Certo, 2006; Lamberton and Minor, 1995; McDaniel and Gitman, 2008; Rodriguez-Dominguez *et al.*, 2009).

Advertising and advertising moralities that are connected to the 4P-problems, such as hazardous products, deceptive pricing, misleading promotion, and bribery, are investigated by business ethics (Smith and Quelch, 1993). Issues are related with the use of client weaknesses or utilize of public relations to stymie critical media and public discourse. It defines the examination of right, wrong, fair, affordable, and appropriate in the business sector. For many years, situations in the field of business relating to moral concerns have been on the increase in a variety of issues, industries, and nations. Customers can participate in the RED campaign's "moral" purchases of AIDS pills, play word games that help the UN World Food Program provide rice to the needy, retweet images of their favourite humanitarian actors, or unleash a superhero caricature to Africa and donate a computer to an African infant through General Mills' "Win-One Give-One" initiative (Richey and Ponte, 2014). Since Prothero's (1998) original problem, Environmental advertising, sustainable advertising, social advertising, and ethical consumption have all influenced new advertising material. Consumers' understanding of moral issues can also be shaped by their demographic history in terms of age, wealth, experience, and so on. Researchers have discovered that as individuals' age and mature, they demonstrate a larger proclivity for morally motivated actions (Chiu, 2003). Given that advertising is still held responsible for encouraging unsustainable levels of consumption, the more focus our field pays to inexperienced/moral advertising, the better it will be in the long run for society's well-being. Therein lays the foundation for a theoretical and practical reexamination of the subject of inexpert/honest advertising. As Prothero (1998) anticipated, there is no evidence of a decline in the field of unskilled branding.

EBM from a global viewpoint

Ethical issues and disputes in overseas business ethics are a major source of worry, necessitating distinct points of view and remedies for each scenario. Furthermore, from an economic and business standpoint, business ethics is often seen as a topic opposed to business and economic concerns based on interests, preserving particular standards in the first place, and based on an extensive range of principles and its own thinking Burnaz *et al.,* 2009; Choi *et al.,* 2010).Different nations may hold differing moral and ethical standards. To effectively affect ethical behaviour, it is preferable to embrace a situational predisposition based on cultural, moral, historical, and personal grounds as opposed to a universal point of view. (Tsalikis, 2007; Tsalikis et al., 2008; Helin and Sandström, 2008). Because cheaply developed nations are expected to have solid ethical standards to maintain the process perpetually viable, there is a widespread belief that developed countries have a greater level of ethical awareness than poor countries. Transparency and the extent of the ethical atmosphere are other important considerations. More open and morally sound company practises will increase customer and business confidence, increasing market trade volume and economic strength. A framework for executing an ethics programme was developed by McDonald and Nijhof (1999), and when paired with a code of ethics, it may encourage morally responsible behaviour in businesses and raise the ethicalness of workers' activities and behaviour. Five essential requirements must be met for a programme to be considered effective in an organisation: (1) knowledge of the formal goals of the organisation and the corresponding informal norms; (2) appropriate decision-making techniques; (3) appropriate commodity allocation; (4) availability of necessary skills; and (5) personal intentions for ethical behaviour. Thus, organizational factors such as code of beliefs are extremely important when combined with other people, personal beliefs, and goals in order to promote ethical culture in the workplace. Similar to this, Doig and Wilson (1998) argue that it is unproductive to use codes of ethics as frameworks for determining ethical behaviour. and that doing so may have less of an impact on employees and managers than could be anticipated.

The table below highlights some of the unethical techniques in Promoting Foodstuffs that are used to entice youngsters, a susceptible element, or an oblivious customer, through advertising.

Table 1. Common tactics in internet food marketing to minors that are typically prohibited by government or self-regulation

Sl. No.	Parameters
1.	Selling low-nutritional-quality meals; failing to provide adequate nutrient information; making false nutritious assertions
2.	Including food advertisements in games and promoting literacy development to intake the recommended foodstuffs
3.	Making a 'BUZZ' about the items and encouraging kids to email advertisements to their pals (i.e., viral-marketing)
4.	Delivering children private label goods that they may utilise after visiting the Internet sites, in addition to linking the digital advertising to other branded exposure levels
5.	'Ad breaks' and reminders that the programme being watched is advertisements are not included.
6.	Bringing chances and rewards to youngsters who may be too immature to register on the Internet sites
7.	Providing a clear enticement to buy (e.g. secret-site access)

People are able to produce and be creative to the fullest extent when they work with a strong belief in the moral validity of their point of view. When engaging in unethical behaviour, on the other hand, people feel compelled to participate in laborious concealment, resulting in lower efficacy and success. Furthermore, a clearly expressed commitment to ethics conveys a strong message that ethical behaviour is seen as a commercial essential. The table below highlights some of the unethical techniques in "Marketing Foods" that are used to entice youngsters, a vulnerable element, or an oblivious customer, in advertisements. A simple logical extrapolation of conventional marketing has been used to describe sustainable marketing (Crane and Henion and Kinnear (1976), Desmond, 2002; Kilbourne, 1998) provided the first definition of all marketing efforts, both those that have exacerbated environmental issues and those that could help address them, are considered to be part of natural marketing. This notion was introduced to assist marketers in responding to societal and environmental issues in order to retain corporate respectability in the context of changing society's norms and the growth of civil society initiatives (Crane, 2000).

ANALYSIS AND SUMMARY

The acquisition of inaccurate or fraudulent data will give rise to ethical problems. Implementing quality standards and controls, as well as delegating the responsibility for high quality to the interviewers themselves, can prevent this. This study also tried to emphasize the problem of boosting customer knowledge regarding ethical corporate practices. Because it must exist in a competitive environment, an organization must be ethical in its behaviour. The following have been found after searching through the secondary literature that is available. In order to maintain its promise to society to act ethically, a company must:

- Safeguard its own interests;
- Safeguard the interests of the business community as a whole;
- Satisfy stakeholder expectations;
- Avoid harm to the general public;
- Cultivate trust with key stakeholder groups;
- Safeguard itself from abuse by dishonest employees and rivals;
- Safeguard their own reputations;
- Safeguard their own staff; and
- Establish a culture of ethical behaviour.

An organization's code of ethics is essential. It should begin with top management and work its way down the organizational chart. Moreover, normative ethics may offer a helpful perspective as well as a group of essential conceptual tools for the creation of sustainable marketing based on design. In recognition of the complexity of the topic of sustainability, which includes challenging political, economic, and ethical issues, all of these ethical perspectives on sustainable marketing have a tendency to place various market participants under somewhat different duties, rights, and obligations. This research considered major ethical challenges in brand management as described in the paradigm of ethics and business (Calle, 2000; Stanforth and Hauck, 2010; Ferrell *et al.*, 2019; Tanveer *et al.*, 2021; Chaturvedi and Mishra, 2022), which contributes a significant amount to the survey on marketing. Any organization's ethical behaviour is comprised of a number of the procedures and policies that govern and oversee how the business operates. It includes a proper balance to uphold the rights of the government, community, shareholders, buyers, and vendors. Businesses that engage in unethical business activities are more likely to fail. As a result, the organization's and brand's image diminishes in the minds of customers.

MANAGERIAL IMPLICATIONS

A socially responsible and ethical behaviour guiding concept must be developed by each business and marketing management. According to the social marketing idea, each manager must go above what is legally and permissible and set standards due to personal decency, business consciousness, and enduring customer satisfaction. As we enter the new millennium, marketing executives will face a slew of new difficulties and possibilities. Technological advancements in every field, from communications, information and technology, and the "World-wide web to health-care and amusement", create numerous marketing possibilities. However, influences in the socioeconomic, cultural, and environmental contexts enhance the constraints on marketing. Businesses must exercise caution in their marketing activities since the ethical commitments and promises made by the organization have a substantial impact on consumer perceptions and intents. Companies who can develop fresh consumer value while still being socially responsible will have a globe to conquer.

Furthermore, businesses have recognized the need of adopting practices that contribute to the creation of a distinct identity as socially responsible. The study also found a substantial association between ethical marketing practices, which serve as the foundation for interactions, and prosocial behavior. While utilizing the goods, the client feels as if they are making a responsible contribution to society. In a business setting where competition is rising and technological standardization is difficult to obtain, successful marketing techniques may be established with a right balance of ethical standards. As a result, corporations operating in emerging economies must recognize the critical need of maintaining ethics in their marketing activities.

REFERENCES

Aguilar, F. J. (1994). Managing Corporate Ethics: Learning From America's Ethical Companies How To Supercharge Business Performance. Oxford University Press: New York, Ny, USA.

Anghel, L. D., Grigore, G. F., & Roşca, M. (2011). Cause-related marketing, part of corporate social responsibility and its influence upon consumers' attitude. *Amfiteatru Economic Journal, 13*(29), 72–85.

Aydin, I. (2003). *Managerial, Occupational And Organizational Ethics*. Pegem Press.

Boulstridge, E., & Carrigan, M. (2000). Do Consumers Really Care About Corporate Responsibility? Highlighting The Attitude - Behaviour Gap. *Journal of Communication Management (London), 4*(4), 355–368. doi:10.1108/eb023532

Brenner, S. N., & Molander, E. A. (1977). Is The Ethics Of Business Changing? *Harvard Business Review, 55*(1), 57–71.

Bretcu, A. (2013). Marketing Ethics And Postmodern Era. Analele Universitatii 'Eftimie Murgu'. *Resita Fascicola Ii Studii Economice, 2013*(1), 202–209.

Brubaker, S. (2007). Ethics And Regulation In Direct Marketing. *Direct Marketing (Bradford), 1*(1), 55–58. doi:10.1108/17505930710734134

Burnaz, S., Atakan, M. G. S., Topcu, Y. I., & Singhapakdi, A. (2009). An Exploratory Cross-Cultural Analysis Of Marketing Ethics: The Case Of Turkish, Thai, And American Businesspeople. *Journal of Business Ethics, 90*(3), 371–382. doi:10.100710551-010-0422-4

Calle, J. (2000). *Ethics In Business*. Accounting Smart Pros. http://Accounting.Smartpros.Com/X12209.Xml

Camenisch, P. F. (1991). Marketing Ethics: Some Dimensions Of The Challenge. *Journal of Business Ethics, 10*(4), 245–248. doi:10.1007/BF00382961

Cavanagh, G. F., Dennis, J. M., & Manuel, V. (1981). The Ethics Of Organizational Politics. *Academy of Management Review, 6*(3), 363–374.

Certo, S., & Certo, S. T. (2006). *Modern Management*. Prentice Hall.

Chaturvedi, C., & Mishra, D. (2022). Competitive Edge Building in Business: An Approach Through Ethical Marketing Practices. In S. Bansal, V. Ahuja, V. Chaturvedi, & V. Jain (Eds.), *Multidisciplinary Perspectives Towards Building a Digitally Competent Society* (pp. 248–261). IGI Global., doi:10.4018/978-1-6684-5274-5.ch014

Chiu, R. K. (2003). Ethical Judgment And Whistleblowing Intention: Examining The Moderating Role Of Locus Of Control. *Journal of Business Ethics*, *43*(1-2), 65–74. doi:10.1023/A:1022911215204

Choi, J. C., Kim, S. W., & Kim, J. B. (2010). Globalizing Business Ethics Research And The Ethical Need To Include The Bottom Of The Pyramid Countries: Redefining The Global Triad As Business Systems And Institutions. *Journal of Business Ethics*, *94*(2), 299–306. doi:10.100710551-009-0258-y

Chonko, L. B. (1995). Ethical Decision Making. In *Marketing*. Sage Publications.

Chonko, L. B., & Hunt, S. D. (1985). Ethics And Marketing Management: An Empirical Examination. *Journal of Business Research*, *13*(4), 339–359. doi:10.1016/0148-2963(85)90006-2

Consoli, J. (1976). *Comparative Print Ads More Credible*. Kershaw.

Cooper, J. M. (1999). Reason And Emotion: Essays On Ancient Moral Psychology And Ethical Theory. Princeton University Press.

Crane, A. (1999). Are You Ethical? Please Tick Yes Or No: On Researching Ethics In Business Organizations. *Journal of Business Ethics*, *20*(3), 237–248. doi:10.1023/A:1005817414241

Crane, A. (2000). Marketing And The Natural Environment: What Role For Morality. *Journal of Macromarketing*, *20*(2), 144–154. doi:10.1177/0276146700202004

Crane, A., & Desmond, J. (2002). Societal Marketing And Morality. *European Journal of Marketing*, *36*(5/6), 548–569. doi:10.1108/03090560210423014

Doig, A., & Wilson, J. (1998). The Effectiveness Of Codes Of Conduct. *Business Ethics (Oxford, England)*, *7*(3), 140–149. doi:10.1111/1467-8608.00100

Donaldson, T., & Werhane, P. H. (1983). Cording, M. Ethical Issues In Business. Pearson Prentice Hall.

Drumwright, M. E., & Murphy, P. E. (2009). The Current State Of Advertising Ethics: Industry And Academic Perspectives. *Journal of Advertising*, *38*(1), 83–108. doi:10.2753/JOA0091-3367380106

Dudiak, J. (2001). The Intrigue Of Ethics: A Reading Of The Idea Of Discourse In The Thought Of Emmanuel Levinas; Fordham University Press: New York, Ny, USA. *Ethics*, *90*(4), 607–622.

Eagle, L. (2009). *Social marketing ethics: report prepared for the National Social Marketing Centre*. Then SMC. https://www.thensmc.com/sites/default/files/public-files/NSMC_social_marketing_ethics.pdf on 22/2/2023.

Evans, D. S. (2009). The online advertising industry: Economics, evolution, and privacy. *The Journal of Economic Perspectives*, *23*(3), 37–60. doi:10.1257/jep.23.3.37

Ferrell, O. C., Harrison, D. E., Ferrell, L., & Hair, J. F. (2019). Business Ethics, Corporate Social Responsibility, And Brand Attitudes: An Exploratory Study. *Journal of Business Research*, *95*, 491–501. doi:10.1016/j.jbusres.2018.07.039

Ford, R. C., & Richardson, W. D. (1994). Ethical Decision Making: A Review Of The Empirical Literature. *Journal of Business Ethics*, *13*(3), 205–221. doi:10.1007/BF02074820

Gaski, J. F. (1999). Does Marketing Ethics Really Have Anything To Say? A Critical Inventory Of The Literature. *Journal of Business Ethics*, *18*(3), 315–334. doi:10.1023/A:1017190829683

Godos-Diez, J.-L., Fernandez-Gago, R., & Martinez-Campillo, A. (2011). How Important Are Ceos To Csr Practices? An Analysis Of The Mediating Effect Of The Perceived Role Of Ethics In Social Responsibility. *Journal of Business Ethics*, *98*(4), 531–548. doi:10.100710551-010-0609-8

Goolsby, J. R., & Hunt, S. D. (1982). Cognitive Moral Development And Marketing. *Journal of Marketing*, *56*(1), 55–68. doi:10.1177/002224299205600106

Hastings, G., Stead, M., McDermott, L., Forsyth, A., MacKintosh, A. M., Rayner, M., Godfrey, C., Caraher, M., & Angus, K. (2003). *Review of research on the effects of food promotion to children*. Food Standards Agency.

Helin, S., & Sandström, J. (2008). Codes, Ethics And Cross-Cultural Differences: Stories From The Implementation Of A Corporate Code Of Ethics In A Mnc Subsidiary. *Journal of Business Ethics*, *82*(2), 281–291. doi:10.100710551-008-9887-9

Henion, K. E., & Kinnear, T. C. (1976). *Ecological Marketing, Chicago, Il.* American Marketing Association. https://Www.Tandfonline.Com/Doi/Full/10.1080/07393148.2017.1304737

Hur, W. M., Kim, H., & Woo, J. (2014). How Csr Leads To Corporate Brand Equity: Mediating Mechanisms Of Corporate Brand Credibility And Reputation. *Journal of Business Ethics, 125*(1), 75–86. doi:10.100710551-013-1910-0

Islam, J. U., Shahid, S., Rasool, A., Rahman, Z., Khan, I., & Rather, R. A. (2020). Impact Of Website Attributes On Customer Engagement In Banking: A Solicitation Of Stimulus-Organism-Response Theory. *International Journal of Bank Marketing, 38*(6), 1279–1303. doi:10.1108/IJBM-12-2019-0460

Jeurissen, R., & Van De Ven, B. (2020). (2996). Developments In Marketing Ethics. *Business Ethics Quarterly, 16*, 427–439. doi:10.5840/beq200616335

Keith, N., Petto, J. C., & Burnett, M. (2008). Ethics In Advertising: Differences In Industry Values And Student Perceptions. *Academy of Marketing Studies Journal, 27*, 33–47.

Khandelwal, U., & Bajpai, N. (2012). Price Fairness And Its Linear Dependence On Consumer AttiTude: A Comparative Study In Metro And Non Metro City. *European Journal of Business and Management, 4*(10), 94–10.

Kilbourne, W. E. (1998). Green Marketing: A Theoretical Perspective. *Journal of Marketing Management, 14*(6), 641–655. doi:10.1362/026725798784867743

Kotler, P. (1972). A Generic Concept Of Marketing. *Journal of Marketing, 36*(April), 46–54. doi:10.1177/002224297203600209

Lamberton, H., & Minor, L. (1995). *Human Relations: Strategies For Success*. Irwin.

Lämsä, A. M., Vehkaperä, M., Puttonen, T., & Pesonen, H. L. (2008). Eff Ect Of Business Education On Women And Men Students' Attitudes On Corporate Responsibility In Society. *Journal of Business Ethics, 82*(1), 45–58. doi:10.100710551-007-9561-7

Lee, J. Y., & Jin, C. H. (2019). The Role Of Ethical Marketing Issues In Consumer-Brand Relationship. *Sustainability (Basel), 11*(23), 6536. doi:10.3390u11236536

Low, W., & Davenport, E. (2005). Has The Medium (Roast) Become The Message? *International Marketing Review, 22*(5), 494–511. doi:10.1108/02651330510624354

Ludlum, M., & Johnson, J. B. (2015). Ethics And Law School Marketing Practices. *South. J. Bus. Ethics, 7*, 89–104.

Malhotra, N. K., & Miller, G. L. (1998). An Integrated Model For Ethical Decisions In Marketing Research. *Journal of Business Ethics, 17*(3), 263–280. doi:10.1023/A:1005711311426

Martin, K. D., & Johnson, J. L. (2010). Ethical Beliefs And Information Asymmetries In Supplier Relationships. *Journal of Public Policy & Marketing*, *29*(1), 38–51. doi:10.1509/jppm.29.1.38

Mcdaniel, C., & Gitman, L. (2008). *The Essential Of The Future Of Business*. South-Western Cengage Learning.

Mcdonald, G., & Nijhof, A. (1999). Beyond Codes Of Ethics: An Integrated Framework For stimulating Morally Responsible Behaviour. *Organizations. Leadership and Organization Development Journal*, *20*(3), 133–147. doi:10.1108/01437739910268406

Mcguire, J. B., Sundgren, A., & Schneeweis, T. (1988). Corporate Social Responsibility And Firm Financial Performance. *Academy of Management Journal*, *31*(4), 854–872. doi:10.2307/256342

Melewar, T. C., & Nguyen, B. (2017). Five Areas To Advance Branding Theory And Practice. *Journal of Brand Management*, *21*(9), 758–769. doi:10.1057/bm.2014.31

Nill, A., & Schibrowsky, J. A. (2007). Research On Marketing Ethics: A Systematic Review Of The Literature. *Journal of Macromarketing*, *27*(3), 256–273. doi:10.1177/0276146707304733

Olins, W. (2014). Brand New: The Shape Of Brands To Come. Thames & Hudson: New York, Ny, USA.

Preston, I. (2010). Interaction Of Law And Ethics In Matters Of Advertisers' Responsibility For Protecting Consumers. *The Journal of Consumer Affairs*, *44*(1), 257–264. doi:10.1111/j.1745-6606.2010.01166.x

Prothero, A. (1998). Green Marketing: The 'Fad' That Won't Slip Slide Away. *Journal of Marketing Management*, *14*(6), 507–512. doi:10.1362/026725798784867680

Reidenbach, R. E., Robin, D. P., & Dawson, L. (1991). An Application And Extension Of A Multidimensional Ethics Scale To Selected Marketing Practices And Marketing Groups. *Journal of the Academy of Marketing Science*, *19*(2), 83–92. doi:10.1007/BF02726000

Resnik, D. B. (2011). What Is Ethics In Research And Why Is It Important. National Institute Of Health.

Riche, L. A., & Ponte, S. (2014). Buying Into Development? Brand Aid Forms Of Cause-Related Marketing. *Third World Quarterly*, *35*(1), 65–87. doi:10.1080/01436597.2014.868985

Rodriguez-Dominguez, L., Gallego-Alvarez, I., & Garcia-Sanchez, I. M. (2009). Corporate Governance And Codes Of Ethics. *Journal of Business Ethics*, *90*(2), 187–202. doi:10.100710551-009-0035-y

Ross, W. D. (1930). *The Right And The Cood.* Clarendon Press.

Schlegelmilch, B. B., & Öberseder, M. (2010). Half A Century Of Marketing Ethics: Shifting Perspectives And Emerging Trends. *Journal of Business Ethics*, *93*(1), 1–19. doi:10.100710551-009-0182-1

Sen, S., Bhattacharya, C. B., & Korschun, D. (2006). The Role Of Corporate Social Responsibility In Strengthening Multiple Stakeholder Relationships: A Field Experiment. *Journal of the Academy of Marketing Science*, *34*(2), 158–166. doi:10.1177/0092070305284978

Sevensson, G., Wood, G., Singh, J., & Callaghan, M. (2009). Implementation, Communication And Benefits Of Corporate Codes Of Ethics: An International And Longitudinal Approach For Australia, Canada And Sweden. *Business Ethics (Oxford, England)*, *18*(4), 389–398. doi:10.1111/j.1467-8608.2009.01571.x

Simon, J., Charles, W. P., & Jon, P. G. (1972). *The Ethical Investor: Universities And Corporate Responsibility*. Yale University Press.

Smith., & Murphy. (2012). A Marketing Ethics: A review of the Field. *Marketing Ethics.* SAGE publications.

Stanaland, A. J., Lwin, M. O., & Murphy, P. E. (2011). Consumer Perceptions Of The Antecedents And Consequences Of Corporate Social Responsibility. *Journal of Business Ethics*, *102*(1), 47–55. doi:10.100710551-011-0904-z

Stanforth, N., & Hauck, W. (2010). The Effects Of Ethical Framing On Consumer Price Perceptions. *Journal of Fashion Marketing and Management*, *14*(4), 615–623. doi:10.1108/13612021011081779

Stohl, C., Stohl, M., & Popova, L. (2009). A New Generation Of Corporate Code Of Ethics. *The Journal of Business.*

Tanveer, M., Khan, N., & Ahmad, A. R. (2021)). AI Support Marketing: Understanding The Customer Journey Towards The Business Development. In *Proceedings Of The 2021 1st International Conference On Artificial Intelligence And Data Analytics (Caida)*, Riyadh, Saudi Arabia. 10.1109/CAIDA51941.2021.9425079

Tarkianen, A., & Sundqvist, S. (2014). Subjective norms, attitudes and intentions of Finnish consumers in buying organic food. *British Food Journal*, *107*(11), 808–822. doi:10.1108/00070700510629760

Taylor, P. W. (1975). *Principles Of Ethia: An Introduction*. Dickerson Publishing Co., Inc.

Thompson, M. (2005). Ethical Theory (Access To Philosophy) (2nd Ed.). Hodder & Stoughton.

Tsalikis, J., & Seaton, B. (2007). The International Business Ethics Index: European Union. *Journal of Business Ethics, 75*(3), 229–238. doi:10.100710551-006-9249-4

Tsalikis, J., Seaton, B., & Li, T. (2008). The International Business Ethics Index: Asian Emerging Economies. *Journal of Business Ethics, 80*(4), 643–651. doi:10.100710551-007-9459-4

Vitell, S. J. Jr. (1986). Marketing Ethics: Conceptual And Empirical Foundations Of A Positive Theory Of Decision Making. In *Marketing Situations Having Ethical Content', Unpublished Dissention*. Texas Tech University.

Yallop, A. (2012). The Use And Effectiveness Of Code Of Ethics – A Literature Review. *International Conference 'Marketing – From Information To Decision, 5.*

KEY TERMS AND DEFINITIONS

Business: Making a living or earning money through the production, acquisition, and sale of items is what it entails (such as goods and services). Additionally, it includes "any activity or enterprise undertaken for profit."

Competitive Advantage: It refers to elements that enable a business to create goods or services more effectively or affordably than its competitors. These elements enable the producing unit to outperform its competitors in terms of sales or margins.

Ethics: The discipline that examines what is ethically good and bad as well as right and wrong is known as moral philosophy.

Marketing Ethics: It entails consciously incorporating moral good and evil into the organization's marketing decision-making, behaviour, and practice.

Marketing: Advertising and market research are both part of the process of promoting and selling goods and services.

Compilation of References

Aali-Bujari, A., Venegas-Martínez, F., & Santillán-Salgado, R. J. (2018). On the stock market-electricity sector nexus in Latin America: A dynamic panel data model. *International Journal of Energy Economics and Policy*, *8*(6), 148–154. doi:10.32479/ijeep.7120

Abbad, M. M., Morris, D., & de Nahlik, C. (2009). Looking under the Bonnet: Factors affecting student adoption of Online Learning systems in Jordan. *International Review of Research in Open and Distance Learning*, *10*(2), 1–25. doi:10.19173/irrodl.v10i2.596

Abbas, H. A., & Hamdy, H. I. (2015). Determinants of continuance intention factor in Kuwait communication market: Case study of Zain-Kuwait. *Computers in Human Behavior*, *49*, 648–657. doi:10.1016/j.chb.2015.03.035

Abbasi, A. G. (2022). *Coordinated Volt-Var control in multiple smart inverters in Smart Distribution Networks for Voltage Regulation* [Master's thesis]. Arctic University of Norway. https://munin.uit.no/bitstream/handle/10037/25764/thesis.pdf

Abbasi, A., Zahedi, F., Zeng, D., Chen, Y., Chen, H., & Nunamaker, J. F. Jr. (2015). Enhancing predictive analytics for anti-phishing by exploiting website genre information. *Journal of Management Information Systems*, *31*(4), 109–157. doi:10.1080/07421222.2014.1001260

Abdou, H. A., & Pointon, J. (2011). Credit scoring, statistical techniques and evaluation criteria: A review of the literature. *Intelligent Systems in Accounting, Finance & Management*, *18*(2-3), 59–88. doi:10.1002/isaf.325

Abdulrahaman, M. D., Alhassan, J. K., Ojeniyi, J. A., & Abdulhamid, S. M. (2018). Security risk analysis management in mobile wallet transaction: A case study of Pagatech Nigeria Limited. *International Journal of Computer Network and Information Security*, *10*(12), 21. doi:10.5815/ijcnis.2018.12.03

Aboagye, J., & Jung, J. Y. (2018). Debt holding, financial behavior, and financial satisfaction. *Financial Counseling and Planning*, *29*(2), 208–218. doi:10.1891/1052-3073.29.2.208

Abrishambaf, O., Faria, P., & Vale, Z. (2020). Aggregation of Consumers Participation in the Ramping of a Demand Response Event. *International Conference on the European Energy Market, EEM*. 10.1109/EEM49802.2020.9221914

Adams, J., Hayunga, D., Mansi, S., Reeb, D., & Verardi, V. (2019). Identifying and treating outliers in finance. *Financial Management*, *48*(2), 345–384. doi:10.1111/fima.12269

Adhikari Egodawele, M. H., Sedera, D., & Bui, V. (2022). A Systematic Review of Digital Transformation Literature (2013–2021) and the Development of an Overarching a-Priori Model to Guide Future Research. In *Australasian COnference on Information Systems*. AIS.

Adikari, A., Burnett, D., Sedera, D., de Silva, D., and Alahakoon, D. (2021). Value Co-Creation for Open Innovation: An Evidence-Based Study of the Data Driven Paradigm of Social Media Using Machine Learning. *International Journal of Information Management Data Insights* (1-2), 100022.

Adjei, J. K. (2015). Explaining the role of trust in cloud computing services. *Info*, *17*(1), 54–67. doi:10.1108/info-09-2014-0042

Adu, G., Alagidede, P., & Karimu, A. (2015). Stock return distribution in the BRICS. *Review of Development Finance*, *5*(2), 98–109. doi:10.1016/j.rdf.2015.09.002

Afini Normadhi, N. B., Shuib, L., Md Nasir, H. N., Bimba, A., Idris, N., & Balakrishnan, V. (2019). Identification of personal traits in adaptive learning environment: Systematic literature review. *Computers & Education*, *130*, 168–190. doi:10.1016/j.compedu.2018.11.005

Agarwal, D. D. K., Bansal, S., Jain, A., & Jain, S. (2021). A Study on Investment Behavior of Individual Investors With Reference To Delhi-NCR. *International Journal of All Research Education and Scientific Methods (IJARESM)*. http://www.ijaresm.com/a-study-on-investment-behavior-of-individual-investors-with-reference-to-delhi-ncr

Aghabozorgi, S., Shirkhorshidi, A. S., & Wah, T. Y. (2015). Timeseries clustering–a decade review. *Information Systems*, *53*, 16–38. doi:10.1016/j.is.2015.04.007

Aguilar, F. J. (1994). Managing Corporate Ethics: Learning From America's Ethical Companies How To Supercharge Business Performance. Oxford University Press: New York, Ny, USA.

Agus, A., Barker, S., & Kandampully, J. (2007). An exploratory study of service quality in the Malaysian public service sector. *International Journal of Quality & Reliability Management*, *24*(2), 177–190. doi:10.1108/02656710710722284

Ahmad Khan, A., Naeem, M., Iqbal, M., Qaisar, S., & Anpalagan, A. (2016). A compendium of optimization objectives, constraints, tools and algorithms for energy management in microgrids. In *Renewable and Sustainable Energy Reviews* (Vol. 58, pp. 1664–1683). Elsevier. doi:10.1016/j.rser.2015.12.259

Ahmad, M. N., Zakaria, N. H., & Sedera, D. (2013). Ontology-Based Knowledge Management for Enterprise Systems. In *Competition, Strategy, and Modern Enterprise Information Systems* (pp. 184–212). IGI Global. doi:10.4018/978-1-4666-2464-1.ch010

Ahmed, Z., Ramakrishnan, S., & Noreen, U. (2017). Financial literacy as competitive advantage for individual investors' decision making. *Advanced Science Letters*, *23*(9), 8988–8993. doi:10.1166/asl.2017.10009

Ajala, K., Sakanko, M. A., & Adeniji, S. O. (2021). the Asymmetric Effect of Oil Price on the Exchange Rate and Stock Price in Nigeria. *International Journal of Energy Economics and Policy, 11*(4), 202–208. doi:10.32479/ijeep.10977

Ajzen, I. (2011). The theory of planned behaviour: Reactions and reflections. In Psychology and Health, 26(9), 1113–1127. https://doi.org/ doi:10.1080/08870446.2011.613995

Akter, S., McCarthy, G., Sajib, S., Michael, K., Dwivedi, Y. K., D'Ambra, J., & Shen, K. N. (2021a). *Algorithmic Bias in Data-Driven Innovation in the Age of Ai.* Elsevier. doi:10.1016/j.ijinfomgt.2021.102387

Alamgir, F., & Amin, S. (2021). The nexus between oil price and stock market: Evidence from South Asia. *Energy Reports, 7*, 693–703. doi:10.1016/j.egyr.2021.01.027

Alchamdani, A., Fatmasari, F., Anugrah, E. R., Sari, N. P., Putri, F., & Astina, A. (2020). The Impact of Covid19 Pandemic on Online Learning Process in the College at Southeast Sulawesi. *JURNAL KESEHATAN LINGKUNGAN, 12*(1si), 129–136. doi:10.20473/jkl.v12i1si.2020.129-136

Aleem, A., & Ryan Sprott, C. (2012). Let me in the cloud: Analysis of the benefit and risk assessment of cloud platform. *Journal of Financial Crime, 20*(1), 6–24. doi:10.1108/13590791311287337

Alenzi, M. (2015). *The Impact of Exchange Rate, Interest Rate and Oil Price Fluctuations on Stock Returns Of GCC Listed Companies* [Thesis, University of Plymouth].

Alexandru, A., Alexandru, C. A., Coardos, D., & Tudora, E. (2016). Big data: concepts, technologies, and applications in the public sector. *International Journal of Computer Electrical Automation Control and Information Engineering, 10*, 1629-35.

Alghushami, A. H., Zakaria, N. H., & Aji, Z. M. (2020). Factors Influencing Cloud Computing Adoption in Higher Education Institutions of Least Developed Countries: Evidence from Republic of Yemen. *Applied Sciences, 10*(22), 8098. doi:10.3390/app10228098

Alimadadi, A., Aryal, S., Manandhar, I., Munroe, P. B., Joe, B., & Cheng, X. (2020). Artificial intelligence and machine learning to fight COVID-19. *Physiological Genomics, 52*(4), 200–202. doi:10.1152/physiolgenomics.00029.2020 PMID:32216577

Almaiah, M. A., Al-Khasawneh, A., & Althunibat, A. (2020). Exploring the critical challenges and factors influencing the Online Learning system usage during COVID-19 pandemic. *Education and Information Technologies, 25*(6), 5261–5280. doi:10.1007/s10639-020-10219-y

Almeida, D., Pasupuleti, J., & Ekanayake, J. (2021). Comparison of reactive power control techniques for solar pv inverters to mitigate voltage rise in low-voltage grids. *Electronics (Basel), 10*(13), 1569. Advance online publication. doi:10.3390/electronics10131569

Alotaibi, S., Mehmood, R., & Katib, I. (2020). The role of big data and twitter data analytics in healthcare supply chain management. Smart Infrastructure and Applications, 267-279. doi:10.1007/978-3-030-13705-2_11

Alqaralleh, H. (2020). On the asymmetric response of the exchange rate to shocks in the crude oil market. *International Journal of Energy Sector Management*, *14*(4), 839–852. doi:10.1108/IJESM-10-2019-0011

Al-Qudah, A. A., Al-Okaily, M., Alqudah, G., & Ghazlat, A. (2022). Mobile payment adoption in the time of the COVID-19 pandemic. *Electronic Commerce Research*. doi:10.100710660-022-09577-1

Alrahhal, M. S., & Abi Sen, A. (2018). *Data mining, big data, and artificial intelligence: An overview, challenges, and research questions.*

Alshehri, K., Ndrio, M., Bose, S., & Başar, T. (2020). Quantifying Market Efficiency Impacts of Aggregated Distributed Energy Resources. *IEEE Transactions on Power Systems*, *35*(5), 4067–4077. doi:10.1109/TPWRS.2020.2979997

Alsheibani, S., Cheung, Y., & Messom, C. (2018). Artificial Intelligence Adoption: Ai-Readiness at Firm-Level.

Altman, E. I. (1983). *A Complete Guide to Predicting, Avoiding, and Dealing with Bankruptcy*. Corporate Financial Distress.

Amani, F. A., & Fadlalla, A. M. (2017). Data mining applications in accounting: A review of the literature and organizing framework. *International Journal of Accounting Information Systems*, *24*, 32–58. doi:10.1016/j.accinf.2016.12.004

Amari, M., & Jarboui, A. (2015). Financial Literacy and Economics Education Among Young Adults: An Observation From Tunisia. *Journal of Business & Finance Librarianship*, *20*(3), 209–219. Advance online publication. doi:10.1080/08963568.2015.978834

Amin, H. (2009). An analysis of online banking usage intentions: An extension of the technology acceptance model. *International Journal of Business and Society*, *10*(1), 27–40.

Anazonwu, H. O., Egbunike, F. C., & Gunardi, A. (2018). Corporate Board Diversity and Sustainability Reporting: A Study of Selected Listed Manufacturing Firms in Nigeria. *Indonesian Journal of Sustainability Accounting and Management*, *2*(1), 65–78. doi:10.28992/ijsam.v2i1.52

Anderson, J. Q., & Rainie, L. (2010). The future of cloud computing. *Pew Research Center's Internet & American Life Project An Initiative of the Pew Research Center*. https://pewinternet.org/Reports/2010/The-future-of-cloud-computing.aspx

Anderson, J. Q., & Rainie, L. (2010). The future of cloud computing. *Pew Research Center's Internet & American Life Project. Pew Research Center*. https://pewinternet.org/Reports/2010/The-future-of-cloud-computing.aspx

Anghel, L. D., Grigore, G. F., & Roşca, M. (2011). Cause-related marketing, part of corporate social responsibility and its influence upon consumers' attitude. *Amfiteatru Economic Journal*, *13*(29), 72–85.

Anubha, J. A., & Hooda, M. (2019). Consumer engagement towards travel websites and purchase intentions. *Journal of Advanced Research in Dynamical and Control Systems, 11*(8 Special Issue).

Archenaa, J., & Anita, E. M. (2015). A survey of big data analytics in healthcare and government. *Procedia Computer Science, 50*, 408–413. doi:10.1016/j.procs.2015.04.021

Arias, C. A., Monroy, C. R., & Guerrero, Y. M. N. (2012). *The New Cloud Computing Paradigm: The Way To It Seen As A Utility.*

Arkorful, V., & Abaidoo, N. (2014). *The role of Online Learning, the advantages, and disadvantages of its adoption in Higher Education*. Undefined.

Armbrust, M., Fox, A., Griffith, R., Joseph, A. D., Katz, R., Konwinski, A., Lee, G., Patterson, D., Rabkin, A., Stoica, I., & Zaharia, M. (2010). A view of cloud computing. *Communications of the ACM, 53*(4), 50–58. doi:10.1145/1721654.1721672

Arowoshegbe, A., & Uniamikogbo, E. (2016). Accounting for Social and Environmental Challenges: A Theoretical Perspective. *Saudi Journal of Business and Management Studies, 1*(3), 143–148.

Asaad, Z. A. (2021). Oil Price, Gold Price, Exchange Rate and Stock Market in Iraq Pre-During Covid19 Outbreak: An Ardl Approach. *International Journal of Energy Economics and Policy, 11*(5), 562–571. doi:10.32479/ijeep.11552

Asadi, Z., Abdekhoda, M., & Nadrian, H. (2019). Cloud computing services adoption among higher education faculties: development of a standardized questionnaire. *Education and Information Technologies, 25*(1), 175–191. doi:10.1007/s10639-019-09932-0

Asante-Korang, A., & Jacobs, J. P. (2016). Big data and pediatric cardiovascular disease in the era of transparency in healthcare. *Cardiology in the Young, 26*(8), 1597–1602. doi:10.1017/S1047951116001736 PMID:28148322

Asgarnezhad Nouri, B., Motamedi, S., & Soltani, M. (2017). Empirical analysis of the financial behavior of investors with brand approach (case study: Tehran stock exchange). *Scientific Annals of Economics and Business, 64*(1), 97–121. doi:10.1515aeb-2017-0007

Awasthi, P., & George, J. J. (2020). A Case for Data Democratization. In *Americas Conference on Information Systems*. Virtual: AIS Library.

Aydin, I. (2003). *Managerial, Occupational And Organizational Ethics*. Pegem Press.

Ayodele, T.O. (2010). Types of machine learning algorithms. *New Advances in Machine Learning, 3*, 19–48.

Azure, M. (2021). *What is cloud computing? A beginner's guide*. Microsoft. https://azure.microsoft.com/en-in/resources/cloud-computing-dictionary/what-is-cloud-computing/#benefits

Babu, M. M., Rahman, M., Alam, A., & Dey, B. L. (2021). Exploring Big Data-Driven Innovation in the Manufacturing Sector: Evidence from Uk Firms. *Annals of Operations Research, 21*(April), 1–28. doi:10.100710479-021-04077-1 PMID:33897083

Bag, S. N. (2020). *Impact of COVID-19 Pandemic on Productivity of Jute Industry: A Case Study*. Fibre2Fashion. https://www.fibre2fashion.com/industry-article/8796

Bag, S. N., & Sinha, R. C. (2021). *Study on Weaving Performance of a Jute Mill in Pre- & Post-COVID Lockdown Periods*. Fibre2Fashion. https://www.fibre2fashion.com/industry-article/8923

Bagchi, B. (2017). Volatility spillovers between crude oil price and stock markets: Evidence from BRIC countries. *International Journal of Emerging Markets*, *12*(2), 352–365. doi:10.1108/IJoEM-04-2015-0077

Bai, J., & Perron, P. (2003). Computation and analysis of multiple structural change models. *Journal of Applied Econometrics*, *18*(1), 1–22. doi:10.1002/jae.659

Balcilar, M., van Eyden, R., Uwilingiye, J., & Gupta, R. (2017). The Impact of Oil Price on South African GDP Growth: A Bayesian Markov Switching-VAR Analysis. *African Development Review*, *29*(2), 319–336. doi:10.1111/1467-8268.12259

Bandura, A. (1997). *Self-efficacy: The exercise of control*. W. H. Freeman and Company.

Ban, G. Y., El Karoui, N., & Lim, A. E. (2018). Machine learning and portfolio optimization. *Management Science*, *64*(3), 1136–1154. doi:10.1287/mnsc.2016.2644

Barrot, J. S. (2018). Facebook as a learning environment for language teaching and learning: A critical analysis of the literature from 2010 to 2017. *Journal of Computer Assisted Learning*, *34*(6), 863–875. doi:10.1111/jcal.12295

Barrot, J. S., Llenares, I. I., & del Rosario, L. S. (2021). Students' online learning challenges during the pandemic and how they cope with them: The case of the Philippines. *Education and Information Technologies*, *26*(6), 7321–7338. doi:10.100710639-021-10589-x PMID:34075300

Bartelmus, P. (1998). The value of nature: valuation and evaluation in environmental accounting. In K. Uno & P. Bartelmus (Eds.), *Environmental Accounting in Theory and Practice*. Kluwer. doi:10.1007/978-94-017-1433-4_16

Baseem & Hagos. (2022). Demand response aggregation. *Active Electrical Distribution Network*, 345-358. doi:10.1016/B978-0-323-85169-5.00008-3

Basher, S. A., Haug, A. A., & Sadorsky, P. (2012). Oil prices, exchange rates and emerging stock markets. *Energy Economics*, *34*(1), 227–240. doi:10.1016/j.eneco.2011.10.005

Baticulon, R. E., Sy, J. J., Alberto, N. R. I., Baron, M. B. C., Mabulay, R. E. C., Rizada, L. G. T., Tiu, C. J. S., Clarion, C. A., & Reyes, J. C. B. (2021). Barriers to Online Learning in the Time of COVID-19: A National Survey of Medical Students in the Philippines. *Medical Science Educator*, *31*(2), 615–626. doi:10.1007/s40670-021-01231-z

Baviskar, A., Das, K., Hansen, A. D., & Menegatos, P. (2021): Loss Minimization in Distribution Network using Wind Power Plant Reactive Power Support. doi:10.36227/techrxiv.14554845.v1

Bayar, Y., Sezgin, H. F., Öztürk, Ö. F., & Şaşmaz, M. Ü. (2020). Financial Literacy and Financial Risk Tolerance of Individual Investors: Multinomial Logistic Regression Approach. *SAGE Open*, *10*(3). Advance online publication. doi:10.1177/2158244020945717

Beckers, B., & Beidas-strom, S. (2015). Forecasting the Nominal Brent Oil Price with VARs — One Model Fits All? *IMF Working Paper, 15/251.*

Beckmann, J., Czudaj, R. L., & Arora, V. (2020). The relationship between oil prices and exchange rates: Revisiting theory and evidence. *Energy Economics*, *88*, 104772. doi:10.1016/j.eneco.2020.104772

Belhadi, A., Mani, V., Kamble, S. S., Khan, S. A. R., & Verma, S. (2021). Artificial Intelligence-Driven Innovation for Enhancing Supply Chain Resilience and Performance under the Effect of Supply Chain Dynamism: An Empirical Investigation. *Annals of Operations Research*, 1–26. doi:10.100710479-021-03956-x PMID:33551534

Bellovary, J. L., Giacomino, D. E., & Akers, M. D. (2007). *A review of bankruptcy prediction studies: 1930 to present*. J Financ Education.

Ben Ameur, H., Ftiti, Z., & Louhichi, W. (2022). Revisiting the relationship between spot and futures markets: Evidence from commodity markets and NARDL framework. *Annals of Operations Research*, *313*(1), 171–189. doi:10.100710479-021-04172-3 PMID:34334864

Benhmad, F. (2012). Modeling nonlinear Granger causality between the oil price and U.S. dollar: A wavelet based approach. *Economic Modelling*, *29*(4), 1505–1514. doi:10.1016/j.econmod.2012.01.003

Benke, K., & Benke, G. (2018). Artificial intelligence and big data in public health. *International Journal of Environmental Research and Public Health*, *15*(12), 2796. doi:10.3390/ijerph15122796 PMID:30544648

Beyer, K., Beckmann, R., Geißendörfer, S., von Maydell, K., & Agert, C. (2021). Adaptive online-learning volt-var control for smart inverters using deep reinforcement learning. *Energies*, *14*(7), 1991. Advance online publication. doi:10.3390/en14071991

Bharati, P., & Chaudhury, A. (2019). Assimilation of Big Data Innovation: Investigating the Roles of It, Social Media, and Relational Capital. *Information Systems Frontiers 21*(6), 1357-1368.

Bhattacharjee, A. (2001). Understanding information systems continuance: An expectation confirmation model. *Management Information Systems Quarterly*, *25*(3), 351–370. doi:10.2307/3250921

Bhatti, S. H., Hussain, W. M. H. W., Khan, J., Sultan, S., & Ferraris, A. (2022). Exploring Data-Driven Innovation: What's Missing in the Relationship between Big Data Analytics Capabilities and Supply Chain Innovation? *Annals of Operations Research*, 1–26. doi:10.100710479-022-04772-7

Bird, K. A., Castleman, B. L., & Lohner, G. (2022). Negative Impacts From the Shift to Online Learning During the COVID-19 Crisis: Evidence from a Statewide Community College System. EdWorkingPapers.Com. https://doi.org/ doi:10.26300/GX68-RQ13

Black, F., & Scholes, M. (2019). The pricing of options and corporate liabilities. In World Scientific Reference on Contingent Claims Analysis in Corporate Finance: Volume 1: Foundations of CCA and Equity Valuation. World Scientific. doi:10.1142/9789814759588_0001

Boero, G., Smith, J., & Wallis, K. F. (2008). Uncertainty and disagreement in economic prediction: The bank of England survey of external forecasters. *Economic Journal (London)*, *118*(530), 1107–1127. doi:10.1111/j.1468-0297.2008.02162.x

Boldanov, R., Degiannakis, S., & Filis, G. (2016). Time-varying correlation between oil and stock market volatilities: Evidence from oil-importing and oil-exporting countries. *International Review of Financial Analysis*, *48*, 209–220. doi:10.1016/j.irfa.2016.10.002

Bollerslev, T., Engle, R. F., & Wooldridge, J. M. (1988). A capital asset pricing model with time-varying covariances. *Journal of Political Economy*, *96*(1), 116–131. doi:10.1086/261527

Bolton, R.J., & Hand, D.J. (2001). Unsupervised Profiling Methods for Fraud Detection. *Credit Scoring and Credit Control, 7*, 235–255.

Bora, D. J. (2019). Big data analytics in healthcare: A critical analysis. Big Data Analytics for Intelligent Healthcare Management, 43-57 doi:10.1016/B978-0-12-818146-1.00003-9

Bosamia, M. (2018). *Mobile wallet payments recent potential threats and vulnerabilities with its possible security measures.*

Bosch-Sijtsema, P., & Bosch, J. (2015). User Involvement Throughout the Innovation Process in High-Tech Industries. *Journal of Product Innovation Management, 32*(5), 793-807.

Bostrom, N., & Yudkowsky, E. (2018). The ethics of artificial intelligence. In *Artificial intelligence safety and security* (pp. 57–69). Chapman and Hall/CRC. doi:10.1201/9781351251389-4

Boubaker, H., & Raza, S. A. (2017). A wavelet analysis of mean and volatility spillovers between oil and BRICS stock markets. *Energy Economics*, *64*, 105–117. doi:10.1016/j.eneco.2017.01.026

Boulstridge, E., & Carrigan, M. (2000). Do Consumers Really Care About Corporate Responsibility? Highlighting The Attitude - Behaviour Gap. *Journal of Communication Management (London)*, *4*(4), 355–368. doi:10.1108/eb023532

Brenner, S. N., & Molander, E. A. (1977). Is The Ethics Of Business Changing? *Harvard Business Review*, *55*(1), 57–71.

Bresciani, S., Ciampi, F., Meli, F., & Ferraris, A. (2021). Using Big Data for Co-Innovation Processes: Mapping the Field of Data-Driven Innovation, Proposing Theoretical Developments and Providing a Research Agenda. *International Journal of Information Management*, *60*, 1–15. doi:10.1016/j.ijinfomgt.2021.102347

Bretcu, A. (2013). Marketing Ethics And Postmodern Era. Analele Universitatii 'Eftimie Murgu'. *Resita Fascicola Ii Studii Economice*, *2013*(1), 202–209.

Britten-Jones, M. (1999). The sampling error in estimates of mean-variance efficient portfolio weights. *The Journal of Finance, 54*(2), 655–671. doi:10.1111/0022-1082.00120

Broby, D., Basu, D., & Arulselvan, A. (2019). The role of precision timing in stock market price discovery when trading through distributed ledgers. *J Business Thought., 10*, 1–8. doi:10.18311/jbt/2019/23355

Brubaker, S. (2007). Ethics And Regulation In Direct Marketing. *Direct Marketing (Bradford), 1*(1), 55–58. doi:10.1108/17505930710734134

Burnaz, S., Atakan, M. G. S., Topcu, Y. I., & Singhapakdi, A. (2009). An Exploratory Cross-Cultural Analysis Of Marketing Ethics: The Case Of Turkish, Thai, And American Businesspeople. *Journal of Business Ethics, 90*(3), 371–382. doi:10.100710551-010-0422-4

Business Standard. (2022). India to have 1 billion smartphone users by 2026: Deloitte report. *Business Standard.* https://www.business-standard.com/article/current-affairs/india-to-have-1-billion-smartphone-users-by-2026-deloitte-report-122022200996_1.html

Butler, T., & O'Brien, L. (2019). Understanding regtech for digital regulatory compliance. In *Disrupting Finance* (pp. 85–102). Palgrave Pivot. doi:10.1007/978-3-030-02330-0_6

Buyya, R., Yeo, C. S., Venugopal, S., Broberg, J., & Brandic, I. (2009). Cloud computing and emerging IT platforms: Vision, hype, and reality for delivering computing as the 5th utility. *Future Generation Computer Systems, 25*(6), 599–616. doi:10.1016/j.future.2008.12.001

Cai, L., Cui, J., & Jo, H. (2016). Corporate environmental responsibility and firm risk. *Journal of Business Ethics, 139*(3), 563–594. doi:10.100710551-015-2630-4

Calle, J. (2000). *Ethics In Business.* Accounting Smart Pros. http://Accounting.Smartpros.Com/X12209.Xml

Camenisch, P. F. (1991). Marketing Ethics: Some Dimensions Of The Challenge. *Journal of Business Ethics, 10*(4), 245–248. doi:10.1007/BF00382961

Canikli, S., & Aren, S. (2019). *Effect Of Financial Literacy And Risk Perception On Individual Investors' Investment Choices.* EPSBS. doi:10.15405/epsbs.2019.01.02.68

Cao, W., & Cao, L. (2015). Financial crisis forecasting via coupled market state analysis. *IEEE Intelligent Systems, 30*(2), 18–25. doi:10.1109/MIS.2015.4

Cardoso, F., Stadler, G., & Mashayekh, M. (2021). *The impact of Ancillary Services in optimal DER investment decisions.* Lawrence Berkeley National Laboratory Recent Work Title. https://escholarship.org/uc/item/112337hb

Cavanagh, G. F., Dennis, J. M., & Manuel, V. (1981). The Ethics Of Organizational Politics. *Academy of Management Review, 6*(3), 363–374.

Certo, S., & Certo, S. T. (2006). *Modern Management.* Prentice Hall.

Ceylan, R., Ivrendi, M., Shahbaz, M., & Omay, T. (2020). Oil and stock prices: New evidence from a time varying homogenous panel smooth transition VECM for seven developing countries. *International Journal of Finance and Economics, September 2018*, 1–16. doi:10.1002/ijfe.2202

Chadha, S. (2022). Why cash circulation in economy hit all-time high in March 2022 despite surge in digital payments, *The Times of India*. https://timesofindia.indiatimes.com/business/india-business/why-cash-circulation-in-economy-hit-all-time-high-in-march-2022-despite-surge-in-digital-payments/articleshow/90562209.cms

Chakraborty, P., Mittal, P., Gupta, M. S., Yadav, S., & Arora, A. (2021). Opinion of students on online education during the COVID-19 pandemic. *Human Behavior and Emerging Technologies*, *3*(3), 357–365. doi:10.1002/hbe2.240

Chand, K., Tiwari, R., & Sapna. (2022). Effect of Perception and Satisfaction on Preference for Mobile Wallet. *FIIB Business Review*. https://doi.org/ doi:10.1177/23197145221077365

Chandrasekhar, C. P., & Ghosh, J. (2018). The financialization of finance? Demonetization and the dubious push to cashlessness in India. *Development and Change*, *49*(2), 420–436. doi:10.1111/dech.12369

Chandy, R., Hassan, M., & Mukherji, P. (2017). Big Data for Good: Insights from Emerging Markets. *Journal of Product Innovation Management, 34*(5), 703-713.

Changchit, C. (2014). Students' Perceptions Of Cloud Computing. *Issues in Information Systems*, *15*, 312–322. doi:10.48009/1_iis_2014_312-322

Charalambous, A., Hadjidemetriou, L., Zacharia, L., Bintoudi, A. D., Tsolakis, A. C., Tzovaras, D., & Kyriakides, E. (2019). Phase balancing and reactive power support services for microgrids. *Applied Sciences (Basel, Switzerland)*, *9*(23), 5067. Advance online publication. doi:10.3390/app9235067

Chatterjee, S., & Barcun, S. (1970). A nonparametric approach to credit screening. *Journal of the American Statistical Association*, *65*(329), 150–154. doi:10.1080/01621459.1970.10481068

Chatterjee, S., Chaudhuri, R., Shah, M., & Maheshwari, P. (2022). Big Data Driven Innovation for Sustaining Sme Supply Chain Operation in Post Covid-19 Scenario: Moderating Role of Sme Technology Leadership. *Computers & Industrial Engineering*, *168*, 168. doi:10.1016/j.cie.2022.108058 PMID:36569991

Chatterjee, S., Chaudhuri, R., & Vrontis, D. (2021). Does Data-Driven Culture Impact Innovation and Performance of a Firm? An Empirical Examination. *Annals of Operations Research*, 1–26. doi:10.100710479-020-03887-z

Chaturvedi, C., & Mishra, D. (2022). Competitive Edge Building in Business: An Approach Through Ethical Marketing Practices. In S. Bansal, V. Ahuja, V. Chaturvedi, & V. Jain (Eds.), *Multidisciplinary Perspectives Towards Building a Digitally Competent Society* (pp. 248–261). IGI Global., doi:10.4018/978-1-6684-5274-5.ch014

Chaudhuri, K., & Daniel, B. C. (1998). Long-run equilibrium real exchange rates and oil prices. In Economics Letters (Vol. 58). doi:10.1016/S0165-1765(97)00282-6

Chaudhuri, R., Chatterjee, S., Vrontis, D., & Thrassou, A. (2021). Adoption of Robust Business Analytics for Product Innovation and Organizational Performance: The Mediating Role of Organizational Data-Driven Culture. *Annals of Operations Research*, 1–35. doi:10.100710479-021-04407-3

Chawla, D., & Joshi, H. (2021). *Degree of awareness and the antecedents of the digital media platform: The case of mobile wallets*. FIIB Business Review., doi:10.1177/23197145211023413

Chen, J., Dougherty, E., Demir, S. S., Friedman, C., Li, C. S., & Wong, S. (2005). Grand challenges for multimodal bio-medical systems. *IEEE Circuits and Systems Magazine*, *5*(2), 46–52. doi:10.1109/MCAS.2005.1438739

Chen, M., Hao, Y., Hwang, K., Wang, L., & Wang, L. (2017). Disease prediction by machine learning over big data from healthcare communities. *IEEE Access : Practical Innovations, Open Solutions*, *5*, 8869–8879. doi:10.1109/ACCESS.2017.2694446

Chin, W. W. (1998). The partial least squares approach to structural equation modeling. *Modern methods for business research, 295*(2), 295-336.

Chiu, R. K. (2003). Ethical Judgment And Whistleblowing Intention: Examining The Moderating Role Of Locus Of Control. *Journal of Business Ethics*, *43*(1-2), 65–74. doi:10.1023/A:1022911215204

Choi, J. C., Kim, S. W., & Kim, J. B. (2010). Globalizing Business Ethics Research And The Ethical Need To Include The Bottom Of The Pyramid Countries: Redefining The Global Triad As Business Systems And Institutions. *Journal of Business Ethics*, *94*(2), 299–306. doi:10.100710551-009-0258-y

Chonko, L. B. (1995). Ethical Decision Making. In *Marketing*. Sage Publications.

Chonko, L. B., & Hunt, S. D. (1985). Ethics And Marketing Management: An Empirical Examination. *Journal of Business Research*, *13*(4), 339–359. doi:10.1016/0148-2963(85)90006-2

Choudhry, T., & Wu, H. (2009). Forecasting the weekly time-varying beta of UK firms: Garch models vs. kalman filter method. *European Journal of Finance*, *15*(4), 437–444. doi:10.1080/13518470802604499

Choudhury, K. (2018). Fearing worst, mobile wallets plan to diversify; loses 45% of user base. *Business Standard*. https://www.business-standard.com/article/companies/fearing-worst-mobile-wallets-plan-to-diversify-loses-45-of-user-base-118033100711_1.html

Churchill, G. A. Jr. (1979). A Paradigm for Developing Better Measures of Marketing Constructs. *JMR, Journal of Marketing Research*, *16*(1), 64–73. doi:10.1177/002224377901600110

Churchill, G. A. Jr, & Surprenant, C. (1982). An investigation into the determinants of customer satisfaction. *JMR, Journal of Marketing Research, 19*(4), 491–504. doi:10.1177/002224378201900410

Clark, L. (2005). Shopping without cash: The emergence of the e-purse. *Economic Perspectives, 29*(4), 34–51.

Coakley, J. R., & Brown, C. E. (2000). Artificial neural networks in accounting and finance: Modelling issues. *Intelligent Systems in Accounting, Finance & Management, 9*(2), 119–144. doi:10.1002/1099-1174(200006)9:2<119::AID-ISAF182>3.0.CO;2-Y

Cohen, J. (1992). A new criterion for assessing discriminant validity in variance-based structural equation modeling. *Current Directions in Psychological Science.* doi:10.1111/1467-8721.ep10768783

Cohen, W. W., Schapire, R. E., & Singer, Y. (1999). Learning to order things. *Journal of Artificial Intelligence Research, 10*, 243–270. doi:10.1613/jair.587

Collins, J., Hammond, M., & Wellington, J. (2002). *Teaching and Learning with Multimedia.* Teaching and Learning with Multimedia. doi:10.4324/9780203441305

Cong, R. G., Wei, Y. M., Jiao, J. L., & Fan, Y. (2008). Relationships between oil price shocks and stock market: An empirical analysis from China. *Energy Policy, 36*(9), 3544–3553. doi:10.1016/j.enpol.2008.06.006

Consoli, J. (1976). *Comparative Print Ads More Credible.* Kershaw.

Cooper, J. M. (1999). Reason And Emotion: Essays On Ancient Moral Psychology And Ethical Theory. Princeton University Press.

Copeland, W. E., McGinnis, E., Bai, Y., Adams, Z., Nardone, H., Devadanam, V., Rettew, J., & Hudziak, J. J. (2021). Impact of COVID-19 Pandemic on College Student Mental Health and Wellness. *Journal of the American Academy of Child and Adolescent Psychiatry, 60*(1), 134–141.e2. doi:10.1016/j.jaac.2020.08.466 PMID:33091568

Coussement, K., & Van den Poel, D. (2009). Improving customer attrition prediction by integrating emotions from client/company interaction emails and evaluating multiple classifiers. *Expert Systems with Applications, 36*(3), 6127–6134. doi:10.1016/j.eswa.2008.07.021

Crane, A. (1999). Are You Ethical? Please Tick Yes Or No: On Researching Ethics In Business Organizations. *Journal of Business Ethics, 20*(3), 237–248. doi:10.1023/A:1005817414241

Crane, A. (2000). Marketing And The Natural Environment: What Role For Morality. *Journal of Macromarketing, 20*(2), 144–154. doi:10.1177/0276146700202004

Crane, A., & Desmond, J. (2002). Societal Marketing And Morality. *European Journal of Marketing, 36*(5/6), 548–569. doi:10.1108/03090560210423014

Cristofaro, M., Giardino, P. L., Misra, S., Pham, Q. T., & Hiep Phan, H. (2022). Behavior or culture? Investigating the use of cryptocurrencies for electronic commerce across the USA and China. *Management Research Review*. doi:10.1108/MRR-06-2021-0493

Cronholm, S., Göbel, H., & Rittgen, P. (2017). Challenges Concerning Data-Driven Innovation. *The 28th Australasian Conference on Information Systems*, (pp. 1-11). Hobart Australia: Australasian Conference on Information Systems

Da Chen, C., Cheng, C. M., & Demirer, R. (2017). Oil and stock market momentum. *Energy Economics*, *68*, 151–159. doi:10.1016/j.eneco.2017.09.025

Dahlberg, T., Mallat, N., Ondrus, J., & Zmijewska, A. (2008). Past, present and future of mobile payments research: A literature review. *Electronic Commerce Research and Applications*, *7*(2), 165–181. doi:10.1016/j.elerap.2007.02.001

Daruwalla, B. (2020). Data Democratization: Balancing Risk Vs Reward through Data Governance. *Data Protection*. Security Intelligence. https://securityintelligence.com/posts/data-democratization-governance/

Das, S.R. (2014). Text and context: language analytics in finance. Found Trends® Finance. 2014;8:145–261.

Das, P. (2011, May). Productivity and Efficiency in the Jute Industry. *Economic and Political Weekly*, *46*(19), 74–76.

Das, P. K. (2016). Environmental Accounting: A Conceptual Study of Indian Context. *International Journal of Social, Behavioral, Educational, Economic, Business and Industrial Engineering*, *10*(8), 2914–2920.

Das, S., Dey, A., Pal, A., & Roy, N. (2015). Applications of artificial intelligence in machine learning: Review and prospect. *International Journal of Computer Applications*, *115*(9), 31–41. doi:10.5120/20182-2402

Dataquest. (2020). *Oxigen launches India's first mobile wallet*. DQ India. https://www.dqindia.com/oxigen-launches-india-s-mobile-wallet/#:~:text=Oxigen%20 Wallet%2C%20launch%20ed%20India's%20the,Transfers%20anytime%2C%20anywhere%20using%20IMPS

Davis, F. D. (1987). *User acceptance of information systems : the technology acceptance model (TAM)*. Deep Blue. https://deepblue.lib.umich.edu/handle/2027.42/35547

Davis, F. D. (1989). Perceived usefulness, perceived ease of use, and user acceptance of information technology. *Management Information Systems Quarterly*, *13*(3), 319–339. doi:10.2307/249008

Davis, F. D. (1993). User acceptance of information technology system characteristics, user perceptions and behavioral impacts. *International Journal of Man-Machine Studies*, *38*(3), 475–487. doi:10.1006/imms.1993.1022

Davis, F. D., Bagozzi, R. P., & Warshaw, P. R. (1992). Extrinsic and intrinsic motivation to use computers in the workplace. *Journal of Applied Social Psychology*, *22*(14), 1111–1132. doi:10.1111/j.1559-1816.1992.tb00945.x

De Gooijer, J. G., & Hyndman, R. J. (2006). 25 years of time series forecasting. *International Journal of Forecasting*, *22*(3), 443–473. doi:10.1016/j.ijforecast.2006.01.001

de Prado, M. M. L. (2020). *Machine Learning for Asset Managers*. Cambridge University Press. doi:10.1017/9781108883658

Deegan, C. (2002). The legitimizing effect of social and environmental disclosures – a theoretical foundation. *Accounting, Auditing & Accountability Journal*, *15*(3), 282–311. doi:10.1108/09513570210435852

Degiannakis, S., Filis, G., & Arora, V. (2018). Oil prices and stock markets: A review of the theory and empirical evidence. *The Energy Journal (Cambridge, Mass.)*, *39*(5), 85–130. doi:10.5547/01956574.39.5.sdeg

Degutis, A., & Novickytė, L. (2014). The efficient market hypothesis: A critical review of literature and methodology. *Ekonom.*, *93*(2), 7–23. doi:10.15388/Ekon.2014.2.3549

Dewan, S., Low, G., & Land, L. (2009). Consumer choice model of mobile banking. *Proceedings of the 20th Australasian Conference on Information Systems*. Monash University, Melbourne. 2-4.

Dhar, V., & Chou, D. (2001). A comparison of nonlinear methods for predicting earnings surprises and returns. *IEEE Transactions on Neural Networks*, *12*(4), 907–921. doi:10.1109/72.935099 PMID:18249921

Dignum, V. (2018). Ethics in artificial intelligence: Introduction to the special issue. *Ethics and Information Technology*, *20*(1), 1–3. doi:10.100710676-018-9450-z

Dixon, M. F., Halperin, I., & Bilokon, P. (2020). *Machine Learning in Finance*. Springer. doi:10.1007/978-3-030-41068-1

Doctor, G., & Joshi, P. (2021). Empowering Cities through Open Data-Open Government Data Initiatives in India. *14th International Conference on Theory and Practice of Electronic Governance*, India. 10.1145/3494193.3494241

Doig, A., & Wilson, J. (1998). The Effectiveness Of Codes Of Conduct. *Business Ethics (Oxford, England)*, *7*(3), 140–149. doi:10.1111/1467-8608.00100

Doko Tchatoka, F., Masson, V., & Parry, S. (2019). Linkages between oil price shocks and stock returns revisited. *Energy Economics*, *82*, 42–61. doi:10.1016/j.eneco.2018.02.016

Donahoe, E., & Metzger, M. M. (2019). Artificial intelligence and human rights. *Journal of Democracy*, *30*(2), 115–126. doi:10.1353/jod.2019.0029

Donaldson, T., & Werhane, P. H. (1983). Cording, M. Ethical Issues In Business. Pearson Prentice Hall.

Drumwright, M. E., & Murphy, P. E. (2009). The Current State Of Advertising Ethics: Industry And Academic Perspectives. *Journal of Advertising, 38*(1), 83–108. doi:10.2753/JOA0091-3367380106

Dudiak, J. (2001). The Intrigue Of Ethics: A Reading Of The Idea Of Discourse In The Thought Of Emmanuel Levinas; Fordham University Press: New York, Ny, USA. *Ethics, 90*(4), 607–622.

Dwivedi, Y.K., Janssen, M., Slade, E.L., Rana, N.P., Weerakkody, V., Millard, J., Hidders, J., & Snijders, D. (2017). Driving Innovation through Big Open Linked Data (Bold): Exploring Antecedents Using Interpretive Structural Modelling. *Information systems frontiers, 19*(2), 197-212.

Eagle, L. (2009). *Social marketing ethics: report prepared for the National Social Marketing Centre*. Then SMC. https://www.thensmc.com/sites/default/files/public-files/NSMC_social_marketing_ethics.pdf on 22/2/2023.

Egodawele, M., Sedera, D., Grover, V., Seneviratne, D., & Sooriyapperuma, B. (2023). "Shooting 'Yohani'to Global Stardom: A Teaching Case of Social Media Strategy of a Top-10 Youtuber," *Communications of the Association for Information Systems, 52*(1), p 21.

Ehtesham, M., & Junaid, M. (2022). Reactive power control strategy for integrated photovoltaic inverter. *International Journal of Power Electronics and Drive Systems, 13*(3), 1713–1720. doi:10.11591/ijpeds.v13.i3.pp1713-1720

Eichler, R., Gröger, C., Hoos, E., Schwarz, H., & Mitschang, B. (2022). Data Shopping—How an Enterprise Data Marketplace Supports Data Democratization in Companies. *International Conference on Advanced Information Systems Engineering*, (pp. 19-26). Springer. 10.1007/978-3-031-07481-3_3

Elliott, R. K. (1992). The third wave breaks on the shores of accounting. *Accounting Horizons, 6*, 61.

Elmer, T., Mepham, K., & Stadtfeld, C. (2020). Students under lockdown: Comparisons of students' social networks and mental health before and during the COVID-19 crisis in Switzerland. *PLoS One, 15*(7), e0236337. doi:10.1371/journal.pone.0236337 PMID:32702065

Engle, R. (2002). Dynamic conditional correlation: A simple class of multivariate generalized autoregressive conditional heteroskedasticity models. *Journal of Business & Economic Statistics, 20*(3), 339–350. doi:10.1198/073500102288618487

Engle, R., & Kelly, B. (2012). Dynamic equicorrelation. *Journal of Business & Economic Statistics, 30*(2), 212–228. doi:10.1080/07350015.2011.652048

Enyi, P. E. (2012). Environmental and Social Accounting as an Alternative Approach to Conflict Resolutions In A Volatile and E-Business Environment. *Journal of Sustainable Development and Environmental Protection, 4*(2), 1–7.

Ericsson. (2022). *Mobile Data Traffic Outlook*. Eric's Son. https://www.ericsson.com/en/reports-and-papers/mobility-report/dataforecasts/mobile-traffic-forecast#:~:text=The%20global%20monthly%20average%20usage,to%20grow%20to%2069%20percent

Etzioni, A., & Etzioni, O. (2017). Incorporating ethics into artificial intelligence. *The Journal of Ethics*, *21*(4), 403–418. doi:10.100710892-017-9252-2

EuropeanCommission. (2020). *The Benefits and Value of Open Data*. EC. https://data.europa.eu/en/publications/datastories/benefits-and-value-open-data

Evans, D. S., Schmalensee, R., Noel, M. D., Chang, H. H., & Garcia-Swartz, D. D. (2011). *Platform Economics: Essays on Multi-Sided Businesses*. SSRN. https://papers.ssrn.com/abstract=1974020

Evans, D. S. (2009). The online advertising industry: Economics, evolution, and privacy. *The Journal of Economic Perspectives*, *23*(3), 37–60. doi:10.1257/jep.23.3.37

F'eraud, R., & Cl'erot, F. (2002). A methodology to explain neural network classification. *Neural Networks*, *15*(2), 237–246. doi:10.1016/S0893-6080(01)00127-7 PMID:12022511

Fabozzi, F., Focardi, S. M., & Jonas, C. (2011). High-frequency trading: Methodologies and market impact. *Review of Futures Markets.*, *9*, 7–38.

Fachkha, C., Bou-Harb, E., & Debbabi, M. (2013). Towards a forecasting model for distributed denial of service activities. In *2013 IEEE 12th Inter- national Symposium on Network Computing and Applications*. IEEE. 10.1109/NCA.2013.13

Fadler, M., & Legner, C. (2022). Data Ownership Revisited: Clarifying Data Accountabilities in Times of Big Data and Analytics. *Journal of Business Analytics, 5*(1), 123-139.

Falabretti, D., Gulotta, F., & Spinelli, L. (2022). Participation of Aggregated DERs to the Ancillary Services Market: A Monte Carlo Simulation-Based Heuristic Greedy-Indexing Model. *Energies*, *15*(3), 1037. Advance online publication. doi:10.3390/en15031037

Fama, E. F., & Blume, M. E. (1966). Filter rules and stock market trading. *The Journal of Business*, *39*(S1), 226–241. doi:10.1086/294849

Fama, E. F., & French, K. R. (1988). Permanent and temporary components of stock prices. *Journal of Political Economy*, *96*(2), 246–273. doi:10.1086/261535

Fama, E. F., & French, K. R. (2004). The capital asset pricing model: Theory and evidence. *The Journal of Economic Perspectives*, *18*(3), 25–46. doi:10.1257/0895330042162430

Fang, C. R., & You, S. Y. (2014). The impact of oil price shocks on the large emerging countries' stock prices: Evidence from China, India and Russia. *International Review of Economics & Finance*, *29*, 330–338. doi:10.1016/j.iref.2013.06.005

Farooq, F., Rathore, F. A., & Mansoor, S. N. (2020). Challenges of online medical education in Pakistan during COVID-19 pandemic. *Journal of the College of Physicians and Surgeons—Pakistan*, *30*(1), S67–S69. doi:10.29271/jcpsp.2020.Supp1.S67 PMID:32723456

Faulkner, X. (2000). *Usability Engineering*. Palgrave.

Fawaz, M., Al Nakhal, M., & Itani, M. (2021). COVID-19 quarantine stressors and management among Lebanese students: a qualitative study. *Current Psychology, 41*(11), 7628–7635. doi:10.1007/s12144-020-01307-w

Fayyad, U., Piatetsky-Shapiro, G., & Smyth, P. (1996). The kdd process for extracting useful knowledge from volumes of data. *Communications of the ACM, 39*(11), 27–34. doi:10.1145/240455.240464

Fernandez-Aller, C., de Velasco, A. F., Manjarres, A., Pastor-Escuredo, D., Pickin, S., Criado, J. S., & Ausin, T. (2021). An inclusive and sustainable artificial intelligence strategy for europe based on human rights. *IEEE Technology and Society Magazine, 40*(1), 46–54. doi:10.1109/MTS.2021.3056283

Ferrell, O. C., Harrison, D. E., Ferrell, L., & Hair, J. F. (2019). Business Ethics, Corporate Social Responsibility, And Brand Attitudes: An Exploratory Study. *Journal of Business Research, 95*, 491–501. doi:10.1016/j.jbusres.2018.07.039

Fischer, J. A., Pohl, P., & Ratz, D. (2020). A machine learning approach to univariate time series forecasting of quarterly earnings. *Review of Quantitative Finance and Accounting, 55*(4), 1163–1179. doi:10.100711156-020-00871-3

Flavian, C., Guinaliu, M., & Lu, Y. (2020). Mobile payments adoption: Introducing mindfulness to better understand consumer behavior. *International Journal of Bank Marketing, 38*(7), 1575–1599. doi:10.1108/IJBM-01-2020-0039

Forbes. (2022). Why Data-Driven Insights Are Critical to Digital Transformation. *Forbes.* https://www.forbes.com/sites/forbesbusinessdevelopmentcouncil/2022/05/10/why-data-driven-insights-are-critical-to-digital-transformation/?sh=67b34fad78c2

Ford, R. C., & Richardson, W. D. (1994). Ethical Decision Making: A Review Of The Empirical Literature. *Journal of Business Ethics, 13*(3), 205–221. doi:10.1007/BF02074820

Franses, P. H., & Van Dijk, D. (2000). *Non-linear Time Series Models in Empirical Finance.* Cambridge University Press. doi:10.1017/CBO9780511754067

Franzoni, A. L., & Assar, S. (2009). *Student Learning Styles Adaptation Method Based on Teaching Strategies and Electronic Media.* JStor. https://www.jstor.org/stable/jeductechsoci.12.4.15

Frecka, T. J., & Hopwood, W. S. (1983). The effects of outliers on the cross-sectional distributional properties of financial ratios. *The Accounting Review*, 115–128.

Fry, K. (2001). Online Learning markets and providers: Some issues and prospects. *Education + Training, 43*(4/5), 233–239. doi:10.1108/EUM0000000005484

Gable, G.G., Sedera, D., & Chan, T. (2008). Re-Conceptualizing Information System Success: The Is-Impact Measurement Model. *Journal of the Association for Information Systems 9*(7), 377-408.

Ganai, A., Naveed Hamid, I., Sudhakar Dwivedi, I., Jyoti Kachroo, I., Manhas, I. J., Hamid, N., Dwivedi, S., Kachroo, J., & Manhas, J. (2019). Influence of packaging elements of ready to eat food products on buying behaviour. ~ *189* ~. *Journal of Pharmacognosy and Phytochemistry*, *8*(2), 189–194.

Gandotra, E., Bansal, D., & Sofat, S. (2015). Computational techniques for predicting cyber threats. *Intelligent Computing, Communication and Devices*, 247–253.

Ganjian-Aboukheili, M., Shahabi, M., Shafiee, Q., & Guerrero, J. M. (2020). Seamless Transition of Microgrids Operation from Grid-Connected to Islanded Mode. *IEEE Transactions on Smart Grid*, *11*(3), 2106–2114. doi:10.1109/TSG.2019.2947651

Gao, Z., Alshehri, K., & Birge, J. R. (2021). On Efficient Aggregation of Distributed Energy Resources. *2021 60th IEEE Conference on Decision and Control (CDC)*, 7064-7069. 10.1109/CDC45484.2021.9683117

Gartner. (2022). *Gartner Identifies Three Imperatives Driving the Top Trends in Data and Analytics for 2022*. Gartner. https://www.gartner.com/en/newsroom/press-releases/2022-03-29-gartner-identifies-three-imperatives-driving-the-top-trends-in-data-and-analytics-for-2022

Gaski, J. F. (1999). Does Marketing Ethics Really Have Anything To Say? A Critical Inventory Of The Literature. *Journal of Business Ethics*, *18*(3), 315–334. doi:10.1023/A:1017190829683

Gastalver-Rubio, A., Romero-Ramos, E., & Maza-Ortega, J. M. (2019). Improving the Performance of Low Voltage Networks by an Optimized Unbalance Operation of Three-Phase Distributed Generators. *IEEE Access : Practical Innovations, Open Solutions*, *7*(7), 177504–177516. Advance online publication. doi:10.1109/ACCESS.2019.2958206

Gay, R. D. Jr. (2008). Effect Of Macroeconomic Variables On Stock Market Returns For Four Emerging Economies: Brazil, Russia, India, And China. *Applied Economics*, *40*(11), 1363–1372. doi:10.1080/00036840600820663

Gefen, D., Karahanna, E., & Straub, D. W. (2003). Trust and tam in online shopping: AN integrated model. *Management Information Systems Quarterly*, *27*(1), 51–90. doi:10.2307/30036519

Geis, J. R., Brady, A. P., Wu, C. C., Spencer, J., Ranschaert, E., Jaremko, J. L., Langer, S. G., Borondy Kitts, A., Birch, J., Shields, W. F., van den Hoven van Genderen, R., Kotter, E., Wawira Gichoya, J., Cook, T. S., Morgan, M. B., Tang, A., Safdar, N. M., & Kohli, M. (2019). Ethics of artificial intelligence in radiology: Summary of the joint European and North American multisociety statement. *Radiology*, *293*(2), 436–440. doi:10.1148/radiol.2019191586 PMID:31573399

Georgios, C. (2022). Distributed methodology for reactive power support of transmission system, Sustainable Energy. *Grids and Networks*, *31*, 100753. Advance online publication. doi:10.1016/j.segan.2022.100753

Ghasemaghaei, M., & Calic, G. (2019). Does Big Data Enhance Firm Innovation Competency? The Mediating Role of Data-Driven Insights. *Journal of Business Research*, *104*, 69–84. doi:10.1016/j.jbusres.2019.07.006

Ghoul, S. E., Guedhami, O. C. Y., Kwok, C., & Mishara, D. R. (2011). Does corporate social responsibility affect the cost of capital? *Journal of Banking & Finance*, *35*(9), 2388–2406. doi:10.1016/j.jbankfin.2011.02.007

Godos-Diez, J.-L., Fernandez-Gago, R., & Martinez-Campillo, A. (2011). How Important Are Ceos To Csr Practices? An Analysis Of The Mediating Effect Of The Perceived Role Of Ethics In Social Responsibility. *Journal of Business Ethics*, *98*(4), 531–548. doi:10.100710551-010-0609-8

Goolsby, J. R., & Hunt, S. D. (1982). Cognitive Moral Development And Marketing. *Journal of Marketing*, *56*(1), 55–68. doi:10.1177/002224299205600106

Goswami, M. (2014). Corporate Environmental Accounting: the issue, its practices and challenges: A study on Indian corporate accounting practices. *IOSR Journal of Business and Management*, *16*(5), 36–42. doi:10.9790/487X-16533642

Granell, C., Mooney, P., Jirka, S., Rieke, M., Ostermann, F., Van Den Broecke, J., Sarretta, A., Verhulst, S., Dencik, L., & Oost, H. (2022). *Emerging Approaches for Data-Driven Innovation in Europe: Sandbox Experiments on the Governance of Data and Technology*, 93-97.

Grover, P., & Kar, A. (2020). User engagement for mobile payment service providers introducing-the social media engagement model. *Journal of Retailing and Consumer Services*, *53*, 101718. doi:10.1016/j.jretconser.2018.12.002

Gujarati, D. (2011). [). Palgrave macmillan.]. *Econometrics By Example*, *I*, 101–102.

Hair, F., Jr., Black, W., Babin, B., & Anderson, R. (2006). 2010 Hair et al.pdf. In Clemson International Institute for Tourism.

Hair, J. F. Black, W. C., & Babin, B. J. (2010). *Multivariate Data Analysis: A Global Perspective*. Google Books. https://books.google.co.in/books/about/Multivariate_Data_Analysis.html?id=SLRPLgAACAAJ

Hair, J. F., Anderson, R. E., Tatham, R. L., & Black, W. C. (1998). *Multivariate Data Analysis*. Prentice Hall International.

Hair, Joe F., & Sarstedt, Hopkins, M., Kuppelwieser, L., & G., V. (. (2014). Partial least squares structural equation modeling (PLS-SEM): An emerging tool in business research. *European Business Review*, *26*(2), 106–121. doi:10.1108/EBR-10-2013-0128

Hallock, K. F., Madalozzo, R., & Reck, C. G. (2010). Ceo pay-for-performance heterogeneity using quantile regression. *Financial Review*, *45*(1), 1–19. doi:10.1111/j.1540-6288.2009.00235.x

Hansen, P. R., Lunde, A., & Nason, J. M. (2011). The model confidence set. *Econometrica*, *79*(2), 453–497. doi:10.3982/ECTA5771

Harland, T., Hocken, C., Schröer, T., & Stich, V. (2022). Towards a Democratization of Data in the Context of Industry 4.0. *Sci 4*(3), 29.

Harris, S. L., May, J. H., & Vargas, L. G. (2016). Predictive analytics model for healthcare planning and scheduling. *European Journal of Operational Research, 253*(1), 121–131. doi:10.1016/j.ejor.2016.02.017

Hartshorne, R., & Ajjan, H. (2009). Examining student decisions to adopt Web 2.0 technologies: Theory and empirical tests. *Journal of Computing in Higher Education, 21*(3), 183–198. doi:10.100712528-009-9023-6

Harvey, C. R., & Liu, Y. (2021). Lucky factors. *Journal of Financial Economics, 141*(2), 413–435. doi:10.1016/j.jfineco.2021.04.014

Hashimzade, N., Myles, G. D., & Rablen, M. D. (2016). Predictive analytics and the targeting of audits. *Journal of Economic Behavior & Organization, 124*, 130–145. doi:10.1016/j.jebo.2015.11.009

Haslem, J. A. (2014). Selected topics in financial literacy. *The Journal of Wealth Management, 17*(3), 47–57. doi:10.3905/jwm.2014.17.3.047

Hastings, G., Stead, M., McDermott, L., Forsyth, A., MacKintosh, A. M., Rayner, M., Godfrey, C., Caraher, M., & Angus, K. (2003). *Review of research on the effects of food promotion to children*. Food Standards Agency.

Hauwanga, A. S., & Musti, K. S. S. (2022). Evaluation of Energy Losses and Costs Based on the Location of PCC in Smart Grids. *IEEE 11th Int. Conference on Communication Systems and Network Technologies (CSNT)*, 76-82. 10.1109/CSNT54456.2022.9787642

Hayashi, F. (2012). Mobile payments: What's in it for consumers? *Economic Review-Federal Reserve Bank of Kansas City, 35*.

He, X., Gokmenoglu, K. K., Kirikkaleli, D., & Rizvi, S. K. A. (2021). Co-movement of foreign exchange rate returns and stock market returns in an emerging market: Evidence from the wavelet coherence approach. *International Journal of Finance & Economics, August 2020*, ijfe.2522. doi:10.1002/ijfe.2522

Helin, S., & Sandström, J. (2008). Codes, Ethics And Cross-Cultural Differences: Stories From The Implementation Of A Corporate Code Of Ethics In A Mnc Subsidiary. *Journal of Business Ethics, 82*(2), 281–291. doi:10.100710551-008-9887-9

Henion, K. E., & Kinnear, T. C. (1976). *Ecological Marketing, Chicago, Il.* American Marketing Association. https://Www.Tandfonline.Com/Doi/Full/10.1080/07393148.2017.1304737

Henrique, B. M., Sobreiro, V. A., & Kimura, H. (2019). Literature review: Machine learning techniques applied to financial market prediction. *Expert Systems with Applications, 124*, 226–251. doi:10.1016/j.eswa.2019.01.012

Henseler, J., Hubona, G., & Ray, P. A. (2016). *Using PLS path modeling in new technology research: updated guidelines*. doi:10.1108/IMDS-09-2015-0382

Henseler, J., Ringle, C. M., & Sarstedt, M. (2015). A new criterion for assessing discriminant validity in variance-based structural equation modeling. *Journal of the Academy of Marketing Science*, *43*(1), 115–135. doi:10.100711747-014-0403-8

Henseler, J., Ringle, C. M., & Sinkovics, R. R. (2009). The use of partial least squares path modeling in international marketing. *Advances in International Marketing*, *20*, 277–319. doi:10.1108/S1474-7979(2009)0000020014

Hertzano, R., & Mahurkar, A. (2022). Advancing Discovery in Hearing Research Via Biologist-Friendly Access to Multi-Omic Data. *Human Genetics*, *141*(3-4), 1–4. doi:10.100700439-022-02445-w PMID:35235019

Herzig, J., Feigenblat, G., Shmueli-Scheuer, M., Konopnicki, D., & Rafaeli, A. (2016). Predicting customer satisfaction in customer support conversations in social media using effective features. *Proceedings of the 2016 Con- Ference on User Modeling Adaptation and Personalization*, 115–119.

Hinds, T.L., Floyd, N.D., & Ueland, J.S. (2021). Policy and Praxis in Data Democratization Efforts: A Case Study of Minnesota State's Equity 2030. *New Directions for Institutional Research 189*(192), 53-70.

Hoehle, H., Venkatesh, V., Brown, S. A., Tepper, B. J., & Kude, T. (2022). Impact of customer compensation strategies on outcomes and the mediating role of justice perceptions: A longitudinal study of target's data breach. *Management Information Systems Quarterly*, *46*(1), 299–340. doi:10.25300/MISQ/2022/14740

Hopf, K., Weigert, A., & Staake, T. (2022). Value Creation from Analytics with Limited Data: A Case Study on the Retailing of Durable Consumer Goods. *Journal of Decision Systems*, 1–37. doi:10.1080/12460125.2022.2059172

Ho, S. M., Hancock, J. T., Booth, C., & Liu, X. (2016). Computer-mediated deception: Strategies revealed by language-action cues in spontaneous com- munication. *Journal of Management Information Systems*, *33*(2), 393–420. doi:10.1080/07421222.2016.1205924

Hossain, M. A., Quaddus, M., Hossain, M. M., & Gopakumar, G. (2022). Data-Driven Innovation Development: An Empirical Analysis of the Antecedents Using Pls-Sem and Fsqca. *Annals of Operations Research*, 1–43. doi:10.100710479-022-04873-3 PMID:36570556

Huang, W., Lai, K. K., Nakamori, Y., Wang, S., & Yu, L. (2007). Neural networks in finance and economics forecasting. *International Journal of Information Technology & Decision Making*, *6*(01), 113–140. doi:10.1142/S021962200700237X

Huang, W., Nakamori, Y., & Wang, S. Y. (2005). Forecasting stock market movement direction with support vector machine. *Computers & Operations Research*, *32*(10), 2513–2522. doi:10.1016/j.cor.2004.03.016

Hu, L., & Bentler, P. M. (1998). Fit indices in covariance structure modeling: Sensitivity to underparameterized model misspecification. *Psychological Methods*, *3*(4), 424–453. doi:10.1037/1082-989X.3.4.424

Hung, A., Parker, A. M., & Yoong, J. (2011). Defining and Measuring Financial Literacy. SSRN *Electronic Journal*. https://doi.org/ doi:10.2139/ssrn.1498674

Hur, W. M., Kim, H., & Woo, J. (2014). How Csr Leads To Corporate Brand Equity: Mediating Mechanisms Of Corporate Brand Credibility And Reputation. *Journal of Business Ethics*, *125*(1), 75–86. doi:10.100710551-013-1910-0

Hussein, E., Daoud, S., Alrabaiah, H., & Badawi, R. (2020). Exploring undergraduate students' attitudes towards emergency online learning during COVID-19: A case from the UAE. *Children and Youth Services Review*, *119*, 105699. doi:10.1016/j.childyouth.2020.105699

Hwang, H. G., Ku, C. Y., Yen, D. C., & Cheng, C. C. (2004). Critical factors infuencing the adoption of data warehouse technology: A study of the banking industry in taiwan. *Decision Support Systems*, *37*(1), 1–21. doi:10.1016/S0167-9236(02)00191-4

Hyun, Y., Hosoya, R., & Kamioka, T. (2019). The Moderating Role of Democratization Culture: Improving Agility through the Use of Big Data Analytics. In *Pacific Asia Conference on Information Systems*. Virtual: AIS Library.

Hyun, Y., Kamioka, T., & Hosoya, R. (2020). Improving Agility Using Big Data Analytics: The Role of Democratization Culture. *Pacific Asia Journal of the Association for Information Systems, 12*(2), 35-63.

Illia, A., Ngniatedema, T., & Huang, Z. (2015). A conceptual model for mobile banking adoption. *Journal of Management Information and Decision Sciences*, *18*(1), 111–122.

Income Tax India. (2022). *Why should I pay tax?* Income Tax India. https://incometaxindia.gov.in/Charts%20%20Tables/Why%20should%20I%20pay%20tax.htm#:~:text=a)%20It%20is%20an%20admitted,too%20small%20for%20our%20country.

International Energy Agency. (2021). *International Energy Agency*. IEA. https://www.iea.org/countries/china

Islam, J. U., Shahid, S., Rasool, A., Rahman, Z., Khan, I., & Rather, R. A. (2020). Impact Of Website Attributes On Customer Engagement In Banking: A Solicitation Of Stimulus-Organism-Response Theory. *International Journal of Bank Marketing*, *38*(6), 1279–1303. doi:10.1108/IJBM-12-2019-0460

Islam, P. T., Manivannan, D., & Zeadally, S. (2016). *A Classification and Characterization of Security Threats in Cloud Computing*. Undefined.

Iyamu, T., & Mgudlwa, S. (2018). Transformation of healthcare big data through the lens of actor network theory. *International Journal of Healthcare Management*, *11*(3), 182–192. doi:10.1080/20479700.2017.1397340

Jadey, S., Girish, S. C., Raghavendra, K., Srinidhi, H. R., & Anilkumar, K. M. (2022). Introduction to cyber security. In *Methods, Implementation, and Application of Cyber Security Intelligence and Analytics* (pp. 1–24). IGI Global. doi:10.4018/978-1-6684-3991-3.ch001

Jain, A., Bansal, S., & Bhardwaj, S. (2022). *COVID-19 Outbreak: A Paradigm Shift in Food and Beverage Industry with Context to Delhi-NCR*. 329–339. doi:10.1007/978-981-19-0357-1_28

Jalal, R., & Gopinathan, R. (2022). Time-Varying and Asymmetric Impact of Exchange Rate on Oil Prices in India: Evidence from a Multiple Threshold Nonlinear ARDL Model. *Finance Research Letters, 103297*, 103297. doi:10.1016/j.frl.2022.103297

Jamil, F., & G. E. K. (2016). The impact of crude oil prices on the economy of developing countries. *International Journal of Economics, Commerce, and Management*, *IV*(11), 11–20.

Janssen, M., Konopnicki, D., Snowdon, J.L., & Ojo, A. (2017). Driving Public Sector Innovation Using Big and Open Linked Data (Bold). *Information Systems Frontiers 1*(2), 189-195.

Jarrow, R. A., & Turnbull, S. M. (1995). Pricing derivatives on financial securities subject to credit risk. *The Journal of Finance*, *50*(1), 53–85. doi:10.1111/j.1540-6261.1995.tb05167.x

Jeble, S., Kumari, S., & Patil, Y. (2016). Role of big data and predictive analytics. *International Journal of Automation and Logistics.*, *2*(4), 307–331. doi:10.1504/IJAL.2016.080336

Jensen, M. C., & Benington, G. A. (1970). Random walks and technical theories: Some additional evidence. *The Journal of Finance*, *25*(2), 469–482. doi:10.1111/j.1540-6261.1970.tb00671.x

Jetzek, T., Avital, M., & Bjorn-Andersen, N. (2014). Data-Driven Innovation through Open Government Data. *Journal of theoretical and applied electronic commerce research, 9*(2), 100-120.

Jeurissen, R., & Van De Ven, B. (2020). (2996). Developments In Marketing Ethics. *Business Ethics Quarterly*, *16*, 427–439. doi:10.5840/beq200616335

Jha, A., & Cox, J. (2015). Corporate social responsibility and social capital. *Journal of Banking & Finance*, *60*(2), 252–270. doi:10.1016/j.jbankfin.2015.08.003

Jiang, Z., & Yoon, S. M. (2020). Dynamic co-movement between oil and stock markets in oil-importing and oil-exporting countries: Two types of wavelet analysis. *Energy Economics*, *90*, 104835. doi:10.1016/j.eneco.2020.104835

Ji, Q., Liu, B. Y., & Fan, Y. (2019). Risk dependence of CoVaR and structural change between oil prices and exchange rates: A time-varying copula model. *Energy Economics*, *77*, 80–92. doi:10.1016/j.eneco.2018.07.012

Johnson, E., & Festus, A. (2021). Environmental Accounting Practices and Environmental Capacity for Sustainable Economy. *International Journal of Business and Management*, *9*(4), 225–232.

Jones, S., Johnstone, D., & Wilson, R. (2015). An empirical evaluation of the performance of binary classifiers in the prediction of credit rating changes. *Journal of Banking & Finance*, *56*, 72–85. doi:10.1016/j.jbankfin.2015.02.006

Joseph, J., & Ramalingam, N. (2022). Digital Payments and GST Revenue. NIPFP. https://nipfp.org.in/media/medialibrary/2022/12/JJ.pdf.pdf

Kalinic, Z., Marinkovic, V., Molinillo, S., & Libanas, F. (2019). A multi-analytical approach to peer-to-peer mobile payment acceptance prediction. *Journal of Retailing and Consumer Services*, *49*, 143–153. doi:10.1016/j.jretconser.2019.03.016

Kanbara, S., & Shaw, R. (2021). Disaster Risk Reduction Regime in Japan: An Analysis in the Perspective of Open Data, Open Governance. *Sustainability, 14*(1), 19.

Kankanhalli, A., Hahn, J., Tan, S., & Gao, G. (2016). Big data and analytics in healthcare: Introduction to the special section. *Information Systems Frontiers*, *18*(2), 233–235. doi:10.100710796-016-9641-2

Karim, M. M., Kawsar, N. H., Ariff, M., & Masih, M. (2022). Does implied volatility (or fear index) affect Islamic stock returns and conventional stock returns differently? Wavelet-based Granger-causality, asymmetric quantile regression and NARDL approaches. *Journal of International Financial Markets, Institutions and Money*, *77*, 101532. doi:10.1016/j.intfin.2022.101532

Kaul, C., Kaul, A., & Verma, S. (2015). Comparative study on healthcare prediction systems using big data. *2015 International Conference on Innovations in Information, Embedded and Communication Systems (ICIIECS)*, 1-7.

Kaur, P., Dhir, A., Singh, N., Sahu, G., & Almotairi, M. (2020). An innovation resistance theory perspective on mobile payment solutions. *Journal of Retailing and Consumer Services*, *55*, 102059. doi:10.1016/j.jretconser.2020.102059

Keith, N., Petto, J. C., & Burnett, M. (2008). Ethics In Advertising: Differences In Industry Values And Student Perceptions. *Academy of Marketing Studies Journal*, *27*, 33–47.

Keller, S., Lancaster, V., & Shipp, S. (2017). Building Capacity for Data-Driven Governance: Creating a New Foundation for Democracy. *Statistics and Public Policy, 4*(1), 1-11.

Khandelwal, U., & Bajpai, N. (2012). Price Fairness And Its Linear Dependence On Consumer AttiTude: A Comparative Study In Metro And Non Metro City. *European Journal of Business and Management*, *4*(10), 94–10.

Khanzode, K. C. A., & Sarode, R. D. (2020). Advantages and Disadvantages of Artificial Intelligence and Machine Learning: A Literature Review. [IJLIS]. *International Journal of Library and Information Science*, *9*(1), 3.

Khayati, S., & Zouaoui, S. K. (2013). Perceived usefulness and use of information technology: The moderating influences of the dependence of a subcontractor towards his contractor. Journal of Knowledge Management. *Economics and Information Technology.*, *3*(6), 68–77.

Khraief, N., Shahbaz, M., Mahalik, M. K., & Bhattacharya, M. (2021). Movements of oil prices and exchange rates in China and India: New evidence from wavelet-based, non-linear, autoregressive distributed lag estimations. *Physica A*, *563*, 125423. doi:10.1016/j.physa.2020.125423

Kibria, M. G., & Tisdell, C. A. (1985, May- June). Operating capital and productivity patterns in jute weaving in Bangladesh. *Journal of Development Economics*, *18*(1), 133–152. doi:10.1016/0304-3878(85)90011-2

Kilbourne, W. E. (1998). Green Marketing: A Theoretical Perspective. *Journal of Marketing Management, 14*(6), 641–655. doi:10.1362/026725798784867743

Kim, C. N., & McLeod, R. Jr. (1999). Expert, linear models, and nonlinear models of expert decision making in bankruptcy prediction: A lens model analysis. *Journal of Management Information Systems, 16*(1), 189–206. doi:10.1080/07421222.1999.11518239

Kim, H., Lee, D.-S., & Ham, S. (2013). Impact of hotel information security on system reliability. *International Journal of Hospitality Management, 35*, 369–379. doi:10.1016/j.ijhm.2012.06.002

Kim, M. K., & Park, J. H. (2017). Identifying and prioritizing critical factors for promoting the implementation and usage of big data in healthcare. *Information Development, 33*(3), 257–269. doi:10.1177/0266666916652671

Kisswani, K. M., & Elian, M. I. (2021). Analyzing the (a)symmetric impacts of oil price, economic policy uncertainty, and global geopolitical risk on exchange rate. *Journal of Economic Asymmetries, 24*, e00204. doi:10.1016/j.jeca.2021.e00204

Kitchens, B., Dobolyi, D., Li, J., & Abbasi, A. (2018). Advanced customer analytics: Strategic value through the integration of relationship-oriented big data. *Journal of Management Information Systems, 35*(2), 540–574. doi:10.1080/07421222.2018.1451957

Klassner, F. (2002, February). A case study of LEGO Mindstorms'™ suitability for artificial intelligence and robotics courses at the college level. In *Proceedings of the 33rd SIGCSE technical symposium on Computer science education* (pp. 8-12). 10.1145/563340.563345

Klein, D., & Ware, M. (2003). Online Learning: New opportunities in continuing professional development. *Learned Publishing, 16*(1), 34–46. doi:10.1087/095315103320995078

Koenker, R., & Hallock, K. F. (2001). Quantile regression. *The Journal of Economic Perspectives, 15*(4), 143–156. doi:10.1257/jep.15.4.143

Koh, B. S. K., Mitchell, O. S., & Rohwedder, S. (2020). Financial knowledge and portfolio complexity in Singapore. *The Journal of the Economics of Ageing, 17*, 100179. doi:10.1016/j.jeoa.2018.11.004

Koivisto, M. (2008). Acceptance of mobile communication technologies in student communities, to appear in special issue on dynamic virtual communities in the information society: Technologies, methodologies, and tools. *International Journal of Web Based Communities, 4*(3), 21–32.

Kolekar, S. V., Pai, R. M., & Manohara Pai, M. M. (2017). Prediction of Learner's Profile based on Learning Styles in Adaptive Online Learning System. [IJET]. *International Journal of Emerging Technologies in Learning, 12*(06), 31–51. doi:10.3991/ijet.v12i06.6579

Konting, M., Kamaruddin, M., & Man, N. A. (2009). Quality Assurance in Higher Education Institutions: Exist Survey among Universiti Putra Malaysia Graduating Students. *International Education Studies, 2*(1). doi:10.5539/ies.v2n1p25

Kotler, P. (1972). A Generic Concept Of Marketing. *Journal of Marketing, 36*(April), 46–54. doi:10.1177/002224297203600209

Kozak, J., Kania, K., Juszczuk, P., & Mitręga, M. (2021). Swarm Intelligence Goal-Oriented Approach to Data-Driven Innovation in Customer Churn Management. *International Journal of Information Management, 60*, 1–16. doi:10.1016/j.ijinfomgt.2021.102357

Kriebitz, A., & Lütge, C. (2020). Artificial intelligence and human rights: A business ethical assessment. *Business and Human Rights Journal, 5*(1), 84–104. doi:10.1017/bhj.2019.28

Krishnan, S. M. (2016). Application of analytics to big data in healthcare. *2016 32nd Southern Biomedical Engineering Conference (SBEC)*, 156-157. 10.1109/SBEC.2016.88

Kuhn, M., & Johnson, K. (2013). *Applied Predictive Modelling Springer*. doi:10.1007/978-1-4614-6849-3

Kumar, A. S., & Chandrakala, D. (2017). An optimal churn prediction model using support vector machine with adaboost. Int J Scientific Res Computer Sci. *Eng and Information Technology.*, 2, 225–230.

Kumar, A., Adlakha, A., & Mukherjee, K. (2018). The effect of perceived security and grievance redressal on continuance intention to use M-wallets in a developing country. *International Journal of Bank Marketing, 36*(7), 1170–1189. doi:10.1108/IJBM-04-2017-0077

Kumar, A., & Seri, S. P. (2014). *Banking on mobile wallet-achieve significant benefits through proactive involvement in mobile wallet*. Infosys.

Kumar, S., Kumar, A., & Singh, G. (2022a). Gold, crude oil, bitcoin and Indian stock market: Recent confirmation from nonlinear ARDL analysis. *Journal of Economic Studies (Glasgow, Scotland)*. doi:10.1108/JES-01-2022-0007

Labadie, C., Legner, C., Eurich, M., & Fadler, M. (2020). Fair Enough? Enhancing the Usage of Enterprise Data with Data Catalogs. *2020 IEEE 22nd Conference on Business Informatics (CBI)*, (pp. 201-210). IEEE. 10.1109/CBI49978.2020.00029

Lakbala, P. (2016). Barriers in Implementing Online Learning in Hormozgan University of Medical Sciences. *Global Journal of Health Science, 8*(7), 83. doi:10.5539/gjhs.v8n7p83 PMID:26925885

Lamberton, H., & Minor, L. (1995). *Human Relations: Strategies For Success*. Irwin.

Lämsä, A. M., Vehkaperä, M., Puttonen, T., & Pesonen, H. L. (2008). Eff Ect Of Business Education On Women And Men Students' Attitudes On Corporate Responsibility In Society. *Journal of Business Ethics, 82*(1), 45–58. doi:10.100710551-007-9561-7

Lazarov, V., & Capota, M. (2007). Churn prediction. *Bus. Anal. Course. TUM Comput. Sci., 33*, 34.

Lee, J. Y., & Jin, C. H. (2019). The Role Of Ethical Marketing Issues In Consumer-Brand Relationship. *Sustainability (Basel), 11*(23), 6536. doi:10.3390u11236536

Lefebvre, H., & Legner, C. (2022). How Communities of Practice Enable Data Democratization inside the Enterprise. In *ECIS 2022 Proceedings*. AIS Virtual Library.

Lefebvre, H., Legner, C., & Fadler, M. (2021). Data Democratization: Toward a Deeper Understanding. *Forty-Second International Conference on Information Systems*, (pp. 1-17). AIS Library, .

Lekha, K. C., & Prakasam, S. (2017). *Data mining techniques in detecting and predicting cyber crimes in banking sector. In 2017 International Conference on Energy, Communication, Data Analytics and Soft Computing (ICECDS)*. IEEE. doi:10.1109/ICECDS.2017.8389725

Leonard, K. (2018). The Role of Data in Business. *Small Business*. https://smallbusiness.chron.com/role-data-business-20405.html

Levy, Y., & Ellis, T. J. (2006). A Systems Approach to Conduct an Effective Literature Review in Support of Information Systems Research. *Informing Science*, 9. doi:10.28945/479

Liang, X., Li, G., Zhang, H., Nolan, E., & Chen, F. (2022). Firm Performance and Marketing Analytics in the Chinese Context: A Contingency Model. *Journal of Business Research*, *141*, 589–599. doi:10.1016/j.jbusres.2021.11.061

Liao, P. H., Hsu, P. T., Chu, W., & Chu, W. C. (2015). Applying artificial intelligence technology to support decision-making in nursing: A case study in Taiwan. *Health Informatics Journal*, *21*(2), 137–148. doi:10.1177/1460458213509806 PMID:26021669

Liao, S., & Yang, L. (2020). Mobile payment and online to offline retail business models. *Journal of Retailing and Consumer Services*, *51*, 102230. doi:10.1016/j.jretconser.2020.102230

Li, L., Lin, Y. L., Zheng, N. N., Wang, F. Y., Liu, Y., Cao, D., Wang, K., & Huang, W. L. (2018). Artificial intelligence test: A case study of intelligent vehicles. *Artificial Intelligence Review*, *50*(3), 441–465. doi:10.100710462-018-9631-5

Lim, K. L., Soutar, G. N., & Lee, J. A. (2013). Factors affecting investment intentions: A consumer behaviour perspective. In Journal of Financial Services Marketing, 18(4). https://doi.org/ doi:10.1057/fsm.2013.23

Lim, S. Y., & Sek, S. K. (2014). Exploring the Inter-relationship between the Volatilities of Exchange Rate and Stock Return. *Procedia Economics and Finance*, *14*, 367–376. doi:10.1016/S2212-5671(14)00725-4

Li, N., & Qian, Y. (2018). The Impact of Educational Pairing and Urban Residency on Household Financial Investments in Urban China. *Journal of Family and Economic Issues*, *39*(4), 551–565. doi:10.100710834-018-9579-2

Lin, A., & Chen, N. C. (2012). Cloud computing as an innovation: Percepetion, attitude, and adoption. *International Journal of Information Management*, *32*(6), 533–540. doi:10.1016/j.ijinfomgt.2012.04.001

Lin, H., & Wang, Y. (2006). An examination of the determinants of customer loyalty in mobile commerce contexts. *Information & Management*, *43*(3), 271–282. doi:10.1016/j.im.2005.08.001

Lin, K. C., & Dong, X. (2018). Corporate social responsibility engagement of financially distressed firms and their bankruptcy likelihood. *Advances in Accounting*, *43*(1), 32–45. doi:10.1016/j.adiac.2018.08.001

Lin, X., Bruhn, A., & William, J. (2019). Extending financial literacy to insurance literacy: A survey approach. *Accounting and Finance*, *59*(S1), 685–713. doi:10.1111/acfi.12353

Little, R. J., & Rubin, D. B. (1989). The analysis of social science data with missing values. *Sociological Methods & Research*, *18*(2-3), 292–326. doi:10.1177/0049124189018002004

Livingston, S., & Risse, M. (2019). The future impact of artificial intelligence on humans and human rights. *Ethics & International Affairs*, *33*(2), 141–158. doi:10.1017/S089267941900011X

Li, Y., & Giles, D. E. (2015). Modelling volatility spillover effects between developed stock markets and Asian emerging stock markets. *International Journal of Finance & Economics*, *20*(2), 155–177. doi:10.1002/ijfe.1506

Lokuge, S., & Duan, S. X. (2023). Exploring the Enablers of Digital Transformation in Small and Medium-Sized Enterprises. Handbook of Research on Business Model Innovation Through Disruption and Digitalization), pp 136-156.

Lokuge, S., & Sedera, D. (2018). The Role of Enterprise Systems in Fostering Innovation in Contemporary Firms. *Journal of Information Technology Theory and Application (JITTA)*, *19*(2), 7-30.

Lokuge, S., Sedera, D., Ariyachandra, T., Kumar, S., & Ravi, V. (2020a). The Next Wave of Crm Innovation: Implications for Research, Teaching, and Practice. *Communications of the Association for Information Systems*, *46*(1), 560-583.

Lokuge, S., Sedera, D., Cooper, V., & Burstein, F. (2021). Digital Transformation: Environmental Friend or Foe? Panel Discussion at the Australasian Conference on Information Systems 2019. *Communications of the Association for Information Systems* (48), 47. 10.17705/1CAIS.04846

Lokuge, S., Sedera, D., Grover, V., & Xu, D. (2019). Organizational Readiness for Digital Innovation: Development and Empirical Calibration of a Construct. *Information & Management*, *56*(3), 445-461.

Lokuge, S., & Duan, S. X. (2021). Towards Understanding Enablers of Digital Transformation in Small and Medium-Sized Enterprises. *Australasian Conference on Information Systems*. AIS.

Lokuge, S., & Sedera, D. (2014a). Deriving Information Systems Innovation Execution Mechanisms. *Australasian Conference on Information Systems*, Auckland, New Zealand.

Lokuge, S., & Sedera, D. (2014b). Enterprise Systems Lifecycle-Wide Innovation Readiness. *Pacific Asia Conference on Information Systems*. AIS.

Lokuge, S., & Sedera, D. (2016). Is Your It Eco-System Ready to Facilitate Organizational Innovation? Deriving an It Eco-System Readiness Measurement Model. *International Conference on Information Systems*, AIS.

Lokuge, S., & Sedera, D. (2019). Attaining Business Alignment in Information Technology Innovations Led by Line-of-Business Managers. *Australasian Conference on Information Systems*, Perth, Australia.

Lokuge, S., & Sedera, D. (2020). Fifty Shades of Digital Innovation: How Firms Innovate with Digital Technologies. *Pacific Asia Conference on Information Systems*, AIS.

Lokuge, S., Sedera, D., Atapattu, M., & Samaranayaka, D. (2016a). Exploring the Role of Is in Agriculture: Creating an Agenda Towards Agri-Informatics. *Pacific Asia Conference on Information Systems*, AIS.

Lokuge, S., Sedera, D., & Grover, V. (2016b). Thinking inside the Box: Five Organizational Strategies Enabled through Information Systems. *Pacific Asia Conference on Information Systems*, AIS.

Lokuge, S., Sedera, D., & Palekar, S. (2020b). The Clash of the Titans: Cio and Lob Engagement in It Innovation. In K. Sandhu (Ed.), *Leadership, Management, and Adoption Techniques for Digital Service Innovation* (pp. 86–102). IGI Global. doi:10.4018/978-1-7998-2799-3.ch005

Lokuge, S., Sedera, D., & Perera, M. (2018). The Clash of the Leaders: The Intermix of Leadership Styles for Resource Bundling *Pacific Asia Conference on Information Systems*, AIS.

Low, W., & Davenport, E. (2005). Has The Medium (Roast) Become The Message? *International Marketing Review*, *22*(5), 494–511. doi:10.1108/02651330510624354

Ludlum, M., & Johnson, J. B. (2015). Ethics And Law School Marketing Practices. *South. J. Bus. Ethics*, *7*, 89–104.

Lusardi, A. (2019). Financial literacy and the need for financial education: Evidence and implications. *Swiss Journal of Economics and Statistics*, *155*(1), 1. doi:10.118641937-019-0027-5

Lv, Q. (2019). The Influence of International Oil Price Fluctuations on Chinese Economy Based on VAR Model. *IOP Conference Series. Earth and Environmental Science*, *371*(5), 052007. doi:10.1088/1755-1315/371/5/052007

Mahastanti, L. A., & Hariady, E. (2014). Determining the factors which affect the stock investment decisions of potential female investors in Indonesia. *International Journal of Process Management and Benchmarking*, *4*(2), 186. doi:10.1504/IJPMB.2014.060407

Mahmoudi, M., Fatehi, A., Jafari, H., & Karimi, E. (2018). Multi-objective micro-grid design by NSGA-II considering both islanded and grid-connected modes. *IEEE Texas Power and Energy Conference,* 1–6. 10.1109/TPEC.2018.8312105

Ma, L., & Pohlman, L. (2008). Return forecasts and optimal portfolio construction: A quantile regression approach. *European Journal of Finance*, *14*(5), 409–425. doi:10.1080/13518470802042369

Malhotra, N. K., & Miller, G. L. (1998). An Integrated Model For Ethical Decisions In Marketing Research. *Journal of Business Ethics*, *17*(3), 263–280. doi:10.1023/A:1005711311426

Malkiel, B. G. (1989). Efficient market hypothesis. In *Finance* (pp. 127–134). Springer. doi:10.1007/978-1-349-20213-3_13

Mankotia, A. (2022). Massive data usage growth in India: Economic survey. *The Economic Times*. https://economictimes.indiatimes.com/industry/telecom/telecom-news/massive-data-usage-growth-in-india-economic-survey/articleshow/89245236.cms?utm_source=contentofinterest&utm_medium=text&utm_campaign=cppst

Marinakis, V., Koutsellis, T., Nikas, A., & Doukas, H. (2021). AI and Data Democratisation for Intelligent Energy Management. *Energies, 14*(14), 43-41.

Marinkovic, V., Đorđević, A., & Kalinić, Z. (2020). The moderating effects of gender on customer satisfaction and continuance intention in mobile commerce: A UTAUT-based perspective. *Technology Analysis and Strategic Management*, *32*(3), 306–318. doi:10.1080/09537325.2019.1655537

Marston, S., Li, Z., Bandyopadhyay, S., Zhang, J., & Ghalsasi, A. (2011). Cloud computing — The business perspective. *Decision Support Systems*, *51*(1), 176–189. doi:10.1016/j.dss.2010.12.006

Martínez-Ramos, J. L. (2018). Provision of Ancillary Services by a Smart Microgrid: An OPF Approach. *Int. Conf. on Smart Energy Systems and Technologies (SEST),* 1-6. 10.1109/SEST.2018.8495883

Martin, K. D., & Johnson, J. L. (2010). Ethical Beliefs And Information Asymmetries In Supplier Relationships. *Journal of Public Policy & Marketing*, *29*(1), 38–51. doi:10.1509/jppm.29.1.38

Martin-Sanchez, F. J., Aguiar-Pulido, V., Lopez-Campos, G. H., Peek, N., & Sacchi, L. (2017). Secondary use and analysis of big data collected for patient care. *Yearbook of Medical Informatics*, *26*(01), 28–37. doi:10.15265/IY-2017-008 PMID:28480474

Mathew, M., Sulphey, M. M., & Prabhakaran, J. (2014). Perceptions and intentions of customers towards mobile banking adoption. *The Journal Contemporary Management Research.*, *8*(1), 83–101.

Mcdaniel, C., & Gitman, L. (2008). *The Essential Of The Future Of Business*. South-Western Cengage Learning.

Mcdonald, G., & Nijhof, A. (1999). Beyond Codes Of Ethics: An Integrated Framework For stimulating Morally Responsible Behaviour. *Organizations. Leadership and Organization Development Journal*, *20*(3), 133–147. doi:10.1108/01437739910268406

Mcguire, J. B., Sundgren, A., & Schneeweis, T. (1988). Corporate Social Responsibility And Firm Financial Performance. *Academy of Management Journal*, *31*(4), 854–872. doi:10.2307/256342

Melewar, T. C., & Nguyen, B. (2017). Five Areas To Advance Branding Theory And Practice. *Journal of Brand Management*, *21*(9), 758–769. doi:10.1057/bm.2014.31

Mell, P., & Grance, T. (2011). *The NIST Definition of Cloud Computing. Computer Security Division*. Information Technology Laboratory, National Institute of Standards and Technology Gaithersburg.

Menkhoff, L., & Taylor, M. P. (2007). The obstinate passion of foreign exchange professionals: Technical analysis. *Journal of Economic Literature*, *45*(4), 936–972. doi:10.1257/jel.45.4.936

Mensi, W., Hammoudeh, S., Reboredo, J. C., & Nguyen, D. K. (2014). Do global factors impact BRICS stock markets? A quantile regression approach. *Emerging Markets Review*, *19*, 1–17. doi:10.1016/j.ememar.2014.04.002

Mensi, W., Hkiri, B., Al-Yahyaee, K. H., & Kang, S. H. (2018). Analyzing time–frequency co-movements across gold and oil prices with BRICS stock markets: A VaR based on wavelet approach. *International Review of Economics & Finance*, *54*, 74–102. doi:10.1016/j.iref.2017.07.032

Merai, M., Naouar, M. W., Slama-Belkhodja, I., & Monmasson, E. (2018). Grid connected converters as reactive power ancillary service providers: Technical analysis for minimum required DC-link voltage. *Mathematics and Computers in Simulation*, *158*, 344–354. doi:10.1016/j.matcom.2018.09.016

Mishra, A., Alzoubi, Y. I., Anwar, M. J., & Gill, A. Q. (2022). Attributes impacting cybersecurity policy development: An evidence from seven nations. *Computers & Security*, *120*, 102820. doi:10.1016/j.cose.2022.102820

Mishra, S. (2015). An Econometric Investigation of Long and Short Run Relationship among Global Crude Oil Price, Exchange Rate and Stock Price in India : *XIMB. Journal of Management*, *12*(2), 1–19.

Mohammed, F., Ibrahim, O., & Ithnin, N. (2016). Factors influencing cloud computing adoption for e-government implementation in developing countries: Instrument development. *Journal of Systems and Information Technology*, *18*(3), 297–327. doi:10.1108/JSIT-01-2016-0001

Mohan, N. (2020). Electronic Payment: Arhtiyas threaten to launch stir in Haryana. *Hindustan Times*. https://www.hindustantimes.com/chandigarh/ electronic-payment-arhtiyas-threaten-to-launch-stir-in-haryana-from-march-30/story-okb Vm0amzc1b3Lb0yYUmNN.html/

Moore, G. C., & Benbasat, I. (1991). Development of an instrument to measure the perceptions of adopting an information technology innovation. *Information Systems Research*, *2*(3), 192–222. doi:10.1287/isre.2.3.192

Moorhead, P. (2023). Data Democratization in a Hybrid World. *Forbes*. https://www.forbes.com/sites/patrickmoorhead/2023/02/23/data-democratization-in-a-hybrid-world/?sh=12b63b192a9c

Mroua, M., & Trabelsi, L. (2020). Causality and dynamic relationships between exchange rate and stock market indices in BRICS countries: Panel/GMM and ARDL analyses. *Journal of Economics, Finance and Administrative Science, 25*(50), 395–412. doi:10.1108/JEFAS-04-2019-0054

Muflih, S., Abuhammad, S., Karasneh, R., Al-Azzam, S., Alzoubi, K. H., & Muflih, M. (2020). *Online Education for Undergraduate Health Professional Education during the COVID-19 Pandemic: Attitudes, Barriers, and Ethical Issues*. Research Square., doi:10.21203/rs.3.rs-42336/v1

Muhammad, A., & Anwar, K. (2020). Online Learning amid the COVID-19 Pandemic: Students' Perspectives. *Online Submission, 2*(1), 45–51. https://www.doi.org/10.33902/JPSP.2020261309

Muilenburg, L. Y., & Berge, Z. L. (2005). *Student Barriers to Online Learning: A factor analytic study. 26*(1), 29–48. doi:10.1080/01587910500081269

Muller, O., Junglas, I., Vom Brocke, J., & Debortoli, S. (2016). Utilizing big data analytics for information systems research: Challenges, promises and guidelines. *European Journal of Information Systems, 25*(4), 289–302. doi:10.1057/ejis.2016.2

Munnukka, J., Uusitalo, O., & Koivisto, V. J. (2017). The consequences of perceived risk and objective knowledge for consumers' investment behavior. *Journal of Financial Services Marketing, 22*(4), 150–160. doi:10.105741264-017-0033-6

Munn, Z., & Qaseem, A. (2018). Disappearance of the National Guideline Clearinghouse: A huge loss for evidence-based health care. *Annals of Internal Medicine, 169*(9), 648–649. doi:10.7326/M18-2216 PMID:30167676

Musti, K. S. (2020b). *Circular Economy in Energizing Smart Cities. In Handbook of Research on Entrepreneurship Development and Opportunities in Circular Economy.* IGI Global., doi:10.4018/978-1-7998-5116-5.ch013

Musti, K. S. S. (2020a). Quantification of Demand Response in Smart Grids. *IEEE India Council Int. Conf. (INDISCON)*, 278-282. 10.1109/INDISCON50162.2020.00063

Musti, K. S. S., Iileka, H., & Shidhika, F. (2020). *Industry 4.0 Based Enterprise Information System for Demand-Side Management and Energy Efficiency. In Novel Approaches to Information Systems Design.* IGI-Global. doi:10.4018/978-1-7998-2975-1.ch007

Musti, K. S., & Kapali, D. (2021). Digital Transformation of SMEs in the Energy Sector to Survive in a Post-COVID-19 Era. In N. Baporikar (Ed.), *Handbook of Research on Strategies and Interventions to Mitigate COVID-19 Impact on SMEs* (pp. 186–207). IGI Global. doi:10.4018/978-1-7998-7436-2.ch009

Nalini, R., Alamelu, R., Amudha, R., & Cresenta Shakila Motha, L. (2016). Financial literacy and its contributing factors in investment decisions among urban populace. *Indian Journal of Science and Technology, 9*(27). doi:10.17485/ijst/2016/v9i27/97616

Nambiar, D. (2020). The impact of online learning during COVID-19: students' and teachers' perspective. *The International Journal of Indian Psychology*. https://www.researchgate.net/publication/343229234_The_impact_of_online_learning_during_COVID-19_students%27_and_teachers%27_perspective

Nandhini, M., & Girija, K. (2019). Customer perception regards e-wallets. *International Journal of Recent Technology and Engineering.*, *8*(4), 4061–4067.

Narayan, P. K., & Narayan, S. (2010). Carbon dioxide emissions and economic growth: Panel data evidence from developing countries. *Energy Policy*, *38*(1), 661–666. doi:10.1016/j.enpol.2009.09.005

Natsir, K., & Arifin, A. Z. (2021). The Effect of Product Knowledge and Influence of Society on Investment Intention of Stock Investors with Perceived Risk as Mediation. *Estudios de Economía Aplicada*, *39*(12). doi:10.25115/eea.v39i12.6022

Naveed, Q. N., Muhammed, A., Sanober, S., Qureshi, M. R. N., & Shah, A. (2017). Barriers effecting successful implementation of Online Learning in Saudi Arabian Universities. *International Journal of Emerging Technologies in Learning*, *12*(6), 94–107. doi:10.3991/ijet.v12i06.7003

Neslin, S. A., Gupta, S., Kamakura, W., Lu, J., & Mason, C. H. (2006). Defection detection: Measuring and understanding the predictive accuracy of customer churn models. *JMR, Journal of Marketing Research*, *43*(2), 204–211. doi:10.1509/jmkr.43.2.204

NewVantagePartners. (2021). Newvantage Partners Releases 2021 Big Data and Ai Executive Survey. The Journey to Becoming Data-Driven. *Data And AI Executive Survey 2021*. Business Wire. https://www.businesswire.com/news/home/20210104005022/en/NewVantage-Partners-Releases-2021-Big-Data-and-AI-Executive-Survey

NewVantagePartners. (2022). The Quest to Achieve Data-Driven Leadership: A Progress Report on the State of Corporate Data Initiatives. *Data And AI Executive Survey 2022*. https://www.newvantage.com/_files/ugd/e5361a_ad5a8b3da8254a71807d2dccdb0844be.pdf

Ngai, E. W., Hu, Y., Wong, Y. H., Chen, Y., & Sun, X. (2011). The application of data mining techniques in financial fraud detection: A classification framework and an academic review of literature. *Decision Support Systems*, *50*(3), 559–569. doi:10.1016/j.dss.2010.08.006

Nguyen, L. S. (2019). Relationship between environmental financial accounting practices and corporate financialrisk: Evidence from listed companies in Vietnam's securities market. *Asian Economic and Financial Review*, *9*(2), 285–298. doi:10.18488/journal.aefr.2019.92.285.298

Nguyen, L. S., & Tran, M. D. (2019). Disclosure levels of Environmental Accounting information and financial performance: The case of Vietnam. *Management Science Letters*, *9*(4), 557–570. doi:10.5267/j.msl.2019.1.007

Ng, W. (2012). Can we teach digital natives digital literacy? *Computers & Education*, *59*(3), 1065–1078. doi:10.1016/j.compedu.2012.04.016

Nie, J., Liu, Y., Zhou, L., Jiang, X., & Preindl, M. (2022). Deep Reinforcement Learning Based Approach for Optimal Power Flow of Microgrid with Grid Services Implementation. *IEEE Transportation Electrification Conf. & Expo*, 1148–1153. 10.1109/ITEC53557.2022.9813862

Nill, A., & Schibrowsky, J. A. (2007). Research On Marketing Ethics: A Systematic Review Of The Literature. *Journal of Macromarketing*, *27*(3), 256–273. doi:10.1177/0276146707304733

Nirmala, R., & Venkatesan, S. (2022). Inverter current control for reactive power compensation in solar grid system using Self-Tuned Fuzzy Logic Controller. *Automatika (Zagreb)*, *63*(1), 102–121. doi:10.1080/00051144.2021.2009653

Niti Aayog. (2020). *Digital Payments: Trends, Issues and Opportunities*. Niti Aayog. http://niti.gov.in/writereaddata/files/documentpublication/DigitalPaymentBook.pdf.

Njuguna, P. K. (n.d.). *Determinants Of Investment Intentions: An Individual Retail Investor's Perspective From Nairobi Securities Exchange*. Research Gate. https://www.researchgate.net/publication/341089225

Nouira, R., Hadj Amor, T., & Rault, C. (2018). Oil price fluctuations and exchange rate dynamics in the MENA region: Evidence from non-causality-in-variance and asymmetric non-causality tests. *The Quarterly Review of Economics and Finance*. doi:10.1016/j.qref.2018.07.011

Nyamtiga, B. W., Sam, A., & Laizer, L. S. (2013). Enhanced security model for mobile banking systems in Tanzania. *International Journal of Technology Enhancements and Emerging Engineering Research.*, *1*(4), 20.

O'Leary, D. E. (2013). Artificial intelligence and big data. *IEEE Intelligent Systems*, *28*(2), 96–99. doi:10.1109/MIS.2013.39

Octaberlina, L. R., & Muslimin, A. I. (2020). EFL Students Perspective towards Online Learning Barriers and Alternatives Using Moodle/Google Classroom during COVID-19 Pandemic. *International Journal of Higher Education*, *9*(6), 1. doi:10.5430/ijhe.v9n6p1

Odugbesan, J. A., Sunday, T. A., & Olowu, G. (2021). Asymmetric effect of financial development and remittance on economic growth in MINT economies: An application of panel NARDL. *Future Business Journal*, *7*(1), 39. doi:10.118643093-021-00085-6

OECD. (2015). Data-Driven Innovation: Big Data for Growth and Well-Being, 1-456. OECD.

OECD. (2020). *The potential of Online Learning for adults: Early lessons from the COVID-19 crisis*. OECD. https://read.oecd-ilibrary.org/view/?ref=135_135358-ool6fisocq&title=The-potential-of-OnlinOnline Learning-for-adults-Early-lessons-from-the-COVID-19-crisis

Offergeld, T., Mattus, N., Schmidtke, F., & Ulbig, A. (2022). On Aggregation Performance in Privacy Conscious Hierarchical Flexibility Coordination Schemes. *Proceedings of the 11th Bulk Power Systems Dynamics and Control Symposium (IREP)*. 10.48550/arXiv.2207.03439

Ogonowski, A., Montandon, A., Botha, E., & Reyneke, M. (2014). Should new online stores invest in social presence elements? The effect of social presence on initial trust formation. *Journal of Retailing and Consumer Services. 21*(4), 482-491. https://doi.org/ conser.2014.03.004 doi:10.1016/j.jret

Ohlson, J. A. (1980). Financial ratios and the probabilistic prediction of bankruptcy. *Journal of Accounting Research, 18*(1), 109–131. doi:10.2307/2490395

Oikonomou, I., Brooks, C., & Brooks, C. (2014). The effects of corporate social performance on the cost of corporate debt and credit ratings. *Financial Review, 49*(1), 49–75. doi:10.1111/fire.12025

Okoye, A. E., & Ngwakwe, C. C. (2004). Environmental Accounting: A convergence of antecedent divergence. Accountancy; Management Companion. Nigerian Accounting Association (NAA).

Olga, S. (2018). *Determinants of customer satisfaction on Chinese and Russian m-commerce markets.* DSpace. https://dspace.spbu.ru/bitstream/11701/12520/1/SharkoMaster Thesis.pdf/

Olins, W. (2014). Brand New: The Shape Of Brands To Come. Thames & Hudson: New York, Ny, USA.

Oliveira, T., Thomas, M., & Espadanal, M. (2014). Assessing the determinants of cloud computing adoption: An analysis of the manufacturing and services sectors. *Information & Management, 51*(5), 497–510. doi:10.1016/j.im.2014.03.006

Oliver, R. L., & Westbrook, R. A. (1993). Profiles of consumer emotions and satisfaction in ownership and usage. *Journal of Consumer Satisfaction, Dissatisfaction & Complaining Behavior, 6*(1), 12–27.

Onel, G. (2005). Testing for Multiple Structural Breaks: An Application of Bai-Perron Test To the Nominal Interest Rates and Inflation in Turkey. *Dokuz Eylül Üniversitesi İktisadi İdari Bilimler Fakültesi Dergisi, 20*(2), 81–94.

Opitz, N., Langkau, T. F., Schmidt, N. H., & Kolbe, L. M. (2012). Technology acceptance of cloud computing: Empirical evidence from German IT departments. *Proceedings of the Annual Hawaii International Conference on System Sciences*, 1593–1602. 10.1109/HICSS.2012.557

Ostern, N. K., & Perscheid, G. (2021). Solve for Blockchain: Toward a Framework for Navigating Blockchain Tensions. In *ICIS 2021 Proceedings* (pp. 1–9). AIS Virtual Library.

Ostrovsky-Berman, E., & Litwin, H. (2019). Social Network and Financial Risk Tolerance Among Investors Nearing and During Retirement. *Journal of Family and Economic Issues, 40*(2), 237–249. doi:10.100710834-018-9592-5

Ou, J. A., & Penman, S. H. (1989). Financial statement analysis and the prediction of stock returns. *Journal of Accounting and Economics, 11*(4), 295–329. doi:10.1016/0165-4101(89)90017-7

Oye, N. D., A.Iahad, N., & Ab.Rahim, N. (2014). The history of UTAUT model and its impact on ICT acceptance and usage by academicians. *Education and Information Technologies 2012, 19*(1), 251–270. doi:10.1007/s10639-012-9189-9

Öztürk, E., Rheinberger, K., Faulwasser, T., Worthmann, K., & Preibinger, M. (2022). Aggregation of Demand-Side Flexibilities: A Comparative Study of Approximation Algorithms. *Energies, 15*(7), 2501. Advance online publication. doi:10.3390/en15072501

Pachamanova, D. A., & Fabozzi, F. J. (2014). Recent trends in equity portfolio construction analytics. *Journal of Portfolio Management, 40*(3), 137–151. doi:10.3905/jpm.2014.40.3.137

Pal, D., & Mitra, S. K. (2019). Asymmetric oil price transmission to the purchasing power of the U.S. dollar: A multiple threshold NARDL modelling approach. *Resources Policy, 64*, 101508. doi:10.1016/j.resourpol.2019.101508

Pańkowska, M., Pyszny, K., & Strzelecki, A. (2020). Users' Adoption of Sustainable Cloud Computing Solutions. *Sustainability 2020, Vol. 12, Page 9930, 12*(23), 9930. doi:10.3390/su12239930

Papapetrou, E. (2001). Oil price shocks, stock market, economic activity and employment in Greece. *Energy Economics, 23*(5), 511–532. doi:10.1016/S0140-9883(01)00078-0

Paripunyapat, D., & Kraiwanit, T. (2018). Financial technology acceptance in Bangkok metropolis and vicinity. *Review of Integrative Business and Economics Research, 8*(3).

Park, C. S., & Han, I. (2002). A case-based reasoning with the feature weights derived by analytic hierarchy process for bankruptcy prediction. *Expert Systems with Applications, 23*(3), 255–264. doi:10.1016/S0957-4174(02)00045-3

Patel, J. (2019). Bridging Data Silos Using Big Data Integration. *International Journal of Database Management Systems, 11*(3), 01-06.

Patnam, M., & Yao, W. (2020). The Real Effects of Mobile Money: Evidence from a Large-Scale Fintech Expansion. *IMF working Paper*, 20/138.

Paul, J., & Criado, A. R. (2020). The art of writing a literature review: What do we know and what do we need to know? *International Business Review, 29*(4), 101717. doi:10.1016/j.ibusrev.2020.101717

Paul, J., Lim, W. M., O'Cass, A., Hao, A. W., & Bresciani, S. (2021). Scientific procedures and rationales for systematic literature reviews (SPAR-4-SLR). *International Journal of Consumer Studies, 45*(4), 1–16. doi:10.1111/ijcs.12695

Paytm. (2020). *About Paytm India*. Paytm. https://care.paytm.ca/hc/en-us/articles/360004846313-About-Paytm-India

Perols, J. L., Bowen, R. M., Zimmermann, C., & Samba, B. (2017). Finding needles in a haystack: Using data analytics to improve fraud prediction. *The Accounting Review, 92*(2), 221–245. doi:10.2308/accr-51562

Perron, B. Y. P. (1989). The Great Crash, the Oil Price Shock, and the Unit Root Hypothesis Author. *The Econometric Society Stable, 57*(6), 1361–1401. https://www.jstor.org/stable/1913712

Pesaran, M. H., Shin, Y., & Smith, R. J. (2001). Bounds testing approaches to the analysis of level relationships. *Journal of Applied Econometrics, 16*(3), 289–326. doi:10.1002/jae.616

Pitra, G. M., & Musti, K. S. S. (2021). Duck Curve with Renewable Energies and Storage Technologies. *13th International Conference on Computational Intelligence and Communication Networks (CICN),* 66-71. 10.1109/CICN51697.2021.9574671

Poeteri, N. A., Simanjuntak, M., & Hasanah, N. (2021). The Investment Intention Among Indonesian Millennials via Peer-to-Peer Lending Applications. *Peer-Reviewed Article Jurnal Keuangan Dan Perbankan, 25*, 2443–2687. doi:10.26905/jkdp.v25i4.6352

Pole, A., West, M., & Harrison, J. (2018). *Applied Bayesian Forecasting and Time Series Analysis*. Chapman and Hall/CRC. doi:10.1201/9781315274775

Prabakaran, S., & Mitra, S. (2018). Survey of analysis of crime detection techniques using data mining and machine learning. In *Journal of Physics:Conference Series* (p. 012046). IOP Publishing. doi:10.1088/1742-6596/1000/1/012046

Praiseye, T., & John, F. (2018). A study on consumer preference towards mobile wallet. *International Journal of Research and Analytical Reviews.*, *5*(3), 185–189.

Prasad Bal, D., & Narayan Rath, B. (2015). Nonlinear causality between crude oil price and exchange rate: A comparative study of China and India. *Energy Economics*, *51*, 149–156. doi:10.1016/j.eneco.2015.06.013

Press Information Bureau. (2022). *Transforming India's Digital Payment Landscape*. Press Information Bureau. https://pib.gov.in/FeaturesDeatils.aspx?NoteId=151163&ModuleId%20=%202

Preston, I. (2010). Interaction Of Law And Ethics In Matters Of Advertisers' Responsibility For Protecting Consumers. *The Journal of Consumer Affairs, 44*(1), 257–264. doi:10.1111/j.1745-6606.2010.01166.x

Prothero, A. (1998). Green Marketing: The 'Fad' That Won't Slip Slide Away. *Journal of Marketing Management, 14*(6), 507–512. doi:10.1362/026725798784867680

Provost, F., & Fawcett, T. (2013). Data Science and Its Relationship to Big Data and Data-Driven Decision Making. *Big data, 1*(1), 51-59.

Raghupathi, W., & Raghupathi, V. (2014). Big data analytics in healthcare: Promise and potential. *Health Information Science and Systems, 2*(1), 1–10. doi:10.1186/2047-2501-2-3 PMID:25825667

Raj, M., & Bansal, S. (2019). Customer Satisfaction In Banking Sector-A Case Study Of H.D.F.C Bank. *International Journal of Research and Analytical Reviews*. http://ijrar.com/

Raj, M., & Bansal, S. (2019). CUSTOMER SATISFACTION IN BANKING SECTOR-A CASE STUDY OF H.D.F.C BANK. *International Journal of Research and Analytical Reviews*. http://ijrar.com/

Raj, M., Jain, A., Bansal, S., & Verma, T. (2018). Non-Performing Assets: A Comparative Study of SBI & ICICI Bank from 2014-2017. *IOSR Journal of Business and Management (IOSR-JBM), 20*(9), 78–84. https://doi.org/ doi:10.9790/487X-2009077884

Raj, M., Verma, T., Bansal, S., & Jain, A. (2018). Performance Of Mutual Funds In India : A Comparative Analysis Of SBI Mutual Funds And HDFC Mutual Funds. *IOSR Journal of Business and Management (IOSR-JBM), 20*, 36–43. https://doi.org/ doi:10.9790/487X-2010013643

Rajab, M. H., Gazal, A. M., & Alkattan, K. (2020). Challenges to Online Medical Education During the COVID-19 Pandemic. *Cureus, 12*(7). doi:10.7759/cureus.8966 PMID:32766008

Raju, B., Jumah, F., Ashraf, O., Narayan, V., Gupta, G., Sun, H., & Nanda, A. (2020). Big data, machine learning, and artificial intelligence: A field guide for neurosurgeons. *Journal of Neurosurgery, 1*, 1–11. doi:10.3171/2020.5.JNS201288 PMID:33007750

Raju, G. A., & Marathe, S. R. (2020). Relationship between crude oil prices and macro-economic variables: Evidence from brics countries. *International Journal of Energy Economics and Policy, 10*(5), 264–271. doi:10.32479/ijeep.9755

Ram & Chand. (2016). Effect of drivers' risk perception and perception of driving tasks on road safety attitude. *Transportation Research Part F: Traffic Psychology and Behaviour, 42*(1), 162–176. 10. 1016/j.trf.2016.07.012

Ran, B., Nutma, J., & Klever, M. (2019). Maximizing the utilization of DERs with the Interflex Aggregation Platform for Flexibility. CIRED-2019 Conference, Madrid, Spain, doi:10.34890/781

Rao, S., Suma, S. N., & Sunitha, M. (2015). Security solutions for big data analytics in healthcare. *2015 Second International Conference on Advances in Computing and Communication Engineering*, 510-514. 10.1109/ICACCE.2015.83

Rao, S., & Troshani, I. (2007). A conceptual framework and propositions for the acceptance of mobile services. *Journal of Theoretical and Applied Electronic Commerce Research, 2*(2), 61–73. doi:10.3390/jtaer2020014

Rasheed, R. A., Kamsin, A., & Abdullah, N. A. (2020). Challenges in the online component of blended learning: A systematic review. *Computers & Education, 144*, 103701. doi:10.1016/j.compedu.2019.103701

Ratten, V. (2014). A US-China comparative study of cloud computing adoption behavior: The role of consumer innovativeness, performance expectations and social influence. *Journal of Entrepreneurship in Emerging Economies, 6*(1), 53–71. doi:10.1108/JEEE-07-2013-0019

Raut, R. K. (2020). Past behaviour, financial literacy and investment decision-making process of individual investors. *International Journal of Emerging Markets, 15*(6), 1243–1263. doi:10.1108/IJOEM-07-2018-0379

Rehman, A., Naz, S., & Razzak, I. (2021). Leveraging big data analytics in healthcare enhancement: Trends, challenges and opportunities. *Multimedia Systems, 1*, 33.

Reidenbach, R. E., Robin, D. P., & Dawson, L. (1991). An Application And Extension Of A Multidimensional Ethics Scale To Selected Marketing Practices And Marketing Groups. *Journal of the Academy of Marketing Science, 19*(2), 83–92. doi:10.1007/BF02726000

Reji, R. (2022). The complexity of payments in rural India, available https://www.cnbctv18.com/views/the-complexity-of-payments-in-rural-india-10742161.htm

Reserve Bank of India (RBI). (2020a). *Benchmarking India's Payment Systems*. RBI. https://m.rbi.org.in/Scripts/PublicationReportDetails.aspx?UrlPage=&ID=923/

Reserve Bank of India. (2020b). *Drivers of Digital Payments: A Cross Country Study*. RBI Bulletin. https://www.rbi.org.in/scripts/BS_ViewBulletin.aspx?Id=18409

Resnik, D. B. (2011). What Is Ethics In Research And Why Is It Important. National Institute Of Health.

Reurink, A. (2018). Financial fraud: A literature review. *Journal of Economic Surveys, 32*(5), 1292–1325. doi:10.1111/joes.12294

Reza, A., Monfared, K., Fathi, S., & Ranjbarian, B. (2017). Perceived risks of individual investors in the capital market: the antecedences and consequences. In Int. J. Business Innovation and Research, 14(2).

Riche, L. A., & Ponte, S. (2014). Buying Into Development? Brand Aid Forms Of Cause-Related Marketing. *Third World Quarterly, 35*(1), 65–87. doi:10.1080/01436597.2014.868985

Riedl, M. O. (2019). Human-centred artificial intelligence and machine learning. *Human Behavior and Emerging Technologies, 1*(1), 33–36. doi:10.1002/hbe2.117

Ringle, C. M., & Sarstedt, M. (2016). Gain more insight from your PLS-SEM results the importance-performance map analysis. In Industrial Management and Data Systems, 116(9). https://doi.org/ doi:10.1108/IMDS-10-2015-0449

Riquelme, H. E., & Rios, R. E. (2010). The moderating effect of gender in the adoption of mobile banking. *International Journal of Bank Marketing, 28*(5), 328–341. doi:10.1108/02652321011064872

Rizk, A., & Elragal, A. (2020). Data Science: Developing Theoretical Contributions in Information Systems Via Text Analytics. *Journal of Big Data, 7*(7), 1-26.

Rizvi, S., & Abu-Saida, A. (2022). Active Power Sharing in a Micro-Grid with Multiple Grid Connections. *Designs, 6*(2), 24. Advance online publication. doi:10.3390/designs6020024

Roberts, B. W., & DelVecchio, W. F. (2000). The rank-order consistency of personality traits from childhood to old age: A quantitative review of longitudinal studies. *Psychological Bulletin, 126*(1), 3–25. doi:10.1037/0033-2909.126.1.3 PMID:10668348

Roblek, V., Mesko, M., Dimovski, V., & Peterlin, J. (2019). Smart technologies as social innovation and complex social issues of the Z generation. *Kybernetes*, *48*(1), 91–107. doi:10.1108/K-09-2017-0356

Rodrigues, L. F., Oliveira, A., Rodrigues, H., & Costa, C. J. (2019). Assessing consumer literacy on financial complex products. *Journal of Behavioral and Experimental Finance*, *22*, 93–104. doi:10.1016/j.jbef.2019.02.005

Rodriguez-Dominguez, L., Gallego-Alvarez, I., & Garcia-Sanchez, I. M. (2009). Corporate Governance And Codes Of Ethics. *Journal of Business Ethics*, *90*(2), 187–202. doi:10.100710551-009-0035-y

Rossi, P. G. (2009). Learning Environment With Elements Of Artificial Intelligence. *Journal of Online Learning and Knowledge Society*, *5*(1), 191–199. doi:10.20368/1971-8829/306 PMID:33809696

Ross, W. D. (1930). *The Right And The Cood*. Clarendon Press.

Rowland, K., & Shrauger, S. (2013). *The coming new way to pay*. Aba Bank Marketing.

Russell, S., Hauert, S., Altman, R., & Veloso, M. (2015). Ethics of artificial intelligence. *Nature*, *521*(7553), 415–416. doi:10.1038/521415a PMID:26017428

Rust, R. T., & Oliver, R. L. (1994). *Service quality: Insights and managerial implications from the frontier*. Scientific Research.

Sabi, H. M., Uzoka, F. M. E., Langmia, K., & Njeh, F. N. (2016). Conceptualizing a model for adoption of cloud computing in education. *International Journal of Information Management*, *36*(2), 183–191. doi:10.1016/j.ijinfomgt.2015.11.010

Sagiroglu, S., & Sinanc, D. (2013). *Big data: A review. In 2013 international conference on collaboration technologies and systems*. CTS.

Sahu, T. N., Bandopadhyay, K., & Mondal, D. (2014). Crude oil price, exchange rate and emerging stock market: Evidence from India. *Jurnal Pengurusan*, *42*, 75–87. doi:10.17576/pengurusan-2014-42-07

Saidu, M. T., Naseem, N. A. M., Law, S. H., & Yasmin, B. (2021). Exploring the asymmetric effect of oil price on exchange rate: Evidence from the top six African net oil importers. *Energy Reports*, *7*, 8238–8257. doi:10.1016/j.egyr.2021.07.037

Saluja, S. (2022). Identity theft fraud-major loophole for FinTech industry in India. *Journal of Financial Crime*.

Salvi, A., Petruzzella, F., & Giakoumelou, A. (2018). Does sustainability foster the cost of equity reduction? The relationship between corporate social responsibility (CSR) and riskiness worldwide. *African Journal of Business Management*, *12*(12), 381–395. doi:10.5897/AJBM2018.8562

Samarasinghe, S. S. U., Lokuge, S., & Snell, L. (2022). Exploring Tenets of Data Democratization. PACIS 2022 Proceedings, (pp. 1-5). Virtual: AIS Electronic Library (AISeL).

Samarasinghe, S., & Lokuge, S. (2022). Exploring the Critical Success Factors for Data Democratization. In *ACIS 2022 Proceedings*. ACIS.

Samsuri, A., Ismiyanti, F., & Narsa, I. M. (2019). Effects of risk tolerance and financial literacy to investment intentions. *International Journal of Innovation. Creativity and Change*, *10*(9), 40–54.

Samudra, M. S., & Phadtare, M. (2012). Factors influencing the adoption of mobile banking with special reference to Pune city. *ASCI Journal of Management.*, *42*(1), 51–65.

Sandryhaila, A., & Moura, J. M. (2014). Big data analysis with signal processing on graphs: Representation and processing of massive data sets with irregular structure. *IEEE Signal Processing Magazine*, *31*(5), 80–90. doi:10.1109/MSP.2014.2329213

Saranya, P., & Asha, P. (2019). Survey on Big Data Analytics in health care. *2019 International Conference on Smart Systems and Inventive Technology (ICSSIT),* 46-51. 10.1109/ICSSIT46314.2019.8987882

Saraswat, G. B., Saraswat, M., Singh, S. K., & Tiwari, R. S. (2022). The Fluctuation in Interest Rate, Exchange Rate and Crude Oil Price and its impact on Stock Market. *YMER Digital*, *21*(01), 484–52. doi:10.37896/YMER21.01/44

Sastry, M. K. S. (2007). Integrated Outage Management System: An effective solution for power utilities to address customer grievances. *International Journal of Electronic Customer Relationship Management*, *1*(1), 30–40. doi:10.1504/IJECRM.2007.014424

Saura, J. R., Ribeiro-Soriano, D., & Palacios-Marqués, D. (2021). From User-Generated Data to Data-Driven Innovation: A Research Agenda to Understand User Privacy in Digital Markets. *International Journal of Information Management*, *60*, 102331. doi:10.1016/j.ijinfomgt.2021.102331

Saxena, A. (2020). Environmental Accounting Practices in India. *International Journal of Scientific Research*, *9*(2), 1014–1016.

Schlegelmilch, B. B., & Öberseder, M. (2010). Half A Century Of Marketing Ethics: Shifting Perspectives And Emerging Trends. *Journal of Business Ethics*, *93*(1), 1–19. doi:10.100710551-009-0182-1

Sedera, D., & Dey, S. (2013). User Expertise in Contemporary Information Systems: Conceptualization, Measurement and Application. *Information & Management, 50*(8), 621–637.

Sedera, D., & Gable, G.G. (2010). Knowledge Management Competence for Enterprise System Success. *The Journal of Strategic Information Systems, 19*(4), 296-306.

Sedera, D., & Lokuge, S. (2019b). Does It Get Better over Time? A Longitudinal Assessment of Enterprise System User Performance. *Information Technology & People, 33*(4), 1098-1123.

Sedera, D., & Lokuge, S. (2019c). From Punctuation to Equilibrium: A Longitudinal Assessment of Enterprise Systems User Performance. Academy of Management Proceedings. Academy of Management Briarcliff Manor.

Sedera, D., Lokuge, S., Grover, V., Sarker, S., & Sarker, S. (2016). Innovating with Enterprise Systems and Digital Platforms: A Contingent Resource-Based Theory View. *Information & Management, 53*(3), 366–379.

Sedera, D., Tan, C.-W., & Xu, D. (2022). Digital Business Transformation in Innovation and Entrepreneurship. *Information & Management, 59*(3), 103620.

Sedera, D. D., Lokuge, S., & Nugawela, S. (2021). How Status Quo Bias Affects Digitalization of Agriculture: A Mixed-Method Study of Agri-Business Ceos. *International Conference on Information Systems*. AIS Library.

Sedera, D., Gable, G. G., & Chan, T. (2004). Knowledge Management as an Antecedent of Enterprise System Success. N.C. Romano (ed.), *Americas Conference on Information Systems*. AIS.

Sedera, D., Gable, G., & Palmer, A. (2002). Enterprise Resources Planning Systems Impacts: A Delphi Study of Australian Public Sector Organisations. *Pacific Asia Conference on Information Systems*, AIS.

Sedera, D., & Lokuge, S. (2019a). Do We Put All Eggs in One Basket? A Polynomial Regression Study of Digital Technology Configuration Strategies. *International Conference on Information Systems*. AIS.

Selim, H. M. (2007). Online Learning critical success factors: An exploratory investigation of student perceptions. *International Journal of Technology Marketing*, *2*(2), 157–182. doi:10.1504/IJTMKT.2007.014791

Seng, W. K., & Hook, L. S. (2001). *Part a Cointegration Test – Ardl Bounds Test*. 1–32.

Sen, S., Bhattacharya, C. B., & Korschun, D. (2006). The Role Of Corporate Social Responsibility In Strengthening Multiple Stakeholder Relationships: A Field Experiment. *Journal of the Academy of Marketing Science*, *34*(2), 158–166. doi:10.1177/0092070305284978

Serafy, S. (1997). Green Accounting and Economic Policy. *Ecological Economics*, *21*(3), 217–229. doi:10.1016/S0921-8009(96)00107-3

Sevensson, G., Wood, G., Singh, J., & Callaghan, M. (2009). Implementation, Communication And Benefits Of Corporate Codes Of Ethics: An International And Longitudinal Approach For Australia, Canada And Sweden. *Business Ethics (Oxford, England)*, *18*(4), 389–398. doi:10.1111/j.1467-8608.2009.01571.x

Shahbaz, M., Gao, C., Zhai, L., Shahzad, F., & Hu, Y. (2019). Investigating the adoption of big data analytics in healthcare: The moderating role of resistance to change. *Journal of Big Data*, *6*(1), 1–20. doi:10.118640537-019-0170-y

Shah, G., Shah, A., & Shah, M. (2019). Panacea of challenges in real-world application of big data analytics in healthcare sector. *Journal of Data. Information & Management, 1*(3), 107–116.

Shah, J. R., & Murtaza, M. B. (2000). A neural network-based clustering procedure for bankruptcy prediction. *Am Bus Rev., 18*, 80.

Shamim, S., Yang, Y., Zia, N. U., & Shah, M. H. (2021). Big Data Management Capabilities in the Hospitality Sector: Service Innovation and Customer Generated Online Quality Ratings. *Computers in Human Behavior, 121*, 106–777. doi:10.1016/j.chb.2021.106777

Sharma, N. (2021). Reliance Jio's cheap data turned India's internet dreams into reality. *Quartz*. https://qz.com/india/2055771/reliance-jios-cheap-data-turned-indias-internet-dreams-into-reality

Sharpe, D. R., & Benfield, D. G. (2015). *Institutional strategies for supporting learners in a digital age*. Taylor and Francis. doi:10.11120/elss.2012.04020004

Shaw, J. (2019). Artificial intelligence and ethics. *Harvard Magazine*, 30.

Shehata, S. M., Abdeljawad, A. M., Mazouz, L. A., Aldossary, L. Y. K., Alsaeed, M. Y., & Sayed, M. N. (2021). The moderating role of perceived risks in the relationship between financial knowledge and the intention to invest in the Saudi Arabian stock market. *International Journal of Financial Studies, 9*(1), 1–16. doi:10.3390/ijfs9010009

Shi, Y., Cui, T., & Liu, F. (2022). Disciplined Autonomy: How Business Analytics Complements Customer Involvement for Digital Innovation. *The Journal of Strategic Information Systems, 31*(1), 1. doi:10.1016/j.jsis.2022.101706

Simon, J., Charles, W. P., & Jon, P. G. (1972). *The Ethical Investor: Universities And Corporate Responsibility*. Yale University Press.

Singhal, S., & Ghosh, S. (2016). Returns and volatility linkages between international crude oil price, metal and other stock indices in India: Evidence from VAR-DCC-GARCH models. *Resources Policy, 50*, 276–288. doi:10.1016/j.resourpol.2016.10.001

Singh, K. (2011). Innovated technology in banking services. *Journal of Internet Banking and Commerce, 16*(2), 1–16.

Singh, N., & Sinha, N. (2020). How perceived trust mediates merchant's intention to use a mobile wallet technology. *Journal of Retailing and Consumer Services, 52*, 101894. Advance online publication. doi:10.1016/j.jretconser.2019.101894

Singh, N., Srivastava, S., & Sinha, N. (2017). Consumer preference and satisfaction of m-wallets: A study on north Indian consumers. *International Journal of Bank Marketing, 35*(6), 944–966. doi:10.1108/IJBM-06-2016-0086

Singh, S. (2014). Customer perception of mobile banking: An empirical study in national capital region Delhi. *Journal of Internet Banking and Commerce, 19*(3), 2–23.

Singh, S., & Srivastava, R. K. (2020). Understanding the intention to use mobile banking by existing online banking customers: An empirical study. *Journal of Financial Services Marketing*, *25*(3), 86–96. doi:10.105741264-020-00074-w

Sitar-Tăut, D.A. (2021). Mobile Learning Acceptance in Social Distancing During the Covid-19 Outbreak: The Mediation Effect of Hedonic Motivation. *Human Behavior and Emerging Technologies, 3*(3), 366-378.

Sivaramakrishnan, S., Srivastava, M., & Rastogi, A. (2017). Attitudinal factors, financial literacy, and stock market participation. *International Journal of Bank Marketing*, *35*(5), 818–841. doi:10.1108/IJBM-01-2016-0012

Smedley, J. (2010). Modelling the impact of knowledge management using technology. *OR Insight*, *23*(4), 233–250. doi:10.1057/ori.2010.11

Smet, A. D., Gagnon, C., & Mygatt, E. (2021). *Organizing for the Future: Nine Keys to Becoming a Future-Ready Company.* McKinsey. https://www.mckinsey.com/capabilities/people-and-organizational-performance/our-insights/organizing-for-the-future-nine-keys-to-becoming-a-future-ready-company

Smith., & Murphy. (2012). A Marketing Ethics: A review of the Field. *Marketing Ethics.* SAGE publications.

Smith, S. W., & Koppel, R. (2014). Healthcare information technology's relativity problems: A typology of how patients' physical reality, clinicians' mental models, and healthcare information technology differ. *Journal of the American Medical Informatics Association : JAMIA*, *21*(1), 117–131. doi:10.1136/amiajnl-2012-001419 PMID:23800960

Smys, S., & Raj, J. S. (2019). Internet of things and big data analytics for health care with cloud computing. *Journal of Information Technology*, *1*(01), 9–18.

Soper, D. S. (2017). *A-priori sample size calculator*. Google Scholar. https://scholar.google.com/scholar?hl=en&as_sdt=0%2C5&q=Soper%2C+D.+S.+%282017%29.+A-priori+sample+size+calculator+for+structural+equation+models+%5BSoftware%5D.+Available+at+www.+danielsoper.+com%2Fstatcalc+%28accessed+28+October+2020%29.&btnG=

Sorescu, A. (2017). Data-Driven Business Model Innovation. *Journal of Product Innovation Management, 34*(5), 691-696.

Spasi, D., Stojanovi, (2013). Sustainability reporting - theoretical framework and practice in the serbian oilindustry, *Economics and Organization, 10*(3).

Srinivasan, P. (2015). Modeling and Forecasting of Time-Varying Conditional Volatility of the Indian Stock Market. *IUP Journal of Financial Risk Management, 12*(1), 49–64. http://0-search.ebscohost.com.wam.city.ac.uk/login.aspx?direct=true&db=bth&AN=109099697&site=ehost-live

Stanaland, A. J., Lwin, M. O., & Murphy, P. E. (2011). Consumer Perceptions Of The Antecedents And Consequences Of Corporate Social Responsibility. *Journal of Business Ethics*, *102*(1), 47–55. doi:10.100710551-011-0904-z

Stanforth, N., & Hauck, W. (2010). The Effects Of Ethical Framing On Consumer Price Perceptions. *Journal of Fashion Marketing and Management*, *14*(4), 615–623. doi:10.1108/13612021011081779

Stieninger, M., & Nedbal, D. (2014). Diffusion and Acceptance of Cloud Computing in SMEs: Towards a Valence Model of Relevant Factors. *2014 47th Hawaii International Conference on System Sciences (HICSS)*, 3307–3316. 10.1109/HICSS.2014.410

Stohl, C., Stohl, M., & Popova, L. (2009). A New Generation Of Corporate Code Of Ethics. *The Journal of Business*.

Su, X., Zeng, W., Zheng, M., Jiang, X., Lin, W., & Xu, A. (2022). Big Data Analytics Capabilities and Organizational Performance: The Mediating Effect of Dual Innovations. *European Journal of Innovation Management, 25*(4), 1142-1160.

Sujith, T. S., & Julie, C. D. (2017). Opportunities and Challenges of E-payment System in India. *International Journal of Scientific Research and Management*, *5*(9), 6935–6943.

Suls, J., & Wallston, K.A. (2008). Social Psychological Foundations of Health and Illness. *John Wiley & Son*s. http://dx.doi.org/ doi:10.1002/9780470753552

Sultana, S., Akter, S., Kyriazis, E., & Wamba, S.F. (2021). Architecting and Developing Big Data-Driven Innovation (Ddi) in the Digital Economy. *Journal of Global Information Management (JGIM), 29*(3), 165-187.

Sultana, S., Akter, S., & Kyriazis, E. (2022). How Data-Driven Innovation Capability Is Shaping the Future of Market Agility and Competitive Performance? *Technological Forecasting and Social Change*, *174*, 121–260. doi:10.1016/j.techfore.2021.121260

Sultan, N. (2010). Cloud computing for education: A new dawn? *International Journal of Information Management*, *30*(2), 109–116. doi:10.1016/j.ijinfomgt.2009.09.004

Summers, L. H. (1985). On economics and finance. *The Journal of Finance*, *40*(3), 633–635. doi:10.1111/j.1540-6261.1985.tb04985.x

Sung, T. K., Chang, N., & Lee, G. (1999). Dynamics of modelling in data mining: Interpretive approach to bankruptcy prediction. *Journal of Management Information Systems*, *16*(1), 63–85. doi:10.1080/07421222.1999.11518234

Sur, A. (2022). India saw 18 million cyber-attacks in first quarter of 2022: Google's Royal Hansen. *Money Control*. https://www.moneycontrol.com/news/business/india-saw-18-million-cyber-attacks-in-first-quarter-of-2022-google-executive-royal-hansen-9084911.html

Syed, A. A. (2021). Symmetric and Asymmetric Influence of Macroeconomic Variables on Stock Prices Movement: Study of Indian Stock Market. *New Challenges for Future Sustainability and Wellbeing*, 319–339. https://doi.org/ doi:10.1108/978-1-80043-968-920211017/FULL/HTML

Tabrizi, B., Lam, E., Girard, K., & Irvin, V. (2019). Digital Transformation Is Not About Technology. Harvard business review, 13, 1-6.

Tackett, J. A. (2013). Association rules for fraud detection. *Journal of Corporate Accounting & Finance*, *24*(4), 15–22. doi:10.1002/jcaf.21856

Talwar, S., Dhir, A., Khalil, A., Mohan, G., & Islam, A. (2020). Point of adoption and beyond. Initial trust and mobile-payment continuation intention. *Journal of Retailing and Consumer Services*, *55*, 102086. doi:10.1016/j.jretconser.2020.102086

Tandon, S. (2022). Millennials in Rural India Shaping Consumption patterns in the hinterland. *Mint*. https://www.livemint.com/industry/retail/millennials-in-rural-india-shaping-consumption-patterns-in-the-hinterland-1553026089886.html

Tanveer, M., Khan, N., & Ahmad, A. R. (2021)). AI Support Marketing: Understanding The Customer Journey Towards The Business Development. In *Proceedings Of The 2021 1st International Conference On Artificial Intelligence And Data Analytics (Caida)*, Riyadh, Saudi Arabia. 10.1109/CAIDA51941.2021.9425079

Tarkianen, A., & Sundqvist, S. (2014). Subjective norms, attitudes and intentions of Finnish consumers in buying organic food. *British Food Journal*, *107*(11), 808–822. doi:10.1108/00070700510629760

Ta, V. D., Liu, C. M., & Addis, D. (2018). Prediction and portfolio optimization in quantitative trading using machine learning techniques. *Proceedings of the Ninth International Symposium on Information and Communication Technology*, 98–105. 10.1145/3287921.3287963

Taylor, S., & Todd, P. A. (1995). Understanding Information Technology Usage: A Test of Competing Models. Https://Doi.Org/10.1287/Isre.6.2.144, *6*(2), 144–176. doi:10.1287/isre.6.2.144

Taylor, P. W. (1975). *Principles Of Ethia: An Introduction*. Dickerson Publishing Co., Inc.

Tehrani, S. R., & Shirazi, F. (2014). Factors influencing the adoption of cloud computing by Small and Medium size Enterprises (SMEs). Lecture Notes in Computer Science (Including Subseries Lecture Notes in Artificial Intelligence and Lecture Notes in Bioinformatics), 8522 LNCS(PART 2), 631–642. https://doi.org/ doi:10.1007/978-3-319-07863-2_60/COVER

Thai, P., Trang, M., & Tho, N. H. (2017). International Journal of Economics and Financial Issues Perceived Risk, Investment Performance and Intentions in Emerging Stock Markets. *International Journal of Economics and Financial Issues*, *7*(1), 269–278. http:www.econjournals.com

The Statesman. (2022). Password attacks rise to 921 per second: Microsoft. *The Statesman*. https://www.thestatesman.com/technology/password-attacks-rise-to-921-per-second-microsoft-1503128467.html

The Tribune. (2022). Mobile cyber-attacks on Indian firms up 845% in last 5 months. *The Tribune*. https://www.tribuneindia.com/news/delhi/mobile-cyber-attacks-on-indian-firms-up-845-in-last-5-months-238994

Thomas, J. S. (2001). A methodology for linking customer acquisition to customer retention. *JMR, Journal of Marketing Research*, *38*(2), 262–268. doi:10.1509/jmkr.38.2.262.18848

Thompson, M. (2005). Ethical Theory (Access To Philosophy) (2nd Ed.). Hodder & Stoughton.

Thrall, J. H., Li, X., Li, Q., Cruz, C., Do, S., Dreyer, K., & Brink, J. (2018). Artificial intelligence and machine learning in radiology: Opportunities, challenges, pitfalls, and criteria for success. *Journal of the American College of Radiology*, *15*(3), 504–508. doi:10.1016/j.jacr.2017.12.026 PMID:29402533

Timmermann, A., & Granger, C. W. (2004). Efficient market hypothesis and forecasting. *International Journal of Forecasting*, *20*(1), 15–27. doi:10.1016/S0169-2070(03)00012-8

Tisdell, C. A. (1983). *Productivity Progress and Learning by Doing in Bangladesh Jute Weaving Industry*. Researcsh Gate. https://www.researchgate.net/publication/303447627

Tiwari, R. (2019). August 15. Direct payment system for grain farmers of Punjab, Haryana soon. *The Economic Times*. https://economictimes.indiatimes.com/news/ economy/agriculture/direct-payment-system-for-grain-farmers-of-punjab-haryana-soon/ articleshow/70686123.cms?from=mdr

Tiwari, R., Chand, K., Bhatt, A., Anjum, B., & Thirunavukkarasu, K. (2021). Agriculture 5.0 in India: Opportunities and Challenges of Technology Adoption. *A Step Towards Society 5.0*, 179-198. https://www.taylorfrancis.com/chapters/edit/10.1201/9781003138037-10/agriculture-5-0-india-rajesh-tiwari-khem-chand-arvind-bhatt-bimal-anjum-thirunavukkarasu

Tiwari, A. K., & Albulescu, C. T. (2016). Oil price and exchange rate in India: Fresh evidence from continuous wavelet approach and asymmetric, multi-horizon Granger-causality tests. *Applied Energy*, *179*, 272–283. doi:10.1016/j.apenergy.2016.06.139

Tiwari, A. K., Dar, A. B., & Bhanja, N. (2013). Oil price and exchange rates: A wavelet based analysis for India. *Economic Modelling*, *31*(1), 414–422. doi:10.1016/j.econmod.2012.11.043

Tiwari, A. K., Trabelsi, N., Alqahtani, F., & Hammoudeh, S. (2019). Analysing systemic risk and time-frequency quantile dependence between crude oil prices and BRICS equity markets indices: A new look. *Energy Economics*, *83*, 445–466. doi:10.1016/j.eneco.2019.07.014

Tiwari, R., Chand, K., & Anjum, B. (2020). Crop Insurance in India: A Review of Pradhan Mantri Fasal Bima Yojana (PMFBY). *FIIB Business Review.*, *9*(4), 249–255. doi:10.1177/2319714520966084

Török, L. (2020). Industry 4.0 from a Few Aspects, in Particular in Respect of the Decision Making of the Management: /Will the New Industrial Revolution Change the Traditional Management Functions? *International Review of Applied Sciences and Engineering*.

Trabucchi, D., & Buganza, T. (2018, September). Data-Driven Innovation: Switching the Perspective on Big Data. *European Journal of Innovation Management*, *5*(22), 23–40.

Tresp, V., Overhage, J. M., Bundschus, M., Rabizadeh, S., Fasching, P. A., & Yu, S. (2016). Going digital: A survey on digitalization and large-scale data analytics in healthcare. *Proceedings of the IEEE, 104*(11), 2180–2206. doi:10.1109/JPROC.2016.2615052

Troilo, G., De Luca, L.M., & Guenzi, P. (2017). Linking Data-Rich Environments with Service Innovation in Incumbent Firms: A Conceptual Framework and Research Propositions. *Journal of Product Innovation Management, 34*(5), 617-639.

Trucíos, C., Zevallos, M., Hotta, L. K., & Santos, A. A. (2019). Covariance prediction in large portfolio allocation. *Econometrics., 7*(2), 19. doi:10.3390/econometrics7020019

Truong, D. (2010). *How cloud computing enhances competitive advantages: A research model for small businesses.* The Business Review, Cambridge. https://www.researchgate.net/publication/273447113_How_cloud_computing_enhances_competitive_advantages_A_research_model_for_small_businesses

Tsalikis, J., & Seaton, B. (2007). The International Business Ethics Index: European Union. *Journal of Business Ethics, 75*(3), 229–238. doi:10.100710551-006-9249-4

Tsalikis, J., Seaton, B., & Li, T. (2008). The International Business Ethics Index: Asian Emerging Economies. *Journal of Business Ethics, 80*(4), 643–651. doi:10.100710551-007-9459-4

Tsay, R. S. (2005). *Analysis of Financial Time Series* (Vol. 543). John Wiley & Sons. doi:10.1002/0471746193

Tse, J., & You, W. (2011). How accurate is the electronic health record?–a pilot study evaluating information accuracy in a primary care setting. In *Health Informatics* (pp. 158–164). The Transformative Power of Innovation.

Tyagi, P. (2022). A whopping 303% jump! India's tax collection growth in last 12 years. *Business Today.* https://www.businesstoday.in/latest/economy/story/a-whopping-303-jump-indias-tax-collection-growth-in-last-12-years-357310-2022-12-22?onetap=true

Ullah, Z., Al-Turjman, F., Mostarda, L., & Gagliardi, R. (2020). Applications of artificial intelligence and machine learning in smart cities. *Computer Communications, 154*, 313–323. doi:10.1016/j.comcom.2020.02.069

Uloli, T., Sadasivam, G. S., & Arthi, R. (2022). Requirements analysis of security and privacy of mobile payments-Indian context. *International Journal of Mobile Communications, 20*(6), 639–658. doi:10.1504/IJMC.2022.125923

Van Binsbergen, J. H., & Koijen, R. S. (2010). Predictive regressions: A present-value approach. *The Journal of Finance, 65*(4), 1439–1471. doi:10.1111/j.1540-6261.2010.01575.x

Van Horne, J. C., & Parker, G. G. (1967). The random walk theory: An empirical test. *Financial Analysts Journal, 23*(6), 87–92. doi:10.2469/faj.v23.n6.87

Veerasingam, N., & Teoh, A. P. (2022). Modeling cryptocurrency investment decision: Evidence from Islamic emerging market. *Journal of Islamic Marketing*. doi:10.1108/JIMA-07-2021-0234

Venkatesh, V., & Davis, F. D. (2000). A theoretical extension of the technology acceptance model: Four longitudinal field studies. *Management Science, 46*(2), 186–204. doi:10.1287/mnsc.46.2.186.11926

Visvizi, A., Troisi, O., Grimaldi, M., & Loia, F. (2021). Think Human, Act Digital: Activating Data-Driven Orientation in Innovative Start-Ups. *European Journal of Innovation Management, 25*(6), 452-478.

Vitell, S. J. Jr. (1986). Marketing Ethics: Conceptual And Empirical Foundations Of A Positive Theory Of Decision Making. In *Marketing Situations Having Ethical Content', Unpublished Dissention.* Texas Tech University.

Walterbusch, M., & Teuteberg, F. (2012). Vertrauen im Cloud Computing. *HMD Praxis Der Wirtschaftsinformatik, 49*(6), 50–59. doi:10.1007/BF03340757

Walther, S., Sarker, S., Sedera, D., & Eymann, T. (2013). Exploring Subscription Renewal Intention of Operational Cloud Enterprise Systems-a Socio-Technical Approach. *European Conference on Information Systems*, AIS.

Wand, Y., & Weber, R. (1995). On the deep structure of information systems. *Information Systems Journal, 5*(3), 203–223. doi:10.1111/j.1365-2575.1995.tb00108.x

Wang, Y., Blobel, B., & Yang, B. (2022). Reinforcing Health Data Sharing through Data Democratization. *Journal of Personalized Medicine, 12*(9), 1380.

Wang, Y., Kung, L., & Byrd, T. A. (2018). Big data analytics: Understanding its capabilities and potential benefits for healthcare organizations. *Technological Forecasting and Social Change, 126*, 3–13. doi:10.1016/j.techfore.2015.12.019

Weber, E. U. (2010). Risk attitude and preference. In Wiley Interdisciplinary Reviews: Cognitive Science, 1(1), 79–88. https://doi.org/ doi:10.1002/wcs.5

Wells, J. (2021). The Intersection of Data Democratization and Security. DBTA. https://www.dbta.com/BigDataQuarterly/Articles/The-Intersection-of-Data-Democratization-and-Security-146091.aspx

Wen, D., Wang, G., Ma, C., & Wang, Y. (2019). Risk spillovers between oil and stock markets: A VAR for VaR analysis. *Energy Economics*, #pagerange#. https://doi.org/S0140988319300568

Wills, M. J. (2014). Decisions through data: Analytics in healthcare. *Journal of Healthcare Management, 59*(4), 254–262. doi:10.1097/00115514-201407000-00005 PMID:25154123

Winkler, D. A. (2020). Role of artificial intelligence and machine learning in nanosafety. *Small, 16*(36), 2001883. doi:10.1002mll.202001883 PMID:32537842

Wolgast, T., Ferenz, S., & Nieße, A. (2022). Reactive Power Markets: A Review. IEEE Access, 10, 28397–28410 . doi:10.1109/ACCESS.2022.3141235

Wong, D. T., & Ngai, E. W. (2022). Linking Data-Driven Innovation to Firm Performance: A Theoretical Framework and Case Analysis. *Annals of Operations Research*, 1–20. doi:10.100710479-022-05038-y PMID:36407941

Wu, X., Zhu, X., Wu, G. Q., & Ding, W. (2013). Data mining with big data. *IEEE Transactions on Knowledge and Data Engineering*, *26*, 97–107.

Xie, Y., & Wu, Y. (2022). Investment Strategy of Reactive Power Compensation Scheme in Wind Turbine Distribution Network Based on Optimal Allocation. *Journal of Sensors*, *2022*, 1–8. Advance online publication. doi:10.1155/2022/7037451

Yallop, A. (2012). The Use And Effectiveness Of Code Of Ethics – A Literature Review. *International Conference 'Marketing – From Information To Decision, 5.*

Yang, K., & Lee, H. J. (2010). Gender differences in using mobile data services: Utilitarian and hedonic value approaches. *Journal of Research in Interactive Marketing*, *4*(2), 142–156. doi:10.1108/17505931011051678

Yang, M., al Mamun, A., Mohiuddin, M., Ali Al-Shami, S. S., & Zainol, N. R. (2021). Predicting stock market investment intention and behavior among malaysian working adults using partial least squares structural equation modeling. *Mathematics*, *9*(8), 873. doi:10.3390/math9080873

Yao, J., & Tan, C. L. (2001). A study on training criteria for financial time series forecasting. *Proceedings of International Conference on Neural Information Processing*.

Yap, C. M., & Ng, B. A. (2019). Factors influencing consumers perceived usefulness of m-wallet in Klang Valley, Malaysia. *Review of Integrative Business and Economics Research.*, *8*(4), 1–23.

Yeh, C. C., Lin, F., Wang, T. S., & Wu, C. M. (2019). *Does corporate social responsibility affect cost of capital in China?* Asia Pacific Management Review.

Yeh, I. C., & Lien, Ch. (2009). The comparisons of data mining techniques for the predictive accuracy of probability of default of credit card clients. *Expert Systems with Applications*, *36*(2), 2473–2480. doi:10.1016/j.eswa.2007.12.020

Yengin, I., Karahoca, A., & Karahoca, D. (2011). Online Learning success model for instructors' satisfactions in perspective of interaction and usability outcomes. *Procedia Computer Science*, *3*, 1396–1403. doi:10.1016/j.procs.2011.01.021

Yin, L., & Ma, X. (2018). Causality between oil shocks and exchange rate: A Bayesian, graph-based VAR approach. *Physica A*, *508*, 434–453. doi:10.1016/j.physa.2018.05.064

Zakrzewska, D., & Murlewski, J. (2005). Clustering algorithms for bank customer segmentation. In *5th International Conference on Intelligent Systems Design and Applications (ISDA'05)*. IEEE. 10.1109/ISDA.2005.33

Zeng, J., & Glaister, K.W. (2018). Value Creation from Big Data: Looking inside the Black Box. *Strategic Organization, 16*(2), 105-140.

Zhang, D., Zhou, L., Briggs, R. O., & Nunamaker, J. F. Jr. (2006). Instructional video in Online Learning: Assessing the impact of interactive video on learning effectiveness. *Information & Management, 43*(1), 15–27. doi:10.1016/j.im.2005.01.004

Zhang, H., Morrison, M. A., DeWan, A., Adams, S., Andreoli, M., Huynh, N., & DeAngelis, M. M. (2008). The NEI/NCBI dbGAP database: Genotypes and haplotypes that may specifically predispose to risk of neovascular age-related macular degeneration. *BMC Medical Genetics, 9*(1), 1–10. doi:10.1186/1471-2350-9-51 PMID:18541031

Zhang, X., & Baek, J. (2022). The role of oil price shocks on exchange rates for the selected Asian countries: Asymmetric evidence from nonlinear ARDL and generalized IRFs approaches. *Energy Economics, 112*, 106178. doi:10.1016/j.eneco.2022.106178

Zhao, Y., & Kamioka, T. (2022). Understanding the Role of Chief Data Officers: Insights from Japanese Companies. PACIS 2022 Proceedings. AIS Virtual Library.

Zhao, Z. (2008). Parametric and nonparametric models and methods in financial econometrics. *Statistics Surveys, 2*(none), 1–42. doi:10.1214/08-SS034

Zhou, S., Qiao, Z., Du, Q., Wang, G. A., Fan, W., & Yan, X. (2018). Measuring customer agility from online reviews using big data text analytics. *Journal of Management Information Systems, 35*(2), 510–539. doi:10.1080/07421222.2018.1451956

Zhou, T. (2013). An empirical examination of continuance intention of mobile payment services. *Decision Support Systems, 54*(2), 1085–1091. doi:10.1016/j.dss.2012.10.034

Zhu, H. (2020). Big data and artificial intelligence modeling for drug discovery. *Annual Review of Pharmacology and Toxicology, 60*(1), 573–589. doi:10.1146/annurev-pharmtox-010919-023324 PMID:31518513

Zillner, S. (2021). Innovation in Times of Big Data and Ai: Introducing the Data-Driven Innovation (Ddi) Framework. In E. Curry, A. Metzger, S. Zillner, J. C. Pazzaglia, & A. García Robles (Eds.), *The Elements of Big Data Value* (p. 289). Springer. doi:10.1007/978-3-030-68176-0_12

Zmijewski, M. E. (1984). Methodological issues related to the estimation of financial distress prediction models. *Journal of Accounting Research, 59*, 82.

Zoričić, D., Knežević, G., Miletić, M., Dolinar, D., & Sprčić, D. M. (2022). Integrated Risk Analysis of Aggregators: Policy Implications for the Development of the Competitive Aggregator Industry. *Energies, 15*(14), 5076. Advance online publication. doi:10.3390/en15145076

Zotoo, I.K., Lu, Z., & Liu, G. (2021). Big Data Management Capabilities and Librarians' Innovative Performance: The Role of Value Perception Using the Theory of Knowledge-Based Dynamic Capability. *The Journal of Academic Librarianship, 47*(2), 102-272.

About the Contributors

Anubha is an Associate Professor at Jaipuria Institute of Management, Ghaziabad, India. Her research interests include Social Media Marketing, Islamic marketing, electronic word of mouth, Advertising, and Consumer Behaviour. Her strengths include data analysis & interpretation. She has published many scholarly "ABS 3 level", "ABDC", "SCI", "SCIE", "Scopus" and "Web of Science" indexed research papers in various journals of Wiley, Emerald, Taylor & Francis, and Sage including Psychology and Marketing, Journal of Islamic Marketing, Journal of Internet Commerce, Global Knowledge, Memory & Communication, Vision and FIIB Business Review. She has been an active reviewer of journals of Elsevier, Emerald, Inderscience and Sage. She has presented papers at various National and International conferences at MDI Murshidabad, IIM Indore, IIT Delhi, XLRI Jamshedpur, and Curtin University. She is also a recipient of the best paper award for two of her papers, one of which was presented at MDI.

Himanshu Sharma is working as an Assistant Professor in Management Department of IILM Institute for Higher Education, Lodhi Road, Delhi. Previously, he has got an opportunity to work as an Assistant Professor in University of Delhi and Jaipuria Institute of Management. He has also worked in an ICSSR funded project. He has completed his Ph.D. in Operational Research from University of Delhi. He has also done his M.Phil. and Masters in Operational Research from University of Delhi. He has his bachelor in Mathematics. His research interests are online marketing, Multi-criteria decision making, path analysis modeling. He has published research papers in reputed journals of Springer and Emerald and contributed chapters in edited books. He has also presented his work in International conferences.

***

Rohit Bansal is working as Associate Professor in Department of Management Studies in Vaish College of Engineering, Rohtak. He is a perseverant, passionate academician cum seasoned professional. He obtained Ph.D. in Management from

Maharshi Dayanand University, Rohtak. With a rich experience of 14 years, he has achieved growth through robust and proactive academic initiatives. He has authored & edited 16 books with renowned national & international publishers including IGI Global USA, Scrivener-Wiley Publishing, De Gruyter, Weser Books, Scholar's Press, Germany etc. In addition to, Dr. Rohit has published 120 research papers and chapters in journals of repute including Scopus indexed as well as edited books. He has also presented papers in 45 conferences and seminars. His area of interest includes marketing management, organizational behaviour, services marketing, customer engagement, digital marketing, human resource management and organizational development. He is on Editorial Advisory Board as a member in 125 national and international peer reviewed journals. He has acted as session chair in many international conferences.

Shruti Bansal has completed her Master's in Business Administration with a specialization in Finance and Human Resource Management from SRM Institute of Science & Technology, Ghaziabad, and qualified for UGC-NET Management in June 2021. Her research interests lie in the intersection of finance and human resource management, and she has published several research papers in various Scopus Indexed Journal, UGC Care listed international and national journals. Additionally, she has presented her research papers at various conferences, further contributing to the field of finance and human resource management.

Paurush Batish is with the School of Computing Science and Engineering, Vellore Institute of Technology, Vellore, India. With a deep interest for research in the field of Big data and soft computing, he has executed few projects and authored a few publications in these areas.

Shobha Bhardwaj is working as an Assistant Professor-School of Management, Institute of Management Studies Ghaziabad (University Courses Campus), Ghaziabad, India. She has been awarded Ph.D. in HR Specialization from SRM Institute of Science and Technology, Ghaziabad under the guidance of Dr. Ajay Jain in 2021. She has also qualified UGC NTA NET (2019) in HR specialization. She has published many research papers and chapters in Scopus, UGC-listed national and international journals in the area of HR and General Management. Besides, she has presented numerous papers at various national and international conferences. She has teaching as well as industry experience of more than five years. Her areas of interest include Employee Psychology, Emotional Intelligence, Competency Mapping, Talent Management, Organization Behavior, Employee Relation and Welfare.

Vyomkesh Bhatt is an assistant professor at Department of Management Studies, G L Bajaj Institute of Technology and Management, Noida and received a Master Of Commerce from D.A.V.(P.G.) College, Dehradun affiliated to H.N.B Garwhal Central University with major in Finance and minor in Marketing. Bhatt graduated with a Bachelor Of Commerce (Honours) with specialization in Financial Management from Uttaranchal University, and has published four research papers in peer reviewed International Journals, two chapter's in edited book, one edited book and two reference books, and regular participation in conference's/workshops. Bhatt takes an active part in Seminar, Webinar and different Conclave organized by leading Universities such as Alagappa University- Karikudi, Manipal University- Jaipur, Lucknow University, MIT-ADT University, etc.

Venkateswarlu Chandu is working as Assistant Professor and is having more than 20 publications.

Jatin Kumar Dhankhar is with the School of Computing Science and Engineering, Vellore Institute of Technology, Vellore, India. With a deep interest for research in the field of Big data and soft computing, he has executed few projects and authored a few publications in these areas.

Amala Gangula is working as Faculty Research Associate in Institute of Banking Personnel Selection, Mumbai, India.

Karuna Gupta is an accomplished company secretary with nearly two decades of experience in both industry and academia. Currently, she holds the position of Associate Professor in Business Management at SRM Institute of Science and Technology, located in Ghaziabad, India. Her academic and professional interests are diverse and include corporate finance, secretarial audit, fintech, blockchain technology, and behavioral finance. Apart from her teaching responsibilities, she has a strong research background with several publications in both national and international journals. Furthermore, Dr. Gupta is an active ICSI (Institute of Company Secretaries of India) member in New Delhi and holds the esteemed position of Chairperson at the ICSI Modinagar chapter.

Ajay Jain is a highly accomplished academic who has been working as an Associate Professor in Business Management at SRM Institute of Science and Technology in Ghaziabad, India for the last 25 years. In addition to his teaching responsibilities, he holds various positions within the institute, including Program Chair for BBA, Area Chair for Finance, Chair for Research, and Chair for the Anti-Ragging Committee. He is also the Chief Editor of the "SRM - IMT Journal of Business and Management Research". With a strong academic background, Dr. Jain holds two master's degrees, one in MBA (Finance) and another in M.Com. He completed his Ph.D. in Finance in 2003. Dr. Jain has published 31 research papers in both national and international journals and has presented numerous papers at various conferences. He has also guided the successful completion of four Ph.D. students and currently guides four more in their research pursuits. Dr. Jain's research interests include various areas within finance such as Mutual Funds, Banking, Financial Services, Non-Performing Assets (NPAs), and Microfinance.

Sapna Jangra is an Assistant Professor, Institute of Management Studies and Research, Maharshi Dayanand University, Rohtak, Haryana, India.

Nghipundaka Jeremia is currently with the Namibia University of Science and Technology. His research interests are in the extended areas of energy systems, forecast and data aggregation studies.

Marimuthu Karuppiah received his B.E. degree in Computer Science and Engineering from Madurai Kamaraj University, Madurai, India in 2003, M.E. degree in Computer Science and Engineering from Anna University, Chennai, India in 2005, Ph.D. degree in Computer Science and Engineering from VIT University, Vellore, India in 2015. Presently, he is a Professor in Department of Computing Science and Engineering, Presidency University, Bengaluru, India. Before joining SRMIST, he was with the VIT University, Vellore, India as an Associate Professor. He has published more than 30 research papers in SCI indexed journals. Also, he has published more than 40 research papers in SCOPUS indexed journals and international conferences. He is a life member of Cryptology Research Society of India (CRSI) and Computer Society of India (CSI), senior member of IEEE and member of ACM. His main research interests include cryptography and wireless network security, in particular, authentication and encryption schemes.

Sachithra Lokuge is a Lecturer in Information Systems at the School of Business at the University of Southern Queensland, Australia. Her work has been published in Information & Management, Communications of the AIS, Information Technology & People, Journal of Information Technology Theory and Applications (JITTA), The International Conference on Information Systems, Academy of Management Conference, The Americas Conference, European Conference and The Pacific Asia Conference on Information Systems.

Debesh Mishra is working as Principal at Sri Polytechnic, Komand (Nayagarh), Odisha, India and is having more than 35 publications.

Swagatika Mishra is working as Assistant Professor in VSSUT, Odisha (India).

K.S. Sastry Musti is presently with Namibia University of Science and Technology, Windhoek, Namibia. He has than 30 years of professional experience. He obtained his BTech in Electrical Engineering from JNTU, Kakinada (A.P.) in 1990, MTech and PhD from NIT, Warangal in the years 1996 and 2002 respectively. Some of his earlier employments include University of the West Indies, St Augustine, Trinidad, ESIGELEC, Rouen, France and Sophia University, Tokyo, Japan. His research interests include Power and Energy Systems, Information Systems and Engineering Education.

K. Pradeep Reddy is working as associate professor and is having more than 20 publications.

Narendra Ryali is working as an Assistant Professor in KL University. He has been awarded with Ph.D. from Andhra University, Visakhapatnam, Andhra Pradesh. He completed his Masters Degree in both Commerce and Management.

Sasari Samarasinghe is a PhD candidate at the University of Southern Queensland, Australia. She has been working as an IT Project Manager for more than 8 years serving local and international clientele. Her work has been published in The Pacific Asia Conference on Information Systems, Australasian Conference on Information Systems, IEEE International Conference on Computer Science & Education, and American Scientific Research Journal for Engineering, Technology, and Sciences (ASRJETS).

Gopal Bihari Saraswat is an associate professor at the Faculty of Management Studies, SRM Institute of Science and Technology at Delhi NCR Campus, Ghaziabad. The professor has more than 15 years of academic experience and has published many research articles in reputed Scopus index journals. He also published a book in the area of finance and banking. He completed his PhD in commerce and is interested in the research areas of financial econometrics, energy econometrics and macroeconomics.

Madhav Saraswat has more than 24 years of academic experience and presently working as Assistant Professor at the Institute of Business Studies, Ch. Charan Singh University, Meerut, Uttar Pradesh, India. Dr. Saraswat had his PhD in Commerce from Chaudhary Charan Singh University and completed PGDBM, M.B.A., M.Com and L.L.B. Prof. Madhav has published several research papers in reputed journals and presented papers at conferences.He is also author of books on economics and finance.

Ramani Selvanambi is an Assistant Professor (Senior) in the School of Computing Science and Engineering at Vellore Institute of Technology (VIT), Vellore, India. He received his B.E in Computer Science and Engineering from MNM Jain Engineering College, Madras University and M. Tech Computer Science and Engineering from Bharathidasan University and Ph.D. in Computer Science and Engineering from Vellore Institute of Technology (VIT), Vellore. He has 12+ years of experience in teaching and 2 years of experience in the Consultancy and Software Industry. He has published about 30 papers in International Journals on Machine Learning, NatureInspired Algorithms, Cryptography and Health Care. His research interest includes Data Mining, Machine learning, Database Systems, Optimization Techniques. He is a member of the Computer Society of India (CSI), IEEE and other technical societies.

Ram Singh is a new Age Innovative Educationist working as a professor at MM Institute of Management, Maharishi Markandeshwar (Deemed to be University), Mullana-Ambala, Haryana. Dr. Singh has a vast teaching and research experience of more than 11 years at the UG & PG courses. Being a researcher, Dr. Singh holds multifarious positions in the field of academics, for instance, he is a member and secretary of the Research Council of Quantum University, member of Editorial Board of various reputed journals in the domain of Accounting, Finance & General Management, Reviewer in IGI Global, Inderscience Journals, member and Chairperson of the Board of Faculty & Board of Study (Commerce & Management), member in Board of Management etc. Besides, Dr. Singh has also been awarded the „Excellent Reviewer Award-2020" by Bilingual Publishing Company Singapore, „Best Doctoral Thesis Award2022" by International Association of Research & Developed Organization, Ghaziabad India, and „National Elite Teacher Award-2022" by International Institute of Organized Research (I2OR) Chennai. Currently his professional affiliation includes a member of four National & International academic organizations i.e. Life Member of the Indian Commerce Association (ICA), Life Member in the International Association of Academic plus Corporate Society (IAACS), Life Member in the Indian Academic Researchers Association (IARA), Life Member in the International Institute of Organized Research (I2OR).

Pravin Singh is an Assistant Professor, Alabbar School of Management, Raffles University, Neemrana, Alwar, Rajasthan.

Rakshit Soni is with the School of Computing Science and Engineering, Vellore Institute of Technology, Vellore, India. With a deep interest for research in the field of Big data and soft computing, he has executed few projects and authored a few publications in these areas.

Govind Sricastava spent 16 years in corporate and academics and served different organizations with different capacities. Having a deeper interest in research and publication and published seven good quality papers, out of which six are Scopus indexed and one is indexed in Web of Science. Conducted two FDPs, One MDP/ SDP and several research workshops on marketing research and data analytics. Reviewer of ABDC list of journals. Presently working on two books, one book chapter and three research papers for high impact factor journal

Rajesh Tiwari is a Professor, Department of Management Studies, Graphic Era (Deemed to be University), Dehradun, Uttarakhand, India.

Ravi Tiwari is an ssociate Professor, Faculty of Management, SRM Institute of Science and Technology, Delhi NCR Campus, Ghaziabad, UP, India.

Priyanka Tyagi is a Research Scholar at SRM Institute of Science Technology, Delhi NCR Campus, Ghaziabad, Uttar Pradesh, India. Her area of specialization is Marketing and Finance. She has recently received the Best Paper award at the international conference on reimaging marketing with the technology (ICRMT 2023) jointly organized by IIM Jammu India and Deakin University, Australia. Her areas of interest include Marketing, Consumer Behaviour, Corporate Social Responsibility, Financial Literacy, Financial Technology, and Artificial Intelligence.

Index

www.ingramcontent.com/pod-product-compliance
Lightning Source LLC
LaVergne TN
LVHW081341300926
849161LV00008B/2045

* 9 7 8 1 6 6 8 4 7 5 6 8 3 *